Contents

List of Illustrations   ix

Acknowledgments   xi

INTRODUCTION
Americans at the Gate   1

CHAPTER 1
"The Age of the Uprooted Man": The United States
and Refugees, 1900–1952   11

CHAPTER 2
"A Mystic Maze of Enforcement":
The Refugee Relief Program   34

CHAPTER 3
"From Hungary, New Americans":
The United States and Hungarian Refugees   60

CHAPTER 4
"Half a Loaf": The Failure of Refugee Policy
and Law Reform, 1957–1965   86

CHAPTER 5
"They Are Proud People": The United States
and Refugees from Cuba, 1959–1966   106

CHAPTER 6
"The Soul of Our Sense of Nationhood":
Human Rights and Refugees in the 1970s   133

CHAPTER 7
Reform and Retrenchment: The Refugee Act of 1980
and the Reagan Administration's Refugee Policies   167

EPILOGUE
The United States and Refugees after the Cold War   197

Notes   207

Index   257

Illustrations

1.1 Senator Patrick McCarran conferring with Senator Lyndon
    Baines Johnson in 1954 (Hank Walker/Time &
    Life Pictures/Getty Images)   28

2.1 Refugee Camp in West Berlin during the early 1950s
    (courtesy of the International Rescue Committee)   36

2.2 Camp Valka message board (courtesy of the International
    Rescue Committee)   49

3.1 Leo Cherne of the International Rescue Committee during
    the Hungarian refugee crisis (courtesy of the International
    Rescue Committee)   76

3.2 The Csillag family (Carl Mydans/Time & Life
    Pictures/Getty Images)   79

5.1 Cuban refugees emerging from the surf (courtesy of the
    International Rescue Committee)   111

5.2 A Cuban refugee meets with a U.S. government official in
    1961 (Michael Rougier/Time & Life Pictures/Getty Images)   122

6.1 A Russian refugee family after arriving in New York City in
    the 1970s (courtesy of the International Rescue Committee)   144

6.2 Aerial view of a boat people refugee camp in fall
    1979 (Leo Cherne/courtesy of the International
    Rescue Committee)   150

6.3 Life in a boat people refugee camp in 1979
    (courtesy of the International Rescue Committee)   153

Acknowledgments

IF THIS LIST of "thank-yous" is long, it is only because numerous institutions, scholars, friends, and family have so generously offered support, encouragement, and advice as I worked on this book.

The staffs of the Truman, Eisenhower, Kennedy, Johnson, and Ford Presidential Libraries were invaluable in aiding my search through their voluminous holdings as I began research. I owe special thanks to Rod Ross at the Center for Legislative Archives who always answered my e-mails and calls about obscure refugee legislation and was ever eager to learn about the project. Thanks as well to the International Rescue Committee, and especially Wynne Boelt and Ed Bligh, for help with photographs.

This book began as a dissertation in the University of Virginia's History Department, whose staff and administration were most helpful. I spent a year working at the Miller Center of Public Affairs at UVA where my friends and bosses Marc Selverstone and Garth Wermter gave me the freedom to begin transforming the dissertation into a book. I owe thanks as well to the Center's American Political Development Program for its support. Matt Lassiter was instrumental in bringing me to the University of Michigan's History Department as a lecturer in 2004–2005, where revisions to the book began in earnest. From 2005 to 2007, I taught at the University of Waterloo in Ontario, Canada, and I owe special thanks to my department chairs, Patrick Harrigan and Andrew Hunt, and to the extraordinary administrators Irene Majer and Nancy Birss, for their support. Finally, thanks to Kevin Kruse, Jeremy Adelman, Judy Hanson, and the Princeton University History Department.

Several scholars and friends took time from their busy schedules to answer questions and to read parts of (and sometimes all of) the manuscript. Many thanks go out to Brian Balogh, Erica Gould, Charles McCurdy, Mel Leffler, Michael Parrish, Gary Gerstle, Brian Gratton, M. Isabel Medina, Joe Crespino, Stephen Porter, Lauren Celello, Matt Kilcoyne, Katie Miller, Josh Mester, Linda Zengerle, and Kurt Hohenstein. I also would like to thank the anonymous reviewers who read the manuscript for Princeton University Press for their engaged comments. Brigitta van Rheinberg and Clara Platter at the Press have been especially helpful and supportive of this book.

A whole host of friends helped me to think about the book—and escape from it from time to time. Thanks to Grace, Sarah, and Emma Hale; Chris and Christine; Robert Vinson; Ethan and Zenobia; Pete Flora; John and

Cat; Brian Campbell; Andre and Meredith; Kurt and Cory; Scott Matthews; Carrie and Spence; Kate Pierce; Laurie Hochstetler; Derek, Shelley, and Alethia; Joe and Jessica; Jen Ross; Jason Zengerle; Bill and Beth Southern; Andy and Mary Moore; Watson and Susanna; Ally and Abe; Aaron and Meg; Eric Vettel; Leonard Sadosky; Ed and Christina; Cindy Aron; Holly Shulman; Gary and Antoinette; Lynne and David; Ken and Liz; Wendy and Rex; Steven and Leslie; and Dan and Mary Jo.

A special shout-out to my D.C. crew who now actually live all over the country. Most of you have listened to me prattle on about this book at one time or another, so thanks for your patience: Andy and Erin Myers; Pat and Tina Saudek Cusack; Jason and Kristen Southern; Matt Kilcoyne and Jenn Enloe; Peter Glennon; Adam Wenchel and Erin Heath; and Josh and Denise Mester.

My family has been marvelously supportive of this project over the years, and I owe them much thanks: Chris and Katie; Marc; John, Maggie, and Tom Bon Tempo; the Bon Tempos and Glennons of Milford, Massachusetts; "Judge" Jim Schreier; Mary Kay Schreier; Tom and Marybeth Celello, Dave and Sara Celello, Lauren Celello, and Alison Celello.

Nelson Lichtenstein, who served as my dissertation adviser, has read these pages more times than I can count. His gentle critiques and comments have made this book much better and he and Eileen have been so supportive of both myself and Kristin. I hope that I can be half the scholar, adviser, mentor, and friend that Nelson has been to me over the last decade.

My parents never failed to ask about the progress of the book or to offer encouragement. (My mom even read the manuscript—twice!) They listened to my worries and fears and shared in my successes. At this point, they probably know enough about the publishing process and the academic job market to open their own consulting business. Needless to say, I would not have been able to write this book without their love and support.

And, of course, this book is dedicated to Kristin. It would not have appeared, or possess whatever strengths it might have, without her counsel, support, patience, and love. I learn every day how lucky I am to have her as a partner. We've had a few adventures over the last few years, and as I write we are embarking on yet another one. I could not imagine sharing it—or my life—with anyone else.

Americans at the Gate

Americans at the Gate

IN THE 1930s, as Europeans fled—and attempted to flee—the horrors of Nazism, the United States closed its doors. The United States' failure to act as a sanctuary in the face of the most infamous refugee crisis in history makes the next sixty years all the more remarkable. In the decades after World War II, over 4 million refugees entered the United States. To be sure, those 4 million represented only a small percentage of the global refugee population, yet viewed from the perspective of the 1930s, they also represented a significant effort to admit and resettle some of the world's refugees.

Americans at the Gate explains how and why the United States admitted those refugees. While the United States' commitment to refugees certainly grew more capacious over the second half of the twentieth century—in terms of both the numbers admitted and their countries of origin—refugee admissions were by no means ever assured. Rather, Americans battled ferociously over the size, shape, and existence of refugee programs and laws. Opposition existed nationally and it bloomed regionally and locally, especially in places like Florida and California, which saw large influxes of newcomers after 1960. Likewise, refugee admissions rested upon a tricky and shifting calculus of American foreign policy concerns, domestic political and cultural considerations, the nation's economic health, the public's receptiveness toward immigrants, and the different ways Americans defined themselves as a nation. As a result, refugee affairs in the United States always have been a distinctly human enterprise, with successes and failures, with mistakes and misunderstandings, and with compassion and miserliness.

Refugees made up only part of the almost 28 million newcomers, the majority of whom were immigrants who legally entered the United States between 1945 and 2000.[1] A vital conceptual distinction differentiates refugees from immigrants, however. Refugees suffer from persecution (or the threat of persecution), which precludes them from returning to their homes or native countries. Immigrants are under no such threat, though they often leave their countries because of adverse political, economic, cultural, or social conditions. In more colloquial terms, refugees are chased out of their countries while immigrants choose to leave theirs. This difference has helped give refugee affairs in the post–World War II era their own unique politics, policy development, cultural resonance, and relationship to foreign policy.

The histories of these two types of newcomers, though, most certainly overlapped. As this book shows, immigration politics and laws served as the backdrop to refugee affairs. The two blocs that contested immigration politics—restrictionists (who generally opposed the entry of immigrants) and liberalizers (who generally supported the entry of immigrants)—also frequently battled over the entry of refugees. Moreover, anti-immigrant sentiment was a persistent, but not overwhelming, presence on postwar America's political and cultural landscape. During these decades, between a third to a half of Americans supported reductions in the entry of immigrants; even greater numbers regularly opposed proposals that would make it easier for newcomers to enter the country. Refugees too felt the sting of this xenophobia. Many Americans felt threatened by the prospect of newly arrived refugees—often of religious, racial, and ethnonational groups poorly represented in the United States—moving into their neighborhoods, going to school with their children, or competing with them for jobs.

But immigration affairs, and significant anti-immigrant sentiment, did not predetermine refugee affairs. Many Americans warmly welcomed refugees, regarding their arrival as consistent with that part of the American tradition that promises succor to victims of persecution. Refugee policymaking, because it was a "national security" issue, was somewhat insulated from anti-newcomer blasts. Likewise, the public could not easily scrutinize refugee affairs because the mechanisms of refugee entry were sometimes obscure and the policymaking process was driven by a relatively small circle of experts, bureaucrats, congressional staffers, and powerful congressional committee chairpersons.[2] One other peculiarity helps explain refugee admissions in an age of restrictionist sentiment. The 4 million refugees who entered between 1945 and 2000 amounted to nearly 15 percent of all newcomers, a figure large enough to notice, but no so large as to overshadow—in the eyes of restrictionists—the greater problem of immigrant entry.

Much of the literature on the United States and refugees has been written by anthropologists, sociologists, political scientists, and legal scholars. Such accounts, worthy as they are, too often lack the very strengths of the historian's craft: deep archival research; contextualization in larger foreign policy, political, social, economic, and cultural trends; and a narrative that explains change over time with attention to historical detail.[3] The few works of history on refugee affairs during the Cold War have established a basic narrative and explanatory framework that emphasizes the link between American foreign policy and the commitment to refugees.[4] This explanation has much merit given the importance of the Cold

War to the United States over the second half of the twentieth century. The U.S. government's decisions about which refugee crises deserved attention—and which required intervention—always took Cold War foreign policy goals into account. Government officials stressed that refugee entry would benefit the nation's diplomacy. Finally, sometimes these refugee programs—the best examples being the American responses to Hungarian and Cuban refugees—were important parts of larger Cold War foreign policy initiatives.

The best-developed area in the history of refugee affairs—the study of American refugee policies in the World War II era (roughly from 1933 to 1952)—avoids such a singular focus on foreign affairs, however. Historians like David Wyman, Leonard Dinnerstein, Michael Marrus, and Haim Genizi have explained American policies toward refugees from the Nazis and the survivors of the Holocaust with well-rounded attention to domestic politics, culture, and economics as well as U.S. foreign policy concerns.[5] This scholarship has much in common with the best of the latest work in immigration history. The hallmark of the "new immigration" history, by scholars like Mai Ngai, Gary Gerstle, Dan Tichenor, and Aristide Zolberg, is its attempt to understand the history of newcomers to the United States within the larger themes—like racial and sexual inequality, the growth and power of the state, and the increasingly transnational nature of American life—that help define the American experience. This new immigration history, though, suffers from a blind spot when it comes to refugees; more often than not, the refugee story is left unaddressed or subsumed under the immigration story.[6]

Americans at the Gate builds and expands upon these insights. Two contentions stand at the center of this book. First, refugee policies, laws, and programs in the post–World War II era were the product of interactions between foreign policy imperatives and domestic political and cultural considerations. As a result, refugee affairs clearly demonstrate that the United States' domestic and international histories should not—and indeed cannot—be disaggregated.[7] Second, the history of refugee affairs cannot be found just in the policy and political battles that produced refugee programs and laws, but must be located as well in the implementation and administration of those programs and laws.

Without question, the Cold War was vital to the construction and maintenance of an American commitment to refugees. Many (but not all) Americans believed that the entry of refugees would provide the nation with an advantage over the Soviet Union in the Cold War. Refugee admissions aided Cold War diplomacy by satisfying American allies and fortifying them in the face of population pressures and refugee flows that caused political, economic, and social instability. Moreover, American leaders believed that refugees—especially those persons fleeing communism, the

Soviets, or their allies—were living symbols of Soviet brutality and communism's failure. Thus, refugee admissions struck a rhetorical blow against the Soviets and reminded the world of the United States' unbending commitment to anticommunism and winning the Cold War. It is little wonder, then, that for much of the post–World War II era, Americans, from presidents to the public, associated refugees with anticommunism. Americans continued to think of refugee admissions as an aspect of foreign policy even when the Cold War and muscular anticommunism waned. In the 1970s, as the Cold War consensus that was birthed more than twenty years earlier shattered, portions of both the political left and right supported refugee entry as an articulation of a post-Vietnam and post-détente foreign policy.

Refugee admissions were part and parcel of the United States' engagement with global issues, but those efforts were also surprisingly unilateralist. The policies, laws, and programs the U.S. government designed to admit refugees were constructed and conducted with little consultation with other nations or with international organizations. Of course, the United States occasionally worked with organizations such as the United Nations to solve refugee problems and to expedite resettlement. Likewise, it frequently and successfully campaigned for other nations to admit refugees. In fact, some countries admitted more refugees as a percentage of their total population than the United States. Ultimately, though, American refugee admissions ran along parallel tracks to the efforts of other nations and organizations, never truly intersecting with them. The history of American refugee affairs is an international history, then, but it is a peculiar one in which the United States acted unilaterally to solve a global problem.

An explanation of the development of refugee policies, laws, and programs that focuses almost exclusively on foreign policy imperatives leaves some curious gaps, though. If foreign policy concerns were the most significant force behind U.S. refugee affairs, then why in the early 1950s, with Cold War tensions running high in Europe, did the Refugee Relief Program (RRP) deny entry to large numbers of eastern and central European refugees seeking admission to the United States? If refugee admissions were such a vital tool in the confrontation with the Soviets, why did the Cold Warrior president Ronald Reagan repeatedly reduce the Soviet and Indochinese refugee quotas in the 1980s? If refugee policies, laws, and programs were purely Cold War foreign policy tools, it stands to reason that the United States would have granted admission to all applicants for RRP visas in the 1950s and maintained high admissions quotas in the 1980s. American foreign policy, then, has played an important, but not the sole and starring, role in the history of American refugee affairs.

Rather, refugee admissions in the post–World War II era were just as strongly rooted in political, cultural, economic and social conditions in the United States as they were in foreign affairs and U.S. foreign policy considerations. Politicians (and the political parties they represented) chose to support or oppose particular refugee programs based in part upon the partisan and electoral advantages to be won. Domestic political developments—like the Red Scare and domestic anticommunism of the 1950s—found their way into debates about potential refugee admissions and institutionalized in the bureaucratic structures of refugee programs themselves. Social changes at home—like the successes of the African American civil rights movement and the women's movement—created a political and cultural environment much more welcoming to refugees, and suggested new reasons why the United States should help refugees; it is certainly no coincidence that the United States only began admitting refugees of color in any appreciable numbers after the freedom movements of the 1960s had reshaped American society and attitudes concerning race and ethnicity.

Perhaps nothing better illustrates the domestic roots of American refugee affairs than the ways in which refugee policies, laws, and programs depended upon, and were undergirded by, evolving notions of American identity and citizenship. Through the first half of the twentieth century, the dominant definition of American identity rested upon ethnonational or racial characteristics. In the post–World War II era, this racialized conception of identity slowly lost ground to one that stressed adherence to particular political and ideological traits. In the 1950s and early 1960s, the politicized definition of "American" emphasized anticommunism, but with the 1960s freedom movements, it came to stress the protection of individual rights and explicitly rejected ethnonational and racial benchmarks. The politicized definition of "American" both fractured and evolved by the 1970s, but many Americans—on the left and right—grounded their vision of national identity in the protection of supposedly universal, individual rights, even as they defined those rights somewhat differently.[8]

Conceptions of American identity infused refugee affairs at all levels. The essential equation at the foundation of American refugee politics roughly mirrored the transformations in American identity. In the 1950s, that equation was "refugee equals European, anticommunist." By the 1970s, it read "refugee equals person (of any nationality, race, religion, or political persuasion) whose human rights are endangered." Advocates and opponents of refugee admissions manipulated notions of national identity to justify their positions—and then tried to shape refugee policies, laws, and programs by inserting specific codicils that reflected these conceptions of national identity. Moreover, officials charged with running refugee programs measured refugee applicants against what they perceived to be "American" benchmarks. This book, then, grounds definitions of American identity in specific refugee policies and laws, in the arguments of their proponents and opponents, in the programs that brought refugees to the United States, and in the work of the officials who administered these programs and actually approved the admission of refugees.

As a result, the history of refugee affairs offers a window onto the history of American identity. Rather than being predominately an ephemeral and rhetorical product of the national imagination and discourse, this book argues that notions of "American" shaped the daily lives of persons living in the United States and those who wanted to join them.[9] The history of refugee affairs also clarifies the bifurcated nature of American identity in the postwar years. Conceptions of national identity after 1945—in refugee politics and American politics and culture generally—often highlighted political beliefs or characteristics. But American identity, as it played out in refugee politics, also centered on a whole universe of attributes—relating to gender, to work, and to consumption—that while politicized also sprung from cultural or social assumptions. Indeed, the very richness of "American"—the multiple and varied qualities assigned to that descriptor—made it both a potent political weapon and a point of conflict in refugee affairs.

The book's second contention is that a fuller and more complete history of refugee affairs requires understanding the implementation and administration of refugee policies, laws, and programs. Most accounts assume that once the Congress or the president announced that the United States would admit "x" number of refugees, then "x" number of refugees were admitted.[10] This book shows that policy formulation or a law's passage was only half the battle. The other half largely took place in particular bureaus of the State Department or the Immigration and Naturalization Service (INS). In Washington, D.C., officials from these departments set up the refugee programs, established admissions guidelines, and chose staff and administrators, while INS and State Department officers stationed in the field ran these refugee programs, including the security screening that each refugee applicant received.

By examining how refugee programs ran on the ground, a new and more complex story emerges. First, a focus on the process by which refugees were (or were not) admitted reinforces the point that refugee entry was never guaranteed; State Department and INS officials in the field and in Washington, D.C., could effectively slow or halt or, in some cases, expedite the admission of refugees. Second, as these government officials went about their tasks, they brought their own ideological, political, and cultural predilections to the daily management, administration, procedures, and workings of refugee programs. It made a difference, in other words, that an ardent anticommunist and ally of restrictionists and red-baiters was the most important American government refugee official in the 1950s, whereas the State Department's leading refugee spokesperson nearly thirty years later was a member of the American Civil Liberties Union, a civil rights movement veteran, and an important proponent of human rights. All of this reinforces an earlier point: American politics and political culture, not just foreign policy, established the tenor of the American commitment to refugees.

The story of refugee affairs is also, then, a study of policymaking and governance in the decades after World War II. Refugee policies, laws, and programs did not originate sui generis; they were built upon or borrowed from prior procedures and programs that admitted newcomers, both refugees and immigrants. Ideological continuity buttressed this procedural consistency. For much of the postwar period, the guiding assumption among policymakers and politicians was that refugees were European and anticommunist. Moreover, the U.S. government's publicity campaigns, undertaken throughout the postwar years to tamp down restrictionist opposition, ascribed to arriving refugees a mix of political (anticommunism) and apolitical (particular gender roles, industriousness, and consumption) traits that resulted in the stabilization of the "refugee equals European anticommunist" equation at the heart of policymaking for nearly three decades. This proved a difficult equation from which to depart—witness the failure (until 1980) of determined refugee advocates to win acceptance of a broader, less Cold War–influenced, commitment to refugees. But policymaking continuity and stability—be it procedural or ideological—had its limits. The implementation of refugee programs repeatedly devolved into battles that reopened some of the basic premises that seemed decided during policy formation (or in the early phases of policy implementation). Moreover, while future programs often inherited the bureaucratic structures and administrative rules of their predecessors, actors stretched and rethought those structures and rules. In the largest sense, then, this book reminds historians of government policies that they need to pay as much attention to implementation and administration as they do to policymaking and the drafting of legislation.[11]

These themes clearly emerged as the United States dealt with refugees during the first half of the twentieth century, the subject of chapter 1. Between 1900 and 1930, anti-newcomer sentiment mounted, best symbolized by passage of the national origins quota immigration system and the failure to aid refugees from Nazism. Restrictionist power began to dissipate slightly after World War II, a conflict that created a refugee crisis of at least 10 million stateless persons in Europe alone. The first step was the 1948 Displaced Persons (DP) Act, which brought about 400,000 refugees to the United States over four years in an attempt to speed Europe's postwar reconstruction. The DP program coincided with the onset of the Cold War, which began to reshape immigration and refugee affairs in the early 1950s. It made its first mark in immigration law with the passage of the 1952 McCarran-Walter Act (MWA) that reformed and bolstered the quota system. The MWA debates revealed the centrality of Cold War national security concerns to both the liberalizer and restrictionist intellectual arsenals and the importance of anticommunism to the politics of immigration policy. Moreover, as conceptions of American identity (as defined by all sections of the political spectrum) came to emphasize anticommunism, both liberalizers and restrictionists stressed how newcomers did—or did not—measure up to benchmark political ideals.

The Cold War, which only deepened the post–World War II refugee problem, had an equally transformative effect upon American refugee affairs. The Eisenhower administration and key liberalizers saw the Refugee Relief Program (chapter 2) and the Hungarian refugee admissions (chapter 3)—the most important refugee programs of the 1950s—as parts of an anticommunist and anti-Soviet Cold War foreign policy. Both programs also had domestic political roots; the former mollified opponents of the MWA and the latter fulfilled at least some of the "liberationist" rhetoric employed by the Eisenhower administration to recruit voters of eastern European backgrounds. These programs, forged in the incendiary domestic politics of anticommunism, reflected the era's powerful anticommunist-centered Americanism. Restrictionists essentially exported the Red Scare–era investigatory state to the RRP, mandating investigations into each refugee's political history and beliefs and effectively establishing an anticommunist litmus test for entry. Their goal was to scuttle the RRP, and they nearly succeeded. But with the Hungarian admissions of 1956 and 1957, the U.S. government relaxed numerous entry requirements in order to speed refugee entry in the face of a mounting diplomatic and public relations disaster after the Soviets crushed the Hungarian Revolution. These programs, which in total admitted nearly 300,000 refugees, underscored three lessons. First, they cemented the basic equation at the heart of refugee politics—and refugee programs in the field—for the next thirty years: refugee equals anticommunist European. Second, both programs were ad hoc responses to refugee crises. Finally, both programs demonstrated how anticommunism bonded foreign policies, domestic politics and culture, and refugee affairs in the 1950s.

During the 1960s, the American commitment to refugees evolved, although its early Cold War–influenced foundations did not shatter. The same could not be said for immigration law, the subject of chapter 4. Liberalizers in 1965 finally succeeded in destroying the national origins quota immigration system. Why did immigration laws liberalize and refugee laws not, despite the strenuous efforts of a fast-developing subset of refugee experts within the liberalizer bloc who wanted permanent, substantial, less Eurocentric, and less Cold War–centered refugee policies? Cold War foreign policy concerns contributed to immigration reform's passage, but more important were the great social and political movements of the 1960s, especially the African American civil rights movement, that celebrated the autonomous, rights-bearing individual and validated a vision of American identity theoretically, at least, absent racist and ethnonational biases. While the domestic revolutions legitimated a less Eurocentric focus in refugee affairs and a definition of refugee focused on the protection of individual rights, Cold War foreign policy concerns buttressed the existing justification for aid to refugees and the established meaning of "refugee."

The entry of 500,000 Cuban refugees between 1959 and 1973, the focus of chapter 5, did even more to reinforce the status quo. Rising Cold War tensions and long-term political and cultural ties between the island and the United States guaranteed an "open door" for fleeing Cubans. With Red Scare political culture receding, the majority of Cubans in comparison to their 1950s predecessors faced less rigorous admissions requirements, a weakened anticommunist litmus test, and less pointed questions about their political history. The Cuban program did bring one remarkable change. The U.S. government essentially condoned divided loyalties among Cuban refugees by allowing them to become citizens while fully acknowledging that many of these newly minted citizens would likely return to a post-Castro Cuba.

A chief legacy of the 1960s political and social upheavals—as well as the stunning foreign policy failures in Vietnam—was the reinvigoration of a human rights movement. Human rights concerns in turn shaped, and were shaped by, the admission during the 1970s of Soviet, Chilean, and Indochinese refugees, the topic of chapter 6. Their entry marked a real break with past policies that had favored admission of European, anticommunist refugees. While Soviet Jews fled communism, Chileans did not, and the Indochinese escaped horrifying circumstances perpetrated by communist governments and genocidal maniacs with no clear political ideology. The politics surrounding the admission of all three groups focused less on the traditional Cold War rationales and more on the American duty to defend and protect human rights. Just as important, some American officials attempted to bring human rights considerations to the fore of the admissions process itself, though with less than complete success.

The apogee and subsequent decline of human rights politics in refugee affairs came in the 1980s, the focus of chapter 7. The 1980 Refugee Act mandated at least fifty thousand annual refugee admissions and defined a "refugee" as a victim of "persecution on account of race, religion, nationality, membership in a particular social group, or political opinion" while omitting any reference to communism or communist states.[12] The Reagan White House's administration of the Refugee Act delivered upon and betrayed the law's promise. In the 1980s, the United States accepted record numbers of refugees and from parts of the world it had previously neglected. But the Administration consistently shrank annual admissions, heeding resurgent antinewcomer sentiments in domestic politics, and proved most hospitable to refugees from communism, which resonated with Reagan's ardent anti-Soviet and anticommunist foreign policy. Nor did the Refugee Act bring an end to controversies over admission procedures, which raged throughout the 1980s over whether those entering the United States actually met the definition of refugee.

At the Cold War's end, the United States annually admitted tens of thousands of refugees and while the superpower conflict passed in the early 1990s, refugee admissions continued in the post–Cold War era. Viewed from the perspective of 1945, this was an extraordinary historical evolution. It was also, as this book demonstrates, a rich history deeply intertwined with continuing battles over immigration and newcomers, a Cold War foreign policy that brought the United States a new and larger role in the world, the civil rights revolution that forever changed American society, the growing power and capacity of the American state, and the triumphs and failures of the human rights movement. The history of refugee affairs, then, is also a history of some of the defining aspects of the modern American experience.

CHAPTER 1

"The Age of the Uprooted Man": The United States and Refugees, 1900–1952

DURING THE FIRST HALF of the twentieth century, refugee problems proliferated around the globe, became more dire and deadly, and garnered more attention internationally and in the United States. In 1957 long-time refugee advocate and former first lady Eleanor Roosevelt, upon reviewing the previous decades' refugee crises and assessing the contemporary problems, declared it "the age of the uprooted man." The United States' response to these catastrophes was characterized largely by neglect. In the twentieth century's first five decades, the American government failed to develop a comprehensive response to refugee problems, and, more often than not, it also eschewed temporary measures.[1]

Foreign policy imperatives and domestic political and cultural concerns explain the malnourished response. U.S. foreign policymakers were either indifferent to refugee crises or judged involvement antithetical to the nation's interests. Domestically, economic concerns, cultural biases, and political calculations fed opposition. Most important, public hostility toward immigrants grew measurably, best symbolized by passage of the 1920s national origins laws that closed the "open door." Between 1920 and 1945, refugees (and immigrants) saw their chances to enter the United States lessened by powerful currents in American political culture that deemed only newcomers of particular ethnonational backgrounds worthy of admission and capable of becoming "American." Even when the U.S. government in the 1930s initiated a few programs to admit European Jews fleeing Nazism, the federal government's bureaucracy consciously worked to slow refugee admissions.

World War II brought paradoxical change to refugee and immigration affairs. During the war, the United States clamped down on refugee and immigrant admissions because of fears that political subversives and saboteurs might enter the country. On the other hand, the war on Nazism discredited the scientific racism that underlay restrictionist thinking. Likewise, a limited but newcomer-friendly brand of political and cultural pluralism emerged at the center of postwar political culture. The war's end, moreover, marked a new chapter in the United States' international history, with the nation committed to rebuilding Europe politically and economically, to demonstrating global leadership, and to fulfilling the responsibilities that victory in World War II created—each of which augured well for aid to refugees. These changes led to the passage of the 1948 Displaced Persons Act that admitted about 400,000 refugees.

The most important change in post-1945 refugee and immigration affairs had just emerged as the DP program came into being: the Cold War. The Cold War made U.S. foreign policy explicitly anti-Soviet and anticommunist and placed new emphasis on the establishment of American credibility in international politics. These developments dramatically altered how policymakers and politicians, as well as the restrictionist and liberalizer blocs, considered the admission of newcomers. The Cold War also made opposition to communism central to the nation's identity, a transformation that restrictionists and liberalizers acknowledged. The Cold War's long shadow first emerged forcefully in the postwar debate over immigration, which, in turn, was a dress rehearsal for the refugee politics and policy battles that began as the Displaced Persons program ended in 1952.

THE UNITED STATES AND REFUGEES BEFORE WORLD WAR II

The twentieth century's most notorious refugee crisis occurred in the 1930s. Germans, both Jews and political opponents of the Nazis, began fleeing immediately after Hitler took power in January 1933. As more of Europe fell to the Nazis in the late 1930s, the exodus spread to the rest of the continent. For the millions who escaped, sometimes only temporarily, many more wanted to leave but could not. The tragic outcomes of this story are well known. International efforts were ineffective or half hearted. Indifference, and sometimes outright opposition, also characterized the U.S. government's efforts to help refugees from Nazism. The paucity of the American response can be traced in large part to the United States' recent history in immigration and refugee affairs.[2]

Immigration politics and laws provided the key backdrop to American refugee policies in the 1930s. The previous decades had been marked by a grand battle that pitted liberalizers who wanted to retain a relatively open door that had allowed the entry of almost 25 million newcomers since 1880 against restrictionists who wanted to shut that door.[3] The liberalizer bloc consisted of recent immigrants themselves, immigrant aid organizations, and social Progressives and pluralist thinkers like Jane Addams and Horace Kallen. They were joined by business interests who believed that unfettered immigration provided cheap labor and encouraged overseas trade. The early twentieth-century liberalizer alliance united Democrats and Republicans from the urban and industrialized Northeast and

Midwest, where many newcomers settled. As a result, the liberalizer bloc's political and electoral foundation was the heart of early twentieth-century urban Progressivism. Politicians in the urban Progressive tradition believed that helping and supporting immigrants was a key part of their social and political agenda, which sought to ameliorate the ills of urban and industrial life that fell so heavily upon newcomers.[4] These politicians, of course, also understood the electoral benefits of satisfying their constituents.

The restrictionist bloc was equally powerful and diverse. Its support also came in part from Progressives, indicative of the elastic nature of that descriptor. The economist John Commons and labor organizations like the Knights of Labor and, later, the American Federation of Labor, argued that immigration depressed working-class wages. Other restrictionists, like Senator Henry Cabot Lodge, were more concerned with the ethnonational origins of immigrants from southern and eastern Europe. Lodge believed that these newcomers threatened the nation's exceptional political and economic institutions and traditions, which were exclusively the product of the white, English-speaking, Anglo-cultured, Protestant settlers. Patriotic societies like the Daughters of the American Revolution and, after the Great War, the American Legion echoed Lodge's assertions. Lodge symbolized restrictionism's power in the northeast, but anti-immigrant sentiment flourished in other parts of the country. On the West Coast, politicians from both parties played to anti-Chinese and anti-Asian prejudices. Most important, southern Democrats increasingly joined the restrictionist camp during the first two decades of the twentieth century. They abandoned the liberalizer bloc after finding that European immigrants did not settle in the South and because restrictionism's ethnonational and racial overtones jibed with the political culture of the Jim Crow South.[5]

The two sides battled ferociously in the decades after 1880 and restrictionists made certain gains, like the exclusion of Chinese immigrants and prohibitions on the entry of anarchists, the diseased, and those deemed "likely to become a public charge." On the whole, though, liberalizers maintained the nation's traditionally inviting policies toward newcomers until the Great War. They prevailed because of national partisan politics, which saw both parties benefit from recent immigrant votes, and because of the structural peculiarities of American political institutions—the absence of congressional immigration committees prior to the 1890s and the overwhelming power of the Speaker of the House until the early twentieth century, to name just two—that stymied restrictionist reform efforts.[6]

Capitalizing on the xenophobic anti-immigrant hysteria and economic problems that struck the United States in the aftermath of the Great War, restrictionists won passage of the national origins quota immigration laws in the 1920s that closed the "open door." The Immigration Act of 1924 allotted 165,000 visas annually—reduced to 150,000 in 1929—to Eastern Hemisphere immigrants; the law did not set a quota for immigrants from the western hemisphere and it continued the ban on Asian immigration. The Eastern Hemisphere quota stood in sharp contrast to the annual admissions of newcomers in the early twentieth century, which regularly topped 1 million. The 1920s laws established a quota system that distributed those visas just as restrictionists wanted: Great Britain received the most annual visa slots (65,721) while countries from southern and eastern Europe received the fewest; Italy, for instance, received 5,802 slots, while Russia received 2,784. This immigration system remained in effect with some modifications until the mid-1960s.[7]

The 1920s immigration debates' most striking component was the ascendance in political culture of a particular vision of national identity that stressed nationality and ethnicity. Restrictionist contentions that southern and eastern Europeans lacked both the ability to transcend their ethnic identities and the essential characteristics of Americans possessed by Anglo-Protestants had hardened by the late 1910s into a supposedly scientific hierarchy of races and ethnicities in which genetically blessed Anglos had secured the highest rung. Eugenic thinking posited that each race and ethnicity had immutable and universal characteristics. Anglos possessed a particular genetic makeup, which all other races and nationalities lacked, that allowed them to develop and practice democracy and self-government—and, thus, to enjoy and appreciate supposed American ideals like freedom, liberty, and equality. The conclusion was clear: if the United States continued to admit immigrants of certain ethnic or national backgrounds, then American democracy would collapse and the country would never live up to its Founding vision. The liberalizer bloc failed utterly in the face of the supposedly scientific and social science-proven, restrictionist arguments, of the difficult economic conditions of the early 1920s, and of concerns about the political allegiances of newcomers.[8]

The national origins quota immigration system made no special accommodations for refugee admissions. This oversight did not occur because the United States had no experience with persons fleeing political or religious persecution. In the eighteenth and nineteenth centuries, the country repeatedly offered succor to persons who, in the twentieth century, would be considered refugees. French émigrés escaping the Revolution, German radicals who fled after the Revolutions of 1848 collapsed, and the famous Hungarian revolutionary Louis Kossuth in 1850 all came to the United States to escape political persecution. Despite the arrivals of these newcomers, the U.S. government in the nineteenth century had no "refugee policy," hardly a surprise since until the 1870s United States had neither an official immigration policy nor the means to control its borders. The arrival of these "refugees" aroused some hostility, in part because of the powerful nativist currents and in part because of concerns that those fleeing Europe held radical political beliefs. Opposition, however, never reached remarkable levels because so few "refugees" came to the United States and because equally strong political and cultural currents demanded a warm reception.[9]

In the twentieth century's second and third decades, the global refugee problem deepened as nationalism and war reshaped the political geography of Europe and Asia. The most significant refugee flows occurred in Germany, in the new states formed out of the rubble of the Austro-Hungarian and Ottoman Empires, and in the Soviet Union. The League of Nations, rather than any one country, led the hunt for solutions. The League appointed a "High Commissioner," Dr. Fridjtof Nansen, to manage relief and resettlement policies—a task he handled so well that the League predicted in 1930 that its refugee work would be over by the end of the decade. The international community's engagement with the Russian and Armenian population flows also led to a generally accepted understanding of the term "refugee." In 1926 the League defined a refugee as a person of "Russian origin" or "Armenian origin" who had lost the "protection of the government" of his or her country and had yet to acquire "another nationality." Under the League's definition, the term "refugee" was inherently political: it applied to persons who lacked "the protection of a government." League policymakers consciously arrived at this distinction because they did not want persons leaving a country for economic reasons considered refugees. Moreover, by identifying refugees as persons of "Russian origin" or "Armenian origin," the League put an ethnonational qualifier on its universal political definition of refugee, which theoretically applied to any person.[10]

While the U.S. government and private groups sent substantial material and financial aid to European refugees in the 1910s and 1920s, the United States made no special efforts to resettle refugees within its borders. Congress occasionally attempted to ease the entry of victims of political and religious persecution. The 1917 immigration law omitted the literacy test for immigrants fleeing political or religious persecution, but did not use the term "refugee." In the 1920s, several proposals emerged in Congress that provided for the admission of Armenian refugees, but this legislation never passed. The stillborn efforts to admit Armenians did fashion in U.S. legal and political circles a workable definition of "refugee." Senate legislation in 1923 defined a "refugee" as a "homeless" Armenian "who shows that he has fled from his home in reasonable apprehension of death or bodily injury at the hands of Turkish troops or the Turkish civilian population since the 1st of August, 1914." The Senate definition highlighted what made a refugee—state persecution and persecution at the hands of another ethnic group—but, like the League definition, left the nature of these persecutions unexplored. Nor, unlike

later definitions in the wake of World War II, did the political beliefs of
the refugee enter into the definition. Instead, the chief attributes ascribed
to "refugee" were vaguely defined persecution and—very telling of the
state of American immigration affairs in the 1920s—race; that is, refugees
were of the "Armenian race."[11]

Foreign policy, political, and cultural dynamics explain the American
government's decisions to ignore refugee problems in the 1910s and
1920s. U.S. foreign policymakers had no compelling geopolitical, diplomatic, or public-relations reasons to support the admission of refugees
and they did not link their key objectives of European economic stability
and disarmament to the solution of refugee problems. Just as important,
the political and cultural environment at home in the 1910s and 1920s
was decidedly unfriendly to the admission of newcomers, including refugees. Refugee admissions were even more unlikely because most of the
world's refugees were from eastern and central Europe and from the Near
East, regions that the nation's restrictionist immigration laws discriminated against. It was also not clear in the 1920s that liberalizers, bruised
and soon beaten in the immigration battles, could muster the energy and
strength to successfully advocate for refugees. The lack of powerful and
organized ethnic organizations to represent these refugees only com-
pounded liberalizer weaknesses.

By the 1930s, as the European refugee crisis grew to awful dimensions,
American immigration laws were restrictive, domestic political culture
was anti-newcomer, and the nation had played little role in solving the
previous two decades' refugee problems. Predictably, then, the United
States' unilateral efforts to help European refugees from Nazism in the
1930s were scant. Until December 1941, most refugees fleeing Nazism
entered the United States via regular immigration procedures. The small
German quota hindered refugee admission as did a variety of bureaucratic
and administrative obstacles. Through most of the 1930s, President
Franklin Roosevelt continued the Hoover administration's policy of strict
enforcement of the "likely to become a public charge" clause in immigration law, which suppressed admissions by permitting government officials
to deny entry to persons they believed might not be able to support themselves. Moreover, to gain a visa, immigrants were required to present consuls with a mass of paperwork and documentation, some of which was
difficult, if not impossible, to acquire. While FDR at various points
throughout the 1930s ordered the State Department to moderate these
restrictions, refugee admissions through the immigration quotas remained a trickle. In 1933 just over 5 percent of the German quota was
used, although this percentage increased slightly every year between 1934
and 1937, reflecting in large part the increased emigration flow from Germany and in small part the Roosevelt administration's efforts to ease

entry. In 1937 just over 42 percent of the quota (about 11,500 visas) was utilized. Legislative efforts to revise or create exceptions to the quotas proved no panacea. In 1938 and 1939 prominent liberalizers introduced bills to admit refugees outside the existing quotas, all of which failed. Congressional temper was so restrictionist in the late 1930s that more bills were introduced to reduce the admissions of immigrants (and refugees) than were introduced to increase those admissions.[12]

Refugee advocates did bring much needed attention to the plight of European Jewry, which led to some small victories in the 1930s. Jewish organizations, labor organizations like the Congress of Industrial Organizations, and politicians from the urban and industrialized Northeast— essentially the heart of the New Deal coalition, minus southern Democrats—vigorously supported refugee admissions. They appealed to the nation's history of providing a haven for the oppressed, reassured that an influx of refugees would not damage the economy, and highlighted the awful plight of the refugees in an attempt to build sympathy for admissions. Their prodding in the late 1930s helped force the Roosevelt administration to action. FDR organized an international conference at Evian, the goal of which was a more concerted international effort to help refugees from Nazism. More important, FDR ordered State Department and INS officials to combine and fully utilize the German and Austrian quotas. As a result, the German quota was more than 85 percent filled between 1938 and 1940. But if the Roosevelt administration rethought aspects of citizenship and the role of government in society, it just as surely brought no such revolution to American refugee affairs. FDR was merely sympathetic and lukewarm toward refugee issues at a time when refugee advocates needed a catalyzing leader who would use his immense political and policy powers to rally popular support, to lobby recalcitrant politicians, and to push hard on a federal bureaucracy full of restrictionists.[13]

Liberalizers failed, however, mostly because of the power and determination of restrictionists. Opposition to refugee admissions ran strongest in the West and South, where Democrats continued, as they had for more than two decades, to oppose the admission of newcomers. Likewise, longtime immigration opponents like the American Legion, the Daughters of the American Revolution, and the American Federation of Labor attacked refugee-aid proposals mercilessly. Restrictionists argued that in the midst of the Depression America's needy deserved the nation's compassion and largesse more than foreigners and that an influx of refugees would take jobs from American workers. Restrictionists also warned that refugee admissions would destroy the quota system. Just as important, strong anti-Semitic currents stiffened resistance to the admission of European Jews. Opponents of an American commitment to refugees in the 1930s consistently highlighted the number of Jews who would be admitted; some explicitly argued that the United States was a Christian nation and that any aid ought to go to Christian, not Jewish, refugees. The message was clear: Jews did not make good Americans. The one exception to the failure of refugee-aid legislation proved the larger point. In 1940 the "Mercy Ships" bill, designed to speed the entry of British (and presumably Christian) immigrants passed without patriotic organizations, usually stalwart restrictionists, registering their objections.[14]

The State Department proved a most important ally of restrictionists in the 1930s, shaping the American government's response to the refugee crisis in two important ways. First, the Department asserted that helping German Jewish refugees—by substantively participating in international efforts and by expediting their entry through regular immigration procedures—would damage U.S. relations with Germany. FDR largely acceded to the argument that it was in the United States' foreign policy and diplomatic interests *not* to help refugees. Second, State Department consular personnel charged with the daily administration of the visa process proved obstructionist and restrictionist, even when ordered by Roosevelt to interpret admissions guidelines liberally. Scholars have attributed the restrictionist implementation of the nation's immigration laws in many, but not all, cases to the anti-Semitism of consular officers in the field and their bosses in Washington, D.C. The admission of refugees, then, was not assured with the passage of legislation or the approval of a specific policy, but when a refugee program was implemented and administered with a liberalizing caste.[15]

WORLD WAR II: REFUGEES AND IMMIGRANTS

World War II strengthened both the liberalizer and restrictionist impulses in refugee and immigration affairs. While Congress and the Roosevelt administration supported some cosmetic programs and laws that allowed at most a few thousand immigrants or refugees to enter, newcomers in the main faced more obstacles to entry during the war years. The national origins immigration system remained in place, although Congress modified it in 1943 to give China an annual quota of 107 visas. This reform had its roots in FDR's argument that the complete ban on Chinese immigration angered the United States' key Asian ally in the war against Japan. A similarly small commitment was made to refugees following the fall of France in June 1940 when the Roosevelt administration launched a crash program that temporarily admitted "political and intellectual" refugees from Germany who had fled to France but now had to leave that country because of the Nazi takeover. The program admitted only 2,000 persons (1,200 in 1940 and another 800 in 1941). The State Department and an advisory committee appointed by Roosevelt likely determined exactly who was a "political" or "intellectual" refugee—perhaps handpicking the particular refugees they wished to admit. Finally, in 1944, FDR ordered the admission of 987 European Jews from camps in Italy.[16]

Neither the Chinese legislation nor the special refugee programs altered the restrictionist caste of American immigration or refugee affairs. The Chinese quota was merely a token gesture that left the quota system in place. Likewise, the State Department's special refugee program of 1940–41 required newcomers to jump through considerable bureaucratic hoops to gain admittance. Applicants had to satisfy the "likely to become a public charge" codicil and they had to obtain a brief biography from an American citizen that testified to their moral character, their past political affiliations, and their ability to contribute to the United States' well-being. Such demands were part of the State Department's obstructionist stance toward European refugees who wanted to come to America. Indeed, beginning in late 1939, the State Department began awarding German quota visas to Germans living in the safety of Cuba and Britain rather than refugees in continental Europe.[17]

World War II also roused fears that recent immigrants and foreign nationals living in the United States (known as "aliens") endangered national security. With the rise of Nazi Germany and the approach of continent-wide hostilities in the late 1930s, fears grew in the United States that foreign subversives—potential immigrants or refugees, recent immigrants from Germany, or even first-generation German Americans—retained their loyalties to Nazi Germany and actively worked to harm the United States. The most public expression of this concern came from Representative Martin Dies (D-TX), who launched the House Un-American Activities Committee (HUAC) to investigate the supposed threat. HUAC's legislative analogue was the June 1940 Alien Registration Act, which provided for government registration and fingerprinting of "aliens" and allowed the deportation of aliens who "advocate, abet, advise, or teach" the violent overthrow or destruction of the U.S. government. Offering a deliberately broad definition of subversive activity, the law failed to identify either particular ethnonational groups or political ideologies as its targets, though Germans and communists in the immigrant community most sharply felt its sting. The American concerns with subversion were not exceptional, of course. Britain and Canada enacted mass internment policies that placed so-called German enemy aliens—both Nazi sympathizers and Jewish refugees—in camps.[18]

The fear of subversion and concern about national security led to important bureaucratic changes in admissions policies for refugees and immigrants. Congress, at FDR's urging, moved the Immigration and Naturalization Service (the bureaucratic successor to the Bureau of Immigration) from the Labor Department to the Justice Department in June 1940, signaling that immigration was more a law-enforcement and "national defense" issue than an economic concern. (The State Department retained its role in issuing visas.) Restrictionists supported this transfer because they detested Labor Secretary Frances Perkins, who had emerged as one of the administration's most steadfast supporters of larger refugee and immigrant admissions.[19]

Even more than Congress, the State Department refashioned American immigration and refugee affairs in light of the war. The State Department's immigration experts repeatedly cited national security concerns as they tightened admissions requirements. In mid-1940, Assistant Secretary of State Breckinridge Long and head of the Visa Division Avra Warren, who oversaw the distribution of visas, directed consular officials to vigorously enforce security provisions so that purported fifth columnists and saboteurs did not enter the United States. In January 1941 the State Department reported to FDR that subversives had already entered the United States via regular immigration procedures and that all visa applicants required thorough security screenings. Reacting to such concerns, six months later Congress authorized several changes to the immigrant admissions process. Consular officials were instructed to deny a visa to an applicant whom they feared endangered public safety. All investigations of visa applicants were centralized in the State Department, setting up a procedure by which a State Department–led interdepartmental committee (with members from the INS, FBI, and Naval and Military Intelligence) offered a recommendation on each applicant's admissibility to consular officers in the field. Those consular officers retained the final say over admission, however.[20]

In the short term, the new restrictions, coupled with the difficulties faced by refugees and immigrants trying to leave Europe during a war, caused admissions of Germans to drop precipitously; in 1941 about half of the German quota was filled, a rate that plummeted below 5 percent after the United States entered the war. Viewed through the long term, the bureaucratic, legislative, and policy maneuvering of 1940 and 1941 highlighted the powerful concern that the admission of refugees and immigrants threatened American national security. Great War–era anti-immigrant legislation—such as the 1917 Immigration Act—did focus on the political allegiances and loyalties of newcomers and the threat they posed to the United States By the early 1940s, though, a new conception of "national security" existed that stressed that the United States could not survive in an increasingly interconnected world dominated by militaristic and totalitarian states bent on conquering the globe. This new concern about national security raised the stakes of refugee and immigrant entry considerably, especially compared to what had been the case in the 1910s;

political subversion by newcomers might be in service of a totalitarian foe bent on world domination. Just as telling, in contrast to the 1920s, when restrictionists argued that most immigrants were unable because of their genetic makeup to practice American democracy, 1930s and 1940s restrictionists opposed newcomer admissions for fear that refugees and immigrants remained loyal to political ideologies antithetical to democracy, liberty, and freedom and thus were subversive risks.[21]

In spite of these restrictionist gains, World War II also strengthened the hand of liberalizers. The barbaric nature of Nazism discredited the scientific racism that underlay much of restrictionist thinking. (Of course, other factors, like changes in social science thinking about the concept of race, also discredited scientific racism.) Just as important, World War II thrust upon the United States a greater role in world affairs. An expanded and more activist internationalist foreign policy placed American immigration and refugee affairs in a different light, forcing policymakers to consider seriously how policies toward newcomers affected American diplomacy and relations with other countries. Indeed, Roosevelt supported the 1943 Chinese immigration legislation because he thought it would help the Sino-American alliance. This dynamic only grew in importance in the decades following World War II.

The Holocaust, whose awful dimensions began to emerge as the war ended, was of course a chief legacy of World War II. In the postwar world, most observers agreed that the failure to help those trying to escape the Nazis in the 1930s had horrible consequences and—although this point was certainly more contentious—that the Allies had not done enough, quickly enough, to halt the Nazis' murder of 6 million Jews. The Holocaust and its memory and meaning, though, had surprisingly little effect on American refugee policies in the postwar years, with two exceptions. In the late 1940s, the Holocaust—and Nazi Germany's forced movement of peoples—led to massive refugee and population problems that the United States addressed through a refugee program. In the 1970s, the memory of the Holocaust colored the arguments of refugee advocates who wanted the United States to admit Soviet Jews and the Indochinese, specifically the "boat people." In the 1950s and 1960s, though, policymakers, politicians, and advocates working on refugee issues only very rarely used the Holocaust as a prod to action in the United States.[22]

POSTWAR EUROPE, DISPLACED PERSONS AND REFUGEES, AND THE EARLY COLD WAR

At the war's end, at least 8 million persons in Germany, Italy, and Austria lacked permanent residences and the protection of citizenship. The United

Nations Relief and Rehabilitation Agency (UNRRA), with support from the United States, headed repatriation efforts in 1945 that returned more than 6 million of these persons to their homelands, often against their will. That same year, after learning of the refugees' horrible living conditions and the strain that their care put on Allied military forces, President Harry Truman ordered the State Department to administer immigration laws liberally so that some of these 8 million might enter the United States. Truman's directive did little to solve the population problem, which only worsened in 1946. Anti-Semitic violence broke out in Eastern Europe, especially Poland, sending more Jews to the Allied-controlled sectors of Germany. Additionally, in 1946 about 4 million Germans (the *Volksdeutsche*) who had been living in eastern Europe began returning to Germany, as mandated by the Potsdam Conference. The majority of these 4 million refugees ended up in western Germany—under U.S. and Allied care.[23]

In August 1946 Truman took a bolder step, supporting a proposal to admit an unspecified number of European refugees outside existing immigration quotas; this legislative seed eventually became the 1948 Displaced Persons Act. Domestic political pressures, especially from the religious and ethnic groups that were key members of the Democratic coalition, contributed to Truman's decision. Jewish organizations, but also several Catholic and Protestant groups, made sure that Truman and congressional Democrats knew the plight of the postwar displaced persons. Likewise, European ethnic societies and organizations representing their suffering brethren lobbied Democrats at both ends of Pennsylvania Avenue for refugee admissions. Truman and the Democrats, then, protected and satisfied key electoral constituents in supporting a DP program.[24]

Concerns about Europe's economic and political future also influenced the Truman administration's policies toward the population problem. At the war's end, the United States desired a solution to the population issue as part of general European reconstruction. Thinking about postwar reconstruction, though, quickly took on new urgency as U.S. leaders began to worry in 1945 and 1946 that European political and economic instability and misery might provide an opportunity for indigenous leftist political movements to win power and to reorient their nations politically and economically toward the Soviet Union. Europe's population problem, already tied in the minds of American policymakers to economic and political stability, became part of the larger calculus of U.S.-U.S.S.R. relations. As relations with the Soviets deteriorated, the Truman administration looked to secure its vital interests in Europe and to demonstrate global leadership, goals that, albeit in small ways, were abetted by the admission of refugees. During the sometimes fierce debates about the displaced persons legislation, then, Secretary of State George Marshall and other officials asserted that a DP program would help U.S. foreign policy goals vis-à-vis the Soviet Union.[25]

The displaced persons proposal energized many of the usual opponents of refugee and immigrant admissions. Restrictionists argued that a displaced persons program would hurt unemployed American veterans. They asserted that it would harm the national origins immigration system, ominously warning that "our political institutions could not survive further dilution of the basic strain of our population." Anti-Semitism reared its head as well. Senator William C. Revercombe (D-WV) apparently declared "We could solve this DP problem all right if we could work out some bill that would keep out the Jews." (To combat rampant anti-Semitic attacks, liberalizers highlighted that the majority of entrants would be Christian and enemies of communism fleeing Soviet domination in eastern Europe.) Restrictionists also asserted that more than a few of those admitted would surely be subversives in the employ of the Soviet Union. Finally, Senator Pat McCarran (D-NV), head of the Judiciary Committee, and ardent restrictionist, used every procedural trick in the Senate rule book in an attempt to prevent passage.[26]

While the liberalizer and restrictionist alliances consisted of many of the same groups as in the 1920s and 1930s, the economic, political, and cultural environment in which they worked had shifted considerably. Refugee advocates after 1945 did not face the crushing unemployment of the Depression years, but rather a fluctuating economy that, in the main, was healthy and growing. President Truman proved more supportive than Roosevelt of a refugee program for foreign policy reasons and because he could not afford to offend key parts of his Democratic base, especially with the 1948 election looming and his poll numbers sagging. Finally, liberalizers also encountered a more favorable domestic environment in which more Americans believed that cultural pluralism offered the best protection and recognition of supposed American ideals. Cultural pluralism, formulated most completely by Horace Kallen at the beginning of the twentieth century but now in ascendancy in the early postwar years, held that immigrants of different ethnicities and from different nationalities could all contribute to the growth of America, each bringing to the nation their own attributes. (Cultural pluralism's political analogue, also in vogue by the late 1940s, saw American politics as a competition among competing interests and groups.)

Pluralism, of course, had its limits. For one thing, as we shall see in examining Hungarian refugees in the 1950s, not all Americans embraced cultural pluralism; many believed that newcomers ought to excise completely their immigrant roots—as their predecessors had in the late nineteenth and early twentieth centuries. Moreover, immigrants in the cultural pluralist structure were assumed to be European, not Asian,

African, or South American. This bias, as the historian Gary Gerstle has noted, was at the root of the public's acceptance of cultural pluralism as the decades of immigration restriction slowed—and in the case of Asians, halted—the entry of newcomers. Finally, while cultural (and political) pluralism certainly endorsed diversity to a degree, these theories also assumed that all Americans shared political, social, and cultural values. Nonetheless, despite—and because of—these limitations, the public accepted the basic tenets of cultural pluralism, a boon to liberalizers for it provided a refutation of racial and ethnic definitions of American democracy, liberty, and identity.[27]

The political and cultural terrain, then, had shifted in favor of liberalizers, who won passage of the Displaced Persons Act in the summer of 1948. The DP Act admitted 202,000 persons over two years within the quota system, a substantial amount but a far cry from the liberalizer goal of 400,000 admissions over four years outside the quotas. Restrictionists won numerous other battles as well. Each visa applicant needed to secure an "assurance" (the law's technical term) from either an individual or an accredited religious or ethnic organization that he would not become a public charge, would have a job that did not displace an American worker, and would have adequate housing. The law, moreover, accepted only those persons who had been in relief and resettlement camps prior to December 22, 1945, shutting out persons who arrived in the camps in 1946 and 1947. The law carved out exceptions for the *Volksdeutsche*, who only had to have entered Germany by July 1, 1948, and for persons from the Baltics and agricultural workers, who received special allotments of visas. Each of these codicils had the effect of giving fewer visas to Jews, and more to the *Volksdeutsche* and those who had fled the imposition of Soviet control in the Baltics.[28]

These restrictionist-leaning codicils angered refugee advocates, but other aspects of the law proved heartening. The law continued the tradition of identifying refugees as victims of particular regimes, in this case "victims of nazi or fascist regimes" or "Spanish Republicans and other victims" of Falangist Spain. ("Displaced persons" were victims of these regimes who had been "deported" or "obliged to leave" because of "forced labour" or "racial, religious, or political reasons.") But the definition also referred to those Europeans who, prior to World War II, were refugees for "reasons of race, religion, nationality, or political opinion." This clause offered a capacious definition of "refugee" by basing refugee status on more generalized persecution, rather than on the actions of particular governments. The definition of "refugee," then, continued to contain both particular and universal elements, with the former often outstripping the latter.[29]

More important, the legislation charged the program's administration not to the State Department or the INS, which had proven so restrictionist before and during World War II, but to the Displaced Persons Commission (DPC), a separate body appointed by the president with the Senate's approval. The DPC administered the program liberally, relaxing security and screening measures in comparison with those of the 1930s. By December 1950, over 200,000 DP visas had been issued—and over 40,000 (20 percent) went to Jews, a percentage equal to their representation in the DP population. This liberal admissions policy came at a high price. A number of ex-Nazis or Nazi sympathizers entered via the *Volksdeutsche* and Baltic quotas, angering refugee advocates. The admission of ex-Nazis was not coincidental or the fault of lax screening procedures, but rather the work of American intelligence agencies who hoped to turn these DPs into agents fit for work behind the Iron Curtain.[30]

Soon after the legislation's passage, liberalizers began pushing for revisions. Senator McCarran unsurprisingly continued his obstructionist tactics and revealed his total distaste for the DP program. Yet revisions to the DP law passed in 1950 and 1951 that extended the program for two years, increased DP admissions by 200,000, and made those who had entered the camps before January 1, 1949, eligible for visas. The changes, however, were not all to liberalizers' likings. The *Volksdeutsche* allotment doubled to over 54,000 persons, and a number of other groups, including Greeks, Italians, and Polish veterans living in Britain, were granted visas, which meant that only about 75 percent of the DP visas actually went to displaced persons in International Refugee Organization camps in Germany. More important, McCarran won control of the program's implementation. After 1950 the DPC shared administrative duties with the more restrictionist-minded State Department and the INS. In addition, McCarran's harassment of DP officials during congressional hearings in 1949 led to stricter enforcement of the screening and security provisions. As historian Leonard Dinnerstein has written, McCarran lost the legislative battle, but won the administrative war. Even so, as Dinnerstein notes, McCarran's efforts to slow the entry of DPs were not "insuperable barriers." When the DP program closed up shop in August 1952, it had brought over 400,000 Europeans to the United States. Despite this success, millions of refugees still languished in Europe—a population that kept growing with the steady defection of eastern Europeans from behind the Iron Curtain.[31]

Was the DP program the United States' first Cold War refugee program? Politicians and policymakers did justify the DP program by citing Cold War foreign policy concerns, and, after 1949, debate around DP admissions increasingly focused on internal security and the fear of communist subversion.[32] But the DP program was not birthed in, or greatly shaped by, the Cold War. Relations between the United States and the Soviet Union did not reach the irreparable and antagonistic breach that characterized the "Cold War" until 1948 (with the Marshall Plan, the division of Germany, and the crisis over Berlin) and 1949 (with the formation of NATO). The DP program, by expanding American involvement in Germany and displaying concern for eastern Europeans, is better seen then as contributing to Europe's division into Cold War blocs. Just as important, American officials cast the program as a humanitarian venture that aided victims of World War II rather than helped victims of communism and the Soviet Union. The legislation itself contained no explicit references to the Cold War or problematic U.S.-Soviet relations, nor did it mention communism. The law defined refugees as victims of Nazi and Falangist regimes, but not of the Soviet Union. (It did refer to the Soviet Union by describing it as the "foreign power" that had annexed the Baltic nations.) The DP Act, in sum, lacked the ideological tensions and Cold War rhetoric that characterized much of 1950s and 1960s refugee legislation.[33]

RESTRICTIONIST TRIUMPH: PASSAGE OF THE 1952 McCARRAN-WALTER ACT

The immigration debates of the early 1950s, in contrast, were deeply colored by the Cold War. Immigration emerged as an issue on the postwar political agenda at the insistence of both liberalizers and restrictionists. The former never abandoned their hopes of reforming or destroying the national origins quotas, while restrictionists emerged from the war even more dedicated to strengthening existing immigration laws.[34]

The liberalizer bloc still rested among liberal Democrats, ethnic interest groups, religious organizations with experience in immigrant resettlement, the Congress of Industrial Organizations, and liberal organizations like Americans for Democratic Action. President Truman, just as with the DP legislation, had a political stake in satisfying these constituencies and thus emerged as a strong supporter of reform. Moderates and liberals from the Republican party—like Representatives Jacob Javits and Kenneth Keating (both of New York)—also remained in the liberalizer camp. To be sure, though, the heart of the coalition was the heart of midcentury liberalism: New Dealers, European white ethnics, Catholics and Jews, and labor. This coalition had passed New Deal legislation in the 1930s, but it was unclear whether it could win immigration reform, especially because southern Democrats did not support the liberalizer agenda as they did some of the important economic and welfare agenda of the New Deal.[35]

Liberalizers believed that the current immigration laws unnecessarily suppressed immigration, codified the racist assumption that only immigrants from northwestern Europe could become "American," and harmed the United States' standing in the world, a particular problem as the nation engaged in the Cold War. While publicly calling for the abolition of the national origins quota system, liberalizer proposals circa 1950 were remarkably moderate. They did not seek to lift the overall ceilings on immigration, nor did they demand the immediate elimination of the quota system. Rather, they called for modifications to the existing immigration laws that would ease immigration from southern and eastern Europe and end the ban on Asian immigration and citizenship.

Returning to the restrictionist side were the American Legion and Daughters of the American Revolution, the AFL, and politicians from the West and the South. Southern Democrats particularly were determined to maintain a precise racial and ethnonational regime at home, through Jim Crow, and in immigration affairs via the national origins quotas. On Capitol Hill, restrictionists looked to Senator McCarran and Representative Francis Walter (D-PA) for leadership. McCarran was the key restrictionist. Seniority had catapulted him to head of the Senate Judiciary Committee in 1943, a position from which he launched blistering attacks on the DP Program. McCarran often sounded like his predecessors, revealing a dislike for all immigrants and refugees and harboring a strong anti-Semitic streak. Abandoning the national origins system, McCarran warned, would "in the course of a generation or so, change the ethnic and cultural composition of this Nation. The times . . . are too perilous for us to tinker blindly with our national institutions." McCarran, therefore, opposed granting eastern, southern, and central Europeans and Asians the same opportunities afforded northwestern Europeans to immigrate to the United States. His nativism, however, differed from early twentieth-century restrictionists. McCarran was Irish and Catholic, which surely would have raised the hackles of his restrictionist predecessors. Likewise, in deference to America's Cold War allies in Asia, McCarran acceded to lifting the ban on Asian immigration and granting Asian nations their own quotas. While McCarran dropped the plainly racist and eugenic arguments of the 1920s and instead vaguely stated that immigrants of certain ethnicities and nationalities endangered the nation's "composition," his legislation made clear his support for national origins policy.[36]

McCarran and his allies added another potent argument in support of restrictionism and national origins: anticommunism. Like many of the most vigorous 1950s anticommunists, McCarran despised New Deal and Fair Deal liberalism, which he saw as evidence of encroaching government paternalism that threatened to bring socialism or communism. McCarran's fears of communist subversion and infiltration from abroad were just as pronounced. He authored the most notorious piece of Red Scare legislation, the 1950 Internal Security Act, which explicitly linked immi-

Figure 1.1 Senator Patrick McCarran conferring with Senator Lyndon B. Johnson in 1954. As president, Johnson signed into law the amendments that destroyed the national origins quota immigration system that McCarran supported in 1952.

grants with communism and warned that the admission of newcomers invited communist subversion and espionage. McCarran justified the legislation by citing national security concerns. The Internal Security Act's principles underlay McCarran's proposed immigration and nationality legislation, which called for exclusion of communists, forbade the naturalization of those immigrants who were professed communists, strengthened immigrant screening requirements, and further facilitated the deportation of aliens. Moreover, McCarran justified retention of the national origins system as an effective weapon in the battle against communism at home and abroad.[37]

McCarran was not only an ideologue and a demagogue, he also was an effective Washington operative. He had close ties to the restrictionists at the State Department, particularly those in the visa and passport offices. Moreover, McCarran stocked the Senate's immigration subcommittee with his own people, especially the powerful counsel to the subcommittee, Richard Arens. Official Washington widely believed that this network of restrictionists had written the McCarran immigration bill and that McCarran's allies in the INS and State Department effectively controlled immigration to the United States. McCarran looked to institutionalize this network's power in new ways as well. His legislation created a Bureau of Security and Consular Affairs in the State Department that McCarran hoped would be beholden to him and other congressional restrictionists. The new bureau's responsibilities entailed not only immigration affairs, but also internal security at the State Department.[38]

In the spring of 1952, liberalizer and restrictionist immigration proposals came up for congressional consideration. McCarran's legislation easily passed the House and the Senate as liberalizer opposition collapsed. The McCarran-Walter Act, named after its congressional sponsors, slightly increased the total number of visas available to immigrants annually. It reaffirmed the quota system designed in the 1920s that favored northern and western European immigrants. It ended the prohibition on Asian immigrants, but granted them very small quotas while maintaining the large quotas for Europeans. The legislation also granted visas, within the quota system, to those immigrants who had skills that the Department of Labor deemed necessary. The MWA enacted strict security provisions designed to thwart the entrance of subversives, including fascists, anarchists, and, most importantly, communists or "supporters of the world communist movement." Finally, it imposed new restrictions on the naturalization of immigrants.[39]

Liberalizers blanched at the legislation and President Truman sent it back to Congress with a stinging veto. Truman supported the end of the ban on Asian immigration, but blasted the low numerical ceiling on immigration and the retention, largely unmodified, of the national origins quotas. "The idea behind this discriminatory policy," Truman wrote, "was, to put it baldly, that Americans with English or Irish names make better people and American citizens than Americans with Italian or Greek or Polish names." National origins thinking, Truman asserted, was "utterly unworthy of our traditions and our ideals," like the "the great political doctrine of the Declaration of Independence that 'all men are created equal' . . . the humanitarian creed inscribed beneath the Statue of Liberty . . . our basic religious concepts, our belief in the brotherhood of man." By the 1950s, this rhetoric was boilerplate, even if honestly and energetically professed; similar sentiments had failed liberalizers repeatedly over the preceding three decades.[40]

Truman more effectively pursued a different tact, identifying "the very people that we want to bring in": immigrants from the United States' allies in the Cold War. Truman found it preposterous that "Greeks, struggling to assist the helpless victims of a communist civil war" and "Turks . . . brave defenders of the Eastern flank" had such paltry quotas. "We do not need to be protected" from eastern European immigrants, Truman continued, but "on the contrary we want to stretch out a helping hand, to save those who have managed to flee into Western Europe, to succor those who are brave enough to escape from barbarism, to welcome and restore them against the day when their countries will, as we hope, be free again." Potential Turkish, Greek, and eastern European immigrants had helped America combat the Soviet threat—and fought and suffered under communism in their homelands—and they deserved the chance to live in the United States. Through their anticommunism, and because of their victimization at the hands of communist governments, they had exhibited the respect for and understanding of American ideals like liberty, freedom, and democracy that all good Americans displayed. Truman's portrayal of newcomers skillfully conflated opposition to and victimization by communism, a tactic that others would use in the future. The essence of his argument, though, was clear: national identity and "American-ness" were not related to national origins or ethnicity, but to a certain set of political ideals and allegiances, including anticommunism.[41]

If American identity in the 1920s had turned on ethnicity and national origins, by the 1950s anticommunism joined, and perhaps even superseded, a limited cultural and political pluralism at the center of national identity. Indeed, pluralism, as previously noted, was by its very nature fractious and divisive. Anticommunism served as a powerful counterforce to these centrifugal tendencies. The danger of centering American identity on anticommunism was that it established a political litmus test and benchmark, one that the staunchest defenders of civil liberties and political freedom pointed out was antithetical to traditions of freedom of thought, expression, and political belief. Truman and American liberals, of course, were much more concerned about this delicate balance than McCarran and his allies, including Senator Joe McCarthy.[42]

Nonetheless, a broad consensus existed on the centrality of anticommunism to the nation's identity. Fear of communism and a belief in the righteousness of anticommunism permeated American society in the early years of the Cold War. Americans across the country visited the Freedom

Train, a traveling exhibition of historical documents from the National Archives designed to celebrate American political ideals and, by inference, to contrast them with their antithesis, the political ideals supposedly embodied in Soviet communism. From their living rooms, Americans watched as Desi Arnaz, a Cuban immigrant, defended his wife Lucille Ball from charges that she was a "red." In perhaps one of the most bizarre displays of anticommunist fervor, a small town in Wisconsin staged a communist takeover to demonstrate to its residents their fate under communism should they abandon their vigilance.[43]

Both political parties sought to use the peculiar and particular dynamics of Cold War politics and culture to their electoral and partisan advantage. In the 1946 midterm elections, Republicans like Richard Nixon in California and Joe McCarthy in Wisconsin mercilessly attacked their Democratic opponents as soft on communism, warning that naive Democratic policies abetted communist subversion at home. As eastern Europe fell to Soviet and communist power, Republicans blasted the Truman administration for allowing Poland, Czechoslovakia, and Hungary to lose their freedom. Republican attacks only increased in the late 1940s and early 1950s after the Soviets successfully tested an atomic weapon, Mao's communists took China, and the Korean War settled into a stalemate. Republican leaders like Senator Robert Taft were more than willing to let backbenchers like Senator McCarthy pursue questionable charges of communist subversion in the federal government for the pain it caused Democrats. At no time was this clearer than in 1950, when McCarthy helped engineer the defeat of Democratic senator Millard Tydings of Maryland, who had tried to derail McCarthy's rise to prominence by questioning the senator's motives and charges. McCarthy smeared and red-baited Tydings, who lost to the Republican Jon Butler. Similar tactics helped Republicans defeat Democrats Frank Graham (NC), Claude Pepper (FL), and Helen Gaughan Douglas (CA) in the 1950 midterms.[44]

Republicans believed such attacks played well with the general electorate—though some evidence also suggested the strategy scared voters—and generally put Democrats on the defensive. Just as important, Republicans hoped that trumpeting an aggressive anti-Soviet foreign policy and the vigorous pursuit of communist subversives at home would help them win the support of Catholics and first- and second-generation eastern Europeans, all of whom traditionally voted Democratic. In the 1952 presidential election, this strategy reached an apogee of sorts. The Eisenhower campaign believed that the white ethnic and Catholic voting blocs of the Northeast and Midwest were up for grabs and that promises of an aggressive foreign policy and vigilance in the face of communist subversion at home was the way to their votes. Thus, Eisenhower played up Truman's failures in the face of the Soviet challenge and the Democrats supposedly weak efforts to fight communist subversion while the presumptive secretary of state, John Foster Dulles, asserted that a Republican administration would try to liberate eastern Europe.

The Truman administration and congressional Democrats, in response, sought to refute charges that they were soft on communism with an aggressive Cold War foreign policy and a vigorous security program at home. The immigration issue also emerged for Democrats as a potent counter to Republican charges. By calling for the end of national origins, Democrats could appeal to those very voters Republicans tried to court and to those voters' state and local leaders—this was still the era of the Democratic, urban political machines—whom the national party depended upon. Truman's 1952 veto of the McCarran-Walter bill, in which the president invoked the bravery of the Greeks and eastern Europeans in the face of the Soviet Union, was a plain attempt to reassure those voters of the Democrats' anticommunist bona fides. (Candidate Eisenhower responded by acknowledging that he wanted to see Congress revisit and revise the new immigration legislation.)[45] Anticommunism, then, by the early 1950s had become a central aspect of national identity, national politics, and partisan electoral strategies, which, in turn, made it central to the immigration issue. Unsurprisingly, it would soon emerge with full force in refugee policies, laws, and programs.

• • •

President Truman's protests went for naught in June 1952 as Congress passed the McCarran-Walter Act over his veto. The MWA, like the 1920s national origins immigration legislation, did not provide for the admission of refugees even as the refugee problem in western Europe only worsened in the spring and summer of 1952. The State Department's Policy Committee on Immigration and Naturalization and key members of the Displaced Persons Committee believed that an overpopulation problem numbering between 1 and 5 million Europeans, both refugees and those deemed "surplus population," afflicted the continent, especially Italy, Germany, and Austria. In World War II's wake, each of these nations suffered from "overpopulation," a somewhat fuzzy calculation of the political and economic resources available to sustain a country's residents, many of whom had been displaced (or forcibly moved) during the war. The near constant arrival of eastern European refugees only exacerbated the "overpopulation" challenge, especially in Germany and Italy.

While government experts disagreed on the severity of the problem, they generally worried—and in some cases, feared—that surplus population and refugees would place such a burden upon existing economic infrastructures that political unrest would follow. An American commitment to ameliorate these demographic difficulties would not only help stabilize western Europe economically and politically, it would boost the United States' international stature. All of these concerns, and possible beneficial outcomes, occurred against the background of the Cold War, which only heightened their importance.[46]

The Truman administration's solution, announced in March 1952, was the "Emergency Migration Program" (EMP). It proposed to admit 300,000 Europeans—mainly Italians and Germans, but also 21,000 "religious and political refugees from communism in eastern Europe"—over three years. Truman told the public that the majority of newcomers who would arrive under the proposed program were refugees from "communist tyranny." Their opposition to communism—and their victimization at the hands of the Soviet Union and its puppet governments in eastern Europe—warranted admission and the opportunity to start a new life in the United States, the same rationale Truman would employ in his early summer veto of the McCarran-Walter Act. But with the 1952 campaign season looming and Congress considering immigration legislation, the EMP's chance at passage dimmed. As the fight over McCarran-Walter intensified in the early summer, the refugee proposal went to the back burner. It finally died in August 1952, a victim of congressional hostility and the sagging spirits of liberalizers.[47] The European refugee problem, though, still remained and it would be taken up again in early 1953 by restrictionists and liberalizers alike. The result was the United States' first Cold War refugee program, the Refugee Relief Program, which in its origins and administration would prove a contentious exercise.

CHAPTER 2

"A Mystic Maze of Enforcement": The Refugee Relief Program

REPRESENTATIVE MANNY CELLER was angry on December 14, 1954, when he stepped off the airplane that brought him home to New York after a five-week overseas tour. The bulk of Celler's travels was spent investigating the United States' preeminent refugee program, the Refugee Relief Program, which offered 214,000 visas to European and Asian refugees. When asked about the RRP, Celler furiously declared that "a good law had been prostituted" and now was a "dismal failure." To gain admittance to the United States, refugees were forced to clear "an obstacle course" of security investigations that, while intended to prevent the entry of communists and political subversives, had become a hunt for communists, rendering the RRP completely ineffective. Celler blamed one person: RRP administrator Scott McLeod. He derided McLeod as a "mere cop" and described his management of the program as "savage, insane, and arbitrary." Celler believed lower-level RRP officials followed McLeod's lead, producing "a McLeod bureaucracy run riot in a mystic maze of enforcement." The congressman promised to press for changes.[1]

The RRP originated in the Eisenhower administration's concerns in the spring of 1953 about Europe's simultaneous refugee and overpopulation problems and their consequences for Cold War diplomacy and foreign policy. While Cold War foreign policy concerns initiated the refugee legislation, the domestic politics and culture of anticommunism dominated its drafting and passage. As in the preceding year's immigration debates, restrictionists questioned and liberalizers extolled the political loyalties—and especially anticommunism—of potential refugees as both blocs embraced understandings of national identity in which anticommunism was a key component. The wrangling over the RRA, then, cemented in the law and in political discourse the association between refugees and European opponents and victims of communism.

In their effort to win the legislation in a Red Scare–dominated political environment, liberalizers agreed to a law that instituted stiff security provisions and mandated exhaustive investigations of each applicant. Scott McLeod took these directives seriously. Under his leadership, the RRP replicated the vigorously anticommunist investigatory state that had scrutinized the lives of thousands of Americans during the Red Scare. In the field, RRP officials realized on a daily basis the association between "American" and anticommunist in their search for refugees to admit to the United States. Applicants, then, did indeed run headlong into a bureaucratic "obstacle course," one that reflected concerns about political loyalty and subversion, and communism and anticommunism—hardly surprising given the tenor of refugee politics in early 1953.

Refugees trickled into the United States during the RRP's first eighteen months at paltry rates that would never culminate in the issuance of all 214,000 visas. While restrictionists celebrated, liberalizers like Celler were apoplectic. By late 1955, however, refugee admissions speeded considerably. No overhaul of the authorizing legislation occurred, but rather many of the program's restrictionist codicils were implemented less rigorously. Because of pressure from liberalizers like Celler, because of the Eisenhower administration's desire to see the program succeed, and because McLeod's influence over the program waned, the RRP's "mystic maze of enforcement" became less fearsome. Restrictionists of course railed that more communists entered the United States because of relaxed enforcement, but to no avail. The domestic political battle over the RRP's implementation eventually was won by liberalizers and the Eisenhower administration.

A Solution to Europe's Population Problem

The State Department's European specialists and migration experts continued to report in early 1953 that population pressures—arising from persons still displaced by the war and the arrival of refugees from the East—threatened political stability and economic growth in Europe. Concerns about maintaining a political and economic balance favorable to American interests in Cold War Europe clearly motivated their thinking just as it had in the late 1940s. In Germany, over a million unsettled refugees endangered long-term economic growth and stability. U.S. officials doubted whether the German government had the political strength or resources to deal with both the existing population (many of whom were living in large camps) and newcomers. In Italy, American experts worried that population pressures—from both refugees and "overpopulation"—might lead to political discontent, which would facilitate the rise to power of the Italian communist party. The upcoming Italian elections in May 1953 sharpened State Department apprehensions.[2]

President Eisenhower and Secretary of State John Dulles did not share the alarmist analysis of lower-level State Department officials, but they quickly determined that the United States needed to make a substantial

Figure 2.1 Through the early 1950s, refugees streamed in to West Berlin, as this crowded camp attests. Fearing that population pressures might create dangerous political and economic instability in western Europe, a growing number of American officials urged refugee admissions.

effort to help solve Europe's population issues for a two reasons: Cold War foreign policy concerns and domestic political considerations. For Dulles and Eisenhower, a program that admitted western European "overpopulation" and refugees would not only relieve suffering in refugee camps, but it would shore up American allies in Italy in advance of the upcoming elections, satisfy NATO allies (who clamored for such action), demonstrate leadership and commitment to European stability, and improve the United States' image overseas.[3]

At the same time, Eisenhower and Dulles understood that refugee legislation was politically attractive because it partially fulfilled the president's vague but repeated campaign promises to revise the MWA, without, however, the task of winning comprehensive immigration reform. A refugee program would ameliorate for a time some of the most objectionable effects of the new immigration law—especially the quotas that discriminated against eastern and central Europeans—hopefully satisfying the voters of eastern- and southern-European descent whom Republicans had courted so aggressively in the previous election. In this light, the refugee legislation was yet another attempt by Republicans to leverage anticommunist and anti-Soviet policies into support from key voting blocs in the American electorate.[4]

The United States was not the only nation (or organization) working to ameliorate Europe's population challenges. The Intergovernmental Committee for European Migration (ICEM), the chief international organization concerned with refugees and migration, facilitated the resettlement (mainly to South America and Canada) of about 150,000 European refugees and migrants in 1952 and 1953, and more than double that number between 1954 and 1957. Canada annually admitted about 100,000 Europeans in the early and mid-1950s, although most of these were European nationals rather than refugees. Britain and Australia were not as generous, but still continued their post-1945 liberal immigration policies toward Europeans, both migrants and refugees. American engagement with these efforts was minimal; the United States helped fund the ICEM, but little else. Moreover, one key difference marked the approaches of the United States and these other nations. The United States tackled Europe's population problem because of foreign policy concerns and because of domestic political pressures, while other nations saw newcomers as skilled and unskilled labor that could help rebuild or strengthen their economies in the war's wake.[5]

In April, Eisenhower asked Congress for emergency legislation to admit 240,000 newcomers over two years. Publicly, the president painted Europe's refugee problem as a foreign policy issue—"[t]hese refugees, escapees, and distressed peoples now constitute an economic and political threat of growing magnitude" to "international political considerations." He left no doubt that those who would receive American aid were victims and opponents of communism, which made them worthy of American help. On this front, Eisenhower and Truman utilized a similar vocabulary, although the former did not assert that refugees would make good citizens because of their anticommunism. Indeed, Eisenhower completely avoided the question of how refugees might adapt to America once admitted. Likewise, Eisenhower avoided any mention of the "overpopulation" issue. Casting the proposal as one to relieve "overpopulation" would have made it appear an immigration bill, as would have forthrightly addressing the assimilation of newcomers. Divorcing refugees from immigrants was good strategy given the power of restrictionists.[6]

Over the next months, various offices and bureaus in the State Department (the Bureau of Security and Consular Affairs, the Visa Office, and the Bureau of European Affairs), representatives from the Immigration and Naturalization Service, members and staff of the House and Senate Judiciary Committees and Subcommittees on Immigration, and the White

House's associate counsel Max Rabb hashed out the legislation's particulars. These players offered different levels of support for the proposal. The State Department's Bureau of Security and Consular Affairs and the Visa Office were generally restrictionist, as were the staffs of key Judiciary Committee members McCarran and Walter, while the State Department's European Affairs Office, the liberalizers on the Judiciary Committees, and the Eisenhower administration supported refugee admissions. This divide produced some intense and intricate wrangling in the spring and summer of 1953, resulting in a bill that privileged the entry of European refugees who were victims and opponents of communism.[7]

Throughout the drafting process, the proposed refugee program remained steadfastly Eurocentric. Germans and Italians consistently received the most visas, with smaller but still significant numbers granted to the Netherlands and Greece. Only after persistent pressure during congressional hearings from the China lobby did the proposal extend visas—in very small numbers—to Asian countries. A codicil granting a few thousand visas to Arab refugees appears to have been the work of members of Celler's Judiciary Committee. The proposal's European focus arose for a few reasons. Policymakers conceived of the "refugee problem" affecting U.S. foreign relations as primarily European, rather than Asian or Middle Eastern—even though significant refugee flows existed in those regions as well. More important, politicians and policymakers were reticent to offer visas to nonwhite and non-European refugees, a bias that of course existed in immigration affairs generally. The Asian and Arab visa allocations in the proposal were mere tokens, then, but ones that also attested to the lingering power of ethnonational discrimination. After all, many Asian refugees were victims and opponents of communism—which Republicans made quite clear in their criticisms of the Truman administration's China and Korea policies—but they found little succor in the U.S. commitment to refugees in the 1950s.[8]

The categories of Europeans to be admitted did change, however. Quite in contrast to Eisenhower's public remarks, the earliest discussions addressed the "overpopulation" problem by granting visas both to refugees and to "nationals," or traditional immigrants. But as the legislation evolved, refugees, escapees, and expellees received more visas, and "nationals" fewer. The term "nationals" eventually disappeared altogether, although "nationals" who wished to emigrate to the United States were not completely left out in the final draft; 15,000 Italians, 2,000 Greeks, and 2,000 Dutch could earn visas by qualifying as relatives of a person living in the United States. McCarran—who did not want an immigrant bill to pass—initiated this switch to a largely refugee-only bill, but the politics of immigration affairs accelerated it. Refugees, escapees, and expellees were different than immigrants or nationals looking to come to

America. Their circumstances as victims of political oppression and persecution established a special claim for admission. By pushing a "refugee" bill, lawmakers could avoid repeating the fiery controversy engendered by the McCarran-Walter Act, while still addressing western Europe's population issue and satisfying the Eisenhower administration's objectives.[9]

Finally, the drafting process demonstrated the politicized nature of the definitions of "refugee," "escapee," and "expellee." "Refugee" developed into a catch-all term that applied to any person living in a noncommunist country who could not return home—and could not be resettled—because of "persecution, fear of persecution, natural calamity, or military operations." Expellees and escapees were kinds of refugees who had been expelled from—or escaped from—the Soviet Union or communist countries in eastern Europe. The definition of "expellee" and "escapee," then, used geography to achieve a distinctly ideological and political caste; expellees and escapees fled from communist countries, ensuring that they would be political opponents of the Soviet Union or its allied governments. The definition of "refugee," on the other hand, was, at least superficially, much more capacious. A refugee had only to be living in a noncommunist country and to be in danger of persecution; the definition lacked a geographical component that stood in for ideology. But since most of the refugees admitted under the bill were escapees and expellees, the definition of "refugee" took on distinctly politicized, and anticommunist, overtones. It was an association that only deepened as Congress and refugee advocates and opponents debated the proposal.[10]

"Not a Question of Nationality": Debating the RRA

Debate on Capitol Hill about the Eisenhower refugee proposal lined up restrictionists and liberalizers in a manner that closely resembled the contests over the DP legislation and immigration reform. The most important changes came on the liberalizer side. Moderate Republicans, led by Senator Arthur Watkins of Utah, pushed enthusiastically for Eisenhower's refugee bill, hoping to give the president an early victory. The American Federation of Labor (AFL) supported refugee admissions, abandoning its usual restrictionist position to satisfy some of its more liberal members and because of the bill's Cold War foreign policy ramifications. They were joined by a litany of religious and ethnic organizations who had long supported refugee admissions and reform of the national origins system. At the Senate hearings on the refugee proposal, twenty of the twenty-one interest groups that testified in favor of admissions were either religiously or ethnically based. Jewish, Catholic, and Protestant organizations showed such strong support that the legislation picked up the moniker "the church bill." Ethnic organizations also offered strong support for a variety of reasons. Italian American groups—like the Sons of Italy and the American Committee on Italian Migration—believed the proposal would bring Italians to the United States who would not get in via regular immigration procedures. Ethnic organizations representing eastern Europeans supported refugee admissions as an anti-Soviet statement and as a way to help victims of communism.[11]

The backing of labor, ethnic organizations, and religious groups highlights the strong links between refugee advocates and the liberal base of the postwar northern Democratic party. Indeed, Senators Paul Douglas (D-IL), Herbert Lehman (D-NY), and Hubert Humphrey (D-MN), along with their counterparts in the House like Representatives Manny Celler and Peter Rodino (D-NJ), emerged as some of the most forceful supporters of refugee admissions. Some, like Celler and Lehman, had worked closely on refugee issues in the 1930s and 1940s. But for many, refugee advocacy also resonated with aspects of their liberalism. Liberals in the mid-1950s had an extensive agenda: national health care, an expansion of the federal government's existing social welfare net, job creation and economic growth, and more federal aid to education. But liberals—especially those mentioned above—increasingly turned their attention to the protection of individual rights and the eradication of ethnic and racial discrimination; witness their concerns with civil liberties in an age of McCarthyism, their growing support for African American civil rights, and their opposition to the national origins quota immigration system. On these scores, refugee admissions served their liberal agenda. Refugee admissions were a back door around the hated immigration system and, more importantly, a direct rebuke to the idea that a person's race or nationality determined their worthiness. In fact, refugees, as victims of persecution, were shining examples of the need to protect individual rights— the rights of immigrants, blacks, *and* refugees. Moreover, these "Cold War liberals" believed it imperative to take a stand against the Soviet Union and its totalitarian abuses; refugee entry provided a means by which they could demonstrate their antipathy toward communism and their devotion to anti-Soviet policies. Finally, the political benefits for liberal Democrats of refugee admissions—satisfying their constituents from urban states and districts that had high percentages of first- and second-generation immigrants from the refugees' homelands—were obvious.[12]

Few observers were confident of the measure's passage, though. Besides the obvious power of restrictionists in Congress, public opinion was divided when it came to refugee admissions. In late 1951, a poll showed that while a strong majority (69 percent) of Americans did not believe that persons escaping the Soviet Union and eastern Europe should be sent back behind the "Iron Curtain," only 43 percent believed that these refugees should "be allowed to come to the United States" or offered some sort of qualified support for admission; 40 percent said refugees should not be allowed entry, and 17 percent expressed no opinion. By the spring of 1953, a national poll showed that public opinion concerning the admission of refugees had not shifted much. Forty-seven percent of respondents supported passage of Eisenhower's proposal, while 48 percent opposed it.[13] The numbers indicated, then, no groundswell for refugee admissions, but rather fairly widespread suspicion.

The refugee bill raised many of the same issues as the DP legislation and the MWA, such as the effects of newcomers upon the economy and the benefits of newcomer admissions for America's position in the Cold War. More important, the refugee proposal's relationship to the McCarran-Walter Act animated discussions. Opposition to the refugee measure came precisely because it seemed that the proposal was designed to undo the immigration law passed just one year earlier. On this score, restrictionists were, of course, correct.[14] But the most prominent issues raised that summer centered on internal security concerns and whether refugee admissions would lead to the entry of communists. In one sense, this concern was nothing new. Restrictionists had argued that the entry of German Jews in the late 1930s, and DPs in the late 1940s, threatened national security by providing a means through which political subversives might infiltrate the United States. But in the early 1950s, at the height of McCarthyism and Red Scare anticommunism—and with all involved very cognizant of the political and electoral gains and pains associated with vigorous support of anticommunist policies at home and abroad—the internal security issue emerged as a powerhouse.

Restrictionists worried that no proven methods existed for accurately assessing the political ideology and intentions of immigrants and that the Eisenhower proposal would only provide communists and subversives with more opportunities to enter. Some refugee opponents adopted the overheated rhetoric of the Red Scare. The American Legion, which had long combined red-baiting and immigrant bashing, saw refugees as a "potential danger to our industrial power and communication installations . . . should the hour strike and we become involved in a war, declared or undeclared, with Russia." Others, like Representative Walter, made the same point without the histrionics: "No amendment can cure the thing that is basically wrong with this law. The thing that is wrong with it is that it is impossible, utterly impossible, to write the kind of language that will give America the security that the American Legion just today said that we need." In the era's extreme anticommunist politics, the internal security card was the most potent in the deck. Restrictionists played it often and to good effect.[15]

The bill's supporters had some answers. Senator Watkins reminded people that refugees would be admitted under the MWA and the Internal Security Act (ISA), laws written by McCarran that contained rigorous security measures designed to prevent the entry of subversives and communists. Watkins essentially asked why refugee opponents like McCarran did not trust the security laws they had written. Watkins' endorsement of these security measures was hardly surprising; he was a member of a party notable for its muscular anticommunism. More revealing, though, was the eagerness with which liberals joined him. Monsignor Edward Swanstrom of the National Catholic Welfare Conference (NCWC), a key refugee-resettlement agency, observed that "there should be no letup in the thorough investigation carried out by our official investigative agencies." Congressmen John Fino, a New York Democrat, nearly taunted restrictionists: "The opponents of this bill say that Commies will come in. Well not if the McCarran-Walter Act is as good as they say it is."[16]

Representative Manny Celler offered the most full-throated and extensive endorsement of the bill's security provisions. This was most surprising. Celler had fought bitterly against both the McCarran-Walter Act and the Internal Security Act, emerging as one of the most prominent critics of the excesses of domestic anticommunism. The thirty-year veteran of the House remarked that "[E]veryone [sic] of the security provisions of the McCarran-Walter Act are applicable to the operations under this bill," concluding "If that is so, then what are we worried about?" But Celler was not finished. He praised the "thorough investigation . . . on every person applying" so "that the consuls are going to know more about the individuals applying under this act than they do about people applying under normal immigration law and will thus be in a far better position to protect American security." Celler closed by praising the federal government's security and intelligence agencies and their ability to prevent the entry of subversives and communists.[17]

Celler and American liberals, as well as Republicans like Watkins, defused the subversion issue by fully embracing the stringent security measures built into the legislation. In practice, then, they endorsed provisions that required both INS and State Department officials to clear an applicant for entry, that obligated both the INS and State Department to submit a written report outlining the applicant's eligibility for entry, and that ordered refugees to account for their previous two years with a documented history. The gambit effectively played into the dominant political discourse of the era, anticommunism. Celler's defense of the refugee bill's security measures—and specifically the program's intention to deny entry to communists—reinforced the association between refugees and anticommunism that Eisenhower (and Truman) established publicly and the drafting process put to paper. The price was high, though, as refugees likely would have to clear substantial hurdles in order to enter the United States.

The discussions about internal security concerns, the potential entry of communists, and the refugees' anticommunism were so charged because they directly engaged assumptions about American identity. Both ethnonational and political definitions of "American" came to the fore during the refugee debates, and they transcended mere opposition or support for the pending refugee measure. Indeed, the ethnonational version of citizenship had not disappeared from either the liberalizer or restrictionist blocs. Judge Juvenal Marchisio of the American Committee on Italian Migration asserted that Italians made good Americans because of their ethnic roots. George Washington Williams, a restrictionist from the patriotic organization the General Society of the War of 1812, agreed enthusiastically with Marchisio that ethnicity foretold American-ness, but he railed against the legal and illegal immigrants—including Puerto Ricans, who actually were citizens—that he believed flooded the United States and could never overcome their ethnicity to become "Americans."[18]

The refugee debates, though, ultimately revealed that the ethnonational conception of national identity had lost ground to a politicized definition of "American" resting upon vigorous anticommunism. To be sure, this dynamic was exaggerated in the refugee discourse because the very notion of "refugee" was political: refugees fled political developments in their homelands. Yet by the 1950s, political culture had changed and the refugee debates existed on the cutting edge of the politicization of national identity. A great number of politicians, patriotic organizations, refugee-aid groups, and private citizens, liberalizers and restrictionists alike, crafted a conception of "American" based on allegiance to political ideologies, specifically anticommunism. They set out to demonstrate that refugees did (or did not) display adequate political bona fides and therefore did (or did not) deserve admission.

A number of key liberalizers explicitly argued that refugees with anticommunist credentials would make the best American citizens. Congressman Stuy Wainwright asserted that it was "not a question of nationality" resting at the center of possible refugee admissions, but rather one of political ideology. Wainwright described "the sort of people we would be taking in": three Czechoslovakian refugees who had been sentenced to forced labor for anticommunist activities, and subsequently had escaped through a 200-meter air shaft in a coal mine; a Hungarian family of five who "swam a river and fled across Hungary" to reach Austria; and a family of three who "crossed the Hungarian-Austrian border, after evading dog patrols, passing over mined areas, and cutting through barbed wire barriers." Manny Celler made an even stronger case. He recalled a recent visit to Berlin in which he "saw these refugees streaming in across the line into West Berlin . . . from East Germany, coming in from Czecho-slovakia, from Poland, and from other subjugated countries." These refu-gees would "make good citizens if we let them into this country" because "they understand the meaning of liberty, they understand how they have been downtrodden, how liberty has been denied to them." Celler contin-ued, "I found they would be only too happy to come here and understand, know, appreciate all the more, freedom of speech, freedom of press, free-dom of religion."[19]

Restrictionists joined Celler and Wainwright in sketching out a defini-tion of "American" freighted with anticommunism, but drew different conclusions about the wisdom of admitting newcomers. A Texas Demo-crat declared "Communism does amount to something in Italy, and if this bill is passed we will get a lot of those in this country. . . . To say the least, they will be of the character of people spineless enough to join the Communists when they thought it was the safest thing to do, and did not fight them." A Florida Congressman—as well as the American Legion—had a solution that would measure refugees' commitments to the anticom-munist benchmark: "I suggest that if we were to put these escapees of proven security risks into special battalions and give them the responsibil-ity of representing us on the Korean front, we could then have a greater opportunity to expect of them that they accept their responsibilities if they come to this country as full-fledged American citizens." A refugee, in other words, could prove his worthiness by battling communism in the most direct manner, serving in Korea.[20]

The Eisenhower refugee proposal, which during the congressional de-bate acquired the name "The Refugee Relief Act" (RRA), was thoroughly steeped in the anticommunism of the early Cold War. Concerns among U.S. foreign policymakers about European political and economic stabil-ity and about America's diplomatic reputation in the face of Cold War competitions with the Soviet Union birthed the bill. During the drafting process, the term "refugee" acquired a distinctly Cold War caste with refugees defined as opponents and victims of communism. Just as striking, the refugee proposal was colored by the domestic politics of anticommu-nism as both restrictionists and liberalizers utilized notions of national identity that equated "American-ness" with anticommunism. The restric-tionist position was unsurprising: refugees might be communists—there was no effective way of knowing for sure—and thus could not become Americans and must not be admitted. To counter this charge, liberalizers embraced the "American equals anticommunist" equation, trumpeted the political bona fides of refugees, and supported a rigorous security-check program to make certain newcomers met these benchmarks.

SETTING UP THE REFUGEE RELIEF PROGRAM

As Congress debated the RRA, the Eisenhower administration worked feverishly to secure its enactment. The RRA finally passed in late July 1953, when the House approved the measure by a 221–185 vote and the Senate by a 63–30 tally. The traditional bipartisan support that attended successful immigration bills determined the outcome. Liberals in both parties supported the measure. They were joined by moderates, especially Republicans, attracted by the bill's small step toward immigration reform, its foreign policy implications, and the desire to see a recently elected president get a piece of "must" legislation. Indeed, huge Republican margins—132–74 in the House and 38–8 in the Senate—demonstrated the determination of the new Republican majorities in Congress to give Eisenhower his bill.[21]

The RRA extended over a three-year period 214,000 special immigration visas outside of the existing McCarran-Walter quota limits. More than 90 percent of these visas were allotted to "refugees," "escapees," and "German expellees," while the rest were set aside for Italian, Dutch, and Greek applicants who had relatives in the United States. Germany alone accounted for 90,000 visas, no doubt because of its strategic importance and because it remained the principal destination for refugees from behind the Iron Curtain. Italy received 60,000 visas, 75 percent of which were allocated for Italian refugees. With the exception of 5,000 Asian and 2,000 Arab refugees, all of the visas went to Europeans. Finally, the RRA placed the administration of the program under McCarran's new bureaucratic creature, the State Department's Bureau of Security and Consular Affairs (BSCA).[22]

The Eisenhower administration hoped that the Refugee Relief Program would begin granting visas swiftly. A quick start was unlikely, however. According to officials with experience managing these types of programs, it might take at least three months to make the RRP operational because of the need to determine the intent of Congress, to write operating procedures, and to recruit staff. Likewise, the law was loaded with complicated and time-consuming codicils. To receive a RRA visa, an applicant needed "assurances" of suitable employment that did not displace an American citizen from a job, of housing that did not dislodge American citizens, and of a guarantee that he would not become a public charge. These "assurances" required an American citizen's sponsorship, which the RRA's administrator verified. Finally, the applicant had to have a passport so that he could return to his country of last residence if he violated any of these conditions. For restrictionists, these provisions aimed to provide a safety mechanism that monitored and controlled the effects of refugee entry. Liberalizers viewed the "assurances" warily. The codicils surely did blunt restrictionist critiques concerning unemployment and vagrancy, but, as Senator Herbert Lehman explained, the assurance requirements were nearly "impossible" to fulfill, and thus desired by restrictionists who hoped to slow refugee admissions.[23]

The RRA, of course, complied with immigration law and thus it barred the feebleminded, the insane, prostitutes, polygamists, and drug addicts, and it banned anarchists, supporters of totalitarianism, and, most important, communists. But the RRA enacted even tougher entry requirements than the nation's preeminent immigration law when it came to an applicant's political beliefs and history. Each applicant signed a pledge that he was not currently, nor ever had been, a communist, anarchist, fascist, or advocate of the overthrow of the American government. Each applicant, moreover, underwent an investigation led by consular and/or immigration officers to determine a refugee's "character, reputation, mental and physical health, history, and eligibility under this Act." Visas would be awarded only to those persons who could give "complete information" about their history over the previous two years, and investigators were expected to question the validity of these histories.[24]

The RRA's requirements ensured that an applicant's political allegiances and histories would come under question, in effect strengthening the political barriers to entry. The Eisenhower administration's decision to let Scott McLeod and the BSCA oversee and administer the security investigations of individual refugees—thus placing the entire RRP under McLeod's purview—only toughened the law's provisions.[25] It would have been difficult to find a more controversial head for the program. A former FBI agent, McLeod served as an administrative assistant to Senator Styles Bridges (R-NH) from 1949 to 1953. In this position, McLeod earned the confidence of Senator McCarran, as well as of Senator Joe McCarthy. In March 1953, the State Department's new undersecretary of state for administration, Donald B. Lourie, offered McLeod the top job at BSCA, although it is not clear that Lourie thought deeply about the appointment.[26]

McLeod was a true believer in the anticommunist cause and he tackled his job as the Department's chief "red hunter" with vigor. He once summarized his mission: "Congress wants heads to roll and I let' em roll. . . . Blood in the streets and all that." McLeod believed every job at the State Department to be a potential security risk and proceeded accordingly, claiming in one interview to have launched investigations of every employee in the Department. McLeod's skills as an anticommunist were matched by his talent for self-promotion. He charmed Bridges and McCarthy and others in the Republican party (as well as the Democrat McCarran) and became quite a popular dinner speaker for conservative organizations like the American Legion. McLeod, though, quickly angered the Eisenhower administration by cooperating with Bridges', McCarthy's, and McCarran's attempt to torpedo the nomination of Charles Bohlen as ambassador to the Soviet Union. Eisenhower thought the McLeod appointment a mistake, but that to dismiss him would only raise "a great big stink." The comment was indicative of the political straddle the administration took in its first year as it struggled to discredit McCarthy yet still vigorously pursue communists and subversives in the federal government.[27]

Eisenhower could have selected a different agency or department, perhaps the INS, to administer the RRA's security investigations. He chose McLeod, despite all of this political baggage because, as the *New York Times* noted, McLeod had "the confidence of those legislators who lean toward caution and conservatism on matters of immigration." The *Times* may have understated the case. A McCarran aide revealed his confidence that McLeod was in the restrictionist camp when—in the wake of the RRA's passage, but before Eisenhower gave McLeod oversight of the entire program—he fairly crowed, "We haven't lost yet. . . . We're going to administer the act." Eisenhower's sop to restrictionists was dangerous, for the White House wanted the program to admit refugees. This was going to be a challenge regardless of who administered the program because of the RRA's complex investigative provisions that favored security over speed. Moreover, as one of the RRP's officials in Europe noted at the program's inception, the legislation was vague about "the extent of the investigation required" and "the standards to be applied." Background investigations would be difficult, as well, because it was "virtually impossible for an American officer to conduct an investigation successfully . . . due to police restrictions and the natural reluctance of people to talk about their countrymen to foreigners." Perhaps no person could have "liberalized" these "restrictionist" stipulations, but with McLeod and his allies making the decisions about staffing and procedures, it was likely that the restrictionist tendencies in the RRA would be emphasized rather than downplayed.[28]

In the late fall of 1953, the RRP began processing refugees for admission. Initial grumbling about the program surfaced in January 1954, not more than five weeks after the first visa was issued to Michael Sonnino of Italy. This discontent only grew more intense over the coming year. The criticism centered on the paltry number of refugees that the program actually admitted. By January 30, 1954, only four persons had entered since the law's passage. At the end of March, that total had risen to six, and by May, all of eight had been admitted. As 1954 ended just over 17,000 visas had been issued to applicants—with nearly 42,000 applicants waiting to be processed. Even though there had been a significant increase in refugee admissions over the second half of 1954, the rate of entry was still well below the predictions offered by McLeod at the beginning of the year.[29]

McLeod and his staff steadfastly defended the program, arguing that the trickle of refugees was explainable and fixable. First, staffing the program, both at home and abroad, was a time consuming process that slowed the flow of refugees. Security checks for potential RRP personnel usually took between sixty and ninety days alone. Second, nations permitting aliens to emigrate to the United States had to sign an agreement with the State Department that guaranteed they would accept the return of a refugee who had obtained his visa illegally. As of February 1954, only two countries, Italy and Greece, had met this qualification; Germany agreed to this condition in April 1954. These diplomatic impasses slowed refugee admissions greatly, McLeod argued. Third, RRP officials claimed that the onerous assurance process had dulled the incentive of Americans to sponsor refugees, resulting in a sponsor shortage. Finally, McLeod admitted that each application took a considerable amount of time to investigate. From assurance processing to visa issuance, he estimated that the average case consumed 126 working days—just over six months![30]

The Eisenhower administration took a few concrete steps to try to increase admissions. In late 1954 Secretary of State Dulles hired Edward Corsi, a New York Republican with experience in immigration matters, in the hope that Corsi could ease the RRP's administrative roadblocks. Corsi lasted only three months—repeatedly clashing with McLeod and Representative Walter, who accused him of being a communist—before Dulles asked him to step aside. The administration also asked Congress to amend the RRA. First, it wanted the assurances or sponsorship provision modified so that organizations, mainly religious and ethnic refugee-aid groups, rather than individuals, could offer "blanket assurances" for large numbers of newcomers. The 1948 DP Act effectively used this "blanket assurance" procedure, and religious and ethnic organizations had clamored for this reform almost since the RRA's passage. Second, the administration wanted to drop the requirement that an applicant present a complete, and documented, two-year history. In short, it had proven too difficult for refugees to provide such detailed, documented information. These reforms were hardly radical—they had been proposed by Senator Lehman a few months earlier—but only the first eventually came to pass.[31]

To the program's most vocal critics—and the greatest supporters of refugee admissions—the chief problem was Scott McLeod. This was the essence of Celler's blistering broadside upon his return from an RRP inspection tour in late 1954. Corsi, who had seen the program up close for months, echoed Celler, claiming that the program's failure arose from its

Figure 2.2 At Camp Valka, near Nuremburg, West Germany, refugees await news of opportunities to emigrate. Camp Valka was home to eastern European refugees in the 1950s and, especially, Hungarians in 1956 and 1957.

being "in the hands of security people." "In their desire to keep security risks out," Corsi continued, "they have kept almost everybody out. Nobody in the refugee relief program has ever had anything to do with refugees." Celler's and Corsi's comments raised questions not only about McLeod's leadership of the RRP, but also about the nature of the admissions process itself. How exactly were certain refugees chosen to receive visas, while others were rejected? What did the investigative process entail? Was there an "obstacle race" and a "mystic maze of enforcement?" Did the "security people" and the "desire to keep security risks out" shape the program—and lead to its poor results?[32]

"POLITICAL CLEANLINESS": THE RRP IN THE FIELD

An RRA visa application had to clear four phases before approval. In the first phase, the BSCA verified the applicant's "assurances" and confirmed that the applicant had documentation guaranteeing readmission to the country the refugee hoped to leave. The applicant also completed a preliminary questionnaire (of sixty-nine queries) that asked for basic facts (birthplace and date, family size, occupational skills, and education) and for political, legal, and medical histories. The questionnaire and documentation phase took, on average, forty working days to complete. In the second phase, a State Department consular officer determined whether the applicant qualified under the RRA as a refugee, escapee, or expellee; an INS officer had to agree with the consular officer's "preliminary determination of eligibility" in order for the applicant to proceed. The applicant also underwent a preliminary health examination to detect communicable diseases like tuberculosis. If these hurdles were cleared, which generally took about fourteen working days, the security investigation—or third phase—began. A subdivision of the BSCA, the Office of Investigations of the Refugee Relief Program (IRP) worked with INS and U.S. military intelligence services to conduct a "thorough investigation" that culminated in a written report of the applicant's "character, reputation, mental and physical health, history, and eligibility." The security investigation averaged forty-two working days. Assuming it uncovered no problems, the fourth phase—a review of the application, a more thorough health exam, a final interview, and the issuance of a visa—took place.[33]

McLeod correctly asserted that finding and verifying sponsors slowed refugee admissions during the program's first eighteen months. Indeed, that phase, which included non-assurance-related activities as well, took roughly two months to complete. But Celler, Corsi, and Lehman had a case, too. The security investigation was the most time consuming, most intrusive, and most discretionary part of the admissions process. It also most reflected the RRP's origins in early Cold War domestic political culture.

The security investigation, conducted by IRP officials and their INS partners, involved the questionnaire, background checks run through various American and foreign intelligence agencies, interviews with the applicant's associates and friends, and interviews with the applicant. Officials solicited two types of information: whether the applicant had misrepresented himself or had presented contradictory information regarding his personal history or his political affiliations. In the first instance, applicants ran afoul of the MWA, which barred applicants who lied on their application or during an interview. In the second instance, the MWA banned communists, anarchists, and supporters of totalitarianism, and the RRA fortified these strictures and authorized officials to dig deeply into an applicant's political allegiances. The RRP bureaucracy, in Washington and on the ground across western Europe and Asia, understood its mission. In a draft of a letter he hoped to send to all RRP personnel, deputy administrator Anthony Micocci outlined to McLeod—and, he intended, eventually the rest of the staff—the ways in which investigations should be pursued. "It is simply not true that this law was intended as a cynical piece of legislation designed to keep migrants out," Micocci wrote. "It was intended to bring certain persons in." But, he continued not two paragraphs later, "We should apply rather severely the criteria in respect to political cleanliness, health requirements and work skills." The key part of uncovering any applicant's political leanings and history—assessing his or her "political cleanliness"—was the interview between the IRP and INS officers and the applicant.[34]

One of these applicants, Gottfried Mahlow, hoped to emigrate with his wife, Erika, from Germany to Frankfort, Kentucky. Born in 1925 and raised near Dresden, which by the 1950s was part of East Germany, Mahlow served in the German army during the war and then spent three years in a Russian prison camp. The Russians released Mahlow in 1948 only after he agreed to join the East German People's Police (or *Volkspolizei*). While a member of the People's Police, he claimed to have been pressured constantly to join the Socialist Unity Party of East Germany (SED), which he finally did in the fall of 1950. Three months later, still in his People's Police uniform, he fled to West Berlin. In either late 1954 or early 1955, Mahlow applied for a RRA visa, which an INS officer refused to grant because of Mahlow's SED membership and because Mahlow had failed to disclose a return trip to East Germany that occurred sometime after January 1951, supposedly to visit ailing relatives. The SED membership violated the MWA's ban on the entry of members of communist or socialist organizations, while the undisclosed visit ran afoul of the bar on aliens who made statements that "willfully" misrepresented "a material fact." State Department consular officers disagreed with the INS, asserting that Mahlow's SED membership was involuntary and that his misrepresentations of the trips to East Germany were of secondary order. As a result, the case went back to Washington, D.C., for concurring opinions from the INS and the State Department. In March 1956, the ruling came down: Mahlow was denied a visa.[35]

Throughout the application process, Mahlow put up a good fight trying to prove his SED membership was short and not representative of his political sympathies. His friends testified on his behalf, offering that "his ideas were always democratic and he completely rejected the Communistic regime. . . . he opposes Bolchevism [sic]." Others spoke of his wife: "Mrs. Mahlow definitely rejected and condemned the communistic ideology and its consequences." Mahlow tried to buttress this portrayal when he interviewed with INS officer Homer Dean in October 1955. Dean actually interviewed Mahlow twice. In their first encounter, they discussed Mahlow's time as a Russian POW and his work for the *Volkspolizei*. Dean repeatedly asked Mahlow about his SED membership, which the German doggedly asserted was involuntary. Dean also asked why Mahlow decided to flee the East. "All members of the Volkspolizei had to attend a SED training course and I did not want to," Mahlow replied, "but then I was told 'if you don't want to you might be brought back to Russia or you would probably have to work in a mine or so,' and for this reason I left the East Zone."[36]

Dean resumed questioning a week later, stating that "a couple points were unclear." In this second interview, Dean much more aggressively and skeptically probed Mahlow's anticommunism. Dean asked Mahlow whether "being selected for consideration as a member of the Volkspolizei could have been because you had convinced your Russian capturers that you favoured communism or were at least sympathetic to communist principles?" Mahlow answered no, pointing out that while a POW, he had once hit (with an "upper cut") a Russian guard who harassed him. "I received four days confinement for it," Mahlow offered. He continued, "I don't think that they thought I would be sympathetic to them" after the incident. Dean pressed on, though, asking "It would seem that it would be a practical thing to do for a person in living as a POW under this circumstances to at least make a token appearance of accepting some of the communist principles in order to make your daily existence a little easier, was that sort of thing practiced among prisoners with whom you were confined?" Mahlow, of course, answered no. Just to make his point clear, Mahlow said at the conclusion of the interview, "may I tell you that I would like to go to the United States, I intend to be a real democrat and that I will be a hard worker."[37]

Other applicants, with circumstances similar to Mahlow's, won RRA visas. Kurt Bruss, an ethnic German born in Silesia in 1903, hoped to settle with his wife in Massachusetts. Bruss was a French POW until May 1947, when he returned home to Goerlitz in eastern Germany. There, he began work as a railroad company clerk and later for the Goerlitz City Administration Housing Office. During this time, he enrolled— involuntarily, he claimed—in the Free German Trade Union (known by its German acronym as FDGB), an organization that Bruss admitted was communist dominated. IRP officials determined that Bruss's FDGB membership was involuntary and that he was, in fact, an ardent anticommunist. INS officer Dean disagreed, arguing that Bruss willingly returned to the Soviet-controlled sector of Germany in 1947 after making no effort to stay in western Germany, that the East German regime considered him so loyal that it allowed him to travel freely to West Germany, and that within five weeks of his arrival back home he had joined the communist-controlled FDGB. With the Bruss application unresolved in the field, the case went back to the State Department and INS in Washington. In early October 1955, both agencies agreed that Bruss's FDGB membership was involuntary and Bruss and his wife earned visas.[38]

The Bruss-Dean interview on May 20, 1955, much like Mahlow's interrogation, quickly moved to the German's post–World War II political affiliations. Dean peppered Bruss with questions like, "Is there any doubt in your mind regarding the opinion that the FDGB was a communist controlled organization?" "Were you a member of the SED?" and "Have you ever been a member of the communist party at any time?" Bruss answered this last question—obviously believing he already had made his thinking clear—with a testy "What do you want to hear?" Bruss of course denounced communism, and Dean pressed him on how long he had held that opinion:

Q. When did you first become opposed to communists?
A. Already in 1947 when I saw what happened there
   (*in Goerlitz—ed.*).
Q. Then if I understand you correctly you were not opposed to a communist form of government until you returned to Goerlitz in 1947?
A. I thought that you would ask this question, I was never a friend of communism but in 1947 I got to know and saw what communism really meant.
Q. How do you explain the fact that you found out in 1947 what communism really meant [but] you continued to reside under communist government and do their work until February of 1953, particularly when you and your wife made two journeys to the West Zone and could have remained there on either one of these occasions?
A. I told you already that my parents were there, and all our relatives, we had our lodging there, I had work. . . . It is true it is my fault that we did not remain in West Germany when we were here making a visit, but as I said I had work etc., and where would it lead if 18 000 000 of people would come to West Germany? I also

told you that my wife wanted to come to West Germany to remain here at an earlier date already but if it was up to me and I thought I would not like to become a public charge and the future in West Germany seemed to me to be just as dark as in the East Zone.[39]

In comparison to Bruss and Mahlow, George Fuad Mantoura's RRA visa application raised other concerns, but it illustrated similar, larger dynamics. Mantoura began the application process sometime in 1955 and qualified as an Arab refugee. His credentials appeared impeccable. He worked in Amman, Jordan, for the United States' Point IV program, which provided technical assistance to underdeveloped nations in the hope of winning their allegiance to the United States during the Cold War. As such, his application enjoyed the support of his Point IV bosses. RRP officials initially denied Mantoura a visa, however. In 1954 Mantoura and his friends took up a mail correspondence with a Danish woman, Kitty Asferg, who claimed to be an artist's model and a collector of nude photographs of men and women. Asferg sent Mantoura some nude photos of herself and asked him to do the same. Mantoura claimed that he foolishly complied and sent Asferg photos that RRP personnel later described as "lewd and lascivious . . . by virtue of the subject's position in the photographs." It is unclear exactly how RRP officials came across this incident—because Mantoura did not tell them—but they ruled him ineligible for a visa because he had misrepresented facts in his application by not revealing he had broken a Jordanian law that forbade the mailing of indecent materials.[40]

Mantoura had not run afoul of the sex police. Indeed, consular officials remarked, "It seems highly unlikely that any element of perversion exists in his personality." Instead, he was officially disqualified on a technicality—lying on his application—and not for perversion. Most interesting, though, was Mantoura's reaction upon learning of the RRP's rejection of his application. Told that he had been denied an RRA visa, but not the exact reason for the ruling, Mantoura first sought to prove he was not a political subversive. "Naturally, my first thought was something of a political nature," Mantoura wrote to an ally in the Point IV program, "but I can assure you that this is impossible." "My political history is nil," he continued. "I have never belonged to, or been associated with, or given my views on, a political party of any nature in any country at any time in my whole life." Only after reviewing his political history—and recalling no transgressions—did Mantoura figure that the Asferg episode may have sunk his case. And even Mantoura's letter can be read as a shrewd tactic to win admission. By emphasizing his "political cleanliness" before addressing his supposed moral failure, Mantoura made sure that his Point IV allies knew of his political bona fides. Mantoura eventually won his visa in October 1956, when the BSCA office in Washington reversed the ruling in the field after establishing that Mantoura had not violated Jordanian laws.[41]

The Mahlow, Bruss, and Mantoura cases, of course, were not typical. They could not be decided in the field and were referred back to Washington for a final decision. But if these cases were extreme, they also were consistent with the RRP's development and basic thrust. These security investigations and interviews, with their emphasis on determining the political allegiances and anticommunism of the refugee applicants, were logical outcomes of the refugee politics and policymaking that began in the early spring of 1953. After all, in crafting the legislation, policymakers and politicians emphasized that refugees admitted under the RRA would be victims and opponents of communism. In debating the legislation, restrictionists and liberalizers reinforced the association between anticommunism and refugees, playing off powerful currents that equated American identity with opposition to communism. Moreover, both restrictionists and liberalizers endorsed strict investigative measures designed to ensure that refugees met the law's political and ideological benchmarks. Finally, the ascension of Scott McLeod as the RRP's head nearly ensured that the law's codicils concerning "political cleanliness" would be enforced rigorously.[42]

The Refugee Relief Program's security investigations, of course, had domestic roots: the investigative state birthed by Red Scare political culture and politics. Just as in the United States, where tens of thousands of Americans—teachers, labor union members, actors and actresses, and federal and local government employees—had their political beliefs, activities, and personal relationships subjected to scrutiny and question, so did prospective refugees. Remarkably, the bureaucracy responsible for an important portion of that "Red Scare"—the State Department's Bureau of Security and Consular Affairs—was the lead investigative body in the RRP. Unsurprisingly, then, the tactics of the domestic Red Scare and the RRP were similar: questions of friends, family, and acquaintances; queries concerning organizational memberships and affiliations; and the personal interview in which the subject explained his/her actions and beliefs. Likewise, the intent of refugee screening and domestic "Loyalty Boards" and the like were similar. Indeed, Homer Dean's question of Kurt Bruss—"Have you ever been a member of the communist party at any time?"—surely echoed domestically. Certainly not all refugees faced the onslaught that Mahlow, Bruss, and Mantoura did. But their cases were, it seems, representative of a larger effort. The paucity and sluggishness of admissions throughout 1954 and 1955, the RRA's intent and its regulations, the program's bureaucratic structure, and the RRP's staffing and leadership—as well as these remarkable cases—all suggest that a political litmus test for admission did exist and that it was enforced.[43]

At the same time, the depth of this political examination was left to officials on the ground. They had their orders from above—and most likely knew of McLeod's predilections—but they determined how aggressively they pursued each case, how pointed their questions were, and how much scrutiny they gave the answers. The Mahlow, Bruss, and Mantoura cases indicate that RRA visa applicants expected scrutiny of their political histories, even if they did not always know how to answer queries to the satisfaction of their inquisitors. The application process—and especially the security investigation—was therefore a delicate dance between RRP officials and refugees, wherein investigators hunted for communists, and applicants presented themselves as vigorous anticommunists.

TURNAROUND

By June 1955—as the RRP reached its half-life—only 21,000 visas had been issued. Moreover, because of a 1954 amendment to the RRA that allowed visas allocated to Italian, Greek, and Dutch refugees to go instead to Italian, Greek, and Dutch relatives of those living in the United States, only 3,300 of those 21,000 visas had gone to actual refugees, those fleeing countries behind the Iron Curtain. During the RRP's final eighteen months, though, admissions improved spectacularly. By the end of 1955, the RRP had issued 72,000 visas, meaning that in the last six months of 1955, 51,000 applicants received visas, triple the rate of issuance in the program's first year. In 1956, the program's last year, visa issuance jumped to a rate *seven times* faster than that of 1954! When the RRP closed up shop at the end of 1956, just over 190,000 RRA visas had gone to refugees and relatives. Eighty-eight percent of the available 214,000 RRA visas had been utilized.[44]

The reasons behind this remarkable turnaround are not entirely clear. It decidedly did not result from remedial legislation of the kind suggested by Eisenhower, Lehman, or Celler, none of whose proposals survived in Congress. Instead, it seems the Eisenhower administration desired increased refugee admissions for political reasons and thus made an important personnel change at the RRP that hastened a flurry of significant administrative changes and, finally, the upsurge in visa issuance beginning in mid-1955. Secretary of State Dulles in early June 1955 appointed Pierce Gerety as deputy administrator of the RRP. Gerety had "policy and operational authority" over the RRP, signifying that he technically replaced McLeod as the program's head. Gerety's appointment was approved by

McLeod and seemed to have been accepted by Representative Walter, the key congressional restrictionist in the wake of McCarran's death in late September 1954. The reasons why Walter and McLeod acquiesced to the Gerety appointment, and to (effectively) McLeod's demotion, remain a mystery. Indicative of the White House's interest in recasting the RRP, Eisenhower and Dulles appeared with Gerety at the press conference announcing his appointment. The *New York Times* observed that the Administration's interest in the Gerety hiring emerged because the RRP's problems had hurt the president's standing among white ethnics, a traditionally Democratic voting bloc into which Republicans had made very real inroads in 1952 and hoped to retain in 1956. These concerns only grew as the election neared and Democrats stepped up their attacks on the Eisenhower administration's refugee and immigration policies.[45]

Gerety's arrival energized the program. He immediately traveled to RRP outposts in Europe in an effort to resolve bureaucratic and technical snags that slowed refugee entry. At the same time, he defended RRP officials in the field, dismissing charges that they were obstructionist. Gerety consistently maintained that the chief hurdle facing the program was finding enough sponsors for applications to satisfy the RRA's assurance requirements. A small but significant change in the sponsorship process helped ease this burden. While the RRA still required an individual to sponsor each refugee—a criterion that all liberalizers hoped to see amended—the RRP began in the summer of 1955 to allow voluntary refugee-resettlement agencies, usually ethnic or religious organizations, to endorse, or in effect to cosign, the sponsorship. Refugee experts believed that this adjustment relieved individuals of the worry that they would have no institutional or organizational aid in the sponsorship process.[46] The turnaround in the RRP, then, at least partially resulted from changes to the assurance process, to the greater attention that Gerety paid to the program's administration, and to RRP officials getting better at their jobs.

Liberalizer charges of obstructionism via the security screening process were not fanciful, however, and it seems that these barriers to entry lessened over the program's final eighteen months. During the program's existence, RRP officials refused just over 31,000 visa applications. Health requirements accounted for about 9,700 (31 percent) of these rejections, refugee status eligibility concerns for over 10,600 (34 percent), "moral security" violations (which was likely a term for homosexuality) for about 5,800 rejections (18 percent), and "political security" concerns for slightly more than 4,100 (13 percent).Of the nations that had the most rejections, "political security" concerns led to 11 percent of German rejections, 15 percent of Italian rejections, 39 percent of Greek rejections, and 7 percent of Austrian rejections. The final tally, then, shows that the number of visa rejections on "political security" grounds was significant though not overwhelming. But visa rejections and the discovery of communists and subversives were not all that restrictionists desired. They wanted a thorough investigation of each refugee in the hopes of stalling entry, of grinding to a halt the admission of newcomers. On this score, they did get investigations, more than 250,000 of them in three years. Officials admitted that about 18 percent of these investigations yielded information "of interest" to U.S. security agencies. And through the program's first eighteen months, admissions were horribly slow, just what restrictionists coveted.[47]

Pierce Gerety, however, was no Scott McLeod. While Gerety had no experience in refugee affairs when he took over as deputy administrator, he had served for a short time as chairman of the International Organizations Loyalty Board, a division of the Civil Service Commission. From this position, Gerety led the security investigations—in search of communists and communist sympathizers—of more than four thousand Americans working for international organizations like the United Nations. It was likely this experience that won McLeod and Walter's assent. But Gerety did not arouse the suspicion and antagonism that McLeod did among Americans who detested the Red Scare's excessive anticommunism. Gerety was not a close ally of Walter, McCarran, or McCarthy, nor did he have ties to the restrictionist network in Washington. Indeed, the liberal New Republic, certainly no fan of McLeod or the Red Scare (or immigration restrictionism), lavished praise on Gerety for his work as head of the Loyalty Board and described his record as "extraordinary." The New Republic's endorsement implied that Gerety, unlike McLeod, would be judicious in enforcing the RRA's security measures.[48]

After June 1955 and the arrival of Gerety, the pace of RRP security investigations most certainly quickened. The stunning rise in the rate of entry via the RRP—admissions in 1956 tallied 118,000 versus 17,000 in 1954—was too large to have been only the product of a more efficient assurance process. Likewise, at the program's end, RRP officials announced that each security investigation had required an average of 10.5 man hours—perhaps two working days. But McLeod, in early 1955 just after the program had been in operation for one year, admitted that the average security investigation took forty-two working days. Again, this large discrepancy points to a quicker and less rigorous security investigation. Finally, restrictionists began grumbling in the summer and fall of 1955 about the need to uphold strict security investigations in the RRP, lest the country be flooded with communists. Senator James Eastland, who as chairman of the Internal Security Subcommittee investigated the RRP security screening process, ominously warned that 30–40 percent of refugees entering West Germany in 1955 were Soviet agents, "sleepers" who would try to infiltrate the United States via the RRP. While liberalizers quickly knocked down Eastland's assertions, the senator's actions indicate his fear that security investigations had gone lax. Eastland, most likely, was correct.[49]

. . .

The Refugee Relief Program marked the United States' first major foray into Cold War–era refugee relief. Initiated because of foreign policy concerns and then conceived in the cauldron of vigorously anticommunist domestic politics and political culture, the Refugee Relief Act cemented the central equation at the heart of refugee politics and affairs: "refugee equals European anticommunist." Opponents and supporters of refugee admissions both agreed to this common ground, though they fought bitterly over how such a standard, especially its political component, ought to be enforced in the field. Liberalizers were appalled by the RRP's investigatory powers and its extensive efforts to prevent the entry of subversives and communists, while restrictionists were reassured—reactions that no doubt reflected their opinions about the slow pace of entries through mid-1955. The RRP's turnaround in its final eighteen months, then, was all the more remarkable and stunning, though it owed more to the implementation and administration of the existing program than to any significant rethinking of the American commitment to refugees. In the next refugee crisis, there would be less time for debate, but plenty of time for recrimination, and ultimately the reinforcement of that central equation.

CHAPTER 3

"From Hungary, New Americans": The United States and Hungarian Refugees

COMPARED TO THE REFUGEE PROBLEMS created by Nazism, by World War II, and by the confluence of Soviet domination of eastern Europe and western Europe's population pressures in the early 1950s, the Hungarian refugee crisis of late 1956 was like a thunderclap. While the former refugee flows evolved slowly over years, swift and stunning events in the fall of 1956—the overthrow of Hungary's Stalinist regime by disaffected socialist revolutionaries followed by a massive Soviet invasion when the new Hungarian government attempted to remove the country from the Soviet Union's military and political orbit—precipitated a flood of Hungarian refugees into Austria and Yugoslavia. In a matter of weeks, a Hungarian refugee problem existed.

The Eisenhower administration quickly launched a program that admitted nearly forty thousand refugees in about one year. Unlike the Refugee Relief Program, which resulted from both foreign policy and domestic political considerations, the American decision to help Hungarian refugees was largely driven by foreign policy concerns. Specifically, the Eisenhower administration calculated that a commitment to Hungarians fleeing Soviet tanks was a strong and clear sign of support for the Hungarian Revolution that, at the same time, would not too greatly damage delicate American-Soviet relations or lead to a larger superpower conflict. Hungarian refugee admissions were remarkable for two reasons. First, the executive branch, to an unprecedented degree, assumed control of American refugee policy, especially with the utilization of a new process, called "parole," to admit refugees. Second, the admissions process focused, like the final eighteen months of the RRP, on admitting Hungarians quickly rather than thoroughly and painstakingly screening them. In other words, speed trumped security. Nonetheless, the Hungarian crisis—in which refugees fled Soviet tanks and soldiers—only bolstered and reinforced the association between "refugee" and "anticommunist."

In the immediate aftermath of the Soviet invasion, the usual restrictionist opposition to refugee admissions receded because of sympathy for the so-called freedom fighters. This relative quiet in immigration affairs did not last long. Opposition to the admission of newcomers resurfaced, and congressional restrictionists levied an old charge: the government's inadequate security screening of refugees had led to the entry of communists. (Later research would show that many refugees, in fact, were communists, or ex–party members, or had long histories in leftist politics.) In response, the Eisenhower administration, refugee advocacy organizations, and even public-relations firms made extraordinary efforts to convince the public that Hungarian refugees had all the qualities of "Americans." Anticommunism served as the foundation of this public-relations campaign, but qualifications based on marriage, family life, employment, and gender emerged just as prominently. If ideas about national identity had shifted from an ethnic to a political basis over the previous decades, the "selling" of the Hungarian refugees demonstrates that "American-ness" circa 1957 was more complicated than a purely political definition might imply. The public-relations campaign also had important refugee policy implications. By painting a particular picture of refugees, the PR efforts effectively narrowed the concept of refugee, reinforcing the basic thrust of the American commitment to refugees.

THE HUNGARIAN REVOLUTION AND THE U.S. RESPONSE

The Hungarian Revolution was part of a wave of political disturbances that rocked the Soviet Union and eastern Europe in the aftermath of Joseph Stalin's death in March 1953. With Stalin's passing, Soviets—including leaders like Nikita Khrushchev—and eastern Europeans began debating the merits of Stalinism and the direction of communism. In East Germany in 1953, workers protested that country's Stalinist regime, leading to Soviet armed intervention that quelled the uprising. Three years later, disturbances broke out in Poland that led to the ascension of a reformist government. Its leaders assured the Soviets that they were committed communists (though anti-Stalinists) and pledged to remain in the Warsaw Pact. The crisis ended without Soviet intervention, but with a Polish version of communism within the Soviet Union's national security objectives.[1]

De-Stalinization also bloomed in Hungary. In the early 1950s, Hungary staggered under a Stalinist leadership that produced a stagnant economy and a political reign of terror. A Moscow-directed political liberalization failed in 1955, though it did encourage a strong reformist movement of journalists, university students and professors, artists, intellectuals, and victims of political purges. Their goal was a communist Hungary without Stalinist excesses. The revolutionary foment accelerated in 1956, inspired by events in Poland. On October 15 and 16, university students protested around the country and demanded more radical reforms, including free elections, a multiparty state, the reinstitution of traditional symbols of

Hungarian nationalism, and state protection of civil rights. While earlier reformers wanted to end Stalinism, it appeared that the students now wanted to end communism in Hungary. A week later, protests broke out all across Hungary. The most visible occurred in Budapest, where workers joined the students and both clashed with the Hungarian secret police. Hungary's Stalinist regime panicked and called for Soviet help, but after the Soviet forces mustered from their garrisons, they pulled back and left the streets to the protestors. The Soviets instead decided to pursue a political solution, installing János Kádár as First Secretary and Imre Nagy, who maintained ties to reformist intellectuals, as premier.[2]

Who were these Hungarian revolutionaries confronting the Kádár-Nagy government? During the uprising, over 28,000 Hungarians joined about 2,100 workers councils, while workers and students quickly set up over 10,000 revolutionary committees. These councils and committees took charge of their local communities, removing party and government officials, destroying symbols of Stalinism, and in some cases negotiating with Soviet troops to ensure their noninterference. Four main streams of thought existed among the revolutionaries. Many intellectuals, students, and workers—and the new premiere, Nagy—supported a reformed socialism. Similarly, a group of noncommunist, nationalist politicians who held power in Hungary from 1945 to 1948 envisioned a socialist Hungary. A Christian-Conservative group that emphasized the ownership of private property coalesced around the jailed church leader Cardinal Josef Mindszenty. Finally, historians have classified the street fighters who battled the secret police and intimidated the Soviet military as having "extreme right-wing" politics. A desire for a lessened, and perhaps a complete withdrawal of the, Soviet presence in Hungary and an inchoate but real Hungarian nationalism cemented these ideologically disparate factions.[3]

The revolution continued moving in a more anti-Soviet direction as October ended. First Secretary Kádár remained allied with the Soviets, but Nagy increasingly adopted radical positions. He permitted the Social Democratic Party to officially reorganize, released from jail the strongly anticommunist Mindszenty, attacked the Stalinist hardliners' decision to call for Soviet troops, and reformed the multiparty coalition government of 1945. In foreign affairs, he withdrew Hungary from the Warsaw Pact, proclaimed Hungary's neutrality, and asked for United Nations protection. Soviet leaders could not abide these actions and they determined that a military solution was their only viable option. On November 4, Soviet troops set out to crush the rebellion.[4]

The Soviets' first target was Budapest. Between ten and fifteen thousand Hungarian men and women—mainly young people and workers—took to the streets against the Soviets. While the Soviets quickly arrested Nagy and gave control of the government to their ally Kádár, the battle for

Budapest lasted three days. Contemporary accounts reported over 20,000 Hungarian dead, a figure accepted in the subsequent historiography of the revolution. While the exact numbers of dead and casualties are impossible to know, historians with access to the latest Hungarian documents now estimate that nearly 2,700 Hungarians died, and over 20,000 were injured. Of the dead, over 1,300 were workers. The Soviets lost nearly 700 soldiers, with more than twice that many wounded. While resistance continued in other parts of the country for a short while, by mid-November, the revolution was over.[5]

The U.S. government closely followed events in Hungary. By the fall of 1956, the bravado of Eisenhower's 1952 campaign promises concerning foreign policy had disappeared. Instead, the administration looked to reinforce U.S. military and political alliances, to halt Soviet and communist expansion in the Third World, and to extend the U.S. military advantage through policies like the New Look. Eisenhower, though, also wanted to decrease superpower tensions. The Administration hoped that Khrushchev's rise might produce a Soviet-American détente and that, with the Soviet rejection of Stalinism, eastern Europe might be able to loose the bonds of Soviet control. Soviet actions in Hungary severely tested but did not shatter the Administration's approach. The White House searched for a moderate response that expressed support for the Hungarian revolutionaries and reminded eastern European satellites that the United States wanted to see them free of Soviet control, but did not sabotage the prospect of improved U.S.-Soviet relations or risk a larger Cold War confrontation. With its Hungarian client state teetering, Eisenhower worried that the Soviet leadership might resort to "extreme measures" or even "precipitate global war" because of its deteriorating position vis-à-vis its satellites. Eisenhower's concern in late October 1956 that the Cold War might spin out of control was not solely the product of events in Hungary. Israel, Britain, and France, acting without American support, attacked Egypt and its nationalist leader Gamel Nasser, setting off what came to be known as the Suez Crisis. Nasser's Egypt had recently deepened ties with the Soviet Union, who after the attacks threatened a nuclear response. In late October, then, the Eisenhower administration attempted to defuse tensions in the Middle East and deal with momentous events in Hungary.[6]

Regarding Hungary, the administration publicly tried to reassure the Soviets. Secretary of State Dulles announced on October 27 that the United States "had no ulterior purpose in desiring the independence of the satellite countries" and would not treat these countries "as potential military allies." Eisenhower repeated this message four days later. On November 2, Eisenhower offered the Nagy government twenty-million-dollars' worth of food and relief supplies, a proposition accompanied by another noninflammatory statement of support: "All America pays tribute in these troubled days to the courage and sacrifice of the Hungarian people in their determination to secure freedom." Eisenhower's and Dulles's public comments reflected the Administration's private decision not to intervene in Hungary. Early in the uprising, the Administration ruled out military assistance, in the form of either intervention or an airdrop of supplies. When the Soviet Union initially mustered its troops from their barracks (only to retreat soon thereafter), Eisenhower rejected CIA requests that it be allowed to airdrop supplies and arms to the rebels. One key practical consideration, moreover, worked against any form of military intervention: the United States could not easily move men or supplies into Hungary.[7]

The Soviet decision to crush the Hungarian Revolution hardly surprised American foreign policymakers; intelligence and diplomatic reports predicted as much. The U.S. government's cautious response to the crackdown resembled its reaction to the revolution. Eisenhower sent a letter to the Soviet leadership asking them to withdraw from Hungary. American efforts in the United Nations (UN) were similarly muted, limited to condemnatory statements. Nonetheless, a desire for better superpower relations did not mean completely ignoring the Soviet invasion of Hungary. Eisenhower and Dulles judged the attack morally reprehensible and indicative of Soviet brutality. It also presented an opportunity to rally world opinion against the Soviets and enhance the United States' image. On this score, the administration ran into some challenges, mainly the critiques emanating from European capitals—and from Hungary—that the United States had encouraged the rebellion through its propaganda and Radio Free Europe broadcasts but refused to aid the rebels in their time of need.[8]

Americans also charged that the United States had encouraged and then abandoned the revolutionaries. This accusation unsurprisingly emanated from the die-hard anticommunist hard right, who had long excoriated Eisenhower for being soft on the Soviets. More politically troubling for Eisenhower, conservative Republicans like Phyllis Schlafly and others who would make up the base of the "New Right" worried that the United States' flaccid response during the revolution was but more evidence of the president's accommodationist foreign policy. Regular Americans may not have shared the anticommunist zeal and suspicions of these political activists, but they too wondered whether the United States had let down the brave Hungarians in desperate times. Many of course remembered that the Administration had campaigned in 1952 on the promise of rolling back communism and liberating eastern Europe. While the Administration had long since abandoned such policies and goals—Eisenhower always having been less enthralled with the idea of a rollback policy than

Secretary of State Dulles—Americans surely recalled the stirring rhetoric, which made the administration's Hungary policy appear especially impotent and hypocritical. (Even if the public had forgotten, Democrats in the 1956 campaign reminded voters that Republicans had failed to deliver a "rollback" of communism in eastern Europe.)[9]

Such reactions can only be understood in the context of the tremendous interest and sympathy the revolution generated in the United States—in part, no doubt, because of the link in political culture between American identity and opposition to communism. For two weeks, the story of the revolution and the bravery and fate of the resistance fighters led the news. Reporting in the *New York Times* and the *Washington Post* easily mingled facts, half-truths, and rumors, but a compelling picture emerged that stressed a few components. First, the Hungarian revolutionaries valiantly fought for their freedom against a mighty Soviet military. This image only reinforced the anticommunist credentials of the Hungarians, many of whom would soon be refugees. Second, while it was unclear what political principles the Nagy government embraced—the *Times* described him as "A Strange Communist"—descriptions of events in Hungary took on a good versus evil dichotomy. Third, and most important, the revolution produced a surge of optimism. It appeared that the Iron Curtain might actually be tumbling and that a decisive turning point in the Cold War—beneficial to the United States—might have been reached.[10]

The Eisenhower administration knew, then, that condemnatory statements alone would not demonstrate leadership. Tangible action was needed. The fifteen thousand Hungarians who by the end of November's first week had sought refuge in Austria offered an opportunity to secure these foreign policy objectives and quiet these domestic concerns. Within a few days of the Soviet invasion, the Eisenhower White House decided to admit some of these refugees to the United States. (An interagency committee of State Department, Defense Department, U.S. Information Agency, the CIA, and lower-level White House officials had discussed refugee admissions since the last week in October, though it is unclear how these talks influenced the White House.) Refugee admissions had several other discrete advantages. The Austrian government (a neutral in the Cold War) offered its wholehearted support; its representatives told the United States that it could not handle a large number of Hungarian refugees, citing the "economic burden" and the "potential political difficulties"—specifically in relations with the Soviet bloc—that such an influx would cause. American officials, moreover, believed that the Soviets would soon shut the borders, thereby limiting the refugee problem's scope and making it easier to ameliorate.[11]

HUNGARIAN REFUGEE ADMISSIONS

The State Department's Bureau of Security and Consular Affairs took up the task of developing a program to bring Hungarians to the United States. Because the annual Hungarian immigration quota of 865 visas was oversubscribed and too small, BSCA officials wanted to admit Hungarians through the RRP, which had about 10,000 "escapee" visas available. Knowing that enforcement of the RRA's security and investigatory provisions would delay entry of the Hungarians into the new year, at which point the RRP visas would no longer be available because of the program's expiration on December 31, 1956, Pierce Gerety suggested that the secretaries of state and defense waive the RRA's requirement that each refugee present a two-year documented history. The BSCA's Scott McLeod wanted to further speed admissions by allowing RRP officials alone to sign the visas rather than requiring a cosignature with INS officials. McLeod's position, such a reversal from his obstructionism in 1953 and 1954, was one of the first indications of the sympathy that Hungarian refugees generated, even among restrictionists. (By the spring of 1956, McLeod also apparently wanted to ingratiate himself with the Administration, and thus toned down his opposition to refugee admissions. McLeod did receive an ambassadorship in the spring of 1957, though it is not clear whether this promotion was in the works in November 1956.) After heated discussions with INS commissioner Joseph Swing, McLeod dropped his suggestion. Finally, officials determined that with these conditions they could process—and therefore admit—five thousand Hungarians by December 31, 1956.[12]

The development of a Hungarian refugee program represented both a break from and a continuation of the RRP. To be sure, the American response to the Hungarian crisis conformed to and reinforced earlier policy decisions that had established the "refugee equals European anticommunist" equation at the heart of refugee politics. But the differences from earlier policies and politics were even more striking. Most glaring, the executive branch dominated policy and program development in late 1956. Neither Congress nor the usual interest groups participated as they had throughout the twentieth century. McLeod, Gerety, and Max Rabb, Eisenhower's refugee man at the White House, did not even brief key congressional experts until November 11, three days after Eisenhower made the policy public! The Administration wanted a refugee program quickly, both to help the refugees in Austria and to reap the public relations and diplomatic advantages it sought. Congressional consultation would only have slowed, or perhaps even halted, the program's development. Speed was important in another way. The policy debates surrounding the RRA, and eventually the law itself, stressed meticulous screening of refugees in an attempt to uncover their political histories and beliefs. As American officials began designing the Hungarian refugee program in November 1956, speed of admissions trumped security concerns. Of course, the RRP had moved in this direction over the previous eighteen months, but the Hungarian crisis strengthened this trend.[13]

Indeed, in a striking difference from 1953 it seemed that no one cared much about the exact political and ideological leanings of the Hungarian refugees who would soon enter the United States. To the State Department, RRP, and INS officials who initially designed the program, the Hungarians encamped in Austria qualified as "escapees," no questions asked. (The 1953 RRA defined an "escapee" as "any refugee who, because of persecution or fear of persecution on account of race, religion, or political opinion fled" from the U.S.S.R or communist eastern Europe and "cannot return because of fear of persecution on account of race, religion, or political opinion.") At the same time, Eisenhower's description of the refugees as "older people, they are women; they are children—and many of them are suffering wounds inflicted by the guns of Imperialist Communism" assumed that the refugees were both victims and opponents of communism, effectively conflating victimization with opposition. Hungarian refugees, of course, defied these easy categorizations. For one, not all of the refugees in Austria were "freedom fighters." Many were Hungarians looking to leave Austria and come to the West, an opportunity the revolution afforded. The numbers bear this out. Tens of thousands of Hungarians took to the streets against the Soviets, but eventually over 200,000 Hungarians fled their country. Likewise, many of the revolution's participants and supporters were socialists, social democrats, or former or current members of the communist party. While these refugees were likely anti-Soviet, many subscribed to political ideologies banned by the RRA and immigration statutes. Ultimately, the power of the "refugee equals European anticommunist" consensus combined with sympathy for the revolutionaries and the need for quick, decisive action to overwhelm any doubts in policymaking and political circles—and to flatten the political-ideological diversity of the refugee population.[14]

At the end of the second week of November, the American refugee program got under way with hopes of distributing two hundred visas a day to Hungarians. So many Hungarian refugees queued up outside the American consulate in Vienna for visas that its staff worked around the clock to process them. Other countries of course joined the United States in admitting Hungarians. Aided by international organizations like the Intergovernmental Committee for European Migration and the United Nations, Canada made the largest commitment, eventually admitting 37,000 refugees. Australia, England, West Germany, France, Sweden, and Switzerland each by the end of the crisis admitted about 15,000. (England and France promised to admit all comers.) Argentina, Brazil, Honduras, Guatemala, and Venezuela welcomed thousands more Hungarians. Such a generous response, compared to previous refugee flows, was needed. Even after the Soviets had crushed the revolution, Hungarians kept pouring over the border; over 10,000 refugees arrived in Austria between November 11 and November 17, bringing the total in Austria to around 25,000. Despite the "open doors" of these nations, the United States remained the most popular destination for Hungarians.[15]

Getting a Hungarian from the queue to an airplane bound for the United States took about four days. A refugee first met with the ICEM to secure transport to the United States, and then with one of the five voluntary agencies (World Council of Churches, the International Rescue Committee, the National Catholic Welfare Conference, the Hebrew Immigration Aid Society, and the Lutheran World Federation) matching each refugee with a sponsorship that satisfied the RRA's "assurances" requirements. These agencies also interviewed each refugee to ensure that the newcomer intended to stay in the United States and could assimilate to American life. Next, the refugee reported to the American consulate for a brief health examination and the beginning of a security check, which was completed in a few days after an interview with American officials. The refugee then returned to the ICEM to board a flight to Camp Kilmer, an old army base in New Jersey that had been reactivated to temporarily house the Hungarians. At Kilmer, each refugee received a more complete health examination, was processed by customs officials, and underwent another round of immigration and security checks before being fingerprinted and photographed. These procedures took about four hours, if no problems arose; later, in response to criticism that it was moving too slowly, the army contended it had reduced this phase to a mere fifty-five minutes. Finally, the voluntary agency that had arranged for the refugee's sponsorship helped relocate the refugee to his/her new home and job.[16]

For the most part, the admission of Hungarian refugees moved fairly smoothly. The first group of sixty refugees arrived at Camp Kilmer on November 21, 1956 and the RRP's Gerety predicted that the five thousand visas allocated for Hungarians would be issued by December 31, although the transportation of those refugees to the United States would not be completed until January. The program proceeded at a quick pace by design and because its administration mimicked the final, rather than the initial, eighteen months of the RRP. Sponsorships proved easy to find, with voluntary agencies reporting large numbers of American volunteers. More important, the security investigations moved along quickly because they were enforced so much less rigorously than during the initial year of the RRP.[17]

The screening program for Hungarian refugees had several components. Voluntary agencies conducted what RRP officials called screening, but their efforts—like those described above and the matching of refugees of certain religious faiths to a corresponding voluntary organization—were unrelated to the enforcement of immigration law. Other aspects of refugee screening appeared geared toward uncovering the political beliefs and backgrounds of the Hungarians streaming into Austria. Austrian police screened refugees at the border and they monitored the refugee camps. RRP officials praised "self-purging among" the Hungarian refugee population in "the form of oral denunciations or anonymous letters or formal communications." This "helpful" mechanism eliminated "many questionable applicants who would require additional processing under normal circumstances." Finally, a visa officer, an immigration inspector, and a Hungarian linguist interrogated the refugee while RRP officials checked the records held by the CIA, the army, and the State Department to ensure that the applicant previously had not run afoul of American intelligence.[18]

These procedures only superficially mirrored the RRP's investigatory mechanisms, however. Officials hoped that each interrogation would take about an hour. They replaced the RRP's extensive "investigations and written reports" with a single form. Pierce Gerety pushed the CIA to complete its internal check of each refugee in only twenty-four hours, a deadline the agency met. And RRP officials apparently streamlined the program even more as it went into the field. In an early proposal of the screening plan, an "independent Hungarian Debriefing Committee" was supposed to "independently interview the references" given by each refugee. RRP officials never implemented this background check. Walter Besterman, Representative Francis Walter's chief aide on immigration and refugee matters, visited the American operation on November 19 and 20 and he returned to describe a security screening interview that was as imprecise as it was quick. While Besterman reported that a "reasonable attempt" was made to follow the dictums of the RRP, he illuminated how speed trumped security. Refugees were shown a list of communist organizations and asked if they had ever belonged. If they answered no, "their answers were accepted at face value." If a refugee answered yes, interrogators attempted to ascertain whether the refugee's membership in the communist organization had come under duress, had been used solely to gain work, or had occurred when the refugee was under sixteen years of age. If any of these qualifications were met, investigators declared the membership involuntary and granted the visa. Moreover, if a refugee from a "family group" failed the security check, he or she was granted special admission to the United States (called parole status, which did not confer a visa) because officials were loath to break up families.[19]

Hungarian refugee admissions in late 1956, then, continued the march away from the investigative state and the anticommunist litmus test established by the early RRP. There were no extensive investigations of refugees, nor, according to Besterman, did RRP officials engage in rigorous questioning designed to uncover the political backgrounds of refugees. This helps explain why one RRP official claimed that the "self-purging" by the Hungarian refugee population was "one of the most effective screening practices in Austria." Refugees likely had knowledge of their campmates' past or present political activities or ideological predilections. In other words, "self-purging" identified the political histories of refugees for American officials who did not uncover them during their rushed screening process. The irony of the screening process, of course, is clear. If American officials had conducted interviews as they had initially in the RRP, they would have uncovered the rather complex political histories of applicants, information that surely would have made them inadmissible. Eisenhower and the policymakers in Washington ignored these details as they designed the policy and program. So did officials in the field.[20]

REFUGEE POLICY INNOVATION: THE "PAROLE" OF HUNGARIAN REFUGEES

No matter how quickly Hungarian refugees earned their visas, that pace could not match the flow of newcomers into Austria. By November 27, 1956, eighty-nine thousand Hungarians had arrived in Austria and a few thousand still entered each day. The Austrian government pleaded with the United States to admit more refugees. The Eisenhower administration and the State Department's BSCA and European experts worked on a solution in the last days of November. On December 1, Eisenhower announced further refugee admissions, which had been rumored for about a week. He authorized the entry of an additional 1,500 Hungarians via the RRP and also ordered the "parole" of 15,000 more refugees into the United States.[21]

Eisenhower's directive took advantage of a little-known codicil in the Immigration and Nationality Act that permitted the attorney general to admit (or "parole") an alien into the United States on an emergency basis if the admission served the public interest. The "parolee" could only remain in the United States at the attorney general's discretion. Because the "parolee" was admitted without a visa, he/she had no official immigration status and could not become a permanent resident or citizen. Eisenhower promised to introduce legislation to "regularize" or "normalize" the immigration status of the parolees, essentially saying that any Hungarian refugee who wanted to stay in the United States would be allowed to do so. During the initial discussions about Hungarian refugee admissions in early November, INS chief Joseph Swing suggested using the parole option, but he lost out, largely because parole was meant to admit individuals, not hundreds of persons a day over a period of months. But by late November, American options were limited. The State Department believed it might be able to offer an additional three thousand RRA visas—Eisenhower decided on half that amount—but to bring even more Hungarians to the States required either utilizing the parole procedure or pursuing special immigration legislation, a request that could be made, at the earliest, when Congress returned for its new session in January 1957.[22]

The decision to parole the Hungarians would in time reshape American refugee policymaking and programs. The parole policy significantly increased the Executive Branch's control of refugee policymaking. It provided Eisenhower with the means to admit Hungarians almost immediately, and a speedy U.S. response to the refugee problem was a chief goal in Washington. The parole procedure's other advantage was twofold: the policy did not require either congressional approval or consultation, nor did Congress have as direct a hand in overseeing its implementation. (Of course, Congress possessed its usual oversight role and it controlled the annual INS appropriation, thus it could indirectly influence parole policy, but only if willing to provoke a confrontation with the Administration.) Eisenhower's problem with Congress in November 1956 was not that restrictionists were looking to sabotage his plans for refugee admissions, but that Congress was out of session. Indeed, restrictionists retreated in the aftermath of the Revolution. Even Representative Walter, no friend of generous refugee policies, lobbied the administration both publicly and privately to admit unlimited numbers of Hungarians after he visited Austria and personally saw the refugee camps. Walter, no political dummy, also understood public opinion. A poll released in December 1956 revealed that only 34 percent of the public believed the United States had admitted "too many" refugees, while 48 percent thought "about the right number" had been admitted, and 11 percent claimed "not enough" had been done. Nonetheless, the parole policy's long-term consequences were potentially staggering. The Eisenhower administration had legitimated a method of refugee admissions that it, or its successors, could control completely—a key advantage because restrictionist sentiment was not likely to remain quiet.[23]

Administration of the parole policy fell to the Immigration and Naturalization Service rather than the Department of State, which had been the lead agency in previous refugee programs. Despite this shift, the Eisenhower White House expected parole to run smoothly because many of the procedural and administrative bottlenecks had been solved in the preceding weeks. Officials apparently contemplated relaxing security screening procedures even more. During the State Department's late-November discussions about the parole option, the consensus was that security screening ought to be conducted once the paroled refugee landed in the United States in order to expedite the entry of Hungarians. This, of course, would have been a significant change from the RRP admission of Hungarians.

It is not clear whether such a reform occurred. The announcement of the parole policy gave no inkling of a change in security screening and the *New York Times* reported that "Officials [in Austria] were told that further relaxation of the process had not been authorized." Only a few days later, however, U.S. personnel in Austria announced that one thousand refugees could be moved to the States per day, in part because the parole procedures had been amended so that no refugees would be screened until they reached the United States. Other evidence indicates that the security screening in Austria resembled the procedures under which Hungarians were admitted with RRP visas. INS commissioner Swing detailed for Representative Walter the parole program's security measures. Swing described immigration officers in Austria conducting "personal interrogations" of each applicant and revealed that even the translators used in these interrogations had been trained both "to ascertain any possible ground for inadmissibility for security reasons" and to detect "suspicious conduct" by the applicant. Swing noted that the medical personnel who did physicals on each refugee were also trained to detect any "suspicious conduct." Finally, Swing pointed out that the Austrian government had infiltrated the Hungarian refugee population with informants who reported any "security threat or problem." Once in the United States, refugees were again interrogated by immigration officers to ferret out any possible security violations, although Swing admitted that the work done in the States was mostly paperwork. Swing's description generally conforms to internal State Department descriptions of the parole program's security screening system, although State believed that the INS no longer ran the refugees' names through the files of American intelligence and military agencies.[24]

While the parole program's exact security screening procedures are less than clear, it is highly unlikely that tougher screening occurred. The priority was speed of entry, rather than close investigations of each refugee to establish his or her political history or background or denial of entry to communists, former communists, or socialists. Indeed, Hungarians entered the United States at quicker rates under the parole program than under the RRP. Just as important, the Hungarian parole program built upon the procedural foundations of the late RRP and the RRP's Hungarian admissions, achieving the same results at the same cost: a marked retreat from the investigatory regime established in 1953.[25]

American efforts, even with the parole of 15,000 Hungarians in early December 1956, could not keep up with the flow of refugees into Austria. By mid-December, 130,000 refugees had arrived in Austria, since late October, and only 50,000 had been evacuated. Refugee relief agencies in the field called on the United States to admit still more Hungarians, advice echoed by Vice President Richard Nixon after his mid-December tour of the refugee camps. On January 1, 1957, Eisenhower announced that the United States would parole additional Hungarians. A week later, the Administration clarified the details, quietly authorizing the parole of 6,814 Hungarians. At the end of January, the White House announced its intention to parole 4,000 more refugees—bringing total admissions to over 30,000. By that point, almost 170,000 Hungarians had entered Austria. In March, April, and May, the entry of Hungarian parolees slowed, but still saw hundreds enter each month, bringing total admissions to over 35,000.[26]

The decisions in late 1956 and early 1957 to parole more Hungarians came as restrictionist grumblings resurfaced. Even when sympathy for Hungarian refugees was at its height in November and December, a significant undercurrent of opposition (slightly more than one-third of those polled in public opinion surveys) to the liberal admissions policy existed. The White House made it known in late November that it had received a "considerable number" of letters opposing additional refugee admissions. The Eisenhower administration took this opposition seriously. Part of the reason it dispatched Nixon to Austria in mid-December was to build support for the refugees. Just as troubling, Congressional restrictionists dropped their backing of Hungarian admissions. During a televised appearance on December 30, Representative Walter claimed that the 6,500 RRA visas had been issued to Hungarian refugees without proper security screening. A few days later, he charged that most of refugees admitted with RRA visas—and thus granted permanent residence—were communists fleeing the true Hungarian freedom fighters. On January 10, Walter said, "All the administrators of the law wanted to do, apparently under orders from high quarters, was to bring in a large number of people quickly, and to worry about who has entered the United States—later." Senator Olin Johnston, acting chairman of the Internal Security Subcommittee, echoed Walter. Johnston, worried that communists had infiltrated the United States in the refugee flow, urged in mid-January that no more Hungarian refugees be admitted until the program had been thoroughly investigated. His staff cited the case of Gregory Lang, who entered the United States in late 1956. Upon receiving a tip that Lang once belonged to the communist party in suburban Budapest, Johnson's staff, the INS, and Camp Kilmer authorities interrogated Lang. Lang at first denied any association with the communist party, but then admitted that he had been a member from 1945 to 1948 and, in the words of Johnson's staff, had "even worked as a card clerk in the office of the political secret police." Lang said that he did not mention this political history on his application for fear he would be denied entry to the United States. After his interrogation, Lang was taken into custody by the INS.[27]

Walter's and Johnston's critiques cast suspicion on all Hungarians, whether admitted under the RRP or via parole. They left somewhat vague their charges that "communists" had entered the U.S., however. Were they concerned that some of the refugees were spies? Or ex-communists who had not repented adequately for their political sins? Or communist-party members? Their comments pointed to all of these possibilities, but the two restrictionists seemed most concerned that officials knew so little about the political histories and affiliations of refugees entering the United States at substantial rates. Their critiques, then, invited a return to the security screening regime that dominated refugee affairs in the early 1950s. Walter's and Johnston's attacks also skillfully exploited public conceptions about the characteristics and ideals a proper American embodied. In the later 1950s, even after the storms of the Red Scare, leveling the charge of communist was still tantamount to declaring the Hungarians "un-American." In this case, the ethnonational backgrounds of the refugees mattered little in comparison to their political backgrounds. (Of course, national origins thinking still motivated a vast number of restrictionists in the 1950s, and for them the political bona fides of newcomers mattered little except as the most expeditious way to uphold their beloved immigration system.) It was this skillful manipulation of the politicized conception of national identity that gave critics of refugee admissions their power in 1957. It also was an effective refutation of—and, indeed, a direct challenge to—Eisenhower's and other liberalizers' contention that Hungarians deserved to come to the United States because they embodied that anticommunist ideal so central to American identity.

Walter backed up his rhetoric by opening congressional hearings in late January that investigated Hungarian refugee admissions. INS head Joseph Swing defended the program vigorously, claiming that only three of the 23,000 Hungarians admitted had been returned to Europe because of past subversive activities. Walter was not satisfied, contending that "the best way to find out who has entered is to let time elapse. During the last 48 hours, I have been advised by highly reputable Hungarians that we should give time for Hungarians themselves to advise us as to who among those who have arrived are desirable and who are undesirable." Resurgent restrictionism highlighted that Hungarian refugees would be welcomed in many quarters with only half-opened and suspicious arms—and that the programs and policies that admitted these refugees would come under increasing fire. The political stakes only grew higher as the Eisenhower administration, recognizing that the Hungarians would not soon return home, introduced legislation to give the parolees permanent residence in the United States.[28]

THE CAMPAIGN TO SELL HUNGARIAN REFUGEES AS AMERICANS

The Eisenhower administration and the voluntary agencies charged with refugee resettlement understood the need to blunt this criticism. In response, they undertook a concerted effort to "sell" the Hungarian refugees to the general public as prospective citizens with all of the qualities that "good Americans" supposedly possessed in the late 1950s. The thrust of these campaigns, which further cemented the connections between refugees and anticommunism, resonated because of anticommunism's centrality to American identity. But the public-relations efforts also stressed particular characteristics involving marriage, gender roles, family life, employment, and patterns of consumption—each of which also informed the concept of "American." While the PR campaign ultimately achieved only mixed success, it did have important policy ramifications, mainly its reinforcement of the basic thrust of refugee affairs in the minds of the public and politicians.[29]

While private refugee organizations like the International Rescue Committee and its indefatigable chairman Leo Cherne worked to burnish the public's perception of the Hungarian newcomers, their efforts paled in comparison to the U.S. government's feverish efforts to reassure Americans that refugees were not very different from them. Nixon's visit to Austria in late 1956 was the most overt and most public of these endeavors, but a more sustained effort soon followed. It is not entirely clear why the Administration was so concerned with counteracting restrictionist criticism and negative publicity, but a few reasons suggest themselves. First, by early 1957, the White House was readying legislation that would revise the McCarran-Walter immigration law as well as provide for permanent-resident status for Hungarian refugees. That package stood much less chance of passage in the face of rising antinewcomer sentiment. Second, the Administration, as it began its second term, likely did not want to find itself embroiled in political problems. Eisenhower, in a November news conference, argued that his victory in the just concluded presidential contest amounted to a "mandate" for his policies and the political philosophy of modern Republicanism. Eisenhower spoke of continuing to put his stamp on American politics, and a spat with some members of Congress over Hungarian refugees would only fritter away this opportunity.[30]

Figure 3.1 Leo Cherne of the International Rescue Committee sorts through donations for Hungarian refugees in the aftermath of the failed revolution. The pile of letters and donations aptly symbolized the American public's enthusiasm and support for the revolutionaries.

The key to these efforts was the President's Committee for Hungarian Refugee Relief (PCFHRR), which Eisenhower established on December 12, 1956, to coordinate the refugee-resettlement efforts of the voluntary agencies, the federal government, and private-sector contributors. Tracy Voorhees, a former undersecretary of the army and American minister to NATO with a talent for organization and administration, ran PCFHRR. From this post, Voorhees oversaw the work of two public-relations organizations, the Advertising Council and Communications Counselors, Incorporated (CCI). CCI understood its charge as garnering positive press for the refugee program and easing the resettlement of refugees by creating "a great national desire to welcome and care for these refugees."[31]

The Advertising Council, founded in 1942, consisted of some of the nation's most influential business leaders from large companies like General Electric, Sears and Roebuck, and IBM. In the 1940s and 1950s, the Council launched hundreds of public-service advertising campaigns to bolster public support for the federal government's domestic and foreign policies and to promote the dynamism and viability of America's economic and political system. The Council's members, as historian Robert Griffith has shown, were generally conservative, but they embraced Eisenhower's moderate Republicanism rather than the anti-statist, anti-New Deal positions of more conservative members of the business community. To sell Hungarian refugees to the public, the Council asked radio and television networks and advertisers to air a public-service announcement during the last weekend of November that would explain the material and spiritual needs of "Hungarian Freedom fighters" and "victims of brutal Soviet repression." In mid-December, the Council coordinated a less traditional campaign, sending eight popular disc jockeys to Austria to visit refugee camps with the hope that they would return to the States with anecdotes that might produce "a better understanding of the refugee story" among the listening public.[32]

The Advertising Councils efforts, though, were minuscule compared to the work of Communications Counselors, Incorporated, a division of the advertising giant McCann-Erickson. Voorhees hired CCI because he wanted the firm to "assist in creating an atmosphere of public acceptance" of refugees. CCI assigned a full-time PR man, Mark Foster, to Camp Kilmer to lead this effort. Foster's and CCI's activities aimed to garner as much positive press coverage as possible of both the American response to the refugee crisis and the refugees themselves. CCI and Foster courted all forms of print media, from newspapers to newsmagazines like *Time* and *Newsweek*, to entertainment magazines such as *Life* and *Reader's Digest*. CCI identified artistically talented Hungarian refugees and placed them in productions and concerts, and on TV. It lobbied TV stations to carry stories on Camp Kilmer and the refugees, even filming interviews with "interesting refugees" and offering the footage to the stations. Finally, CCI pushed magazines and newspapers to carry features on Hungarian refugees, and the latter to write editorials sympathetic to the newcomers.[33]

CCI's—and the Advertising Council's—campaign culminated in late January and early February of 1957 when it launched a media blitz "to tell the story of the Hungarian refugees in terms of 'human interest.' " The publicity effort was part of "refugee week" or "Welcome Refugee Neighbor" week, which Foster hoped would convince American families "to adopt a refugee family and help them become good Americans." Foster and his staff distributed press kits to over five hundred newspapers and wire services, pushed for coverage of refugee resettlement on television shows like *The Ed Sullivan Show, Tonight, What's My Line*, and *Meet the Press*, and looked to get the stories of Hungarian refugees into *Look, Reader's Digest*, the *Saturday Evening Post, Time, Life*, and *Sports Illustrated*. CCI's goals, before and during the media blitz, were summarized by a CCI staffer working with *Life* magazine on a story that would "help the American people realize that Hungary has a rich and proud cultural past, and that the refugees are not dopes coming from a cultural vacuum, just because they don't know much English. . . . Help the American people to realize that the refugees can contribute something *of their own* to enrich our culture, and help the Hungarians realize that Americans realize it" (emphasis in original). While such comments suggest that the PR campaign exhibited a cultural pluralist ethos, in fact the vast majority of stories pushed by CCI stressed assimilation, the casting away of Hungarian traditions, and the quick adoption of the American way of life. "New Americans"—rather than Hungarian Americans—came from Hungary.[34]

In an article revealingly titled "They Pour In . . . And Family Shows Refugees Can Fit In," *Life* chronicled the resettlement of the Csillag family, some of the first refugees to arrive in the United States. The Csillags settled down in a two-story duplex in Indianapolis, visited the grocery and department stores, watched TV in their living room, sent their children to school, and played in their front yard. Pal Csillig happily took a night-shift job at a bakery in town. Mrs. Csillig, readers learned, enrolled the children in school, went shopping for groceries, and washed the family's clothes in a new washer. A *Life* photographer captured these activities. While one caption revealed the Csillags' amazement at living in the "land of plenty"—the family supposedly exclaimed "Just think, only use it once" upon learning how to use Kleenex—the thrust of the story portrayed them as easy and happy converts to American life.[35]

Foster and the Eisenhower White House particularly liked the approach taken in a January 22, 1957, article in *Look* magazine, so much so that Foster ordered 100,000 copies of it for distribution during "refugee week." The article's title, "From Hungary—New Americans,"

Figure 3.2 The Csillag family—Hungarian refugees who settled in Indianapolis—were the subject of a *Life* magazine story. The article emphasized the Csillag's easy conversion to life in their new country.

explained Foster's and the White House's enthusiasm. A series of photo essays and captions, as well as a short essay, told the stories of a number of different Hungarians. *Look* declared of the family of Arpad C.—last names were withheld for security reasons—"Seven days after arriving in the United States, this weary refugee family was transformed into four ecstatic Minnesotans." What made "New Americans"? Arpad C. had a job assembling lawnmowers. The family lived in a nice home, and were pictured going off to church, full of smiles, to "pray for Hungarians still to come." *Look* wrote under a photo of "Clowning Suzie," peering through the holes in some Swiss cheese, "Family loves French fries, TV, despite language difficulty." Other refugees delighted in wearing new hats and shirts and were enchanted by "cha-cha-cha music, ice-cube trays, modern plumbing."[36]

The *Look* and *Life* articles explicitly portrayed each of these refugee families as American as their new next-door neighbors. While this conception of American identity was much more nuanced than those offered during early 1950s debates about refugee and immigration legislation, it was just as surely colored by the Cold War. In describing Arpad C.'s family and the Csillags, there was surprisingly little overt trumpeting of anticommunism, although *Life* did publish a picture of one of the Csillags' children standing at attention in school for the Pledge of Allegiance. Instead, both *Life* and *Look* emphasized that each family exhibited typical 1950s gender roles: the father had a job, the mother stayed home, and the kids went to school. Just as important, these "new Americans" embraced their adopted country's materiel abundance, like washing machines and Kleenex. Likewise, Hungarian refugee families eagerly picked up on American popular culture by watching television and dancing the cha-cha-cha. In short, these portrayals stressed that Hungarian families embraced the same qualities and cultural and social forms—consumers (of products), fans of American popular culture, and observant of the proper roles of husband, wife, and children where the man earned the money and the woman cared for children and home—as 1950s middle-class Americans.[37]

This emphasis on marriage, gender roles, materiel and popular culture, and consumption was not without an important political context, one that ultimately reinforced the anticommunism of Hungarian refugees. As the historian Elaine Tyler May has explained, 1950s Americans believed that their level of material abundance, produced by a social and economic system that protected the femininity of women and wives, demonstrated the superiority of the United States over the Soviet Union. The Soviets, most Americans believed, had none of these material comforts, nor did they value gender roles that Americans thought beneficial. In May's telling, then, the 1959 "kitchen debate" between Vice President Nixon and Soviet leader Khrushchev was, in effect, a proxy war in which butter (homes, families, and appliances) replaced guns as both superpowers attempted to demonstrate the superiority of their societies. The campaign to "sell" Hungarian refugees to the public picked up on this dynamic, albeit a few years before Nixon's visit to Moscow. By showing that Hungarians embraced social, economic, and cultural norms common to 1950s America—norms that were antithetical to life under communism—these refugees were shown to be anticommunist and thus American, but without crude political slogans. It is little wonder that Foster, CCI, and the PCFHRR were pleased with the *Life* and *Look* articles.[38]

The PR campaign's portrayal of Hungarian refugees, as a result, stressed a key element of political pluralism in 1950s America: anticommunism. At the same time, CCI's work dramatically highlighted the limits of cultural pluralism. A cultural-pluralist approach would have welcomed the Hungarians—and celebrated some elements of their culture and history—as another ethnonational component in the American populace.

Instead, CCI stressed how easily and eagerly the refugees shucked off their Hungarian ways and assimilated to the dominant social and cultural mores of life in the United States. This surely was the message encapsulated in "From Hungary, New Americans" and countless other pieces that the CCI encouraged and disseminated. The fact that CCI, a sophisticated public-relations firm, believed this to be the most effective way of ensuring a warm welcome for the Hungarians testifies to the lingering hold of the melting-pot assimilationist ethos in American life.

The media blitz ended in early February 1957, but the efforts of Communications Counselors and the Advertising Council continued through the end of March, when the Eisenhower administration shut down the publicity drive. The effectiveness of the effort is hard to judge. In the very short term, the campaign seemed to have had a positive effect. Media coverage of Hungarian refugees in the first months of 1957 was very upbeat; there were very few stories about newcomers failing to adapt to life in their communities. More important, as both the administration and Tracy Voorhees noted publicly, the United States managed to resettle over 35,000 refugees in a matter of months without provoking a massive outcry. Yet, in the first months of 1957 the traditional balance between restrictionists and liberalizers among the public reasserted itself in refugee affairs. A poll from the spring of 1957 asked Americans, "What do you think the effect of the refugees will be on this country?" Only 26 percent answered that the refugees would help the country, while 21 percent answered that the refugees would have no effect at all, and 32 percent believed they would be a "bad influence." Americans, then, had in no way embraced the Hungarians, but neither had they completely rejected them. The muddle in public opinion about immigration and refugee affairs reappeared only six months after the stirring events of the Hungarian Revolution and as the public-relations campaign ended. Thus, perhaps the prudent conclusion is that the Advertising Council and CCI helped in the short term to create a more favorable environment for refugees—aided, surely, by sympathy-inducing circumstances of the refugee flow—but did little to alter long-standing opinions concerning the entry of newcomers.[39]

The public-relations campaign, though, did affect the direction of refugee affairs. The effort helped cement in the minds of politicians, policymakers, and the public the basic idea that refugees, above all, had to measure up to anticommunist benchmarks. Thus, the PR campaign reinforced the narrow definition and concept of "refugee" established in the early 1950s, thereby making future policy innovation or reform that much more challenging. This form of "policy feedback" via the public-relations effort buttressed the anticommunist foundations of America's commitment to refugees that policies like the RRP and the Hungarian admissions had helped establish.

Americans, but Citizens? The Battle over Status Normalization

Restrictionism's comeback in 1957 was also powered by Eisenhower's controversial proposals for immigration reform. The Administration wanted Congress to increase annual admissions by almost seventy thousand persons and it wanted more immigration visas made available to the southern and eastern European countries whose quotas were filled. This combination of reforms would essentially build more flexibility into the national origins immigration system, but avoid a full-fledged drive to rewrite the law. Traditional restrictionist politicians and groups quickly defended the existing immigration laws, a bitter backlash that did not portend well for the reform agenda. Appended to this immigration proposal were several refugee policy requests. The Eisenhower administration asked Congress to authorize parole of up to 62,000 refugees annually. While the White House used foreign policy concerns to justify this measure, the decision to seek congressional sanction for parole also grew from the Administration's unease about paroling hundreds or thousands of refugees, rather than individuals, as the codicil originally intended. Finally, Eisenhower wanted Congress to resolve the sticky legal question of the Hungarian refugees' immigration status. The Hungarian parolees, admitted without visas, had no official status and could not become permanent residents or citizens, as could refugees (and immigrants) with visas. The Eisenhower administration foresaw this problem when it instituted the parole program and promised to try to "regularize" or "normalize" the Hungarians.[40]

Despite the efforts of immigration liberalizers in Congress, and the Administration's threat that it would admit fewer refugees until Congress acted, Eisenhower's ambitious refugee and immigration legislation stalled in 1957. Senator John Kennedy's (D-MA) compromise measure slightly revised some of the MWA's provisions regarding who could enter the United States, and it authorized the issuance of unused RRA visas to "refugees-escapees" from the Soviet bloc—giving the legislation its name, The Refugee-Escapee Act—but it neither made the substantive alterations to immigration law that Eisenhower wanted nor addressed the immigration status of Hungarian parolees. Eisenhower signed the bill on September 11, 1957, although he called it "a disappointment" and noted that it was "particularly regrettable" that Congress failed to address the Hungarian status issue. The defeat was hardly surprising. Restrictionist sentiment was still powerful, especially in the South, and committee heads like Representative Walter (House Subcommittee on Immigration) and Senator Eastland (Senate Judiciary Committee) easily bottled up the legislation they opposed, even if their fellow committee members from an increasingly liberalizer Democratic party desired reform and the end of national origins policy. Restrictionists harped on the supposed unemployment problems caused by newcomers, an especially effective parry with the country in the midst of an economic slump. As for the proposed annual parole of 62,000 refugees, Capitol Hill balked at giving the executive branch free hand in refugee admissions; House and Senate leaders were not about to officially sanction a parole process that disempowered them.[41]

In the case of status normalization for Hungarian parolees, Representative Walter and Senator Johnston seemed intent on delaying and defeating the measure. Even before Eisenhower made public his immigration agenda, Walter announced that no movement would occur on status normalization until he had carefully studied the entire Hungarian program. The congressman held true to his word. He designed his own immigration bill (which was not that different from the Kennedy bill that ultimately passed) in response to the Eisenhower proposal and refused to include any provision for Hungarian status normalization. Walter and his allies objected to status normalization because they feared that inadequate and improper security screening had allowed communists to enter the United States. Walter cited the case of Samuel Gombos, a thirty-seven-year-old parolee who had been deported because he had served in the Hungarian secret police. Other refugees turned in Gombos to American officials, who determined that his admission violated the MWA's ban on the entry of communists. The INS countered that Gombos was an anomaly because only nine Hungarians had been deported for communist affiliation.[42]

Walter, of course, used Gombos as an excuse to sink status normalization. The congressman's motivations, though, were multilayered. He certainly was not bucking public opinion, which by the end of the summer of 1957 was evenly split on whether to regularize the immigration status of Hungarians; a poll showed that 42 percent favored passage of status normalization while 43 percent opposed it. In addition to the political gains to be won, Walter also likely relished reasserting his voice in refugee affairs, which had been dominated by the executive branch in the aftermath of the Hungarian Revolution. Walter's chief staffer even admitted privately that while Walter intended to oppose permanent residence for Hungarians in 1957, the congressman would introduce his own status normalization plan the following year. Walter seemed to want the Eisenhower administration to twist in the wind, not to permanently block Hungarians from legal residence. Likewise, Walter truly believed that the U.S. government had not properly screened the Hungarians and he wanted some sort of review procedure built into the status normalization process.[43]

Just the same, most fascinating about Walter's maneuvering in 1957 was his reliance on a thoroughly politicized definition of "American" that parolees would have to meet, as exemplified by Gombos and his deportation on grounds of past communist activity and affiliations. Walter's chief accomplice, Senator Johnston, a die-hard supporter of national origins policy in 1952, highlighted political histories and not ethnicity in objecting to the Hungarians' entry. Certainly, Johnston and other restrictionists used anticommunism to mask their support for national origins, but few argued so brazenly in 1957 that Hungarian parolees were not fit to be permanent residents (or Americans) because of their ethnicity. The admissibility of Hungarian refugees for permanent residence in the United States rested upon political, and not ethnonational, qualifications. These discussions, then, reinforced the association of both "refugee" and "American" with political ideology and allegiance—and specifically with the rejection of communism.

In 1958, though, Congress passed a law granting the parolees permanent residence provided they met certain conditions. It was the sole victory for Eisenhower on his immigration and refugee affairs agenda, as Congress again rejected his calls for reform of the national origins system. The status normalization measure was fairly straightforward. Michael Feighan—Democratic representative from Ohio, member of the House Immigration subcommittee, and restrictionist—offered a proposal in which a Hungarian parolee, after living two years in the United States, would present him- or herself to the INS for an investigation, as if he or she was applying for a visa. Assuming the parolee earned clearance, then he or she would be granted permanent residence, retroactive to his or her parole date. This meant that the two years spent in the United States as a parolee counted toward the normal five-year wait to apply for citizenship. If the Hungarian did not receive INS clearance, he or she would be subjected to regular deportation proceedings. The Hungarian parolees would be admitted outside existing quotas, but under the MWA's exclusionary political (and medical) provisions.[44]

The Administration quickly got behind the Feighan bill, abandoning its own initiative. Feighan's bill sailed through the House (passing on a voice vote) and the Senate before becoming law in late July 1958. Why did the measure pass so easily? Most likely because of Walter's support for a bill that addressed the concerns he had outlined since early 1957. In this sense, Walter won the status normalization fight: the INS would conduct investigations of each Hungarian parolee to make sure that they qualified under the McCarran-Walter Act. Walter in 1958, moreover, declared himself satisfied with the screening of parolees upon their entry into the United States after reading Attorney General William P. Rogers's final report on that process, in which Rogers noted that only a few Hungarians had been deported. Of course, the INS had contended all along that only a few of the parolees were subversives or communists.[45]

• • •

The U.S. government had admitted 38,000 Hungarian refugees by the end of December, 1957. Just over 6,000 received RRA visas, while the attorney general paroled in the remaining 32,000. The most important policymaking implication of the Hungarian refugee program was that it legitimated the parole mechanism, allowing the president to admit refugees without congressional approval. The Hungarian admissions, like the second half of the RRP, demonstrated how speed could replace security as the guiding principle of an American refugee program. Important continuities, however, remained. "Refugee" was still synonymous with anti-communism, both in the definition of the term and in its practical application. Not only did the policy development and implementation aspects of Hungarian admissions reinforce this association, so did the extensive public-relations efforts that "sold" refugees as "good Americans." Likewise, restrictionist power, after retreating for a few months in the aftermath of the revolution, reasserted itself rather quickly. In the coming years, though, restrictionists would be tested as never before in immigration affairs because of immense changes in domestic politics and culture, and in foreign affairs. How the revolutions of the 1960s affected the American commitment to refugees is the question to which we now turn.

CHAPTER 4

"Half a Loaf": The Failure of Refugee Policy and Law Reform, 1957–1965

IN THE 1960s, the politics of newcomers focused both on the effort to overturn the national origins quota immigration system and on the admission of hundreds of thousands of refugees from Cuba. While these two episodes occurred contemporaneously, they did not influence each other as much as one might expect. The debates over immigration heated up in 1964 and 1965 during a lull in the Cuban migration, which helped keep the latter from informing the former. Just as important, the Cubans, like the Hungarians, for the most part did not enter under existing immigration law or a specific refugee law, but instead were paroled into the United States. This chapter, then, examines the overall state of the American commitment to refugees—the policies, laws, and programs in place to provide for regularized entry of refugees—in the era of immigration reform, from the late 1950s through the mid-1960s. The following chapter explores in depth the Cuban refugee crisis over roughly those same years.

Liberalizers, as we shall see, finally succeeded in destroying the national origins quota immigration system in 1965. It was a signal moment that over time brought about a demographic revolution in the United States. As the push for immigration reform mounted in the late 1950s and early 1960s, the United States' commitment to refugees built on its 1950s foundations. Refugees gained entry to the United States via special exceptions to immigration law (the 1957 Refugee-Escapee Act), special refugee laws (the 1960 Fair Share refugee law), and special procedures (the parole policy initiated by President Eisenhower that continued under Presidents Kennedy and Johnson). At the same time, a cadre of refugee experts, a subset of the larger liberalizer community, launched several attempts to expand the scope of that commitment. They sought to enlarge the definition of "refugee" so that it recognized that refugees came from all over the globe and were not just victims of political persecution at the hands of communists. Refugee advocates, quite simply, wanted to move away from the "refugee equals European anticommunist" equation. They failed. Instead, the new immigration law, passed in 1965, reified the existing definition of "refugee" and set aside 6 percent (or just over 10,000 visas) of the nation's yearly immigration quota for refugees. It was a numeric victory that confirmed rather than reversed the refugee politics of the 1950s.

Why did immigration laws and policies liberalize while refugee laws and policies remained largely unchanged? Two factors—Cold War foreign policy concerns and a domestic political and cultural environment energized by the rights-based liberalism of the 1960s, specifically the civil rights movement—pushed along immigration reform. For refugee experts urging reform, the changes in domestic politics and culture augured well for a turn away from Eurocentric refugee policies and a reorientation of the definition of "refugee" so that it recognized universal political rights. But the Cold War consensus also held in the mid-1960s, ultimately stalling efforts to move the American commitment to refugees away from its anticommunist roots. U.S. refugee policies had been built in the postwar years on both domestic and foreign policy rationales. In 1965, that foreign policy reasoning still stood strong.

Restrictionists and Liberalizers in the 1960s

On Capitol Hill in the early 1960s, Representative Walter remained the chief restrictionist. But if Walter was on the offensive in the early 1950s, he increasingly found himself in a reactive stance toward the end of the decade, defending his immigration system from attacks. Walter willingly liberalized the MWA around the edges (largely by reforming technical aspects of the law) in order to preempt a total assault. Part of this strategy also was to support the admission of a limited number of refugees in the hope that this concession would satisfy immigration liberalizers and refugee advocates.[1] Liberalizers, of course, never wavered in their desire to end national origins, and Walter's passing in May 1963 meant that they no longer had to contend with their crafty and determined opponent.

Congressman Michael Feighan (D-OH) assumed Walter's spot as head of the Immigration Subcommittee. A Harvard Law School graduate who came to Congress in 1943, Feighan represented a district outside of Cleveland that was home to a large eastern European immigrant community. He had to tread carefully on immigration issues, therefore, a lesson he seemed to forget in 1964 when his obstructionist record on immigration reform almost lost him his congressional seat in the Democratic primary. Like Walter, Feighan was stridently anticommunist, openly concerned about communist subversion, and generally supportive of restrictions on immigration. Feighan also despised key liberalizers like President Kennedy; Abba Schwartz, Kennedy's choice as director of the State Department's Bureau of Security and Consular Affairs; and Representative Manny Celler, putting another roadblock in the path toward reform. But Feighan was less wedded to the national origins quota system than Walter and more receptive to reform. Feighan's ascension to the head of the Immigration Subcommittee, then, opened the door to immigration reform just a crack.[2]

In the Senate, restrictionism had a distinctly southern twang. Senator James Eastland, a Democrat from Mississippi, chaired the Immigration and Naturalization subcommittee and the full Judiciary Committee, and any reform effort needed to pass under his gavel. Questions of race were never far from the minds of southern restrictionists during discussions of immigration and refugee policy reform in the 1960s. Like their predecessors, southern restrictionists saw the dismantling of the segregationist and national origins regimes as attacks on political and social orders that privileged whiteness and notions of Anglo-Saxon superiority. For the most part, though, southern Democrats avoided explicitly discriminatory statements as they defended the existing immigration law. Few in the restrictionist camp were more die-hard supporters of national origins theory than Senator Sam Ervin of North Carolina. While Ervin was sure by 1965 that immigration reform would occur, he believed the national origins immigration system "desirable" because it admitted the descendants of those "who made the greatest contributions to the culture and development of America."[3]

Despite such bland pronouncements, Ervin occasionally let slip his discomfort with the idea of persons of color entering the United States as easily as newcomers from Europe. In the spring of 1965, Ervin and the immigration subcommittee hosted a variety of ethnic interest groups. The senator celebrated Italians and Greeks as the types of immigrants who made good Americans, demonstrating just how far the restrictionist position had developed since the 1920s. Ervin noted that "the culture and tradition of the Greek people are similar to those of the people who founded the United States. . . . Democracy first made its appearance in Greece." The senator then compared Greek immigrants to potential immigrants from the Congo, relating a story he claimed his secretary had read a few years ago. "A reporter in the American press," Ervin began, "who had gone over and appraised the readiness of the Congolese people for self government, wrote back that the people said 'We are going to get freedom and democracy. . . . We do not know whether it comes in packages or not, and whether we ought to go to the post office of the express company to get our package of freedom and democracy.' " Ervin concluded the story with a question: "Now, you certainly agree with me that people that have that idea of freedom and democracy are not quite as ready to be assimilated into American life as people who come from a civilized nation like Greece or France or England or any other older nations"?[4]

But the votes on immigration and refugee matters in Congress during the early 1960s revealed the degree to which southern politicians stood nearly alone in their attempt to forestall *any* changes in immigration law and refugee policy. In the 1965 Senate vote on immigration reform, eighteen nays were recorded; sixteen came from southern Democrats. The nativist side of Republicanism that flourished in the Midwest and Northeast during the first half of the twentieth century had dissipated, replaced by moderate and liberal Republicans like Eisenhower and New York's senators Jacob Javits and Kenneth Keating, who supported immigration reform and refugee admissions. Instead, southern restrictionists were joined by the emerging conservative New Right of the Republican Party. While 1964 Republican presidential candidate Barry Goldwater kept relatively quiet on the prospect of immigration reform, his vice-presidential candidate, Representative William Miller (NY), blasted the drive to overturn national origins.[5]

Indeed ultraconservative political organizations such as the Liberty Lobby, the National Council for Individual Freedom, and the Catholic Anti-Communist League lined up with traditional restrictionist (and politically conservative) groups like the Daughters of the American Revolution, the American Coalition of Patriotic Societies, the American Legion, and the Veterans of Foreign Wars. Influential conservative journals with politics similar to Goldwater's opposed immigration reform as well. In the September 1965 *National Review*, author Ernest Van Den Haag questioned liberalizers' attacks on national origins principles, offering that "perhaps" ethnicity was not linked to "ability, behavior, or achievement." Van Den Haag—certain that the national origins quota immigration system would not survive long—suggested a reform proposal, but one that would have made liberalizers apoplectic: the entry of 40,000 immigrants annually. (Most reform bills admitted at least 200,000 immigrants per year.) The *National Review* departed from this ultra-hard-line stance only when it came to refugees. In the early 1960s, it ran several stories that praised refugees from communism and urged their admission. The *Review*'s refugee position was more liberal than Walter's and Feighan's, but its prescriptions for immigration policy were much more restrictionist than anything those two representatives ever offered. But even on refugees, it should be noted, the conservative Right was not united; the *American Mercury*, another conservative journal, adopted a vigorous anti-refugee stance.[6]

Liberalizers in the early 1960s were nearly as tumultuous a lot as their opponents. In the House, Manny Celler remained the dean of liberalizers, joined on the front lines by congressmen from urban, immigrant-heavy districts. In the Senate, liberals like Hubert Humphrey (D-MN), Ted Kennedy (D-MA), Phil Hart (D-MI), and John Pastore (D-RI), were joined by moderate and liberal Republicans, including Senators Jacob Javits (NY), Leverett Saltonstall (MA), and Clifford Case (NJ). This ideological and partisan diversity stretched to the White House, where Presidents Eisenhower, Kennedy, and Johnson all supported liberalization. The liberalizer camp also included stalwart interest groups from the 1950s, including labor unions, ethnic associations and organizations, religious groups, and refugee- and immigrant-aid agencies. In the 1960s, though, rights groups like the ACLU offered their support as well.[7]

There was something of a generational and ideological change under way among Democrats in the liberalizer block, however. New Dealers like Herbert Lehman (who retired in 1957) and Manny Celler, who were at the forefront of the bloc through the 1950s, gradually ceded their places to senators like Ted Kennedy, Robert Kennedy, and Hubert Humphrey. These Democrats, even more than their predecessors, increasingly tied their liberalism to racial issues and civil rights. Liberalizer interest groups mirrored this transition. Labor and religious organizations were at the forefront of progressive politics in the 1960s, pushing for civil rights laws, an end to segregation, the extension of government benefits like health care to America's needy, and a substantive war on poverty. Even if liberalizers shared this political-ideological foundation, little unanimity existed about exactly what they wanted to replace the national origins immigration system with. Liberalizers could not agree on whether they should reform or destroy the existing system, what would take its place if they chose to destroy it, and whether the national origins system should be replaced in phases or in one fell swoop. The morass of proposals was often staggering and confusing, more testimony to the difficulty liberalizers faced in winning reform.[8]

THE ROAD TO IMMIGRATION REFORM, 1959–1965

Liberalizers in the late 1950s and early 1960s continued their push to topple the national origins quota immigration system, but without much success. Reform proposals originated from the Eisenhower, Kennedy, and Johnson White Houses, as well as from Congress. As his second term wore on, Eisenhower's immigration proposals increasingly appeared half-hearted and perfunctory—and Congress received them as such. Congressional liberalizers likewise failed in their attempts to push reform forward. Given Senator John F. Kennedy's immigration record, his election to the White House in November 1960 quite reasonably offered liberalizers hope. Immigration reform, however, quickly proved the least of Kennedy's considerable worries. During its first two years, the Kennedy administration remained almost deathly quiet on the issue, believing that restrictionists like Eastland and Walter would kill the proposals in committee and that other domestic issues, especially relating to the economy, were higher priorities. Kennedy, moreover, confronted a barrage of Cold War foreign policy issues that pushed immigration reform to the back burner until 1963. In July of that year, the Administration finally sent its immigration proposal to Congress. Largely written by the Justice Department, the plan called for the phase-out of the national origins system over five years, a concession to the State Department, which worried that allies like England and Germany would object to the sudden loss of their privileged quotas. Two other facets of the proposal were interesting. First, it granted visas to Western Hemisphere immigrants on a nonquota basis, as the national origins system had. Second, it permitted the president to admit a certain number of refugees annually. The immigration proposition floundered, however, even though Walter's death in late May removed a key opponent of reform.[9]

Kennedy never got a chance to try to push his immigration bill through Congress in 1964. Instead, that task fell to Lyndon Johnson, whose record on immigration and refugee matters was mixed. In 1952 LBJ supported the McCarran-Walter Act and voted to overturn Truman's veto of that legislation. But Johnson, in the 1930s had worked behind the scenes to help European Jews fleeing Nazism, and, subsequently, he had supported the 1953 Refugee Relief Act and the 1957 Refugee-Escapee Act. By 1964 LBJ championed immigration reform for political reasons, particularly because he believed that victory in the 1964 presidential election required that he win the votes of white ethnic Democrats. While Johnson quickly and with much public fanfare adopted Kennedy's immigration initiatives—announcing in his Texas drawl that the United States "should not be asking 'In what country were you born' "—the result was the same at the end of 1964: another year without immigration reform.[10]

The year 1965 proved different, however. Johnson's landslide victory over Goldwater in the 1964 presidential campaign gave LBJ a mandate that he was determined not to waste. Immigration reform was one of the issues he wanted to pass. The new Congress, moreover, was the most liberal since the height of the New Deal, with sixty-five new members, many from the left of the Democratic party. LBJ, who surely knew such moments of political opportunity were fleeting, had unprecedented congressional backing for his ambitious liberal agenda. But the major changes in the calculus of immigration politics came from the restrictionist side in 1965. Restrictionists Feighan and Eastland still controlled the two key congressional committees, but they and their allies understood that liberalizers had the votes to pass a reform package. As a result, restrictionists altered their position in the hope of winning concessions rather than submitting completely. Feighan announced in a speech to the ultrarestrictionist American Coalition of Patriotic Societies that he would acquiesce to the end of the national origins immigration system, but that he wanted a worldwide limit on immigration (rather than just a limit on immigrants

from the Eastern Hemisphere, as under the current system) and a preference system that favored, first, immigrants with relatives who were U.S.
citizens; second, immigrants with needed skills; and third, refugees.[11]

Following Feighan's admission that a deal was possible, the White
House, congressional liberalizers, and restrictionists spent the next
months haggling over its shape. To assure passage and tamp down restrictionist obstructionism that might delay or derail the reform effort, the
White House eventually bowed to many restrictionist demands, including
an admissions system based on family reunification and a cap on Western
Hemisphere immigrants. (The State Department objected to the latter,
fearing that a ceiling would anger South and Central American allies.)
Likewise, liberalizers, including Manny Celler, constantly asserted that
the new immigration law would neither result in a huge jump in annual
admissions nor even a significant change in the countries from which newcomers came to the United States. These reassurances were particularly
salient because they addressed public concerns about immigration in
1965. Polls showed that about two-thirds of the public wanted to maintain—or even reduce—annual immigrant admissions. At the same time,
when asked to identify the "most and least desired immigrants," Americans approved of the entry of Canadians, the English, Scots, and Scandi-
navians, while demonstrating much less enthusiasm for the admission of
immigrants from eastern Europe, the Middle East, Asia, and Russia. (Immigrants from Africa were not even listed in this survey.)[12]

The liberalizer victory of 1965 was built not just on presidential leadership, a powerful political coalition, and astute bargaining. It also was
founded in two important arguments that were particularly relevant in
American politics and culture. As they had in the early 1950s during the
battles over the McCarran-Walter Act, liberalizers harnessed the United
States' anticommunist, Cold War foreign policy to their cause. In explaining the need for reform, Johnson repeated liberalizer claims that
abolishing national origins would strengthen America's Cold War position. Administration officials echoed these assertions throughout 1964
and 1965, arguing that a new immigration statute would enhance America's image as leader of the free world and would placate allies—and potential allies—whose citizens were discriminated against under existing
U.S. immigration laws. As the immigration debate entered its end game
in Congress, liberalizers pounded home these points. The McCarran-Walter Act was "a target for communist propaganda," and the national origins policy made "our effort to win over uncommitted nations more difficult," railed Senator Jacob Javits. "In the volatile area of world relations,
it is difficult enough to maintain a peaceful balance, without the unneces-
sary millstone of an outmoded and outdate immigration policy hanging
around our necks," assured a congressman from New Hampshire. De-

stroying the national origins quota system "would enhance America's image as a leader of the free world . . . and thus take a significant stride forward in our international relations," declared another congressman.[13]

Liberalizers made clear that the newcomers admitted under the reform law would still have to clear provisions meant to exclude communists. Celler insisted, "There can be no fear of Communists or subversives entering this country. The same safeguards that are in the law with reference to internal security are maintained . . . not changed one iota." Andrew Biermiller, a former member of Congress and the AFL-CIO's chief lobbyist, commented, "Certainly we are not admitting Communists under the bill. This takes care of a great many undesirable people," he continued, "so when I talk about not being worried about the country of origin, I am certainly not trying to do away with the restriction on the admission of Communists or other subversive elements." On this point, Celler and Biermiller worked from the assumption that good Americans were not communists, playing to the currents in American identity that still resonated with anticommunism. But their comments also suggest that anticommunism's centrality to American identity had by the mid-1960s become in some respects pro forma. Liberalizers rarely trumpeted the anticommunism of immigrants, as Truman had in his stirring veto of the McCarran-Walter Act, nor did they make as clear and strident connections between "good Americans" and anticommunism as their liberalizer predecessors had nearly fifteen years earlier. Liberalizers, then, deemphasized but did not abandon the anticommunist argument as they pressed the case for the end of the national origins immigration system and the destruction of ethnonational discrimination.[14]

More so than Cold War foreign policy concerns, the major impetus for immigration reform in 1965, as numerous scholars have noted, came from the great liberal reform movements of the era: the civil rights movement, the quest for a "Great Society," and the beginnings of the "rights revolution."[15] These political movements—and the grassroots activism they embodied or inspired—recast the relationship between the individual and state and society. The civil rights movement sought an end to Jim Crow, full citizenship rights for African Americans, a color-blind Constitution, and a society freed from racial discrimination. Civil rights protests throughout the 1950s and 1960s—black college students leading "sit-ins" at segregated lunch counters all over the South, for example—embodied and engendered a sense of "rights-consciousness" among many Americans, who now demanded that their political and individual rights receive acknowledgement, protection, and respect. In turn, disaffected white college-age students, emboldened and inspired by the civil rights movement, protested what they saw as a society organized and run by a "power elite" determined to protect the status quo in politics, the economy, and foreign affairs. The "New Left," as these student activists came to be known, looked to break the country out of what it saw as a stultifying consensus by glorifying the power of the individual and pointing to the individual's ability to change society.

Civil rights organizations and protests and the New Left were grassroots movements, but the effort to define, protect, and promote individual rights during the 1960s also reached some of the most significant and traditional organs of political power. The Supreme Court outlined an expansive notion of individual rights, most notably in decisions such as *Gideon v. Wainwright* (1963), which helped protect the rights of alleged criminals, and *Griswold v. Connecticut* (1965), which established a constitutional right to privacy. Congress, at LBJ's urging, passed landmark civil rights legislation in 1964 and 1965. Even the rhetoric of President Johnson's "Great Society" described a nation in which individuals enjoyed the material, cultural, and spiritual fruits of America's largesse. In practical policy terms, the "Great Society" sponsored medical insurance that protected the infirm, and antipoverty programs that empowered individuals to make better lives. Undergirding such programs were sociological theories—like "maximum feasible participation," which aimed to enlist community members in the effort to rebuild and re-empower their neighborhoods—consonant with "rights-consciousness."

The signal accomplishment of the social and political movements of the 1960s was to take the U.S. Constitution's promises of rights—to freedom of religion, to freedom of assembly, to freedom of speech, to due process, to trial by jury, and to "equal protection under the law"—and extend them to all Americans, regardless of race, national origins, or sex. These political and cultural movements and these governmental and legal reforms were so momentous because they also represented a rethinking of American identity. In the 1950s, anticommunism and the precepts of pluralism, both cultural and political, guided how many Americans thought about governance, the composition of American society, and the meaning of "American." These concepts and ideologies gave definition and structure to ideals like freedom, equality of opportunity, liberty, and democracy. The civil rights movement, the New Left, the rights revolution, and the promises and hopes of the "Great Society" all helped break this consensus down in the early 1960s, in large part by highlighting the racialized, gendered, ethnocentric, and antidemocratic limitations of pluralism and anticommunism. In its stead a conception of American identity arose that stressed an expansive notion of individual rights and aimed to eliminate legal, political, social, and cultural discrimination and inequity based on race, ethnicity, religion, and (in the intervening years) gender and sex.[16]

Of course, cultural-pluralist arguments did not disappear entirely from the liberalizer arsenal in 1965. Ethnic organizations—including many of the same groups, like the American Committee on Italian Migration, which held center stage in 1952—asserted that immigrants of different ethnicities and nationalities could all contribute to the growth of America, each bringing to the nation its own contributions. But the basic thrust of the immigration reform effort—to make the law measure immigrants solely on their individual merits (rather than as members of an ethnic, racial, or national group) and to protect an individual's right to come to the United States regardless of national origin—resonated with this larger transformation within American politics and culture, which turned away from pluralism.[17]

To legitimate immigration reform, and to let it bask in the reflected glow of the civil rights movement, liberalizers repeatedly linked their proposal to the 1964 Civil Rights Act, the 1965 Voting Rights Act, and, even more generally, in the words of Senator Hiram Fong, to the "significant progress in desegregating our public schools, housing, business, and public accommodations, and protecting the voting rights of all citizens." Others drew an even more explicit connection to the "rights revolution" and emerging rights-consciousness. Senator Ted Kennedy claimed that "this immigration legislation is fundamentally based on the dignity of the individual. It is in keeping with the growth of a stronger national policy as regards individual rights . . . enacted by the Congress in recent years." Senator Robert Kennedy echoed his brother:

> we are past that period in the history of the United States when we judge a person by his last name or his place of birth or where his grandfather or grandmother came from. . . . I hope we shall start anew to judge people on what their merit is, on what they can contribute to the country. . . . That is the whole philosophy of the immigration bill, and that was the whole philosophy of the civil rights bills of 1963 and 1964 and the voting rights bill of 1965.

Finally, Representative Leonard Farbstein (D-NY) summed up both of the Kennedys' assertions: "the inherent worth and dignity of the individual man . . . is at present the dominant sentiment of this Congress, and indeed, of the Nation." The public, according to some surveys, seemed to agree. Poll numbers demonstrated that Americans wanted an admissions policy based not on the immigrant's country of origin, but on his "occupational skills," and, to a lesser extent, on whether he already had family in the United States. Of course, given the preference displayed by the public in polls for white immigrants of European descent, it seems the majority of Americans who supported the basic principles behind immigration reform were less comfortable with the particular outcomes it might produce.[18]

The reform package, which President Johnson signed into law on October 3, 1965 at the Statue of Liberty, recast immigration law. It phased out, over a three-year period, the national origins preference system. The new system instead capped the number of visas allotted per year to regions outside the Western Hemisphere at 170,000, while offering 120,000 visas per year to immigrants from the Western Hemisphere. All visas would be offered on a "first come, first served basis" within a seven-level preference system that prioritized the entry of immigrants with family members already in the United States and, to a lesser extent, those with needed job skills.[19] While national origins quotas were now history, restrictionists were not despondent. They had managed to a remarkable degree to shape the reform effort, and even could argue that they had wrested control of immigration affairs away from the White House. Feighan, Ervin, and other restrictionists, for instance, got their Western Hemisphere limit and they won their desired preference system, one that emphasized family reunification. Feighan believed that giving priority in admissions to immigrants whose relatives were already in the United States would guarantee that future immigrants would come predominantly from Europe—and not Africa, Asia, or the Middle East—because most Americans in 1965 were from Europe. In this way, he hoped the new law would preserve the ethnic and cultural makeup of the United States that the national origins system had created over the previous forty years. The American Legion agreed, remarking to its members that while the quota system was struck down, "the national origins system wasn't. . . . nobody is quite so apt to be of the same national origins of our present citizens as are members of their immediate families."[20]

Both restrictionists and liberalizers could not have been more wrong. After 1965 fewer Europeans chose to come to the United States (largely because of economic prosperity and political stability in their homelands), so their percentage of the 170,000 Eastern Hemisphere visas declined. Their spaces were taken up by non-Europeans. From 1960 through 1964, the United States admitted just over 1.4 million immigrants. Over 800,000 came from Europe and Canada, while 485,000 came from Latin America, and 114,000 came from Asia. Fifteen years later, during the period from 1975 through 1979—only six years after the new immigration system went into full effect—immigrants from Europe and Canada numbered 429,000, while just over 992,000 came from Latin America, and over 918,000 came from Asia. Indeed, by 1976, over 50 percent of the legal immigrants to the United States came from Mexico, the Philippines, Korea, Cuba, Taiwan, India, and the Dominican Republic. In addition, the new immigration system allowed close relatives to enter outside of the quotas, which resulted in an additional 100,000 immigrants per year to enter in the decade following 1965. The 1965 immigration reform law did as much—and perhaps more—to reshape the United States as the national origins laws had in the 1920s.[21]

THE FAILURE OF REFUGEE POLICY REFORM

Immigration reform in 1965 also altered American refugee laws and policies. The seventh preference in the new immigration-preference system set aside 6 percent (10,200) of the 170,000 Eastern Hemisphere slots for refugees. These refugees would not be granted visas, but would be offered "conditional entry," meaning that after two years in the United States (and provided they passed an INS inspection), they would become permanent residents, the status conferred by a visa. While Feighan hoped that this annual admission would make the parole procedure obsolete—a growing concern as the executive branch paroled hundred of thousands of Cubans in the early 1960s, as we shall see in the next chapter—the law did not restrict or eliminate the president's parole power. Just as important, the 1965 law defined a refugee as an alien "who . . . because of persecution or fear of persecution on account of race, religion, or political opinion [has] fled . . . from any Communist or Communist-dominated country or area, or . . . from any country within the general area of the Middle East . . . and [is] unable or unwilling to return to such country or area on account of race, religion, or political opinion . . . or are [a person] uprooted by catastrophic natural calamities . . . who [is] unable to return to [his or her] usual place of abode." The definition was, as scholars John Scanlan and Gil Loescher have noted, "ideologically based" because it privileged the admission of refugees from communism.[22]

Even with these revisions, the 1965 law consolidated and borrowed from, more than broke with, the previous fifteen years of American refugee policies and laws. The 1965 definition of "refugee" closely resembled the definition offered in the 1957 Refugee-Escapee Act, which set out that a refugee had to flee from "Communist, Communist-dominated, or Communist-occupied" areas or the "general area of the Middle East." (The 1957 definition, in turn, clearly descended from the 1953 RRA.) Likewise, by 1965 the United States had made a permanent annual commitment to the admission of refugees. In 1960, under pressure from the Eisenhower administration to make sure that the United States participated substantively in the United Nations' "World Refugee Year"—an effort designed to gain attention for, and action on, global refugee crises—Representative Walter facilitated passage of new refugee legislation.

Walter's bill strove to help close the European refugee camps that had been open since World War II's end. It established a two-year program to admit European refugees currently under the care of the United Nations High Commissioner for Refugees. The legislation adopted the 1957 definition of "refugee-escapee," but further circumscribed which refugees could enter by admitting only refugees under the UNHCR's mandate, which by and large covered particular European refugees. Walter's law specifically authorized the attorney general to parole annually into the United States a total number of refugees equal to 25 percent of the refugees resettled outside the United States during the previous year. The 25 percent formula necessarily limited admissions, but also allowed the United States a public-relations victory by allowing it to claim that it took its "fair share" of the world's refugees. Walter's law quickly became known as the Fair Share refugee program, and two years after its passage, Congress extended it indefinitely. The Fair Share law and the 1965 immigration reform, though, shared an important premise: the total number of refugees to be admitted was a pittance.[23]

These refugee laws and policies of the late 1950s and early 1960s did not go unchallenged. Instead, a portion of the liberalizer bloc that had considerable expertise on refugee issues began to push harder than their compatriots for a greater and different American commitment to refugees. Just as a restrictionist network functioned in the 1940s and early 1950s, a refugee advocacy network came into being a decade later. This subset of the liberalizer bloc consisted of religious and labor groups, politicians and former policymakers, and refugee aid organizations that had been loosely allied in the previous decades as they argued for greater U.S. involvement in refugee issues. In the late 1950s, they organized to push with new vigor for their goals. This community of refugee experts differed from their immigration-liberalizer compatriots because the latter were content with the singular goal of killing the national origins immigration system and often avoided dealing substantively with refugee issues because they feared that it might distract from the immigration battle. Refugee advocates pushed on both fronts, and especially on the latter.

Chief among these refugee advocates was the U.S. Committee for Refugee (USCR), which was formed in 1958 to keep refugee problems at the forefront of public attention and to coordinate federal government policies with private efforts at refugee relief. USCR members included key members of the liberalizer bloc, like George Meany of the AFL-CIO, former senator Arthur Watkins, General Arthur Gruenther of the American Red Cross, and former Eisenhower staffer Max Rabb; Watkins and Rabb had played key roles in the RRA's passage in 1953. In late 1957 the International Rescue Committee (IRC) formed the Zellerbach Commission, a fact-finding and advocacy organization that spent the next two years urging the United States and its allies to work together to close European refugee camps, an endeavor that came to fruition in 1960 with the passage of the Fair Share refugee law. At the same time, religious organizations like the American Friends Service Committee and Catholic Relief Services, both with long experience in resettling refugees, joined the USCR and IRC in advocating for more expansive U.S. refugee programs and for more government spending. Each of these organizations, committees, and groups had extensive contacts with State Department and INS officials charged with administering U.S. refugee programs, which gave them a voice and an ear in policymaking circles. Moreover, these refugee advocates happily supported the work of international organizations that tackled refugee problems, like the United Nation's High Commissioner for Refugees and the ICEM.[24]

This community of refugee advocates and experts repeatedly decried the piecemeal refugee laws of the late 1950s and early 1960s as paltry or "half a loaf," in the telling words of Senator Watkins in 1957. In that year, refugee advocates settled for "half a loaf," but in the coming years it seemed too meager a meal. Their main goal was revision of the definition of "refugee," which they believed would in turn enlarge America's commitment to refugees. This impulse ultimately failed, but it demonstrated a movement afoot to expand the nation's refugee policies beyond the consensus of the 1950s and early 1960s. That effort—as well as the influence of refugee experts—would gain momentum in the 1970s.[25]

Driving these liberalizers was an understanding that the size and scope of the global refugee problem was changing dramatically. In the late 1940s and early 1950s, most government policymakers and refugee advocates agreed that the majority of the world's refugees were located in Europe, and to a lesser extent, in the Middle East and Asia. By the 1960s it was becoming clear that the European problem had diminished in size— indeed the point of Fair Share legislation was to close European refugee camps—but that several crises burgeoned in Asia, Africa, and Latin America. Moreover, many of these crises, like the one in India and Pakistan and several in Africa, were the products of local political, cultural, and economic circumstances and not the Cold War. In 1962 the United Nations described the European refugee problem as "residual," but it also reported that the number of African refugees had grown by at least 300,000 over the preceding two years. In 1964 the refugee expert for the World Council of Churches, an organization with a long history of resettling refugees, noted "We are now faced with the problem of refugees who are by and large nonwhite and by and large non-Christian . . . and it remains to be seen how we will react." One year later, the U.S. Committee for Refugees' annual report declared of the global refugee problem:

"we are only beginning to see the awful consequences in human terms of intercommunal, intertribal, and international strife."[26]

Confronted with these trends, refugee advocates worked to broaden both the legal definition and common understanding of "refugee" beyond its Eurocentric and anticommunist core. Edward Snyder of the American Friends Service Committee contended in 1957 that a "regular procedure should be established to deal with large groups of refugees in the future," and he expressed support for the Eisenhower proposal (eventually defeated) that called for sixty thousand annual refugee admissions via parole. "It would seem, however," he continued, "that the provisions might be broadened to include refugees from any form of political, radical, or religious persecution." Edward Marks of the U.S. Committee for Refugees made similar points three years later, arguing that the United States should "allow the admission of some refugees from all parts of the world where there are refugees." Marks added, moreover, "that refugee status is not limited to the stateless but should also apply to persons displaced from their land of usual abode because of their nationality." Here he cited Italian nationals forced to leave Tunisia after that nation's independence from French colonial rule in 1956, an example that allowed Marks to observe that not only communism produced refugees. In his words, "Victims of the rising tide of nationalism, as well as those who flee from communism, should qualify as uprooted refugees." Others drew upon the example of Italians fleeing the new nationalist government of Tunisia, but pushed for an even more radical expansion of the definition of refugee. Long-time refugee advocate Monsignor Edward Swanstrom of Catholic Relief Services remarked of Italian refugees from Tunisia: "It is tragic the way they are being treated. They are deprived of all means of earning a livelihood. The only opportunity they have for earning a living is to get out of the country."[27]

Both Swanstrom and Marks bucked the founding principles of American refugee law and policy. Traditionally, the laws—and policymakers—had defined refugees as persons from communist countries fleeing persecution. Built into this definition—as seen during the RRP and the Hungarian Revolution—was the assumption that refugees were both victims and opponents of communism. Swanstrom and Marks, however, wanted victims of nationalism included as refugees, a revolutionary change that would have committed the United States to help refugees who came from places in the world undergoing nationalist revolutions in the 1960s, mainly the "Third World" of Africa, Asia, and the Middle East. Swanstrom, though, seemed to push the definition of "refugee" even farther. He kept it broadly rooted in the political by asserting that refugees were persons denied the protection of their homeland's government, which in fact had been the basis of the idea of "refugee" since the 1920s. But whereas existing refugee law conceived of the denial of government protection in terms of political or ideological persecution—and this too had been the case since the 1920s—Swanstrom based it on the inability to earn a "living" or "livelihood." In this case, Swanstrom merged the definition of refugee with the traditional conception of immigrant that had emphasized the immigrant's search for better economic conditions and opportunities.

Powerful political actors also contributed to the push to broaden the definition of "refugee." The Kennedy administration wanted the Fair Share law amended in 1963 so that refugees could be admitted from outside the limited mandate of the UNHCR. More important, the Kennedy 1963 immigration-reform proposal defined refugees as "persons oppressed or persecuted, or threatened with oppression or persecution, because of their race, color, religion, national origin, adherence to democratic beliefs, or their opposition to totalitarianism or dictatorship, and to persons uprooted by natural calamity or military operations who are unable to return to their usual place of abode." By considering victims of military operations or natural disasters refugees, the definition returned to prominence two key aspects of the interwar-era definition of "refugee" that largely had gone missing in the intervening four decades. While "opposition to totalitarianism and dictatorship" encompassed refugees fleeing communist countries, it also opened the door to refugees from noncommunist countries, as did the clause that identified refugees as persons persecuted because of their "adherence to democratic beliefs." Opposition to or victimization by communism was not even mentioned in the definition, nor was there a geographic qualifier that served as an ideological limit, as the 1950s definitions of "refugee" contained. The Kennedy proposal, as did the proposals of refugee advocates in the liberalizer community, offered a bifurcated definition that included victims of both communism and other forms of persecution.[28]

The attempts by those in the refugee-advocacy community to reset the boundaries of the American commitment to refugees floundered, however. Each of these thrusts to widen the definition of refugee was met with a parry from key restrictionists intent on halting a change to the status quo. Representative Feighan admitted that the refugee problem was a permanent fixture of international politics, a point that many refugee advocates made. But he refused to budge from the idea that communism produced refugees. "I believe we must face up to the prospect that the likelihood exists," Feighan said, "that so long as a conspiracy of communism continues its tyranny against people we will have refugees who will plead with us for political and religious asylum." Feighan, in other words, believed it was the "conspiracy of communism," not the "rising tide of nationalism" or being "deprived of a livelihood" that produced refugees. Other restrictionists joined Feighan in this defense of the status quo. In

1965 arch-restrictionist John Trevor, Jr., of the American Coalition of Patriotic Societies acceded to the entry of refugees from communism, but only refugees from communism. Given his organization's consistent opposition since the 1930s to the admission of any refugees at all, Trevor's position in 1965 was all the more remarkable. The *National Review* echoed Feighan and Trevor, Jr., when it weighed in on the prospect of immigration reform in 1965 and encouraged the admission of only refugees from communism. In sum, it would have been very difficult to push restrictionists beyond this position in the early 1960s.[29]

In addition to restrictionist intransigence, those who wished to enlarge the U.S. commitment to refugees more often than not did their cause more harm than good. Liberalizers were unable to settle on one expanded definition of "refugee" that they all could fight to win. The differences between Marks's, Swanstrom's, and the Kennedy administration's proposals were significant, and divisions like this were lethal against determined opposition. Too often refugee experts never made a clear case for reform, or even described the refugee crises consistently. Deputy Undersecretary of State Roger Jones, appearing before Congress in 1961, depicted the "refugee problem" as "anything but static. . . . It is continually changing in its nature, its dimensions and in its location. . . . it will continue to exist as long as conditions exist which create it—political tyranny, international conflicts, and tension." Jones then identified refugees from Africa, Asia, and South America as worthy of American aid and visas. But Jones quickly returned to the standard rationale that had developed in the 1950s to justify an American commitment to refugees. "Our sustained interest in and concern for the stateless, unsettled victims of Communist oppression will keep alive the hopes of the refugees and escapees who have been successful in evading border guards, the mined stretches of 'no man's land,' and have reached asylum in a friendly country." Jones's phrases and images were littered with the Cold War: border guards, the mined "no-man's-land," and the victims and opponents of communist oppression. Jones's most vivid description of refugees cut against the policy outcome he hoped to achieve.[30]

Similar confusion marked a special twenty-one-page report on the world refugee problem published in the December 1960 issue of the *Rotarian*. A variety of leading refugee experts offered their assessments of the world's refugee crises and outlined potential solutions. As a whole, the report suggested the global dimensions of the refugee problem, pointing out that the largest refugee problem manifested itself on the border between India and Pakistan, where 5 million homeless and helpless suffered. But the experts' commentary revealed little consensus on solutions and, even worse, belied the report's introductory claim that "there are common elements in the problem wherever it exists." Irwin Canham, editor of the *Christian Science Monitor*, declared "the chief cause of the refugee problem is the existence of totalitarian tyranny in some countries which force people to flee." George Warren, a long-time State Department expert on refugees, on the other hand, asserted that "Refugee problems will continue to arise as long as basic human and civil rights are denied to particular races or religious and political groups." Oscar Handlin, a Harvard University professor, Pulitzer Prize winner, and expert on the history of American immigration, only identified European refugees and argued that the "refugee is a pawn in our world-wide struggle with Communism." On the page opposite Handlin, Francis Sayre, chairman of the U.S. Committee for Refugees, did not describe any refugees from communism—although he invoked the Cold War by urging more aid for refugees from the "nations of the free world"—and described the "really desperate refugee situations" in the Middle East, North Africa, Pakistan, and Asia.[31] Taken together, these assessments left unclear whether aid should go to refugees from "totalitarian tyranny" or those lacking "basic human and civil rights" because of their race, religion, or political beliefs. Likewise, readers were left to wonder whether the United States should direct its efforts toward Europe or the Middle East, Africa, and Asia. Refugee advocates had too many answers and too many variables.

The lack of a clear or defined reason to overturn the status quo was the most important reason why refugee advocates failed in their attempt to widen the American commitment to refugees. Since World War II, refugee policies and laws had been justified by a mix of domestic political and cultural concerns and by foreign policy imperatives defined by the Cold War. In the 1960s, refugee advocates made progress, albeit slight, on only one of these fronts. The refugee reform agenda was consonant with the goals of the domestic political and social revolutions brewing in the 1960s. The aim of aiding refugees from all over the globe—not just Europe—paralleled the drive to end ethnonational discrimination in the admission of newcomers. To paraphrase LBJ, refugee advocates believed that the United States ought not to be asking "in what country do you live?" Moreover, this domestic political, cultural, and social environment legitimated a more capacious definition of refugee that looked, above all, to protect the rights of individuals threatened by persecution. On these scores, the refugee reform agenda encountered a domestic environment conducive to success. Yet to a striking degree, refugee advocates failed to capitalize on this language or these themes as they pressed their case. Whereas liberalizers speaking in favor of immigration reform were only too happy to reference the civil rights movements and the rights revolution, the refugee branch of the liberalizer camp rarely if ever trafficked in these themes. It was a lost opportunity.

At the same time, refugee advocates encountered an important and likely insurmountable obstacle on the foreign policy front. The Cold War consensus that helped found and justify American refugee policies and laws in the early 1950s was still very much in force in the mid-1960s. Two examples will suffice. President Johnson's decision in early 1965 to order American ground forces to Vietnam was greeted, on the whole, with commendation rather than condemnation; the majority of the American public would only begin questioning American involvement in Southeast Asia in 1968. Even more germane, critics of the national origins quota immigration system justified reform by pointing to the benefits that would be obtained for America's Cold War foreign policy. The central contention of all the prescriptions of refugee advocates—that viewing refugee problems through the lens of the Cold War was counterproductive and outdated—ran counter to this Cold War consensus. (In this way of thinking, one of the key conditions for immigration reform—Cold War foreign policy objectives—actually reinforced the status quo in refugee policy that refugee experts so wanted to move against.) Roger Jones's muddled reasoning and the dissonance inherent in the survey of world refugee problems reveals the difficulty even the experts themselves encountered when they tried to move refugee politics away from its Cold War foundations. It is not clear, moreover, that the public would have supported such wholesale changes. A 1959 poll asking whether the United States should admit some of the 15 million refugees "from different parts of the world" who "have been forced to leave their home countries or have fled for various reasons" showed that 60 percent of those surveyed answered in the affirmative, while 31 percent wanted no admissions at all. Such numbers must have been heartening for refugee experts, for the question did not specify refugees from communism. Yet, six years later, when asked if the immigration proposal ending national origins quotas (that eventually became law) ought to provide for the entry of refugees from communism, 64 percent of those polled said yes, while 23 percent answered no. The 1965 law, of course, ultimately reflected this bias toward the admission of refugees fleeing communism.[32]

. . .

The destruction of the national origins immigration system and the inauguration of a new immigration policy in 1965 were powered by the Cold War and, more importantly, the domestic and cultural revolutions sparked by the civil rights movement, the "Great Society," and an emerging rights-consciousness—each of which ultimately helping to alter conceptions of American identity. Consolidation, rather than sweeping change, came to American refugee affairs in the mid-1960s, in spite of the efforts of refugee advocates. The domestic and cultural environment augured well for refugee policy and law reform, but the refugee aid community failed to fully seize the moment. At the same time, the foreign policy climate remained solidly rooted in the Cold War, a blow to the refugee reform agenda. This same mixture of continuity and change marked the United States' major refugee issue of the 1960s: the exodus of refugees from Cuba.

CHAPTER 5

"They Are Proud People": The United States and Refugees from Cuba, 1959–1966

IMMIGRATION REFORM IN 1965 did not substantively address the hundreds of thousands of refugees arriving from Cuba. The U.S. government's decision in early 1959 to admit Cubans fleeing Fidel Castro's revolution grew through the following decade into a massive commitment that by and large conformed to precedent. Cuban refugees, like their predecessors in the 1950s, were of European descent and opposed communism. While Cuba's importance to the Cold War virtually ensured an American response to the refugee problem, a mix of domestic political and cultural concerns also explained U.S. actions. Cuban refugees entered the United States via an admissions process administered by the INS and State Department that bore striking similarities to 1950s refugee programs, especially in its reliance on the "parole" authority. Finally, the U.S. government launched an extensive effort to publicize the arrival of Cuban refugees in the best possible light, largely by emphasizing the refugees' "American" qualities.

The commitment to Cuban refugees, though, also represented a significant departure.[1] While the admission of European refugees in the 1950s engendered opposition nationally, hostility to the entry and arrival of Cuban refugees was largely contained to southern Florida and Miami throughout the 1960s. More striking, entry requirements loosened considerably on a number of fronts. Gone were the days of screening out refugees who did not have guarantees of jobs or homes or were likely to become public charges; instead, the federal government launched a comprehensive resettlement program that supported refugees until they were comfortably resettled with jobs and housing. The INS and State Department still administered a security investigation that required Cubans to declare their opposition to communism and Castro, and some evidence suggests that the INS, which hired some of the most vigorous anticommunists in the Cuban refugee community to assist in the screening process, had more than a passing interest in the political pasts of Cuban refugees. But the government did not prohibit the entry of former communists or Castro supporters, nor did investigators appear to devote much energy to uncovering the political histories of parole applicants. Instead, the focus of the security check became the detection of subversives, usually defined as agents of the Castro government. Thus, while the ghosts of Scott McLeod and the investigatory state could not be exorcised so easily, the anticommunist political litmus test of the early 1950s continued to recede as it had during the Hungarian refugee crisis.

The arrival of Cuban refugees also led to a rethinking of notions of citizenship. In 1966, Congress looked, as it had in 1958 for Hungarians, to clarify the immigration status of Cuban parolees. With passage of the Cuban Status Adjustment Act, refugee advocates opened a path toward American citizenship for Cuban refugees, who were described as easy converts to American life because of their self-sufficiency, hard work, and anticommunism. In the debates over this legislation, the refugees' anticommunism was still considered a mark of their potential for membership in the American nation, but those political bona fides often were treated as pro forma—and as less vital than cultural or social attributes. In this way, then, the Cuban admissions, like the immigration debates of 1965, demonstrated again the fading importance of anticommunism in American life. Most remarkably, the Cuban Status Adjustment Act led politicians, refugee advocates, and Cuban refugees themselves to endorse a bifurcated citizenship in which Cubans might become permanent residents or citizens while still planning to return to the island. Status normalization, in the case of Cuban refugees, condoned divided loyalties. No previous refugee group, or immigrant group for that matter, had been granted such leeway.[2]

Cuban Refugee Flows and American Responses, 1959–1973

On New Year's Eve 1958, the Cuban dictator Fulgencio Batista fled to the Dominican Republic. One day later, the 26th of July Movement, an insurgency led by Fidel Castro, took control of Havana. In the immediate aftermath of the Revolution, the new government (including Castro) was uncertain of its precise ideological and programmatic course. Some Cubans had no interest in discovering the Revolution's future. Fearing for their safety, a few hundred Batista officials and personal friends of the deposed dictator immediately fled to the United States. Those with visas were admitted as temporary visitors, while the rest, lacking documents, were paroled. As the Cuban revolution increasingly fell under Castro's control in the coming months and years—and as he and his allies shaped the island's politics, economics, and social structures—other Cubans decided to depart rather than remain. The refugee flow was not constant, however. It broke down into four phases that corresponded both to changes on the island and to developments in Cuban-U.S. relations. (The

flow did not correspond to the seismic changes in immigration law oc-
curring at the same time.) The first phase began with the fall of the Batista
regime and ended when the United States broke diplomatic relations with
Cuba in January 1961. Phase two lasted from January 1961 to the onset
of the Cuban Missile Crisis in October 1962, when Castro forbade the
departure of Cubans for the United States. The third phase occurred between October 1962 and November, 1965, ending with Castro's unilateral decision to allow Cubans to depart for the States. The refugee flow's
final phase lasted until 1973, when the United States withdrew from an
agreement that governed the arrival of Cubans. Unlike previous crises, in
which U.S. allies offered considerable aid, the Cuban refugee challenge
was met largely and almost exclusively by the United States.[3]

In the first two years following Batista's fall, Castro solidified his hold
on power and developed his reform program. After becoming prime minister in February 1959, he slowly but surely forced right-leaning moderates
and liberals from the government and assiduously removed anticommunists from his ruling coalition. At the same time, Castro forged closer ties
with Cuban communists, whom he saw as his most reliable allies in the
struggle to transform the island's political economy. Castro's policies, like
his political allies, came increasingly from the left. An ambitious nationalization program began in May 1959 with the Agrarian Reform Act that
expropriated large farms, most of which produced sugar, and continued
with the nationalization of all major industries and businesses the following year. Foreign economic interests, and especially American companies,
suffered because of their heavy investments in the island's industries. In
addition to the nationalization program, Castro's inflammatory rhetoric
aggravated the United States. As Cuban-American relations deteriorated,
Castro slowly built bridges to the Soviet Union by reopening diplomatic
relations and signing a commercial treaty in early 1960.[4]

The Eisenhower administration initially was optimistic about post–
Batista Cuba's prospects. It recognized that the island needed major economic and social reforms, and Castro appeared serious about carrying
them out. The honeymoon lasted barely a year. Frustrated by Castro's
nationalization program, suspicious of his political alliances, troubled
by his rapprochement with the Soviet Union, and worried about his influence throughout the Caribbean basin, the Eisenhower administration in
1960 began working actively against Castro. Besides economic counter-
measures, the American government began planning covert operations to
remove Castro. Unsurprisingly, American-Cuban relations deteriorated
in a volley of accusatory rhetoric and economic warfare. The final breaks
occurred in late 1960 and early 1961. The Soviet Union began providing
Cuba with economic aid and arms in the fall of 1960. In January 1961,
Cuba ordered reductions in the size of the American embassy's staff,

and the United States responded by canceling diplomatic and consular relations. Ten days later, Castro declared the socialist nature of the Cuban Revolution.[5]

Castro's social, political, and economic policies caused nearly 100,000 Cubans to flee to the United States in the two years following Batista's fall. Most arrived in 1960, and unlike the Batista supporters who fled Cuba in the early days of 1959, these refugees were often Batista opponents who had grown disaffected with Castro. Largely from the upper and upper-middle classes, they were owners and managers of large firms, professionals, merchants, and representatives of foreign companies. They fled because of the revolution's leftward political turn and because their economic well-being and status depended on fast-disappearing foreign, mainly American, investment. The White House never seriously considered any other policy than admitting the Cubans to the United States and allowing them to remain indefinitely, which was consonant with the Eisenhower White House's admissions of other refugees from communism. Refugee admissions, the Eisenhower administration believed, would help secure the Castro government's demise and thus the containment of Cuba's revolutionary contagion. Cuban refugees highlighted (to the world generally, and to Latin American nations particularly) Castro's economic and political failures and made clear the United States' concern for victims of communism. At the same time, the Eisenhower administration needed Cuban refugees to man a potential invasion force that the president had approved in March 1960. Finally, the Eisenhower administration admitted these refugees believing that—because Castro was destined to fall—they would reside only temporarily in the United States.[6]

After the diplomatic break in January 1961, Cuban-American relations deteriorated. Castro continued his economic reforms and embrace of leftist politics, while President Kennedy largely maintained Eisenhower's Cuban policies, including support for a U.S.-organized invasion of the island by Cuban refugees. An open secret in both countries, the Bay of Pigs invasion took place in April 1961. Castro routed the refugee invasion force and used the attack as a pretext to round up his government's opponents, both suspected and real, strengthening his hold on the island. With no remaining illusions about U.S. policies toward Cuba, Castro declared himself a Marxist-Leninist and reinforced his alliance with the Soviets. With these events, the exodus of refugees from Cuba grew significantly. Between January 1961 and October 1962, roughly 150,000 refugees arrived in the United States, a group that included fewer upper-class elites than during the first phase and many more from the Cuban middle class. These refugees fled in large part because they had lost hope that the Castro government might topple. The Kennedy administration, like its predecessor, accepted these refugees without question and fully aware that

Castro's government appeared more stable. Almost certainly, the Administration's decision to admit these refugees helps explain how refugee advocates like State Department official Roger Jones, as we saw in the previous chapter, might conceptualize refugees as Cold War victims of communism even as he argued for the reform of American refugee law in summer 1961.[7]

The second phase of the refugee migration ended with the Cuban Missile Crisis of October 1962, during which Castro halted commercial air travel between the island and the United States. Cubans could now only get to the United States by first traveling to a third country and applying for a visa, by being so ill and in need of medical care that the Red Cross brought them to the United States, or by crossing the Florida Straits by boat. This third phase lasted three years, during which between 30,000 and 50,000 Cubans arrived in the United States. Thus, just as the debate over immigration reform heated up, the refugee flow from Cuba slowed considerably. The majority of Cubans entering between 1962 and 1965 were skilled and unskilled blue-collar workers, fishermen, and agricultural laborers who came to the States because they were dissatisfied with the Castro government's imposition of food rationing and compulsory military service in 1962 and 1963.[8]

The Cuban refugee flow's nadir ended in the fall of 1965 after Castro announced that all who wanted to leave could do so from the port of Camarioca on Cuba's northern-central coast. Castro allowed the exodus because he relished presenting the United States with an unforeseen refugee crisis and because he hoped to quell the domestic discontent that had arisen from tough economic times and the Cuban government's expropriation of all privately owned businesses. The post-1965 refugees were largely working-class or middle-class Cubans (small business people and merchants, as well as skilled and semiskilled workers) and they fled not because they were political opponents of the Cuban government, but because they thought better economic opportunities lay to the north. Cubans living in the United States immediately set sail for the island, picking up nearly five thousand friends and relatives in two months. This disorderly and dangerous exodus—Cuban exiles often commandeered small crafts of questionable seaworthiness—led the American and Cuban governments to negotiate a "Memorandum of Understanding" in November 1965 that arranged for regular air flights of refugees. With this agreement, both governments for the first time placed restrictions on who could make the journey. The United States prioritized the entry of Cubans who already had relatives in the States, while the Cuban government refused to let men of military age, those they deemed essential to the economy, and political prisoners leave the island. President Johnson, as he signed the

Figure 5.1 Two Cuban refugees, with their boat anchored off-shore, emerge from the surf.

immigration-reform package into law, pledged to accept any and all Cuban refugees, a decision that given the policy precedents was, in the words of two prominent scholars, "probably inevitable." Johnson, moreover, did not know that the refugee flow would last eight years and bring over 275,000 migrants to the United States. By 1973, when the United States withdrew from the "Memorandum of Understanding" because fewer Cubans wanted to come to the States, about 500,000 Cubans had entered the United States since 1959.[9]

How closely did the Cubans admitted in these years fit the prevailing definition of "refugee"? The 1957 Refugee-Escapee Act, which was the last major piece of refugee legislation that passed before the Cuban exodus began, defined a "refugee" as "any alien who, because of persecution or fear of persecution on account of race, religion, or political opinion, has fled or shall flee" from a communist country or area and who cannot return. This legal definition of "refugee" clashed with the reality of Cuban migration. Each Cuban did flee a communist country, and large numbers of refugees left Cuba because they disagreed with the Revolution's political course or because they did not want to live under a communist government. But the vast majority of Cubans were not fleeing a particular act of persecution or fear of a particular act of persecution. Rather, Cubans arriving in the United States fit the general understanding of "refugee" prominent in that era's political culture: Cubans seemed to be both victims and opponents of communism and its effects. Moreover, equally large numbers of Cubans fled because of Castro's economic policies and because they believed better economic opportunities lay in the United States. Cubans, then, shared much with traditional immigrants who left their homelands in search of superior economic prospects. To be sure, Cubans could claim such economic motives were part and parcel of their anticommunism, but it was also clear to most observers that these were migrants searching for economic gain. In this sense, the Cubans were the first large refugee group to muddy the distinction between economic and political refugees, a distinction that would only grow in importance in the coming decades, especially as Haitians and the Indochinese tried to enter the United States.[10]

Cuban refugees' opposition to communism reinforced the most important justification for their admission. Cold War foreign policy concerns surely drove the Eisenhower administration's decisions to admit Cuban refugees, and these concerns just as certainly sustained that commitment through the Kennedy and Johnson presidencies. While Cuban admissions did not directly affect superpower relations, U.S. policymakers no doubt believed Cuban refugee admissions weakened the Soviet Union's greatest ally in the Western Hemisphere. Moreover, successive U.S. administrations believed that if refugee admissions weakened Castro, they in turn helped contain the spread of communism in the Americas, as Castro was considered its main proponent. Finally, Cuban refugees, like their European counterparts, had dramatic propaganda value as vivid examples (to the world and to the peoples of the Americas) of communism's and Castro's failings.

The Cold War's influence on Cuban refugee admissions emerges in even sharper relief when considering the case of Haitians fleeing François Duvalier's oppressive, corrupt, and brutal government. In the late 1950s, Haitians began leaving the island, an exodus that grew to thousands of upper-class and middle-class businessmen and professionals during the 1960s. The U.S. government generally accommodated the Haitians, many of whom, of course, arrived as proper immigrants. But the United States also admitted Haitians on nonimmigrant visas throughout the 1960s and rarely deported them after those visas expired. Some Haitians, then, were granted "virtual refugee status" in the words of scholars Gil Loescher and John Scanlan, but no special efforts were made to help those fleeing the island. Unlike Cubans, Haitians needed visas to enter the United States (rather than entering via parole). The INS, American politicians, and policymakers did not consider Haitians victims of political persecution at the hands of the Duvalier regime. Finally, the Haitians never received the vast federal government resettlement aid that flowed to Cubans. Quite simply, these discrepancies arose because Haiti, unlike Cuba, had no important place in Cold War geopolitics and ideological warfare. Duvalier was not a communist, but an American ally. While the Eisenhower, Kennedy, and Johnson administrations recognized—to different degrees—Duvalier's flaws, each saw him as a bulwark against communism and Castroism in the Caribbean. The Cold War, then, earned Cuban refugees the special treatment that Haitians fleeing their island failed to receive.[11]

But currents in domestic culture and politics, not just the Cold War, also help explain the Cuban policy. As the refugee flow grew in 1960, Eisenhower's decision in favor of admissions was eased because of the cultural affinity—what historian Louis Perez has called "ties of singular intimacy"—between the United States and Cuba. Throughout the twentieth century, well-to-do Cubans had traveled to Miami to shop, to vacation, and even to send their children to school. Americans, on the other hand, frequently visited Cuba to soak up the sun and gamble. The island held a special place even in the minds of Americans without the financial means to visit. In the postwar United States, Cuban baseball players and boxers were American sports heroes, the popular television show *I Love Lucy* starred America's sweetheart Lucille Ball and her real-life husband, Desi Arnaz, a Cuban, and the cha-cha-cha dance craze that swept the United States in the 1950s had its roots in Cuba. In short, a romanticized and idealized vision of Cuba existed among Americans. This element was not present, for instance, in Hungarian-American relations (or U.S. relations with Haiti for that matter).[12]

This affinity also contained a political dimension. Americans had long fashioned themselves as the island's protectors, a paternalistic tone that survived the Roosevelt administration's 1934 decision to abrogate the Platt Amendment (which demanded that the Cuban constitution grant the United States the legal right to interfere in the island's affairs). This paternalism streaked the political culture of U.S.-Cuban relations and heightened the political costs (in Eisenhower's case) of not admitting Cuban refugees, or (in Kennedy's and Johnson's cases) of reversing course. Again, the United States had no such paternalist history with Hungary.[13]

JFK and LBJ, moreover, worked under an additional political constraint: discontinuing the policy of unfettered Cuban admissions would likely have aroused charges from the political right that they were soft on communism and did not have the mettle to conduct the Cold War. As historian Frederik Logevall has shown, both Democratic presidents wished to avoid that charge as they dealt with Vietnam, and it is not implausible that similar considerations entered their minds as they addressed Cuba, which aroused just as strong public passions. The majority of the public-opinion polls from the period focus on the Kennedy administration's handling of Cuba and reveal consistent public support, if also a segment of the public that desired a more aggressive approach. While the Gallup Polls never explicitly asked about Kennedy's refugee policies, it stands to reason that the public considered refugee programs when rating the president's handling of Cuba.[14]

These factors point to the ways in which the entry of Cuban refugees during the early and mid-1960s ultimately did little to help the contemporary efforts to reform the basic principles underlying refugee policies and laws. Cuban admissions—and as we shall later see, some of the publicity efforts on their behalf—were always founded in the Cold War and anticommunism and designed to reward victims and opponents of communism. They were, in other words, products of the aforementioned Cold War consensus that helped construct the post–World War II commitment to refugee admissions. Thus, just as refugee advocates geared up to reform that very commitment, the United States reinforced it via the Cuban admissions.

Finally, the peculiarities of the Cuban refugee flow defused objections that might have arisen in the American public about the race of the newcomers. Cuba, of course, was a multiracial society; the 1953 census—while suffering from the same weaknesses as other census data that attempt to measure a population's racial composition—found that "blacks" made up 27 percent of the island's inhabitants. The refugees who arrived in the United States between 1959 and 1973, however, were overwhelmingly "white." Three explanations account for this dynamic, but they all have their roots in the Batista-era political and economic hierarchies in which "whites" maintained privileged positions and "blacks" were relegated to the lowest strata. First, the vast majority of the initial tens of thousands of Cuban refugees escaping the island were from the upper and middle classes, and thus mostly white. Second, as the exodus continued through the 1960s, the phenomena of chain migration also took hold, wherein Cuban exiles in the United States encouraged their relatives on the island to escape as well. This chain migration also meant that whites dominated the refugee flow throughout the 1960s. Third, "black" Cubans saw new opportunities—many of which were realized—in the Revolution and in the Castro government's programs to improve their lives, and thus had fewer reasons to leave in the years after Batista's fall.[15]

"WE WOULD DEAL WITH THE DEVIL HIMSELF": ADMISSIONS STANDARDS FOR CUBAN REFUGEES

The Eisenhower, Kennedy, and Johnson administrations each decided that the United States should accept large numbers of Cuban refugees, but how open was the "open door?" No consensus exists among scholars about the rigors of the admissions process. Contemporaries wondered about the admissions policies as well. As Senator Phil Hart (D-MI) noted in 1963, "the mail some of us in the Senate receive—I would suspect that all of us receive—reflects a concern on the part of a good many Americans that the security screening involved in the admission of Cuban refugees is lax, and that we are in fact permitting into this country Castro and Soviet agents."[16]

The fluctuations in U.S.-Cuban relations complicated the admissions process. With the United States and Cuba maintaining normal diplomatic and consular relations until January 1961, a Cuban could go to the American consular offices on the island and apply for either a visa or a nonimmigrant visa. (A regular visa allowed a person to stay permanently and eventually become a citizen, while a nonimmigrant visa had an expiration date; tourists, students, and businesspersons often held nonimmigrant visas.) With both kinds of visas, Cubans could travel to the United States, but those with nonimmigrant visas had to return to Cuba after their visas expired. Instead of forcing Cubans with expired nonimmigrant visas to return, the U.S. government allowed them to remain in the United States (called a "visa overstay") if they claimed that they could not return to Cuba as long as the Castro government remained in control. After January 1961, Cubans could not just visit the American embassy to apply for a visa. Instead, their friends and relatives in the United States filed a request with the State Department and INS for a "visa waiver," an administrative mechanism by which the attorney general waived the visa requirement for entry to the United States. If the visa waiver was granted, then the applicant was notified (by his or her relatives), and the applicant would arrange for transportation to the United States. After arriving, the Cuban would apply for parole and refugee status. Under this system, the number of Cuban parolees increased dramatically in 1961, and parole became the main mechanism for Cuban entry into the United States through the 1960s.[17]

The Cuban Missile Crisis choked the flow of refugees and complicated the admissions process. Cubans who arrived in the United States via third countries (mainly Spain and Mexico) already had visas in hand. Those who escaped from the island and landed without papers in Florida were granted a visa waiver and then applied for parole. Refugees who had the Castro government's permission to depart—those who were U.S. citizens or were humanitarian cases—went through a process wherein the Cuban government gave the names of departees to the Swiss Embassy, who passed along the names to the United States for approval. When Cuba reopened travel to the United States in late 1965, the "Memorandum of Understanding" that governed the refugee flow again utilized the Swiss as a consular go-between. Cuba and the United States drew up lists of Cubans whom it would permit to leave or allow to enter. The two countries exchanged these lists through the Swiss, and the persons named on both lists applied for visa waivers. If they received the waiver, the U.S. government arranged for transport from Cuba to Florida, where the Cubans were paroled into the United States as refugees.[18]

All Cuban refugees were screened by the Immigration and Naturalization Service and the State Department. The screening process was relatively similar across each of the refugee flow's phases even as the mechanics of entry varied. The State Department and the INS ran security screenings on Cubans who applied for visas or nonimmigrant visas (between 1959 and 1961) and for visa waivers (after 1961). A Cuban received his or her visa or waiver only if the State Department and the INS concurred on the security clearance. After obtaining the visa or waiver, the Cuban submitted to an initial health inspection and INS inspection immediately before traveling to the United States. In the United States, the refugee received a more complete health inspection and a complete security screening.

On average, a Cuban refugee faced three separate security checks conducted by State Department and INS officials. These checks aimed to elicit intelligence on current affairs in Cuba and information that might disqualify a refugee from entry. In the first check, the State Department and

INS searched their Caribbean "look-out" books for the applicant's name; the INS book compiled the names of some 65,000, mostly Cuban, individuals barred from entering the United States because they were subversion threats. The second security check occurred immediately before the refugee departed Cuba for the United States, as the applicant's name again was checked against the updated "look-out" books. The individual interrogations of refugees—hallmarks of the RRP and the Hungarian Program—constituted the third and final security check. After landing in the United States, all male Cuban refugees went to the mothballed Opa-Locka military base outside of Miami for questioning. (The government closed the Opa-Locka facility in October 1962 after the slowdown in refugee arrivals and instead questioned Cuban refugees at the INS offices in Miami. Opa-Locka reopened after the resumption of the refugee flow in late 1965.) The key INS form used in the interrogation, SE-180, asked only for basic information: name, address, age, occupation in Cuba, military rank (if any), marital status, and "reasons claimed for being unable to return to country of nationality." As a result, officials conducting the individual interviews shaped each investigation. James Hennessy, a high-ranking INS official in the early 1960s, claimed that officials had a "sixth sense" that alerted them to "various subterfuges, frauds, and attempted frauds" perpetrated by Cubans. Mario Noto allowed that "There may be some difference" in the questions asked a Cuban parolee as opposed to a Tibetan parolee.[19]

Noto acknowledged that Cuban refugee applicants were asked about "past activities, affiliations, pedigree, activities engaged in." Investigators looked to prevent the entry of criminals of "persons . . . with a criminal potential," unsurprising given U.S. immigration laws that excluded those who had engaged in criminal activity. Immigration officers also searched for threats to "internal security" (Noto's words) or spies, saboteurs, and agents of the Castro government in the refugee flow. Investigators rejected Cuban parolees most often on the ground that the applicant was an espionage threat or an agent of the Castro government. Noto said of those Cubans refused parole: "Most of the cases seem to center around an approach that has been made to the Cuban national while in Cuba . . . to report data back to some people back in Havana. And most of them were untrained in espionage work."[20]

Espionage was a high standard, one which involved actively working for the Castro government and spying on the United States. INS and State Department officials also investigated an applicant's political history, specifically his affiliations with political parties, organizations, and ideologies. The controversy surrounding one refugee, Colonel Mariano Faget, underscores the INS's interest in the political backgrounds and histories of Cuban refugees. Faget arrived in the United States in 1959, fleeing the revolution in Cuba. He had good reason to flee. For twenty years, Faget served in various positions for the Cuban secret police, and in the mid-1950s directed the Batista regime's Bureau of Repression of Communist Activities (BRAC), which under Faget's leadership vigorously pursued Cuban communists with a program that some said involved murder and torture. By late October 1961, the public learned that Faget now worked for the INS as an interpreter and interrogator of Cuban refugees arriving in the United States. The Justice Department acknowledged that Faget was in their employ, saying that he was at the screenings "to keep Castro agents from coming into the United States." Another official described Faget's role (and his past) less delicately: "To get this job of screening done properly, we would deal with the devil himself." But dealing with the devil quickly became a political problem. Cuban refugee groups in the United States complained that the colonel seemed more interested in investigating the role that refugees may have played in the downfall of the Batista regime than he did in eliciting intelligence on the Castro government or uncovering saboteurs and spies.[21]

The Faget controversy was part of the Cuban refugee groups' larger objection to the U.S. government's screening processes. Cuban refugee organizations simply could not understand why some of their compatriots were being held by the INS. They cited in particular the case of Dr. Augusto Fernandez Code, who headed an underground cell organized in advance of the Bay of Pigs invasion. With the invasion's failure, Castro sent Fernandez to jail. Upon his release, Fernandez fled to the United States. But following his interrogation at the INS facility at Opa-Locka, he was placed in detention at an INS facility in Texas, with no comment from the INS about his status or future. Fernandez's allies in the Cuban refugee population said that the only possible objection to Fernandez may have been the doctor's visits to Poland and Bulgaria in early 1960.[22]

The INS's and the Justice Department's screening methods and procedures were coming under suspicion when it became public that Colonel Faget—who had pursued (and perhaps tortured) Cubans in the 1950s—was now a key INS official in the screening of some of those very same Cubans! Officials at the Justice Department and INS tried to defuse this mounting public-relations problem by insisting that Faget never questioned refugees by himself—a characterization that Cuban refugees disputed—but to no avail. The INS's James Hennessy downplayed Faget's role, saying he was in the "part-time employ" of the INS and that while all intelligence was "grist to our mill," Faget's insights were weighed accordingly. The Kennedy White House apparently tried to quell the controversy by having Faget removed, but the INS objected. Faget's employment was under review, the INS admitted, but his job was not in danger. After all, as an INS spokesperson said, "We can use the information in his possession." Pierre Salinger, President Kennedy's spokesperson, tried to remove the Administration from the fray by declaring, "This is not a White House matter." Finally, the Senate Democrat Joseph Clark of Pennsylvania called for a clean slate, a review of the entire screening process.[23]

In late November, a little more than a month after the Faget controversy surfaced, the Justice Department announced new procedures for screening Cuban refugees. A committee consisting of representatives from Cuban anti-Castro refugee groups operating out of Miami—supplied with INS information—would help screen refugees. That committee's first task was a review of sixteen refugees held by the INS, which resulted (with INS concurrence) in the release of four. At least one of the committee members, Dr. Roberto Hernandez of the anti-Castro refugee group the Cuban Revolutionary Council, reportedly had worked on the screening of refugees with INS officials in the past. This would be the "standard procedure" in the future, a Justice Department spokesman said.[24]

The INS's partnership with Cuban refugees like Faget was hardly surprising; after all, Hungarian refugees assisted in the screening of their fellow refugees in 1956 and 1957. The Faget controversy and its resolution somewhat clarified the intent and goals of INS screening procedures. The INS valued Faget and the screening committee because they held detailed knowledge of the political histories and allegiances of the refugees—and thus could cull from incoming refugees information about Castro agents planted in the refugee flow and about the current political situation on the island. Faget, after all, had spent the better part of twenty years uncovering these histories for the Cuban secret police, while the members of the screening committee had extensive ties to the broad-based movement that overthrew Batista and sustained the Revolution in its early months and years. Faget and the committee, in essence, served as the INS's eyes into the past and current political affiliations of Cubans coming to the United States. It was never clear, though, whether Faget and the committee reviewed each Cuban entering the United States, some of the refugees in the flow, or just particular cases flagged by the INS.

Thus, despite the presence of Faget and the three-tiered security screening, the Cuban program represented a further retreat from the rigid entry requirements of the early 1950s. Close examination of an applicant's political history was an integral part of screening investigations during prior refugee programs. Investigators did try to ascertain a Cuban refugee's political affiliations and activities; the role, if any, that an individual might have played in the years-long struggle against Batista; and a refugee's relationship to Castro's revolutionary movement. But in contrast to those previous programs, these efforts (Faget and the committee aside) appeared even less rigorous than before, and the INS and State Department did not bar from entry those refugees with prior political affiliations with revolutionary, leftist, or communist organizations. Representative Arch Moore asked INS officials in 1963 whether "mere support of or passive activity on behalf of Castro was sufficient for disqualification? In other words, was inquiry made as to how active they were in behalf of Castro's revolution? . . . If it was, was it merely a notation and not a disqualification for remaining in the United States?" Noto answered that participation in the Revolution did not disqualify a Cuban from entering the United States as a refugee and that Cuban refugees could be disaffected Castro supporters. The United States welcomed Cubans, in Noto's telling, who "actually and genuinely sought refuge in the United States as refugees from communism." Cubans, then, like their refugee predecessors, still had to proclaim their anticommunist bona fides to win refugee status, but they did not have to explain away their political histories. Cuban refugee Deborah Carrera recalled years later: "I felt compelled to give it all up and leave my country because I realized that I could never teach communism. . . . When we first got to Miami, the first thing [the immigration authorities] did was interview me. I declared my self against Fidel."[25]

The admissions statistics support the contention that the security screening was neither a formidable bar to entry nor an impediment meant to slow admissions. The "look-out" books, rather than the face-to-face interview, apparently denied the most Cubans entry. The INS and State Department both had to clear the refugee through their books, and INS official Noto revealed in July 1963 that the State Department and the INS failed to concur in 1,013 cases and that 742 of those disagreements involved refugee suspected of subversion. (State Department officials contradicted Noto, saying that the number of nonconcurrences was "in the scores rather than the hundreds.") Even with Noto's higher number, the percentage of nonconcurrences was incredibly low given the roughly 250,000 refugees who had entered since early 1959. The INS, for the most part, dissembled when asked about the numbers of Cuban refugees it turned away during the interview phase. But when pressed in July 1963, Noto revealed that only twenty-nine Cubans had been deported "on strict subversive grounds" after their interviews.[26]

Cuban refugees also faced fewer obstacles to entry than their predecessors because the federal government dropped the sponsorship and "assurances" requirements of the 1950s. RRP entrants—as well as the 5,000 Hungarians who entered under the RRP—needed a sponsor who assured that the newcomer would not become a public charge and would have housing and employment. Hungarian parolees faced no such legal obligations, but they were assigned a sponsoring agency in Austria before they even spoke with consular officials, which effectively mirrored the RRP's assurances codicil. Under the Cuban refugee program, sponsorship and "assurance" qualifications disappeared entirely from the admissions process. A Cuban refugee did not have to demonstrate a guarantee of a job or housing in order to enter the United States, nor was the refugee obligated to meet with a sponsoring agency before departing Cuba.

The Cuban Refugee Program:
"Selling" the "Benefits" of Cuban Refugees

Cuban refugees were not left to fend for themselves, however. Instead, the federal government assumed a new and more prominent role in refugee resettlement. While the Eisenhower administration largely left resettlement efforts in the hands of private agencies and state governments, President Kennedy ordered the Department of Health, Education and Welfare (HEW) to launch a comprehensive resettlement program, the Cuban Refugee Program (CRP). The CRP provided welfare payments to needy Cuban refugee families, funded job retraining programs for unemployed Cubans, and offered Cubans basic health services, in addition to covering the costs incurred by the four voluntary organizations (the Hebrew Immigrant Aid Society, the International Rescue Committee, the Catholic Relief Services of the National Catholic Welfare Conference, and the Church World Service) assisting in resettlement efforts. The growth of the CRP's budget as it tackled these tasks was remarkable. While the Eisenhower White House in 1960 spent $1 million to aid in resettlement, the Kennedy administration spent over $214 million between fiscal years 1961 and 1966; in 1963, the CRP's budget was over $56 million—$40 million on welfare and services alone.[27]

Besides the basics of resettlement, the CRP looked to manage and build public support for the American commitment to refugees. The annual admission of tens of thousands of Cubans in the first half of the 1960s did not produce sustained national protests, indicative of the power of Cold War justifications for the program and the cultural and political affinities shared by many Cubans and Americans. Opposition to the newcomers existed, however. On the national level, some of this opposition was likely the simmering anti-immigrant sentiment that consistently manifested itself in American society. During the 1960s, at least one-third of the public surveyed in polls consistently opposed the entry of newcomers, the base of support that restrictionists appealed to in their efforts to derail reform of the nation's immigration laws.

More troubling to the Eisenhower and Kennedy White Houses and the CRP, though, was the suspicion and grumbling that emanated from southern Florida in the early 1960s. The Eisenhower and Kennedy administrations and the State Department fielded complaints, especially from Florida's congressional delegation, about the stresses refugees placed on

Figure 5.2 An American government official, on the left, engages in an apparently heated discussion with a Cuban refugee during the resettlement process in 1961.

Miami's economic and social structure. The *Miami Herald* reporter Juanita Green told Congress at the end of 1961 of Miamians "growing" ill will toward Cubans. She traced this "xenophobia" to the perception that the newcomers received generous welfare payments, to a tightening job market, and to the further stresses that Cubans placed on Miami's already overburdened school system. There was much truth to these complaints. Unemployment, already a problem in southern Florida, jumped to over 7 percent in 1962. While the federal government agreed to cover half the cost of schooling the nearly 25,000 Cuban children in Florida schools by 1963, state and local governments struggled to fund the rest. Additionally, Florida set its maximum welfare payment for a native family at $81 a month, while federal officials (in concert with the state government) set the monthly maximum for Cuban families at $100. Finally, a *Miami Herald* editorial in late November 1961 highlighted cultural differences, pointing out that "many refugees don't realize they are giving offense simply by doing as they used to do in Cuba. We are thinking of such small things as speaking loudly and letting radios play music loudly, particularly late at night. Most Miamians go to sleep earlier than is customary in Cuba."[28]

The CRP responded to these complaints and reports of public discomfiture by attempting to resettle refugees outside of Florida and by launching a public-relations campaign to tamp down opposition to Cubans. The

CRP's resettlement project had mixed success. In September 1961, only eight thousand Cubans had been resettled outside of Florida. By May 1963, that number had grown to just under sixty thousand—more than one quarter of all refugees admitted—a percentage that grew minimally in the following years. To speed resettlement, the CRP, private voluntary agencies, and a host of observers with keen knowledge of refugee politics believed it necessary to establish a positive image of Cuban refugees in the American public's mind. Officials worried that the resettlement effort sometimes sparked opposition, rooted in fears of job competition, in communities that received Cubans. *Miami Herald* reporter Greene recommended "more publicity to assure Americans that only legitimate refugees are allowed in and only the needy receive aid." Senator Hart expressed concern "that we have not clicked in that same dramatic style in portraying the Cuban problem" as the American government did with the Hungarians. While encouraging communities across the United States to open their doors to resettled refugees was the immediate aim of the CRP's PR campaign, these efforts also more generally had the effect of justifying, and inoculating from criticism, the U.S. government's magnanimous admissions policies.[29] Thus, while the resettlement operation birthed the national public-relations campaign, an additional benefit was the positive light the campaign would shine on Cuban refugee admissions writ large.

The CRP's publicity campaign began in late 1961, but it was not a carbon copy of its Hungarian predecessor. The Cuban effort did not involve private-sector advertising firms to any great extent—the Advertising Council's involvement, for instance, was minimal—nor was it as aggressive or comprehensive as the Hungarian public-relations campaign. Just as important, CRP officials faced a difficult task. Almost a year earlier, the State Department's Bureau of Inter-American Affairs tried, without much success, to publicize the United States' aid to Cuban refugees. As one veteran of that effort noted, the "desire to see Cuban refugees given as much public-media treatment as were the Hungarian ones a few years ago is impossible of fulfillment" largely because the Soviet Union was not involved directly in this crisis, nor was there a "shooting war." "Press, Radio, and TV representatives" in the United States, as a result, displayed "only a relatively restrained interest."[30]

CRP officials established what they called "a systematic information, publicity, promotional . . . program." CRP publicists, who included several veterans of the Hungarian campaign, targeted newspapers, magazines, radio, television, and trade journals. (They also provided state governments with information about the Cubans in the hope that this would open up resettlement opportunities.) In the first eight months of 1962, the CRP sent two mass mailings of materials highlighting both the government's resettlement efforts and the successful adjustment that Cuban refugees had made to the United States. In all, nearly four thousand mailings went out to editors of daily newspapers and local and syndicated columnists while a similar effort attempted to reach radio and television stations. Public-relations personnel at the Cuban Refugee Program also produced films for broadcast on American television, coauthored articles for magazines like *Reader's Digest*, and sent TV and radio announcers scripts of questions they could use to conduct interviews with local politicians about the resettlement process. In each of these cases, CRP publicity officials tried to maintain tight control over—or, at least, shape—the portrayal of refugees.[31]

The CRP's PR campaign stressed that Cubans were victims and opponents of communism. This tactic had two important advantages. First, it refuted charges that the Cuban newcomers merely sought economic opportunities and were not legitimate refugees from communism. Second, the portrayal of Cubans as victims of communism reinforced, and resonated with, the United States' anti-Castro crusade policies. CRP officials, and their superiors at HEW, then, were extremely pleased with the August 1964 publication of "The Dramatic Story of How Heroic Men, Women and Children Brave Terror and Torture to Escape from Red Cuba" in *Parade* magazine, a Sunday supplement to many of the nation's major newspapers. The article's roots were in the CRP's publicity work, and thus it stands as a prime example of what the campaign hoped to accomplish. CRP information officer Philip Holman laid the groundwork for the article in early July when he sent *Parade*'s Jack Anderson a group of stories—"some tragic, some with happy endings," Holman noted—centered on Cubans fleeing the island by boat. This was "[p]robably the most dramatic continuing aspect" of the refugee crisis, Holman told Anderson. One month later, "The Dramatic Story . . ." appeared under Anderson's byline. The piece described refugees attempting to "escape across the Cuban Wall, a far more dangerous, more murderous barrier of water" than the Berlin Wall that European refugees traversed. Anderson depicted "Machine Gun Alley," a "tragic sea lane" in which "Castro's Russian-built patrol boats swarm," attacking refugees fleeing Cuba. The "Cuban Reds" even illegally entered British territory to capture nineteen escapees, some of whom they later executed.[32]

Anderson's story employed broad generalizations and eschewed subtlety. His account stressed that Cuban refugees deserved admission and aid because of the persecution they had endured at the hands of a communist government and its security forces. Anderson did not address the intricacies of Cuban communism or the complex details of Cuba's political and social revolution, but rather merely referred to Cuba as "Devil's Island." Likewise, Anderson asserted the anticommunist credentials of the refugees—thus the importance of his metaphor of the "Cuban

Wall"—rather than revealing the complex political histories of Cuban refugees. Readers were left with only one conclusion after reading the harrowing tales of escape: the Cubans coming to the United States were anticommunists and victims of the Castro regime's persecution. In this way, they were the logical successors to the European refugees admitted throughout the 1950s.

The publicity campaign also stressed the work ethic of Cuban refugees, perhaps even more vigorously than the newcomers' political traits. While it is not entirely clear why CRP officials chose this tact, they likely wished to counteract some of their own handiwork. The federal government's welfare activities for Cuban refugees successfully helped penniless Cubans stay out of abject poverty after they arrived in the United States. But the size of the program—and the publicity it received—also risked creating a hostile response. The dynamic was most acute in Florida, where Miami residents grew increasingly resentful of the government largesse the Cubans received. CRP officials likely worried that such resentment might spread to other parts of the nation, causing resettlement opportunities to dry up as communities outside of Florida closed their doors to what they perceived as Cuban welfare kings and queens. While this fear was largely unstated in the CRP's internal conversations about the publicity campaign, it explains the national scope of that campaign and the energy with which it was pursued. The willingness of refugees to work hard, then, became a staple of the CRP's propaganda plan.

To this end, the CRP ordered 150,000 copies of an editorial from the *Saturday Evening Post* titled "Our Refugees from Castroland." The author pointed out that while refugees received welfare benefits, they "are proud people who do not want to live off the Government." Most emblematic of the willingness of Cuban refugees to work were the "doctors, architects, and engineers" who "have taken jobs as busboys, parking-lot attendants, and bootblacks." About one year later, *Newsweek* published "Iowa, Si!" which covered much the same ground. "Iowa, Si!" told the story of Vincent Rangel, a lawyer who had been imprisoned by Castro before he fled for the United States in the fall of 1960. Unable to work as a lawyer in America, Rangel enrolled in a CRP-funded program that trained Cuban refugees to be high school Spanish teachers. Rangel underwent (as *Newsweek* described it) "eight tough, concentrated weeks of study" and was assigned to Grinnell High School in Grinnell, Iowa. Rangel declared himself "overjoyed" to be earning $5,400 a year as the high school's new Spanish teacher—even though he, like other new Cuban refugee teachers, was underemployed. Both articles offered a clear—and supposedly reassuring—message. Cuban lawyers, doctors, and businessmen were willing to work in less glamorous and well-paying jobs than their years of training and experience had prepared them for. Cubans did not want government aid—even though a number did receive welfare checks—and would take menial jobs to avoid dependency. The CRP not only sought permission to reprint "Iowa, Si!," but in the hope of duplicating the article's basic thrust, it also considered lobbying regional and local media outlets to run stories on Cuban refugees who became high school Spanish teachers.[33]

The phrase "our refugees," though, raised the question of how easily Cubans adapted to their new surroundings. "Iowa, Si!" implied that Rangel and his family were comfortable in corn country. Rangel's new students cheerfully told *Newsweek* that the cultural gap had closed: "We'll get along just fine. . . . He'll probably learn just as much from us as we will from him." The coup de grâce of Rangel's assimilation to the United States and to the Midwest, however, was a most personal decision: he changed his first name from Vincente to Vincent. Or, as *Newsweek* would have its readers, and the CRP, it's audience believe, from Cuban to American. CRP officials likewise praised Juanita Greene's "excellent article on the integration of Cuban refugees" that appeared in the April 25, 1965, *Miami Herald*. Greene noted that the refugees understood that "there'll be no quick return to their homeland, so with a sigh, a shrug, and a laugh, refugees settle down to stay." Cuban refugees were "industrious, hard working, possessed of a trait historically admired by Americans—the desire to get ahead"—and willing to sacrifice. Greene told the story of Ruben Cruz, who owned a furniture business in Cuba but worked as a busboy and waiter in Florida until he and his brother saved enough money to open a small electric-appliance business out of the back of a van. To buttress her point, Greene also highlighted the marked decreases in the number of Cuban welfare recipients, as well as the drop in government welfare expenditures.[34]

Gender roles were another aspect of refugee assimilation that the Cuban campaign, like the Hungarian publicity effort, addressed, although the former did so more obliquely and with a slightly different message than the latter. "Iowa, Si!" tellingly left unsaid whether Mrs. Rangel worked outside the home, an omission that gave the impression that her husband worked while she cared for their four children in their eight-room home. Greene, though, highlighted instances in which Cuban women worked outside the home. "A young pretty bride now works as a secretary in the daytime and helps her husband in a drug store at night." Likewise, Greene's readers met Mrs. Olga Rionda, who co-owned a bakery with three other refugees and worked seven days a week. The CRP, then, portrayed Cuban families as "traditional" family units in which the husband worked while the wife stayed at home with the children as well as families in which both spouses worked. While these portrayals were undoubtedly better received in a nation that was beginning publicly to reevaluate gender roles, the CRP's portrayal of women in and out of the home served another, more pressing purpose. In both cases, the activities of Cuban women reinforced the CRP's central contention that the refugees wanted to—and, in fact, did—avoid welfare and dependency. Thus, it was not large-scale cultural change like the 1960s women's movement, admittedly still in its infancy, that led to this varied picture of Cuban women, but the CRP's concern about welfare.

Greene's story, in addition to other parts of the *Miami Herald*'s coverage, also suggested that the adjustment had been far from seamless. Unlike "Iowa, Si!" Greene did not describe Cuban refugees as culturally assimilated. Instead of offering anecdotes about Cubans Americanizing their names, Greene described the development of a Cuban enclave in Miami that held fast to its cultural and social roots. It was a "Cuban colony," complete with "Cuban cafés," "bodegas for vegetables like yucca and malanga," restaurants "offering blacks beans and rice, or ropa vieja . . . or the malt drinks, or that bland custard flan." Cuban pop music could be heard on the radio, and the island's movie stars appeared on screen at local theaters. Greene summed up: "The Spanish signs in neon, the Latin music, the hot sun glaring on scrubbed cements, the little outdoor cafes serving tiny cups of coffee and guava pies—all proclaim Havana expatriated." Greene's description of unabashedly Cuban communities in Miami called into question the integration of Cubans into American life.[35]

STATUS NORMALIZATION FOR CUBAN REFUGEES IN 1966

The question of the integration and adaptation of Cuban refugees attracted congressional attention in 1966 when Congress moved to address and clarify the legal status of the newcomers. As parolees, the Cubans were not in danger of being deported, but neither were they permanent residents or citizens of the United States. Cuban refugees, as a result, rested in citizenship limbo. Status normalization, essentially an effort to move parolee toward permanent residence (or, eventually, U.S. citizenship), was not a new issue; Hungarians had their status normalized in 1958, and discussions about doing the same for Cubans began in the early 1960s. In 1965 the Johnson administration had indicated support for status adjustment, but refrained from pushing the issue with the battle for immigration reform ongoing. By 1966 that battle was over and the Johnson White House again addressed the status adjustment issue, but now with a new set of circumstances: a renewed refugee flow under the "Memorandum of Understanding" that saw thousands of Cubans entering the United States.[36]

The newly arriving Cubans further complicated the politics and policies behind status adjustment because Florida politicians and community leaders began voicing anew their concerns about the refugees' effects on Florida's economy and welfare net. Leaders in Florida's black community quickly emerged as some of the loudest critics. A member of the Congress of Racial Equality explained, "The Negroes plain don't like it—they are very much afraid that this is going to cost them jobs." The NAACP echoed these concerns about employment, and the Johnson administration understood them to be real. A White House aide working on the effects of Cuban newcomers on southern Florida's economy found that the unemployment rate for Cubans in Miami was 5 percent, but 13 percent for blacks. This disparity only intensified the black community's anger at the federal government's extensive funding for Cuban newcomers, and the relatively paltry aid received by African Americans. Occasionally, violence and scuffles broke out between blacks and Cubans on the streets, which only fueled rumors of larger, more violent confrontations. In the next major refugee crisis, the arrival of the Indochinese in the late 1970s, blacks would levy many of these same charges. In the short term, though, federal officials and the White House believed they needed to act. HEW secretary John Gardner told LBJ, "Even with our best efforts Miami is going to have problems with the Cuban refugees. . . . And if trouble comes, they will blame the Administration . . . but we'll be better off if we can point to sincere efforts to help." [37]

Thus, the Johnson administration pledged to increase aid to Florida and gave assurances that the state would benefit from economic development programs under the Public Works and Economic Development Act of 1965 and the Economic Opportunity Act of 1964. Moreover, the federal government made clear its intention to continue subsidizing local, municipal, and state programs that provided refugees with welfare, health care, and educational opportunities. But federal money and programs were not enough. Cubans, because they were not permanent residents, were not eligible for some of these programs, including particular sections of the Economic Opportunity Act. Likewise, they were banned from some jobs—from practicing as a doctor to being a barber—because state licensing requirements mandated that an applicant have permanent resident status. Government officials and private-sector resettlement experts concluded that status normalization, or the granting of permanent-residence status to Cuban parolees who had been in the United States for a certain amount of time, would ameliorate many of the problems plaguing the Cuban community and worrying Floridians. CRP officials hoped, moreover, that new economic opportunities afforded by permanent residency would keep Cubans off the dole and would expedite resettlement around the country. [38]

Congress passed the Cuban Status Adjustment Act of 1966 with relative ease. The debate lacked the histrionics of the Hungarian Adjustment Act and it failed to inspire the passions of the immigration reform movement that targeted national origins principles. Two main issues emerged. First, the Johnson administration, the State Department, and congressional advocates worried that status normalization might be misinterpreted as acceptance of a communist, Castro-led Cuba. Thus, status normalization supporters at the White House and Foggy Bottom, and on the Hill, consistently restated and reinforced the U.S.'s anticommunist, anti-Castro foreign policy. Second, law and policymakers resolved that Cuban parolees could count their time in the United States toward the mandatory five-year residency requirement that presaged citizenship. The final statute, then, was relatively straightforward. Cuban refugees who entered the United States after January 1, 1959 (as parolees or as visa overstays) could apply to be permanent residents, and eventually American citizens. Cubans were allowed to count up to thirty months of their time in the United States toward satisfying their five-year residency requirement for citizenship—and thus could become citizens in two and a half years.[39]

Status normalization, in the words of one of Senator Ted Kennedy's aides, would "lead them down the road toward citizenship." Status normalization advocates, then, stated unequivocally and repeatedly that Cubans, in the words of Mayor Thomas Dunn of Elizabeth, New Jersey, "are proud people—and make good Americans." Time and again, testimonials highlighted a mix of political and apolitical characteristics—work ethic, dedication to family, and opposition to communism—that Cubans brought to American communities. All of these qualities, of course, mirrored those that the CRP "sold" during its public-relations campaigns. Anticommunism did not emerge as a central and important factor during the status normalization debates, a clear contrast to the Hungarian deliberations of eight years earlier when the political allegiances of Hungarians were the key factor in proving that Hungarians would make good Americans. Instead, similar to the 1965 immigration-reform debates, most participants seemingly assumed the anticommunism of Cuban refugees.[40]

Status normalization offered Cubans the option of American citizenship, but it also raised another set of questions. From the onset of the Cuban flow, American officials had reassured refugees that they could return to the island should Castro fall. As an inducement to spur Cuban relocation away from Miami, the government even offered to pay for the return of Cubans to a post–Castro Cuba. Officials reiterated this promise throughout the mid-1960s, even as it became clear that Castro might be in power for longer than either the refugees or the U.S. government desired. But what should happen when Cuban refugees who had been granted permanent-residence status—or even citizenship—decided they wanted to return to a post–Castro Cuba? In other words, could the U.S. government allow Cubans to become citizens and, at the same time, endorse the right of these Cubans to return to the island? During the status adjustment debates, the answer clearly was yes.

Some observers failed to see any problem at all. The CRP's John Thomas noted that while refugees were "first and foremost . . . citizens of Cuba," they should be allowed to make a temporary "declaration of intent" that began the citizenship application process so that they qualified for particular jobs in certain states. Thomas, in other words, openly encouraged Cubans to play with the elastic nature of the procedures by which newcomers became citizens. William vanden Heuval of the International Rescue Committee estimated that 80 percent of those granted permanent residence likely would head back to Cuba if Castro was overthrown and accepted that Cubans might want both permanent resident status and a return to Cuba. Vanden Heuval correctly drew a distinction between permanent resident status and citizenship, noting that a refugee could live in the United States as a permanent resident without becoming a citizen, and without casting aside allegiance to Cuba. But vanden Heuvel's distinction between citizenship and permanent residence was a fine one, for surely a number of Cubans would take the final step into U.S. citizenship. What if those recently minted American citizens wanted to return to a post–Castro Cuba?[41]

American government officials stated clearly that they were comfortable with this arrangement. Undersecretary of State George Ball said of Cuban refugees, "They want to go back to Cuba. They want to rebuild their country and they will do so when the opportunity—." Representative William T. Cahill (R-PA) cut Ball off and said, all this was true, then "why should we grant to these people American citizenship?" Ball's answer was simple: "In the meantimes, I think we should give them the option of being able to live in this land as good citizens of the United States even though some of them will ultimately return." Ball was not alone in endorsing U.S. citizenship for Cubans that did not require the newcomers to divest all loyalties and allegiances to their homeland. The restrictionist-leaning representative Frank Chelf essentially endorsed Ball's position, accepting that Cubans might renounce their newly granted American citizenship should the opportunity to return to Cuba present itself. "There are those who also thought that once they came and adopted our country or accepted American citizenship that maybe they would never go back, but I have never felt that way about it," he began. "The Cubans are a very proud people, a patriotic people, and I dare say if they thought there was a possibility—those good Cubans that are here now— of overthrowing Castro, the march would be on back to Cuba."[42]

It was a stunning formulation of American citizenship, one that failed to require absolute and unwavering allegiance to the United States. No other previous refugee or immigrant group had been granted—in such a

public forum—such leeway in defining their loyalties. This unique circum-
stance can be attributed in part to the peculiarities of the Cuban refugee
situation. The refugees' homeland lay only ninety miles away, the U.S.
government had pledged its opposition to Castro and hoped for his overthrow, and important segments of the Cuban community in the United
States fully believed that the collapse of Castro's government was forth-
coming. Each of these factors encouraged Cubans to see themselves as
exiles and temporary residents of the United States. In these ways, the
Cold War and Cuban-U.S. relations shaped Cuban refugee integration
into the United States and allowed for a peculiar definition of citizenship.
The clearest contrast surely lay with Hungarian refugees who—while
forced to flee from Soviet tanks, and admitted because such action served
foreign policy goals—had only the vaguest of hopes of a return home,
and received no such official encouragement. It was no small irony, either,
that for most Americans the Cold War and its politics demanded greater
allegiance to the nation, witness the Red Scare and the pressures on previous refugee and immigrant groups to Americanize. For Cubans, though,
the Cold War and its politics made possible publicly sanctioned dual citizenship and dual loyalties.[43]

Viewed from the perspective of domestic politics and culture, the ac-
knowledgment of dual loyalties seems less surprising, though. On a number of fronts in the mid- to late 1960s, Americans of different political
and cultural leanings began rethinking their ties to and membership in
the American nation. The most inflammatory example came from African
American leader Malcolm X who famously declared in 1964, "No, I'm
not an American. I'm one of the 22 million black people who are the
victims of Americanism." In urging blacks to recognize the naïveté of
the biracial civil rights movement's dreams of universal brotherhood
and the impossibility of whites ever treating blacks as equals, Malcolm X
demanded that African Americans direct their loyalties not toward the
"American dream" but toward a separate and distinct African American
community. Of course, this sentiment drew upon decades of black nationalism, but it attained new power in the civil rights era and would become
even more prevalent in the hands of Black Power advocates after 1966.
Malcolm X was not the only one to stretch the boundaries of national
identity in the 1960s. Less explosive, but perhaps just as controversial,
the Supreme Court's 1967 decision in *Afroyim v. Rusk* found that the
U.S. government, because of the Fourteenth Amendment, could not
strip an American citizen of his citizenship; the individual, instead, had
to take positive action to divest himself of his citizenship. The *Afroyim*
opinion, written by Justice Hugo Black and constructed largely as a defense of individual rights, opened the door for Americans to hold dual
citizenship. While neither radical black politics nor the landmark *Afroyim*

decision played a role in the passage of the Cuban Status Adjustment Act, all three taken together illuminate the ways in which public discussion of allegiance and loyalty among Americans (and applicants for citizenship) took new turns in the 1960s, a trend that would continue into the next decade.[44]

• • •

The admission of over half a million Cubans in the 1960s easily stood as the United States' largest and most sustained commitment to refugees in the post–World War II years. The American government's response to the Cuban refugee flow mixed old and new. Cubans may not have qualified strictly under the legal definition of "refugee" elaborated in 1957, but as self-styled (and American government–styled) victims and opponents of communism, they conformed quite well to the basic tenets of American refugee affairs established in the 1950s. At the same time, the CRP's publicity efforts resembled those of the 1957 Hungarian campaign as they reinforced in the public's mind a definition of refugee that stressed both political (anticommunism) and apolitical (industriousness and self-sufficiency) characteristics. But the American government's response to Cuban refugees showed how refugee policies and programs were in flux in the 1960s. The admissions process was more similar in style than substance to that of the 1950s. The housing and employment assurances mandated by law in the RRP (and by custom in the Hungarian Refugee Program) were absent from the Cuban program and while investigators certainly still inquired after the political histories and pasts of Cuban refugees, American government officials focused on blocking the entry of Castro's agents rather than barring admission to former communists or Castro supporters. The anticommunist political litmus test, then, continued to recede from its 1950s heyday, leaving open to debate its importance in the future and, indeed, the integrity of the barriers to entry faced by refugees. Likewise, the curious 1966 status normalization debates condoned divided loyalties among Cuban refugees applying for permanent residence and American citizenship, a remarkable but explainable departure from precedent. It remained to be seen how this would affect refugee programs—and debates about refugee policy—during the 1970s.

CHAPTER 6

"The Soul of Our Sense of Nationhood": Human Rights and Refugees in the 1970s

THE CUBAN REFUGEE flow dissipated in the early 1970s, but the United States soon confronted two new refugee problems: Soviet Jews seeking to emigrate to the United States and refugees fleeing Vietnam, Laos, and Cambodia. On the face of it, the decisions to admit Soviet Jews and the Indochinese look unsurprising. After all, both groups were fleeing communist states, which since 1953 had proven reason enough for entry into the United States. Their admission, though, was a departure because it disturbed the "refugee equals European, anti-communist" foundation of post–World War II American refugee policies. For the first time, the United States admitted substantial numbers of nonwhite refugees. Just as important, refugee advocates justified the entry of both groups not only by referring to the refugees' anticommunist bona fides or by describing them as victims of communism, but, more prominently, by claiming that admissions protected and upheld human rights principles. The rise of human rights principles in refugee affairs was largely the work of members of Congress, who, for the first time since the early 1950s, returned with vigor to refugee policymaking.

A combination of events at home and abroad brought new attention to human rights concerns and principles in 1970s America. Domestically, the continued reorientation of American identity in the aftermath of the political, social, and cultural upheavals of the 1960s resonated with the universal and individualized precepts inherent in "human rights" and opened up intellectual space in American political culture for human rights politics to take hold. It was no accident, then, that some of the most forthright advocates of centering the American commitment to refugees around human rights principles were veterans of the black civil rights and feminist movements. Debates about America's role in the world were even more vital to the ascendancy of human rights. The political and cultural liberal left argued that in the wake of Vietnam and the destruction of the Cold War anticommunist consensus human rights ought to guide American foreign policy. Meanwhile, a subset of conservatives, the neoconservatives, saw human rights principles as a vehicle to discredit détente and to reinvigorate a muscular, confrontational anti-Soviet foreign policy. These different agendas helped produce some common ground: larger refugee admissions based on the protection and promotion of human rights. Both the liberal left and the neocons (with some exceptions for those on the right) believed that refugee admissions would strengthen their larger efforts to recast American foreign policy. The strange alliance strengthened the American commitment to refugees, human rights, and the latter's effect upon the former, even though the left and right had vastly different foreign policy agendas.

Admissions procedures in 1970s refugee programs also evolved, though not in entirely new directions. The 1975 Indochinese refugee program, which offers the best insight into the "on the ground" workings of 1970s refugee programs, saw diminishing enforcement of both the anticommunist political litmus test and, especially, the security check for "subversives"—hardly a surprise given the development of admissions procedures since the 1950s. More surprising, but consonant with the times, congressional liberals in 1975 reformed the admissions process to reflect human rights concerns. To win entry, refugees signed a pledge that they had never persecuted another person on the grounds of race, religion, ethnicity, or political persuasion; violation of this codicil could lead to exclusion. This reform amounted to a litmus test of a sort, though one not nearly as powerful (or restrictive) as the anticommunist benchmarks established by an earlier generation. During the 1970s, then, the advances and limitations of the human rights movement in the United States became very clear, especially in refugee affairs.

The Reemergence of Human Rights in the United States

World War II and its aftermath brought human rights concerns to the fore in both American and international politics. President Roosevelt consistently framed American participation in the war as an attempt to protect human rights. In the immediate postwar years, human rights concepts received concerted international attention via the United Nation's Human Rights Commission, which in 1948 produced the Universal Declaration of Human Rights (UDHR). The UDHR, the founding document of the modern human rights movement, enumerated a remarkable list of political, economic, social, and cultural rights that belonged to all humans "without distinction." The postwar human rights revolution withered, though, largely because of the Cold War. In international politics, the two superpowers increasingly ignored the UDHR's principles. American foreign policy in the early Cold War centered not on human rights, but on geopolitics, anticommunism, and the strategy of containment. The rising tide of domestic anticommunism and Cold War political culture, meanwhile, nearly buried human rights politics domestically. In 1949, indicative of how the era's anticommunism delegitimated certain ideological and political options, the president of the American Bar Association derided the UDHR as a "pink paper" that would "promote state socialism, if not communism, throughout the world." Yet, human rights principles did survive, if not flourish, in some of the efforts of African Americans to win full civil rights in the late 1940s and early 1950s.[1]

In the early 1970s, after nearly two decades of hibernation, human rights reemerged fully in the United States. The era's domestic politics and culture, as compared to the late 1940s, were much friendlier to human rights principles. The political and social revolutions of the 1960s accorded new legitimacy and power to the protection of individual rights, ultimately reshaping American identity around these principles. By the 1970s the effects of this transformation were clear. The feminist, environmental, and gay-rights movements all grew in this fertile, rights-revolution milieu—as did a human rights movement that stressed the political, legal, and social rights of the individual. The rise of multiculturalism—and its effects on American identity—also helped human rights find a place in American political culture. On the political and cultural left, multiculturalists rejected constructing American identity around traditional "American" political or civic ideals and instead suggested that group identity could be constructed out of more particular stuff like cultural or ethnic traditions or universal (rather than "American") political ideals. Multiculturalists embraced a number of approaches, but their key precepts were that American identity was not as rigidly defined or conceived as it had been in the 1950s and early 1960s and that it could be re-imagined outside the physical (and intellectual) borders of the United States. In this intellectual ferment, human rights concerns, which were necessarily universal and transnational, could find a place.[2]

The Vietnam War and the Nixon administration's foreign policies proved even more important to the reemergence of human rights. The Vietnam War's critics, who grew substantially after 1968, found the war's conduct and the U.S. government's support for a series of corrupt and abusive South Vietnamese leaders morally repugnant. For instance, the 1971 disclosure of Operation Phoenix, a program in which the CIA partnered with South Vietnamese forces to eliminate the Vietcong by abducting (and then jailing in horrible conditions) or assassinating them, poignantly symbolized the war's appalling immorality. Many of the war's opponents turned to human rights principles as a necessary antidote. More important, America's failure in Vietnam—and the domestic discontent it fomented—brought an end to the anticommunist consensus that had guided American foreign policy since the late 1940s. In this vacuum, human rights were given a new hearing.[3]

Concurrent with, and in part because of the growing public dissatisfaction with the American role in Vietnam, the Nixon administration embraced new foreign policy approaches. With their détente strategy, President Nixon and Secretary of State Henry Kissinger looked to manage relations with the Soviet Union—and lessen superpower tensions—in an era when the U.S. fortunes in the Cold War had declined. Nixon and Kissinger hoped to regain the diplomatic initiative and advantage by negotiating with the Soviets on a variety of military and economic issues, including arms control, trade, and technology transfers; by strengthening U.S. alliances with western Europe; and by building ties to China. An unstated but clearly understood rule of détente was that neither the Soviets nor the Americans would interfere in the other's internal affairs. Another part of the Nixon administration's plan to reverse America's Cold War slide centered on enlisting the support of "Third World" governments who were vigorously anticommunist and pro-American. This policy often found the United States allied with brutal right-wing dictators who ruled their countries with both iron wills and fists. In Chile, for instance, the Nixon administration (and the CIA) helped undermine the democratically elected socialist president Salvador Allende and cheered his overthrow by the anticommunist rightist general Augusto Pinochet, who inaugurated a military dictatorship. In both the détente and "Third World" initiatives, U.S. foreign policy ignored the domestic abuses of its allies (like Pinochet) and its adversaries (the Soviet regime). Nixon and Kissinger (and later President Ford) did make nods toward human rights. The climax of this effort was the 1975 Helsinki Accords, which contained a "basket" that highlighted some human rights issues, allowing Ford and Kissinger to claim that they had called the U.S.S.R. to account on human rights. On the whole, though, they viewed the promotion of human rights as secondary to accruing advantages in geopolitics.[4]

In a unique political moment, both the American left and right hammered the Nixon administration's foreign policies. Critics on the left—including opinion journals like the *Nation* and the *New Republic* and influential liberal Democrats like Senator Edward Kennedy and Congressman Donald Fraser—cited both the conduct of the wars in Southeast Asia and the cozy relations with right-wing dictators like Pinochet when they declared Nixon's foreign policy morally bankrupt. Kennedy and Fraser, two of the administration's strongest critics, downplayed the Soviet and communist threats and feared a return to the geopolitics of the early Cold War. They instead wanted U.S. foreign policy to stress international cooperation (through the United Nations); to work vigorously to help the world's needy; and to identify, criticize, and punish human rights violations committed by American allies and foes. Kennedy, Fraser, and their allies insisted that the rights enumerated in the UDHR were worth defending and integrating into U.S. policies. To make this point, Fraser held a series of high-profile congressional hearings in which he—often with Kennedy testifying as a witness—examined the ways in which 1970s foreign policy failed to reflect human rights principles. Following Fraser and Kennedy's lead, and fearing that the Nixon and Ford White Houses had little interest in human rights, Congress passed a series of laws that essentially required the State Department to report on human rights abuses around the world; the first of these reports appeared in 1978 (and they continue today). Through hearings and the reports, human rights issues gained both valuable publicity and an institutional and bureaucratic foothold.[5]

Congressional human rights activism, and the attendant direct and forceful critiques of the White House, was part and parcel of the larger liberal-left agenda. In addition to rethinking American foreign policy, 1970s liberals wanted to expand government welfare programs, solidify and extend the political and legal gains of the rights revolution, and cleanse American politics of corruption. Kennedy and Fraser were leaders in these efforts, but they were also anomalies, having entered Congress in 1962 and 1963, respectively. Their allies, and the main source of support for these initiatives, came from a new generation of influential liberals who entered office in 1972 and 1974 (the famed "Watergate Babies") as part of a broad reaction against the Vietnam War and Nixon's administration.[6]

This liberal coalition believed, in part, that the road to their policy agenda lay in the institutional reform of both Congress and the presidency. Congress, in their view, had become sclerotic. As the historian Julian Zelizer has detailed, younger, more aggressive congressional liberals pushed to reform Congress itself, especially its committee structures, to combat the power of entrenched and more conservative older members—most of whom were Democrats—who stalled the newcomers' agenda. The liberal left also set its sights on the power of the presidency, which it believed (in the famous words of the scholar Arthur Schlesinger, Jr.) had achieved "imperial" powers in the decades after World War II. With the immense powers of the office, presidents (from both parties) had slowed or halted domestic reform and led the country into horrible and deadly foreign policy quagmires like Vietnam. The revelations concerning Watergate only cemented the belief that the White House had to be reined in and that Congress needed a more aggressive role in policymaking. Partisan discord sharpened these struggles over executive power in the first half of the 1970s; young liberal Democrats were, in perhaps a bit of understatement, very angry with Republicans like Nixon, Ford, and Kissinger over Watergate and the endgame in Vietnam. Their anger, moreover, had the distinct electoral advantage of firing up their constituents, who were just as disgusted with those signal events of the early 1970s.[7]

Congress took several steps to roll back presidential power. With the 1974 Congressional Budget and Impoundment Control Act, Congress both weakened the president's hand in fiscal policy (by requiring him to win congressional approval for any budgetary impoundment) and strengthened its own hand on such issues (by creating institutional mechanisms that increased Capitol Hill's ability to oversee the budget). Likewise, the War Powers Resolution of 1973 and the 1972 Case Act curbed the White House's foreign policymaking powers. Kennedy's and Fraser's human rights activism was of the same ilk. At a very basic level, the human rights agenda allowed congressional liberals like Fraser and Kennedy to make crystal clear their political and policy differences with the White House. Likewise, pressing for human rights required increased congressional oversight of foreign policy, the domain of the chief executive in the post–World War II era, and demanded that the White House heed Congress's policy priorities. Refugee affairs, as we shall see, over the 1970s became increasingly intertwined with, and a vehicle for, human rights issues for the liberal left. Refugee affairs therefore also emerged as a way to protest the larger direction of American foreign policy, to hopefully curb the power of the White House, and to draw attention to the fresh politics and policies embraced by the new generation of liberals in Congress.

A small but growing faction of conservatives, called the neoconservatives, joined the denunciation of Nixon and Kissinger. Neoconservatives came of age politically in the 1930s as socialists and then transferred their support in the 1940s to the Democratic party's liberal principles and aggressive anticommunist foreign policy. By the late 1960s and early 1970s, neoconservatives had rejected the Democrats' embrace of Great Society liberalism and drift away from vigorous anticommunism. Some of these neocons left the Democratic party completely, though others retained their long-time party affiliation while pushing their agenda. Neocons, though, found little to like in Nixon's foreign policy either. They despised what they saw as Nixon and Kissinger's excessively conciliatory search for détente with the Soviet Union. Neocons charged that Nixonian diplomacy too often condoned, rather than condemned, Soviet actions and ideology, thereby legitimizing communism and Soviet power. They asserted that a reinvigorated, muscular anticommunism should rest at the core of U.S. foreign policy toward the Soviets, with confrontation replacing negotiation. As such, neocons wanted American leaders to publicly condemn the Soviet Union's human rights abuses. Neocons, as a result, not only sparred with the Nixon administration, but also with Democrats like Kennedy and Fraser who saw human rights as a path away from Cold War anticommunism. Instead, neocons blended Cold War anticommunism and anti-Soviet foreign policy with human rights principles—although the latter were subservient to the former. Thus, rather than praise the 1975 Helsinki Accords as a human rights victory, the neoconservatives rejected the Accords as a concession to Soviet control of eastern Europe and totalitarianism in the Soviet Union. In the coming decades, as the Soviet Union and its empire of vassal states collapsed, Soviet and eastern European opponents of the Kremlin's rule pointed to the Accords, and specifically their human rights considerations, as a turning point that legitimated and energized the opposition behind the Iron Curtain.[8]

The reemergence of human rights in the 1970s among elite politicians, policymakers, and ideologues paralleled what historian Ken Cmiel called "a phenomenal burst of human rights activism" among grassroots organizations. The U.S. branch of Amnesty International (AIUSA) best exemplified the growth of grassroots activism. After nearly going bankrupt shortly after its formation in 1965, AIUSA grew from 6,000 members in 1970 to 35,000 members in 1976. In those same years, a staff of one grew to fourteen, and offices opened in New York City, Chicago, San Francisco, and Washington, D.C. Most important, AIUSA's work became well known to thousands of Americans who contributed to its letter-writing campaigns that aimed to free "prisoners of conscience." AIUSA had much more in common politically and ideologically with Kennedy and Fraser than it did with neocons. Pressing human rights cases against state-sponsored repression, they had few qualms about taking on allies of the U.S. government as well as working for the victims of communist oppression. Over the next two decades, Human Rights Watch and the Lawyers Committee for Human Rights, formed in 1975 and 1978, respectively, would grow to rival AIUSA's influence. Older organizations, like the bipartisan Freedom House, turned their attention more fully to human rights. Founded in the early 1940s with the mission of combating fascism and Nazism, Freedom House switched its energies to promoting black civil rights and combating communism in the 1950s. By the 1970s it was tracking global human rights abuses and persecution based on religious beliefs. It continued that work in the 1980s and 1990s, but with closer association with, and support from, conservatives.[9]

Just how popular were human rights principles by the mid-1970s? Ken Cmiel's comparison of the human rights movement to the feminist, gay-rights, and environmental movements seems appropriate. These movements were popular and fast growing in the 1970s, to be sure, but they never captured the support of a majority of Americans. Feminists, for instance, suffered a shattering defeat with the failure of the Equal Rights Amendment, while the gay-rights movement never came close to achieving mainstream acceptance. Likewise, Amnesty International had only 35,000 members in a nation of over 200 million citizens. But human rights organizations like AIUSA did grow phenomenally during the 1970s and even laid the ground for other organizations to join the cause. Moreover, because of Amnesty's letter-writing campaigns, human rights came to the attention of more than just the group's members. Politicians like Kennedy, Fraser, and the neocons (and later Senator Henry "Scoop" Jackson and President Jimmy Carter) saw human rights principles not only as good policy, but as effective politics. Thus, the very apparent limitations of human rights politics should not obscure the larger picture: by the early 1970s, human rights was back on the political agenda.[10]

Human Rights and Refugees: Soviet Jews and Chileans

The two most prominent refugee crises of the early 1970s—Jews fleeing the Soviet Union and Chileans hoping to escape the Pinochet government—illustrate the ascendancy of human rights concerns in refugee affairs. In the 1960s and 1970s, the Kremlin toughened its long-standing policies restricting the rights of Jews to emigrate. The Soviet government denied departure to so many Jews—and so many others were discriminated against by other Soviet citizens just for wanting to leave—that they earned their own moniker, the refuseniks. American Jews—well organized in a variety of interest groups, growing in political power, and increasingly concerned about maintaining Jewish identity—deemed such discrimination unacceptable and worked tirelessly to expose it and push for change. Moreover, because Jews were a key part of the Democratic party's electoral coalition, they instantly gained the attention of certain politicians and policymakers. Though their protests had little political impact in the late 1960s, by the early 1970s, a growing number of politicians from across the ideological and partisan spectrum picked up the cause. Jewish groups and their political allies urged the Nixon administration to forcefully pressure the Soviets to ease Jewish emigration and to facilitate entry of the refuseniks to the United States. Democratic representative Ed Koch stated in 1971 that the United States "should extend the same kind of humanitarian compassion and opportunity to these Jews" as it did for Hungarians and Cubans in previous decades, revealing that the Jewish emigration issue was conceived as a refugee problem. The Nixon administration instead utilized quiet diplomacy to encourage the Soviet Union to relax its emigration stance, a tactic that may have contributed to the Soviet decision in 1972 to allow 35,000 Jews to depart. But the Administration's efforts were muted; it clearly wanted to avoid risking its carefully crafted détente with the Soviets by publicly getting behind Jewish emigration.[11]

Discreet diplomacy became more difficult to pursue in late 1972 after the Soviets imposed further restrictions on Jewish emigration. Senator

Henry "Scoop" Jackson, a conservative Democrat from Washington with an eye on a 1976 presidential run, responded by attempting to link Soviet emigration policies to pending legislation that formally embodied the trade agreements reached at the May 1972 American-Soviet summit. Specifically, Jackson crafted an amendment that tied Soviet access to American trade credits to the liberalization of the Soviet Union's emigration policies. If Jackson had his way, neither the Soviets nor Nixon would get their trade agreement unless the Kremlin allowed Jews to emigrate. Jackson's gambit quickly picked up major congressional support—and equal amounts of disdain from the Nixon administration. In 1973 the trade bill, complete with Jackson's amendment, passed the House by overwhelming numbers, forcing both the Soviets and the Nixon White House to accommodate the senator. In 1974 Jackson, the Nixon (and then Ford) administrations, and the Soviet government engaged in complex negotiations that resulted in the Soviet Union's offering a general endorsement of its citizens' right to emigrate. Jackson boisterously declared victory and announced that sixty thousand Jews would be allowed to leave the Soviet Union annually (which only angered the Soviets, who had made no such commitment). Jackson's triumph was short-lived. In December 1975 the Soviets withdrew from the trade agreement, citing the onerous obligations implicit in Jackson's amendment. Soviet Jewish emigration peaked in 1973 at 35,000 and continued a steady downturn: 21,000 in 1974; 13,000 in 1975; and 14,000 in 1976. In sum, about 30,000 of those emigrating Soviet Jews came to the United States during the entire decade.[12]

The most striking aspect of this episode was the prominence of human rights principles. Even before Jackson began his crusade, defenders of Soviet Jews framed the Kremlin's emigration policies as a human rights issue. In 1971 a representative from one Jewish organization asserted, "we say that every Jew who wants to leave the Soviet Union must have the right to leave. This is his inalienable right. It is a very elementary right he must be able to exercise." That same year, Representative Jack Kemp (R-NY), who would embrace the neocon agenda in the 1980s, simply declared, "It is a human rights issue," while Rep. John Anderson (R-IL) noted that "30,000 human beings . . . are being denied basic human rights and freedom to emigrate to lands where these rights would be honored." Jackson, though, pushed these arguments most aggressively, as human rights concepts colored almost of all his attacks on the Soviets and his exhortations in favor of admitting Soviet Jews. He hailed his amendment as a chance to "advance the cause of human rights . . . to reaffirm on the part of the American people the commitment to individual liberty . . . to bring the blessings of liberty to those who have asked only for the chance to find freedom in a new land." At other times, "I simply say that after a lapse of twenty-five years, it is high time they implement the Universal Declaration of Human Rights. . . . It says, among other things, that a person shall have the right to leave a country freely."[13]

With the question of Soviet Jewish emigration, human rights entered refugee politics with full force. But not all human rights talk flowed from the same sources. Jackson had strong neocon leanings and he increasingly found himself marginalized among Democrats when his foreign policy views seemed more in tune with the "Cold Warriors" of the Truman administration than post–Vietnam War Democrats. Jackson too rejected the policies of détente that marked Nixon's diplomacy and generally believed that strength and confrontation—rather than negotiation and accommodation—were the only ways to deal with the Soviets. In this larger ideological framework, Jackson's declarations that the United States had to protect the human rights of Soviet Jewish refugees were understandable: a generous American refugee policy was another weapon in the Cold War against the Soviet Union, and human rights were a bludgeon to use against both Nixon and the Soviets. Of course, this stance put Jackson at odds with some of his allies who advocated human rights for different reasons. Kennedy, Fraser, and liberal opinion-makers like the *New Republic* and the *Nation* got behind the Jewish emigration issue in large part because it fit the liberal left's embrace of human rights as a foundation for a post–Vietnam, post-anticommunist American foreign policy. (To be sure, Kennedy, Fraser, and Jackson all understood the importance of Jewish Americans to the Democratic party and no doubt appreciated the potential electoral gains.) Amnesty International supported Soviet Jews as part of its larger campaign to free political prisoners, regardless of their political views or geopolitical value, around the globe. But Amnesty understood the Cold War context of the Soviet Jewish issue; its legal officer perceptively noted in 1973 that "Because the human rights problems here [*the Soviet Union*] have been exploited for cold-war purposes in the West," it was even more difficult to work with the Kremlin on the issue of political prisoners.[14]

The disjuncture between human rights and refugee advocates on the liberal left and those on the conservative right emerged most clearly in the American response to refugees looking to depart Chile after the 1973 coup. Pinochet's new government launched a campaign of terror (jailings, torture, mass incarcerations, and murders) directed against Allende supporters, both Chileans and exiles from neighboring countries whom Allende had invited to Chile to escape persecution in their own countries. Estimates vary, but, at the least, thousands of Chileans and foreign nationals hoped to escape Pinochet's persecution. In the coup's aftermath, Latin American and European countries worked with international organizations, especially the United Nations High Commission for Refugees, to secure safe passage and asylum for Chileans and other foreign nationals. The Nixon administration did nothing to help. Instead, it looked to stabilize the Pinochet government and normalize U.S.-Chilean relations. Only belatedly, in June 1975, did the Ford administration set up a small parole program—aiming to process four hundred cases—for Chilean refugees.[15]

The stalled American response, though, was not for a lack of effort on the part of liberals like Kennedy and human rights organizations like Amnesty International. A few weeks after the coup, Kennedy held hearings to call attention to the Pinochet government's human rights abuses and to urge the United States to respond by denying military aid to Chile. Kennedy asserted, "There is little doubt that Chileans and foreign residents alike have suffered . . . the gross violation of their human rights"— resulting in a growing refugee problem. Kennedy wanted the United States to open its doors "to a reasonable number of political refugees from Chile," noting, "We have done this time and again . . . and there is no reason why we cannot do it at the present time." Kennedy and his allies repeated this refrain throughout the mid-1970s, with remarkably little success until the 1975 parole program. They were not joined, though, by the neoconservatives whose support for human rights and refugee admissions stopped when it came to calling anticommunist, pro-American rightist dictators to account. Indeed, the CIA in 1973 asked Senator Jackson to block Senate investigations into the agency's role in the coup. The conservative (rather than neoconservative) *National Review*—while repeatedly blasting the Kremlin's human rights abuses and calling for a U.S. refugee program that admitted Soviet Jews—ridiculed critiques of the Pinochet government, downplayed evidence of its human rights violations, and said nothing about an American commitment to refugees fleeing Chile.[16]

The Soviet and Chilean refugee problems confirmed an important trend. The human rights revolution in refugee affairs—like the evolution of refugee policies in the 1950s and 1960s—resulted from a combination of foreign policy and domestic political and cultural concerns. Both episodes also heralded something new. First, the human rights arguments from the liberal left amounted to a serious attempt to move refugee politics away from its Cold War origins. This was, by 1975, only partly successful, unsurprising given the neoconservatives' embrace of human rights as another tool in the Cold War. Yet, new ideological territory had been reached and new powerful arguments held sway. Second, Congress, rather than the executive branch, was central to the rise of human rights in refugee affairs. This activism began to reverse the preceding nearly two decades of refugee policymaking, which saw the executive branch, and especially the White House, dominate. Congress would continue to reassert its voice in refugee policymaking through the second half of the 1970s.

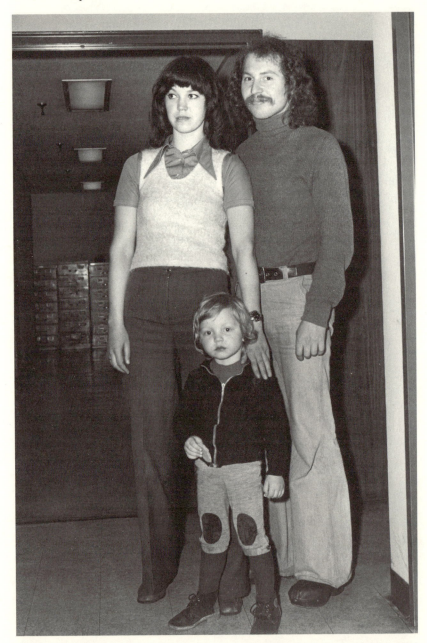

Figure 6.1 The International Rescue Committee helped resettle this Russian refugee family during the 1970s. Between 1970 and 1975, tens of thousands of Russian refugees came to the United States.

THE SAIGON EVACUATION

After 1975, American attention turned to the millions of refugees streaming out of Vietnam, Cambodia, and Laos, where new regimes consolidated their power in the aftermath of the region's colonial and postcolonial wars. The refugee problems largely broke into three phases. The first coincided with major American involvement in the Vietnam War, roughly from 1965 to 1975. The second ran from the fall of South Vietnam in May 1975 to the end of 1976, when the American government shut down its refugee relief operations aiding those who fled in the aftermath of Saigon's collapse. The final phase began in the middle of 1977 and lasted until the early 1980s, a period most remembered for the "boat people."

American involvement in the conflict between North Vietnam and South Vietnam—as well as U.S. military activities in Laos and Cambodia—helped displace millions. By 1971 the violence, political strife, and economic and cultural devastation wrought by the war had created over 6 million refugees in South Vietnam (since 1965); over 700,000 refugees in Laos (since 1962); and a smaller, but growing, refugee population in Cambodia. American policy toward these refugees eschewed mass admissions to the United States and instead focused on providing food and medical aid as well as material and financial resources to resettle refugees in their native countries. The American government viewed these tactics as humane and compassionate—and, more important, as consonant with a larger strategy to stabilize and reinforce American allies in the region. To have begun the wholesale resettlement of refugee populations in the United States would have been interpreted—by both the American public and allies in South Vietnam, Laos, and Cambodia—as a vote of no-confidence in the war effort.[17]

The American approach to the region's refugees changed completely with the fall of the South Vietnamese government in May 1975 and the complete pullout of American interests. But even as the South Vietnamese government teetered in early 1975, American officials and politicians hardly agreed upon a course of action. The Ford administration unsuccessfully lobbied Congress for further military aid that might stabilize the South Vietnamese government. The State Department's Indochina experts, meanwhile, already had begun to prepare for an American evacuation, although it was not until mid-April that upper-level State Department officials joined in these discussions. Here, though, was the genesis of an American commitment to Indochinese refugees. In addition to withdrawing nearly four thousand Americans from Saigon, the planning called for the United States to evacuate about eighteen thousand Vietnamese currently employed by the United States. Fears ran high in the State

Department that the new communist government might seek retribution against those Vietnamese with ties to the United States. Such concerns, of course, made it odd that the original planning failed to evacuate either former employees or the dependents of then current employees.[18]

In late April, with South Vietnam about to collapse, President Ford authorized the evacuation of up to 200,000 Vietnamese whom the Justice Department then would parole into the United States. By authorizing funds for the evacuation and resettlement with the 1975 Indochina Migration and Refugee Assistance Act, Congress essentially approved these large admissions, though it did not debate the numbers to be admitted. This larger commitment included fifty thousand spots for "high risk" Vietnamese, including then current and former employees of the U.S. government, "individuals with knowledge of sensitive U.S. intelligence operations," political leaders and intellectuals who might be targeted by the new regime, and "former communist defectors." The attorney general quickly expanded the "high risk" category to include employees of American firms and voluntary agencies operating in South Vietnam, as well as the rather poorly defined "participants in U.S. government sponsored programs." Beginning on April 21 and continuing into early May, the American military evacuated 65,000 Vietnamese. Another 65,000 managed to secure their own transport out of the country—often on boats— and the U.S. military took them into protective custody.[19]

In hindsight, the most amazing aspect of the 1975 Vietnamese refugee admissions might be that they occurred at all. The United States had no overarching foreign policy interests at stake in allowing Vietnamese refugees to enter the United States. The American public wanted nothing more than to wash its hands of Southeast Asia, and refugee admissions forestalled, even if for only a short time, that end. Several polls indicated that the majority of Americans did not support a large-scale program that would bring refugees to the United States. Part of this opposition surely was long-standing nativism, but some of it also flowed from the particularities of the Vietnamese refugee crisis. (One reporter traced the opposition to refugee admissions to "public misinformation," including the belief that the program would bring 3 million, rather than a few hundred thousand, Indochinese to the United States) Finally, unlike the Soviet Jewish–emigration issue, no ethnic groups lobbied relentlessly for refugee admissions. Ultimately, the impetus behind the admission of tens of thousands of Indochinese refugees was remarkably simple. The White House, Congress, the State Department, and the U.S. military felt a keen sense of responsibility and guilt toward those Vietnamese who had loyally supported the United States during the war, an obligation made more acute by fears that a retributive bloodbath might occur after South Vietnam's collapse. It was this sense of responsibility—felt strongest at the lower levels of the State Department and the military, but soon reaching to the highest levels of the political and military establishment—that forced action.[20]

The central political actors confronting the Vietnamese refugee problem defined "responsibility" in quite distinct manners, however. Senator Kennedy led the push for substantial refugee admissions in 1975. "We have no moral commitment to any army in Indochina . . . to this or that government, to this or that official or political faction," Kennedy said. "Our only true remaining moral obligations are with the people, to the millions of people in Indochina who cry for help." Kennedy believed that, "As never before, America shares in their crisis." A "moral" bond with those "who cry for help" defined Kennedy's conception of American responsibility, not U.S. foreign policy imperatives, past alliances, or a duty to aid victims of communism. On the other hand, foreign policy and political concerns were central to President Ford. As Ford pushed Congress in early 1975 to approve further military aid for South Vietnam, he stressed the American responsibility to uphold its political and military commitment to South Vietnam. With the fall of Saigon, such thinking colored Ford's understanding of American "responsibility" for refugees: America would fulfill its responsibility to South Vietnam not by sending military and economic aid but by accepting refugees. Reminding Americans of the Hungarians and Cubans, Ford declared, "Now, other refugees have fled from the Communist takeover in Vietnam. These refugees chose freedom. They do not ask that we be their keepers, but, only, for a time, that we be their helpers."[21]

Kennedy and Ford offered a clear contrast. Kennedy saw aid to Vietnamese refugees as based in a moral responsibility to alleviate suffering, a higher duty exclusive of aiding allies, of winning the Cold War, or of fighting communism. In doing so, he highlighted a sense of universal rights and obligations consonant with his belief in human rights. Ford saw American responsibility to refugees as an important part of the United States' political and military alliances and actions during the war. While Ford managed to avoid muscular anticommunism and Cold War jingoism, Vietnamese refugees, in his telling, were direct descendants of Hungarian and Cuban refugees; they were, then, equally the products of the Cold War, and thus deserving of American aid. In Ford and Kennedy's conceptions of responsibility, the two central justifications for an American commitment to refugees since the onset of the Cold War loomed large: refugees were victims of communism or of human rights abuses. But of course Vietnamese refugees were not the same as Hungarians or Cubans because they were not of European descent. The admission of Vietnamese refugees broke the decades'-old racial barriers in American refugee affairs. This occurred, all in all, without much fanfare. None of the political fireworks that accompanied the destruction of the national origins system in 1965 were present in 1975. An interesting historical parallel, however, was at work. In 1965 reformers argued that national origins quotas damaged the American effort in the Cold War and offended valued political and civic traditions recently reinvigorated by the civil rights movement. One decade later, similar rationales brought the first substantial group of non-European refugees to the United States, even if offered by rivals with distinctly different political and ideological outlooks.

THE BOAT PEOPLE

By the end of 1975, the American refugee operations precipitated by Saigon's fall had concluded, and both policymakers and the public believed that U.S. involvement in Indochinese refugee problems largely had ended. In fact, it had just begun. North Vietnam's triumph in spring 1975 was accompanied by the communist Pathet Lao's victory over the American-supported government of Laos and by the murderous Khmer Rouge's triumph in Cambodia. Over the next two years, tens of thousands of refugees fled (by foot and boat) from Vietnam, Laos, and Cambodia to Thailand, Malaysia, and Indonesia, each of which established huge refugee camps. The United States responded on several occasions by paroling several thousand refugees, some directly from the camps and others rescued at sea. All of these refugee admissions, though, were small in scope and believed to be part of a cleanup process connected to the 1975 admissions. By late 1977, however, that view began to change. State Department officials determined that this makeshift approach was ineffective as the refugee flows grew slightly in numbers and the camps showed no signs of shrinking. President Jimmy Carter, who had defeated Ford in 1976, ordered the State Department to devise a new policy within three broad guidelines: first priority in refugee admissions would go to those with family ties to the United States or those with needed skills (mimicking the priority system in immigration laws); refugee admissions should be large enough to take pressure off American allies like Thailand and Indonesia; the United States should not commit itself to a large, open-ended refugee program.[22]

In January 1978 Carter ordered the parole of 7,000 refugees. Three months later, he committed the United States to the entry of 25,000 refugees over the following year, although that program was not announced until June because of funding problems. In sum, though, these were minor paroles that hewed to Carter's earlier guidelines and helped him navigate a difficult political environment. Strong opposition to admissions existed in Congress and the general public. Congressman Joshua Eilberg (D-PA)—

who led the Immigration Subcommittee of the Judiciary Committee—loudly and consistently questioned the legality of the parole procedure, and the White House shied away from challenging him. Polling in late spring 1977 showed that 79 percent of Americans wanted immigration levels reduced or maintained at current levels. Finally, the Carter administration feared that arriving refugees would likely be unskilled workers, thus forcing working-class whites—an integral part of the Democratic electoral base—to compete with the newcomers in a generally unhealthy economy battered by unemployment and inflation.[23]

Carter's policies, though, were rendered completely ineffective when the refugee flow intensified in late 1978 in the face of three events. First, Vietnam invaded Cambodia, forcing Cambodian peasants to the Thai border in search of safety. Second, the Pathet Lao stepped up its extermination campaign directed against Laotians formerly allied with the United States. In total, 300,000 refugees fled from Cambodia and Laos, with 200,000 of them headed to Thailand, which already had camps totaling 150,000 refugees. Third, the refugee situation grew even more desperate as ethnic Chinese called the Hoa fled Vietnam because of increasing government persecution and inflamed anti-Hoa sentiment among the Vietnamese population. Evidence strongly suggests that the Vietnamese government began orchestrating the departure of the Hoa, in part to collect an emigration tax. While over 160,000 Hoa left for China, tens of thousands set sail in leaky crafts for Thailand, Malaysia, Indonesia, and even the Philippines and Japan. These were the boat people. In the last three months of 1978, nearly fifty thousand boat people arrived in different ports. Their numbers grew in 1979: 13,000 in March; 26,000 in April; 51,000 in May; and 56,000 in June. These figures accounted only for refugees who successfully made landfall and registered at refugee camps, not the estimated additional 25 percent to 50 percent who perished at sea. Worse still, many boat people who miraculously made it to land were turned away by government authorities already overloaded with refugees. The Thai and Malaysian governments' refusals to accept refugees had one more horrible consequence: ships that came across boat people were reluctant to rescue them for fear that they would not be allowed to come to port by the Thai or Malaysian governments who did not want to assume responsibility for the refugees. Boat people, then, were literally pushed back to sea.[24]

By 1979 an immense human tragedy had unfolded. The international community's response was paltry and ineffective. The Southeast Asian governments and international organizations that set up the sprawling refugee camps left them underfunded. Resettlement efforts, especially among industrialized nations, faltered almost from the very beginning. Between April 1975 and May 1979, Britain resettled 1,500 refugees; West

Figure 6.2 Leo Cherne of the International Rescue Committee took this aerial photo while touring refugee camps in southeast Asia in 1979. The sandy, white beaches and the pleasant palm trees belie the desperation of the boatpeople who inhabited the camp.

Germany admitted 3,000; and Canada 11,000. France and Australia, with totals of 50,000 and 20,000 respectively, stood out for their contributions. The United States tried to rally international action, with modest success. At the G-7 conference in Japan in June 1979, President Carter won concessions for increased funding for the U.N. High Commissioner for Refugee's budget for Indochinese refugee problems, as well as promises from the G-7 to step up resettlement efforts. (Carter's announcement that the United States would admit fourteen thousand refugees a month no doubt helped convince the international community to respond with greater efforts.) One month later, at a conference in Geneva, Switzerland, held under the auspices of the United Nations, the major industrialized nations agreed to set up new, better-provisioned refugee camps, to speed resettlement, and to actively rescue boat people in distress on the high seas.[25]

The United States' unilateral efforts to deal with the Indochinese refugee crisis, which easily outpaced those of other nations, began in earnest in the fall of 1978. In November the United States announced plans to admit another 21,000 refugees over the next six months. In April 1979, as the crisis intensified, the Carter administration planned to parole 7,000 refugees a month. Not three months later, Carter doubled the monthly parole number to 14,000. Within one year, the United States moved from admitting 2,000 parolees per month to 14,000 per month. By the end of 1980—the high point of the refugee influx that saw over 166,000 Indochinese enter—the United States had admitted, beginning with the Saigon evacuation, about 400,000 Indochinese. Admissions continued through the early 1980s, although they annually numbered in the tens, rather than hundreds, of thousands.[26]

The basis of the Carter administration's expansive commitment to the boat people, and the Indochinese languishing in the camps, lay in its belief that their suffering was unacceptable. Carter described this latest round of refugees as "a challenge to the conscience of the world" that required action. Secretary of State Cyrus Vance argued that "[w]hat we face in Southeast Asia is first and foremost a human tragedy of appalling proportions," while his deputy Richard Holbrooke asserted that "refugees are in flight from intolerable circumstances." In outlining their rationales behind the growing parole numbers, Carter and his administration always first presented the humanitarian reasoning. Quite simply, they saw refugee admissions—and U.S. leadership within the international community as the boat people crisis deepened—as protecting and promoting human rights.[27]

Such reasoning jibed with important parts of Carter's foreign policy, his personal politics, and his understanding of American identity. During the 1976 presidential campaign, Carter had vowed repeatedly to integrate human rights principles into American foreign policy. His commitment was sincere, personally held—and good politics in the mid-1970s. In office, Carter found execution of a human rights agenda difficult. Certain countries—like China, the Soviet Union, and Iran—proved too important strategically to risk offending them by criticizing their human rights violations. Others, like Cuba, Cambodia, and North Korea, could not be pressured by the United States, which did not have diplomatic or economic relations with these nations. Moreover, while Carter's chief foreign policy advisers battled ferociously over global strategy—National Security adviser Zbigniew Brzezinski argued that the Administration should focus on superpower relations and containment of the Soviet threat, while Secretary of State Cyrus Vance wanted to deemphasize such concerns, believing that not all regional conflicts and issues sprang from the Cold War—they both were ambivalent in regard to human rights. The National Security Council's and the State Department's bureaucracies divided over larger strategic question as well as whether to push human rights concerns aggressively. Thus, Carter experienced only mixed success in making human rights a centerpiece of U.S. foreign policy. In 1978 Carter began favoring the Brzezinksi approach, a trend that accelerated in 1979 as Soviet aggression in the Third World seemed to mount.[28]

Nonetheless, even as the Administration's human rights agenda experienced difficulties, the boat people crisis presented an opportunity on just that score. Addressing a meeting of human rights activists and organizations at a December 1978 White House ceremony commemorating the thirtieth anniversary of the signing of the Universal Declaration of Human Rights, Carter linked an American commitment to refugees to human rights. With the boat people crisis deepening, Carter declared, "Refugees are the living, homeless casualties of one very important failure on the part of the world to live by the principles of peace and human rights." "To help these refugees is a simple duty," Carter continued, one that meant aiding those fleeing from American friends (like Chile and South Africa) and foes (the Soviet Union and Cambodia), even if such aid angered those nations' governments. He concluded, "Human rights is the soul of our foreign policy. And I say this with assurance, because human rights is the soul of our sense of nationhood." In this remarkable statement, Carter crystallized the centrality of human rights to refugee affairs and indicated that the United States had a "simple duty" to refugees independent of the Cold War, of anticommunism, of Cold War alliances, or of geography. Most telling, he asserted that the protection of human rights was, at its base, part of the nation's very core. "Human rights is the soul of our sense of nationhood" was a long way from the ways in which both liberalizers and restrictionists during the early 1950s had injected anticommunism into their conceptions of national identity.[29]

Nongovernmental actors urging admissions and aid for the boat people also stressed the protection of human rights, the alleviation of misery and suffering, and the defense of individual lives. The liberal Catholic magazine *America* noted that helping the boat people would "recover the value of human life that too often seems to have been lost" while the Protestant weekly the *Christian Century* declared "The suffering of the boat people is an outrage to our common humanity." (In the late 1970s, Catholic and Protestant refugee-relief organizations remained mainstays of the refugee advocacy community and these publications supported their efforts.) The Citizens Commission on Indochinese Refugees (CCIR), which brought together a collection of refugee advocates from across the political spectrum—including the International Rescue Committee's Leo Cherne, African American activist Bayard Rustin, and conservative ideologue and future head of the CIA William Casey—was the most prominent advocate of admissions. Through the television and newspaper reports it encouraged and sometimes planted, the CCIR relayed in painful and frightening detail the life-threatening circumstances most boat people faced. One member of the IRC described the strategy: "Don't let them drown, is what I keep repeating."[30] Few encapsulated the argument that neglect of Indochinese refugees was a crime against humanity—or, in other words,

Figure 6.3 Hundreds of thousands of boatpeople languished in refugee camps throughout southeast Asia in the late 1970s, precipitating a massive humanitarian crisis. Refugee advocates, often citing human rights principles, argued that the United States had a responsibility to help end the suffering.

that something essential about the human condition was being violated in the waters off Vietnam as refugees perished in the face of the world's indifference—than a *Washington Post* editorial from June 1979:

> The world has got very good—very skilled and very adept, really—at spotting these great mass abuses of populations. But only from a distance of about 40 years. Up close its different. Then no one can see. . . . Thousands upon thousands more Indochinese are drifting around in flimsy boats to nowhere, starving, drowning. The thing about all this is not that its politically awkward or economically burdensome or diplomatically tricky. The thing about it is that it is happening—*now*, to real people. And the world—including and especially the world that could help—can't quite get the thing in focus.[31]

Foreign policy considerations of a more traditional sort also informed the boat people parole decisions of 1978 and 1979. Richard Holbrooke, the Carter administration's expert on Indochina, repeatedly asserted that the refugee problems of the late 1970s endangered regional "political and economic stability" and threatened American allies in ASEAN (the Association of South East Asian Nations, consisting of Thailand, the Philippines, Singapore, Malaysia, and Indonesia). Holbrooke especially worried that the Vietnam-Cambodia conflict, which had sent thousands of refugees to the relative safety of Thailand, might actually spill into that nation, the United States' strongest ally in the region and ASEAN's linchpin. For Holbrooke and his boss Vance, ASEAN was a mechanism by which the United States could protect its political and fast-developing economic interests in the region. Holbrooke's concerns about ASEAN reflected his and Vance's belief that U.S. foreign policy ought not to view all global challenges through the lens of the Cold War. Yet, in explaining American actions regarding the boat people, Holbrooke did address some Cold War concerns, though almost as an aside. Holbrooke noted with concern that the developing Soviet-Vietnamese alliance might exacerbate regional instability. While Holbrooke did not link Soviet activity in the region to the refugee crisis, he intimated that an American presence to alleviate the refugee crisis might serve as part (along with ASEAN) of an effective counterweight to the Soviets.[32]

More traditional Cold War–influenced arguments for refugee admissions also appeared in 1978 and 1979. President Carter and State Department officials with years of Southeast Asian experience believed that the United States had a special responsibility to help the boat people because of the United States' involvement in Indochina's wars over the previous three decades. The *New York Times* ("Our Vietnam Duty Is Not Over") and the *New Republic* ("Vietnamese and Cambodian refugees have the strongest possible claim on our compassion, since we are largely responsible for their plight"), among other supporters of admission, echoed this argument. Carter also described the boat people as both victims and opponents of communism, reasoning that had been employed since the early 1950s. Facing a hostile question from an Iowa community-college student in 1979, Carter described boat people as "persecuted by a Communist government in Vietnam, which has taken away from them their basic rights." Moreover, he asserted that the boat people were "more philosophically attuned to us than they are to the Communist regime that's taken over."[33]

This Cold War rhetoric heartened conservatives and neoconservatives, who supported boat people admissions. The *National Review* came out in favor of the admission of Indochinese refugees, as did the political commentator—and former Nixon-administration staffer—Patrick Buchanan, who urged a greater American role in solving the boat people crisis. Many of these conservatives chose not to employ even the language of human rights, and instead derided liberals for considering those principles as the source of America's commitment to refugees. The *National Review* abandoned any such "rights-talk," emphasizing instead the evils of communism that had made the Indochinese refugees. Buchanan mocked the human rights pretensions of President Carter while supporting the entry of the Indochinese: "And then Mr. Human Rights should bribe, pressure, cajole, threaten, urge our allies, clients, and friends to provide homes for these hundreds of thousands—as we ourselves have done and should continue to do." Buchanan wanted a continued American effort in refugee affairs because he believed it would reassert U.S. primacy in global politics generally and, in particular, demonstrate the flaccidity of the international community, especially the United Nations.[34]

Buchanan's, the *National Review*'s, and Carter's Cold War–influenced comments, though, were not representative of the larger debate surrounding admission of the boat people. The *Post* editorial, which did not mention that the Indochinese were fleeing a communist government and instead stressed saving lives, was more typical—and indicative of the way in which Cold War rationales that underpinned previous refugee programs had receded by the late 1970s. It was a process that began in the early 1970s and matured with the agony of the boat people. In 1953 Catholic refugee expert Bishop Edward Swanstrom justified U.S. intervention in the European refugee crisis by describing a "world . . . involved in an ideological struggle in which darkness and tyranny are fighting against freedom and human dignity." Times had changed and the new message was clear. The Catholic magazine *America* declared in 1978, "The human tragedy of the Indochinese refugees should transcend political or ideological conflicts." Indochinese refugees deserved help from the United States—and even admission—not because of their political beliefs, but because the United States had a duty to ameliorate human rights abuses like those taking place in Southeast Asia.[35]

"TOTAL CONFUSION EXISTS": ADMISSIONS STANDARDS FOR INDOCHINESE REFUGEES

The admissions process facing Indochinese refugees continued to evolve as well, in some ways reflecting the changing foundations of the American commitment to refugees. In 1975 Vietnamese were airlifted from South Vietnam or picked up at sea by the navy and brought to American-run refugee camps in Guam or the Philippines. At these sites, refugees interviewed with INS officials to determine their place in the preference system, underwent a series of security checks, submitted to a health check, and were matched with sponsoring agencies. Refugees then flew to the United States where they lived in one of four U.S.-government camps before resettlement. In the post-1977 parole programs, refugees largely undertook the same journey. At camps in Indonesia, Malaysia, and Thailand, State Department officials (assisted by representatives from the voluntary agencies) conducted preliminary interviews and screening to determine who was eligible under the appropriate parole policy. Eligible refugees then flew to the United States for resettlement. This simple route lengthened slightly in the summer of 1979 when the State Department opened "Refugee Reprocessing Centers" in the Philippines, Thailand, and Indonesia. At these centers, parolees learned English, were introduced to American social and cultural mores, and worked in mock jobs meant to introduce them to American work culture. Only after this forced assimilation were refugees resettled. This aspect of refugee resettlement points to lingering power of the assimilationist ideal in American life and governance, even in the 1970s when—as we shall later see—others made real efforts to promote a cultural-pluralist ethos.[36]

Before winning admission, Indochinese refugees needed to qualify under the preference system and satisfy a security check. Post-WWII refugee programs only sporadically had used preference systems, which gave priority entry to certain refugees. The Hungarian and Cuban programs essentially accepted all comers and did not employ preferences, but the RRP gave priority entry to refugees with skills needed in the United States and second priority to those with relatives in the United States. For Indochinese refugees, the preference system emerged as an obstacle to entry largely because the applicant pool was so large and the number of parole slots relatively small. In April 1975 the government developed its preference categories rather quickly and somewhat haphazardly. The Justice Department's initial instructions outlined three preference categories: 4,000 orphans; between 10,000 and 75,000 Vietnamese who were relatives of American citizens and permanent residents; and up to 50,000 "high risk" Vietnamese—a catchall meant to provide for the admission of Vietnamese who had closely supported the United States during the war. Officials in the field, however, soon reported that more than half the refugees under U.S. care—farmers, fishermen, small businesspeople, local police, and soldiers—did not fall into a preference category. To get these persons into the United States, the INS created a new category, called "other," for "men, women, and children without a country." The head of the INS, Leonard Chapman, explained, "The choice is to force them to return to the land they fled for fear of persecution, leave them at sea, or accept responsibility for them." Chapman's telling formulation revealed the assumption that all who wanted to leave Vietnam in 1975— including Vietnamese with little connection to the United States as well as those motivated by economic considerations—were fleeing persecution from the new government, no questions asked.[37]

The post-1977 parole programs were slightly more complex. They capped total admissions and often allotted those slots among different nationalities or between boat people and land refugees. In addition, the programs' preferences evolved over time. The 1976 parole of eleven thousand Vietnamese, Cambodian, and Laotians had three preference categories: relatives of U.S. citizens and permanent residents; former U.S. government employees in supervisory positions; and refugees "who worked closely with U.S. forces on U.S. missions," or who went to U.S. schools, or who possessed "personal accomplishments or eminence" that would benefit the United States. For the 1977 parole of fifteen thousand refugees, a fourth category was added for "refugees who do not fall within one of the preceding categories, but in whose case there are obvious compelling humanitarian reasons for parole." But in the 1977 parole, the preference system was only in place for land refugees; boat persons were exempt and admitted on a first-come, first-served basis. Subsequent paroles in 1978 and 1979 held to this system, with some slight adjustments.[38]

The preference systems—and specifically the determination of whether a refugee fell into a preference category—were vital to the admissions process. Matching a refugee to a preference category required State Department and INS officials to delve into an applicant's work and family history, as well as—for some refugees like intellectuals and defectors—political histories. It was a difficult task given the desire to resettle refugees quickly and because, as the ever widening preference list suggested, officials struggled to fit all refugees into a preference category. Congressional observers in 1975 took a cynical view of the admissions process: "Total confusion exists over the parole categories. . . . In a desperate attempt to expedite procession . . . INS officers are simply expanding the practical definition of "high risk" to fit almost anyone. . . . The parole categories mean little in practice, and it is doubtful ever meant much in theory, when they were first presented to the Judiciary Committees as *fait accomplis* on April."[39]

The categories, however, were not meaningless because they indicated once again the elastic nature of American refugee policy. The imperative of refugee admissions drove American officials, both in the field and in Washington, to reconfigure and sometimes create anew preferences that more accurately reflected those persons under American care. What did this mean for the definition of "refugee"? Many of those admitted after 1975—such as ex-officials of the South Vietnamese government or the pro-American governments that fell in Cambodia or Laos—certainly had a fear of persecution from the new regimes. Likewise, the ethnic Chinese who fled Vietnam claimed persecution at the hands of the Vietnamese government. Others—like the fishermen and street vendors who escaped in 1975—were likely not under an imminent threat of persecution. Rather, these refugees did not want to live under these new regimes and took the opportunity to leave; in this sense, they were quite similar to the Cuban refugees of the mid-1960s. As a result, the U.S. government in

1975 widened the "high risk" category to include all those "men, women, and children without a country" who could not return for fear of persecution, even though many of those persons had made themselves stateless—and made themselves targets of persecution should they return—by their act of escape. The preferences, then, reflected both the desire to admit refugees from Vietnam, no matter their circumstances, and the assumption that any person fleeing Vietnam was (or would be in the future) subject to persecution.

Notions of human rights also infiltrated the preference process. The development of the preference for persons who were refugees because of an "obvious compelling humanitarian reason" clearly acknowledged the importance of human rights principles to the idea of "refugee." This broad category—which allowed for the admission of boat people or land refugees in the late 1970s facing forcible repatriation to the killing fields of Laos, Cambodia, or Vietnam or being towed back to the high seas in questionable crafts—affirmed that refugee admissions targeted those whose human rights were in danger of violation. It also, more cynically, showed how those who ran the refugee program could use the universal principles inherent in human rights to their advantage in establishing a bureaucratic loophole that would admit more refugees.

The Indochinese refugee programs, like its predecessors, screened each applicant. The best evidence on the security checks that the Indochinese faced in the late 1970s comes from the 1975 evacuation of Saigon. Three broad categories of offenses could disqualify a refugee from admission: violations of social norms (polygamy, for instance); a criminal record; or offenses that were political in nature (being a communist) or endangered American national security. In the refugee camps in Guam and the Philippines, the INS began an investigation of all refugees over the age of seventeen, checking its own records and the files of the State Department, Defense Department, Central Intelligence Agency, Federal Bureau of Investigation, and the Drug Enforcement Agency. Refugees who were relatives of either American citizens or permanent residents could be brought to the United States before completion of a full screening, so long as it was completed after their arrival. Likewise, Vietnamese refugees who worked for the U.S. government and had already successfully cleared a security check were exempt from another investigation. If "derogatory information" came to light during these background checks, the INS allowed the applicant to respond to the charges. The INS in Washington then decided the applicant's fate.[40]

Many with knowledge of the investigation process found it burdensome. INS officials in the field could not handle the heavy workload and paperwork that accompanied each application—both made especially difficult by the need to request information from several government agencies. As one official at Eglin Air Force Base (one of four refugee resettlement centers in the United States) noted in a telegram, "FULLY UNDERSTAND AND SUPPORT NEED FOR SECURITY CHECK, BUT PLEAD FOR MAXIMUM EFFICIENCY, MINIMUM TURNAROUND." Voluntary agency officials meeting with President Ford's aides echoed this frustration, complaining about the "delays in out-processing refugees because of the lack of security clearances." Other observers found the screening processes troubling for precisely opposite reasons. Notes from a General Accounting Office (GAO) report on screening processes in Guam skeptically registered, "Little screening, per se. Ask for birth certificates, marriage licenses, ID cards, etc. If don't have, are processed anyway. . . . Supposedly check for 'undesirables' but few have surfaced. . . . Screening officers work through Vietnamese interpreters (refugee volunteers) who may not be translating properly. That is, would have Vietnamese interests at heart rather than U.S. interests." The GAO concluded, "INS has not identified any 'undesirables' and is ill-equipped to do so under the local, temporary conditions on Guam."[41]

The INS's statistics about the investigations offer another window onto the screening process. In May 1977, the INS reported that of the 130,000 refugees paroled into the United States after Saigon's fall in 1975, 60 percent underwent security checks (which represented all parolees who were over seventeen years old). Four thousand "hits" occurred, according to the INS, with 538 of those proving worthy of further investigation. Of those, 445 were deemed to have insufficient evidence to press charges. But five were found excludable by an immigration judge, four for criminal offenses, and one for subversion. Eight others were waiting to go before an immigration judge, five for criminal charges, one for polygamy, and two for subversion. This left eighty cases still under investigation: twenty-one for criminal offenses, one for polygamy, eighteen for drug violations, and forty for subversive activities.[42]

These statistics on security screening told several stories. Investigators clearly looked for criminals, drug dealers, and subversives (communists or persons who, once in the United States, might engage in activities detrimental to U.S. national security, like spying). They did not find many in the over 75,000 refugees they screened, given that only 4,000 (about 5 percent) warranted further scrutiny. Moreover, the INS cleared the vast majority of those 5 percent. Two possible conclusions suggest themselves: either the "hits" information was faulty—which was not outside the realm of possibility given how many "hits" were eventually cleared—or investigators were lax in pursuing leads, also a possibility given the enormous task of clearing tens of thousands of refugees in a short time. But just as clearly, when officials did launch a more in-depth screening, they were most interested in political affiliation or subversion. In the cases still pending in 1977, the largest category was "subversive," a trend substantiated repeatedly by previous INS reports on the 1975 admissions. But the most important conclusion to draw from the INS statistics and the contemporary observations was that security screening was not a deterrent to entry.[43]

The INS claimed its screening procedures protected against the entry of refugees who were communists or might pursue subversive political activities. Ambassador L. Dean Brown, the public face of his Administration's 1975 evacuation efforts, took several congressional questions about the possibility of "communist infiltration" via the refugee flow. Brown indicated that refugees were asked whether they were communists and he promised that the security check would prevent the entry of communists, noting of all refugees, "They will be checked. . . . No person will be admitted to the United States until there has been a security check through our own system." While some in Congress questioned Brown's confident assurances—wondering in one instance how effective immigration screening could be if it relied on the same techniques that "did not keep out some 30,000 people who were in the Communist security services, but who penetrated the entire Vietnam Government"—Capitol Hill seemed largely uninterested in the problem of subversion, the possible entry of communists, and the political backgrounds of the parolees.[44]

Human Rights and the Admissions Process

The 1975 refugee program did develop a new exclusionary principle: human rights abuses. The chief proponent of this change was Representative Liz Holtzman, a young liberal from New York City who well represented the new, reform-minded face of liberalism within the Democratic party in the early 1970s. Holtzman was a civil rights activist in the 1960s, a vocal member of the women's movement, and an ardent opponent of the Vietnam War. She challenged long-time refugee and immigrant advocate Manny Celler in the 1972 Democratic primary. Holtzman charged that Celler's long tenure, stretching back to the 1920s, left him out of touch with his constituents and in debt to powerful interests. Besides stressing her commitment to transparent governance, Holtzman blasted the octogenarian's support of the Vietnam War; his opposition to the Equal Rights Amendment; and his failure to push for consumer, education, and environmental legislation. The upstart Holtzman defeated Celler and won his seat in Congress.[45]

Holtzman quickly emerged as a Nixon critic, opponent of the Vietnam War, and—like Kennedy and Fraser—a supporter of reorienting U.S. foreign policy around human rights; a respect for human rights, according to Holtzman, was a necessary antidote to the barbarism brought on by the Vietnam War. From her seat on the House Immigration Subcommittee, she paid close attention to refugee issues. As the Indochinese refugee program got under way, Holtzman asked the INS and the Ford Administration if safeguards were in place to prevent the entry of Vietnamese who had misappropriated American funds during the war or were "responsible for running the tiger cages, or who were engaged in torture of political prisoners." Government officials admitted admissions policies and guidelines did not prevent the entry of individuals who engaged in these activities *and* had a clean criminal record. (The U.S. government could deny parole status to any refugee convicted of a crime.)[46]

Holtzman was not satisfied. She first pressed the INS to ask refugee applicants if they had tortured persons because of their political beliefs or if they had misappropriated American funds. The INS agreed to establish a "regulation" to exclude those who have committed "war crimes," but Holtzman insisted that all applicants sign an oath that they "had not engaged in any persecution or torture of anybody on account of political opinion or race, religion, national origin or the like." If information came to light that the applicant had lied about participating in such activities, then they would have committed perjury—and thus could see their parole application rejected or their parole revoked. Holtzman's pressure resulted in an italicized statement at the bottom of form G-646, which all parolee signed, requiring each refugee to sign an oath that read "Further, I have never ordered, assisted or otherwise participated in the persecution of any person because of race, religion, or political opinion." (Holtzman and the INS had agreed to drop the language about misappropriation of funds, making persecution the only focus of the statement.)[47]

Holtzman drew attacks for her efforts. Senate Republicans argued that the sworn statement was unprecedented and that pressing refugees, who "are in need of every bit of dignity and human kindness that can be afforded them at this stage of their disrupted lives," was "demeaning." One of the strongest denunciations came from the *Wall Street Journal*, which accused Holtzman (and liberals more generally) of "A Meanness of Spirit" and of racism for failing to extend American aid to all Indochinese refugees. Holtzman brushed aside such criticisms, believing higher principles were at stake. Holtzman's antitorture codicil in refugee admissions flowed from her belief that American foreign policy—and the United States itself—needed to reflect and respect human rights. At the center of Holtzman's objections to the entry of refugees with a history of persecuting others lay conceptions of American identity. Here, Holtzman's conceptions of "American-ness," like her views on U.S. foreign policy, jibed with the liberal left's attempts during the 1970s to ground national identity in universal, rights-based principles. Holtzman stated "[P]ersons who stole American funds or who operated the tiger cages or assassinated in "Operation Phoenix" are undesirable. . . . I would hope that there is some way in which we could see that they are not permanently part of this country, that they do not become eligible for permanent residence or citizenship." Holtzman added, "I do not want their lives jeopardized, but I believe we ought not to offer our country as a haven for these people." Holtzman was even more direct in responding to the *Journal*'s critiques: "I have on numerous occasions pointed out that America should not be a haven for Nazi war criminals. I believe, similarly, that we should not welcome people who have committed despicable acts of persecution in Vietnam." A respect for human rights, for Holtzman at least, was a necessary condition for entry into the United States as a refugee, and, indeed, for opening the door to become "American."[48]

Holtzman's push for a clause in the refugee admissions process that protected human rights signified the continuing human rights revolution in refugee affairs and Congress's determination to reassert itself in refugee policy. But the limitations of Holtzman's gambit were just as clear. Holtzman and the INS left unclear the mechanisms by which human rights abuses might be detected. If she wanted to prevent the entry of persons who had committed these types of offenses, she should have demanded that the INS actively pursue an investigation—complete with interrogations—similar to those launched by the RRP in its hunt for communists in the 1950s. The comparison with the RRP is apt. McCarran constructed, and McLeod oversaw, an admissions process geared toward establishing an anticommunist litmus test for refugees. Holtzman had no such success in bending the refugee admissions process to the principles of human rights. She never succeeded, it seems, in ensuring that a human rights codicil would be implemented in a rigorous manner. Given the importance of shaping how refugee programs "ran on the ground"— as the previous twenty-five years of refugee programs made clear—it was hardly surprising that by December 1975 no refugees were denied entry to the United States on the grounds that they falsified their oath regarding persecution.

BACKLASH

The Indochinese refugee admissions were never popular with the public. Polls between 1975 and 1977 consistently showed that the majority of Americans opposed the 'entry of refugees, making the Ford and Carter administrations' advocacy of various parole programs even more politically courageous and dangerous. While hostility was more intense in certain parts of the United States—California, for instance—it existed in all regions. As the boat people's agony deepened in 1978 and 1979, public opposition to admissions slightly lessened. In August 1979 only 32 percent of Americans surveyed wanted to see immigration laws relaxed to ease the admission of the boat people, compared to 57 percent who opposed such measures. At the same time, though, 47 percent of Americans claimed they would like to see boat people live in their communities, versus 40 percent who said they would not. While nativism, racism, and disgust with the Vietnam War contributed to the reaction, a sluggish economy marked by unemployment problems consistently fueled anti-refugee sentiment through the late 1970s. Moreover, cultural tensions between natives and newcomers rose after 1979, in large part because the boat people (as opposed to the Indochinese admitted in 1975) had poorer language skills and educations, as well as less familiarity with American customs.[49]

In 1975 two issues particularly highlighted the public's reticence about, and sometimes opposition to, the Indochinese arriving in the United States. First, part of the federal government's resettlement scheme matched each refugee family with an American sponsor who would help the newcomers adapt to their surroundings. In the months after the Saigon evacuation, the government struggled to find sponsors, which it attributed to a lack of support for refugee admissions. Second, members of Congress and state and local politicians worried that the social and economic burdens of resettlement would fall mainly upon state and local governments. Californians seemed most concerned, understandable given that the state quickly emerged as the primary destination for Indochinese refugees. Slightly more than 20 percent of the 1975 Indochinese resettled in California—and nearly one-third of the 1976–80 Indochinese refugees followed them. Welfare officials in California noted in September 1975 that more than half of the state's seventeen thousand Vietnamese refugees received a state welfare check, and they estimated that three-quarters of the state's refugees would by year's end. Californians worried as well that state schools could not cope with the influx of refugee children—or the strain they would put on California's education budget. As the rate of Indochinese resettlement in California accelerated in the late 1970s, so did the protests and concerns of elected officials and the general public. In this way, California's experience with the Indochinese mimicked Florida's reaction to the arrival of Cubans in the 1960s.[50]

The persistent opposition and developing backlash to the arrival of the Indochinese became the problem of two government agencies. First, the Interagency Task Force on Refugees (IATFR), formed in early May 1975 and headed by Julia V. Taft of HEW, oversaw and coordinated the various government agencies involved in Indochinese admissions and resettlement. Second, the President's Advisory Committee on Refugees (PACR), a committee of prominent Americans headed by former ambassador to Belgium John D. Eisenhower, focused on building public support for the Indochinese admissions and resettlement. PACR's efforts were clearly modeled on the citizens' commissions that Truman and Eisenhower had formed for the Displaced Persons program and Hungarian admissions, respectively. PACR and the IATFR's missions and tasks overlapped, producing debilitating tensions between Taft and Eisenhower that worsened through the spring and summer of 1975.[51]

PACR and the IATFR, like their predecessors during the Hungarian and Cuban refugee crises, understood the need to rally public opinion. PACR and IATFR wanted to encourage sponsorship offers from the public in the hopes that this would increase resettlement opportunities for refugees—and thus more quickly bring the program to a close. Political considerations drove the resettlement imperative and the desire to close the program. The Ford White House, and its contacts at PACR and IATFR, were concerned that the resettlement efforts, should they continue to lag, might harm Ford politically. PACR took the lead in establishing a publicity program. It discussed a series of television spots to promote resettlement with the Advertising Council—who had publicized the 1957 Hungarian Refugee Program—but determined that such a campaign would commence too late (September 1975) to be effective. PACR did reach an agreement in late June 1975 to hire Educational Systems Corporation (ESC), a Washington, D.C.-based firm, to lead the Indochinese publicity effort. The feud between the IATFR and PACR by that point had reached poisonous levels, and the former killed the ESC contract.[52]

The Indochinese refugee program's PR machine died prematurely, but ESC's proposals were still revelatory. ESC urged the development of a series of short television spots featuring famous Americans—President and Mrs. Ford, labor leader George Meany, and pop star John Denver—asking the public to extend a warm welcome to the Indochinese and to consider aiding in resettlement. ESC thought carefully about how to present the refugees to the public. It wanted to "focus . . . on the individuality of the refugees. . . . They will not be presented as a faceless, hopeless mass of people." The American people, according to ESC, needed to understand that the Indochinese were not so different from previous "political refugees" because these newcomers, as their predecessors, had "a positive attitude towards this country" and "democratic values." Moreover, ESC's proposals also had an intriguing cultural component. The company rejected portraying the Indochinese as fully embracing American cultural and social mores because "[A]lthough we pride ourselves on being a melting pot, observers of the American scene have increasingly commented on our ability to retain aspects of our heritage as a nation of immigrants." ESC continued, "This uniquely American knack for fashioning a coherent national identity, while preserving ethnicity, is a tremendous source of strength."[53]

The contrast with previous refugee-publicity campaigns could not have been clearer. While ESC's efforts to "sell" refugees to the American public never advanced past the planning stages—and thus never dealt with issues of gender relations or consumer culture as did the "selling" of Hungarian and Cuban refugees—the 1975 proposal did have distinct political and cultural components. ESC wanted Americans to know that the Indochinese believed in "democratic values" rather than merely portraying them as victims and opponents of communism. (To be sure, however, some watching the advertisements would have interpreted "democratic values" in an anticommunist light, but ESC's proposals did not make any effort to push viewers to this conclusion.) There would be no analogue of "From Hungary, New Americans" either. Being "American," ESC seemed to think, meant holding on to one's ethnic and cultural identity and celebrating diversity. Later publicity efforts regarding the boat people would utilize the same formulation. In a 1979 speech defending the admission of the boat people at a meeting of an Italian-American organization, President Carter asserted: "Whatever our race or religion or form of nationality, we have kept some of our original character, even as we've learned to live and to work together as Americans. We are not a melting pot. We are more like a pot of minestrone." ESC's PR plans, as well as Carter's speech, indicated the ways in which notions of American identity—both its political and cultural components—had been transformed by the mid-1970s.[54]

· · ·

The U.S. government's policies and programs that admitted Soviet Jewish refugees and Indochinese refugees in the 1970s disrupted the very foundation of post–World War II American refugee policies, the equation "refugee equals European anticommunist." Nowhere was this clearer than in the emergence—through the handiwork of members of Congress and an odd alliance of the left and right—of human rights concerns and principles in refugee politics and, to a lesser extent, in the admissions process. There were limits, though, to the changes that came in the 1970s. Of course, human rights principles did not vanquish Cold War rationales in refugee affairs. Rather, the two coexisted, sometimes uneasily. And while the American commitment to refugees may have expanded, that expansion was hard won, and the product of peculiar political circumstances. Finally, the persistent and widespread opposition to the entry of the Indochinese highlights that while refugee advocates had new and powerful arguments and a more conducive political and cultural environment in which to work, they had not cleared the field of refugee restrictionism. After all, if American identity had fully absorbed the substance of the rights revolution, then refugee restrictionism, it stands to reason, would not have been so powerful. Likewise, opposition to refugee admissions highlights the failure of human rights to fully dent the American political consciousness (or "soul," to use Carter's term) in the late 1970s. If Americans had fully embraced the politics of human rights, they would have opened their arms widely to receive the boat people, for there were surely no more pitiable victims of human rights abuses in the late 1970s. Perhaps Americans believed in human rights enough to help some of the Indochinese, but not enough to welcome them warmly or without complaint.

CHAPTER 7

Reform and Retrenchment: The Refugee Act of 1980 and the Reagan Administration's Refugee Policies

As the Indochinese refugee crisis stretched on through the late 1970s, the push for systemic reform of American refugee laws gained momentum. For advocates of refugee admissions, the ad hoc, successive paroles highlighted the need for an overhaul of the basic commitment to refugees. For skeptics of refugee admissions, those paroles pointed to the executive branch's abuse of the parole codicil and symbolized an immigration system out of control. This debate over refugee affairs, moreover, came as immigration politics deadlocked. The larger liberalizer community by 1980 increasingly felt it was on the defensive, yet the restrictionist alliance was still disorganized and nowhere near as powerful as it once was—or would become in the near future. These factors paved the way for passage of the Refugee Act of 1980, which provided for the annual admission of over fifty thousand refugees from all over the globe. Just as important, that law replaced the Cold War–influenced, anticommunist-centered definition of "refugee" with one much less grounded in early Cold War political ideology. These reforms were long-standing goals of refugee advocates who argued vociferously that refugee policy should flow, at least in part, from human rights principles. The law also had much to recommend it to restrictionists and opponents of refugee admissions, including legally mandated consultations over refugee admissions between the executive and legislative branches and the possibility of the end of mass admissions.

The Refugee Act proved a flawed instrument, however, in two important regards. First, the Reagan administration shaped admissions under the Refugee Act to conform to its anticommunist, anti-Soviet foreign policy agenda rather than to the human rights-based principles inherent in the 1980 legislation. As a result, the vast majority of refugees (and asylees) entering the United States came from communist countries or were fleeing communist persecution. Thus, the Refugee Act, as implemented by the Reagan administration, represented a significant retreat from the human rights moment in refugee affairs that produced the law. Second, admissions during the 1980s declined precipitously, underscoring that while the Reagan administration wanted to admit refugees from communism, it just as ardently wanted to shrink admissions in total.

RESTRICTIONISTS AND LIBERALIZERS IN THE
LATE 1970s: A DIVIDED LOT

By the late 1970s, as immigrant admissions swelled in the aftermath of the 1965 reforms, restrictionism revived, a resurgence that matured by the mid-1980s. Immigration opponents could be found all over the United States, but the heart of restrictionism had shifted from the American South to the West and Southwest. Restrictionism retained its bipartisan flavor as some liberal Democrats, many with ties to the black community, wondered whether newcomers hurt job opportunities for minorities and soaked up needed government funds. But leadership in the restrictionist bloc often fell to Republican conservatives, including some (but not all) of the "New Right." Conservatives worried about the strain that Asian and Latino immigrants placed on already stretched social programs and whether these newcomers could ever become "American." The movement also drew new energy from recently formed organizations like the Federation for American Immigration Reform (FAIR), which emerged in the late 1970s and immediately began shaping public debate through its well-disciplined and organized lobbying efforts. FAIR repeatedly questioned the abilities of newcomers to assimilate culturally to the United States, a critique whose racial and ethnic undertones echoed early twentieth-century restrictionists. Finally, the growing numbers of immigrants arriving illegally—which some estimates put at over 250,000 annually—powered restrictionist growth (especially in the Southwest) and fed restrictionist fears. Public-opinion surveys throughout the United States confirmed that restrictionists might find a sympathetic ear, a sentiment that liberalizers, who believed themselves on the defensive by the end of the 1970s, essentially endorsed.[1]

Immigration liberalizers had similar partisan, ideological, and regional diversity. In Congress, liberal Democrats like Senator Ted Kennedy and Representatives Peter Rodino (NJ) and Liz Holtzman (NY) led the liberalizer bloc. The AFL-CIO, the NAACP, the ACLU, some of the leading liberal interest groups of the late 1970s, still belonged to the liberalizer camp as well. For Democratic politicians, then, support for the immigration-liberalizer position went hand in hand with courting some of the building blocks of their party's electoral coalition. They were joined by pro-business organizations like the National Association of Manufacturers and free-market conservatives who wanted a loose labor market. The most important newcomers to the liberalizer bloc were the Mexican-American and Latino organizations that formed in the 1970s "rights revolution." These groups pushed for capacious immigration laws and for the protection of recent immigrants' political, economic, and social rights. The liberalizer camp's big split came on illegal immigration; Rodino, Kennedy, labor, and African American groups pushed for a crackdown on employers who hired undocumented workers, while business and Latino organizations resisted. This issue stymied much of the immigration legislation of the late 1970s and early 1980s.[2]

As before in the twentieth century, immigration affairs informed refugee politics. Most important, the rising anti-immigrant sentiment of the late 1970s contributed to and reinforced opposition to refugee admissions; the arguments of politicians opposed to refugee entry, for instance, drew on this growing unease about immigration. But immigration concerns did not determine refugee affairs in the late 1970s and early 1980s. After all, a major refugee law passed in 1980, while no such immigration legislation escaped Congress until 1986. Unlike immigration restrictionists, opponents and skeptics of refugee admissions were not an organized constituency in the late 1970s, nor did they perfectly replicate the immigration-restrictionist bloc. For starters, no organizations existed with the sole goal of reducing refugee admissions in the same way that FAIR targeted immigrant admissions. FAIR, as well as other restrictionists, subsumed refugee admissions into its antinewcomer agenda, a tactic that matured in the 1980s as immigration opponents increasingly identified refugee admissions as part of the larger newcomer problem. Likewise, opponents of refugee admissions displayed a remarkable diversity of perspectives and political and ideological leanings; no archetypal opponent of refugee admissions existed.

Some foes of refugee admissions—largely from the South—worried that refugees would never adapt to life in the United States. Those who raised this issue were the intellectual heirs to Senators Lodge and Ervin and the patriotic organizations of the 1920s, but with one significant difference: they established few overt links between ethnicity and/or race and political fitness. Instead, they focused on cultural and social assimilation. Senator Jesse Helms (R-NC) in 1975 acknowledged that "only the most callous would deny that we have a responsibility towards" Indochinese refugees, but the assimilation question bothered him. Helms explained, "[T]his Nation has experienced more and more social problems as a result of the melting-pot theory. . . . There is the feeling that the traditions of our ethnic groups are being undermined, as well as the sense of identity and community. . . . There is widespread concern over the adaptability of such a group to American values. . . . There is the language question." Helms's arguments contained a singular thread: he doubted that Indochinese refugees could become "American." As such, Helms tapped into potent and powerful sentiments emerging not just among his base of conservative southern voters, but among many in the middle class and in the white working class of the Northeast and Midwest—the latter often the children or grandchildren of European immigrants. They worried that the recent arrivals to the United States harmed its culture and "values" and, indeed, bilingual education emerged as an important and divisive issue in the 1970s to white ethnic voters. Such concerns powerfully harmonized with the larger sense of fragmentation that many of these same Americans felt as they contemplated the political, cultural, and social effects of the 1960s. Helms and other conservative Republicans, like the Californian Ronald Reagan, understood this discomfort among voters and made it a key feature of their successful campaigns. Helms's description of the refugee problem, then, was part of the larger critique of American society that helped power the conservative ascendancy of the 1980s.[3]

Another group of opponents of refugee admissions objected to the amount of federal funding earmarked for refugee resettlement programs as the nation's economy sagged and its resources appeared quite limited. Representative Frank J. Sensenbrenner, a conservative Republican from Wisconsin at the beginning of what would be a long career in politics, wondered, "At a time when our unemployment rate is going up, when we are spending about $1 billion per year for refugee resettlement costs, the people of the United States are warm, they are hospitable, but there also is a limit to how much we can afford at a time of rampant inflation and deficit budgets." (Helms had made some of these same allegations, but buried them beneath his vehement rejection of the possible assimilation of Indochinese refugees.) By acknowledging the limits of American munificence, Sensenbrenner actually hit quite a potent political chord. Americans in the 1970s came to understand that the country's economic capacity, its ability to solve persistent social problems, and its access to natural resources, was, in fact, limited. The years of economic growth, unfettered political power, and general optimism that marked the first two decades after 1945 came crashing down in the 1970s. Sensenbrenner tapped this angst-ridden vein in American political culture as he argued against a continued expansive American commitment to refugees on the basis of the limits of American economic and political power that were evident to most in the country.[4]

Other skeptics of an American commitment to refugees also understood the politics of limits, but drew different conclusions. Some liberals argued that American citizens—especially the urban, African American poor—rather than resettled refugees deserved first call upon government aid. The NAACP, of course, made similar charges in the 1960s regarding government funding for Cuban refugees, but in the 1970s the political environment had changed so that such arguments gained more traction. In particular, a welfare-rights movement, in which organizations like the National Welfare Rights Organization asserted that access to welfare was a "right" for all Americans, powerfully defended (on the basis of citizenship) an expansive welfare system that aided poorer Americans. Representative John Conyers, a liberal African American Democrat from Detroit, crystallized these concerns in 1975, asserting that the Indochinese would compete with blacks for scarce jobs and gobble up needed government funds. Conyers asked, "Should we spend them on Vietnamese 'refugees' or should we spend them on Detroit 'refugees'?" If the Vietnamese received more funds than the black, urban poor, "We will be saying to all the poor and deprived and disadvantaged and unemployed Americans that they have no needs this Government is bound to recognize." Conyers, like Sensenbrenner, understood that federal dollars were in short supply, but while conservatives wanted to cut funding to all welfare and social programs, Conyers wanted that money allocated to American citizens who needed the government's helping hand.[5]

Finally, the perceived abuse of the parole codicil motivated many congressional opponents of refugee admissions. Head of the House Subcommittee on Immigration, Joshua Eilberg (D-PA), believed that the Ford and Carter administrations had manipulated the parole power by using it to admit hundreds of thousands of refugees. While the Ford and Carter administrations gave Congress, as a courtesy, the opportunity to approve these parole plans beginning in 1975, Eilberg still believed the paroles perverted the original intent of the codicil—the admission of small numbers of individual refugees who served national security objectives. The American government's successive paroles of the Indochinese in the late 1970s particularly disturbed Eilberg, whose suspicion boiled over in August 1977 when Attorney General Griffin Bell testified that while even he harbored doubts about the legality of paroling thousands of refugees at once, Congress could do nothing to halt such a move. Eilberg fired back that parole was an "extralegal procedure." Eilberg's critiques are important for a few reasons. First, his ire was consonant with other attempts by Congress throughout the 1970s to reinsert themselves into refugee policymaking. Second, Eilberg was not an outright opponent of refugee admissions looking to close the nation's borders; he had voted repeatedly in the 1970s to approve refugee entry. Instead, he wanted a system in place that would allow for the entry of refugees in an orderly fashion rather than ad hoc paroles that seemingly occurred every six months without congressional mandates.[6]

The refugee advocacy community, meanwhile, had grown and matured during the 1970s, in large part because of the ongoing Indochinese refugee crisis. While some conservatives pushed hard for the admission of Soviet Jewish and Indochinese refugees, they did not participate in the effort to win systemic reform of refugee policy. Thus, the heart of the refugee advocacy community remained the liberal left. In Congress, Senator Edward Kennedy and Representative Liz Holtzman continued to play key roles, and they could count on support from the Carter White House. The National Catholic Welfare Conference, the Hebrew Immigrant Aid Society, and Church World Service—staffed with policy experts and veterans of previous refugee programs—argued vociferously for an expansion of admissions and government spending on resettlement activities. Long-standing refugee advocacy groups like the U.S. Committee for Refugees and the International Rescue Committee were joined by newcomers like the Citizens Commission on Indochinese Refugees. Labor unions like the AFL-CIO continued their support for the admission of refugees, even in markedly harder times than in the 1960s. Finally, rights groups like Amnesty International and the ACLU came out in favor of increased refugee admissions. Absent from this alliance, though, were ethnic groups, with the exception of Jewish groups working on Soviet emigration issues. Well represented in refugee politics in the 1950s and 1960s, by the late 1970s the "white ethnic" organizations of southern, central, and eastern Europe had retreated from refugee affairs in part because their ethnicities made up only a small part of the global refugee population, in part because they had pushed for refugee admissions as a backdoor around the national origins quota system, and in part because by the 1970s white ethnics were less inclined to support admission of newcomers from the so-called Third World.

The refugee advocacy community wanted to reshape and formalize the American commitment to refugees. Kennedy's description of his goals for refugee policy in 1970, "a comprehensive asylum policy for refugees" that would "broaden the definition of a refugee from its present European and cold war framework to include the homeless throughout the world—in South America, southern Africa, and elsewhere," neatly summarized the agenda at the end of the decade. The Indochinese admissions had demonstrated that the racial and ethnic biases to refugee admission had diminished. But refugee advocates believed that a more capacious commitment to refugees that both covered the globe and protected human rights required that the statutory definition of refugee (which was nearly identical to the one written in the early 1950s) abandon its references to Cold War political ideology and geography. Reformers also wanted fifty thousand refugees admitted annually and a mechanism in the new law by which the president could admit even more; the 1965 immigration law had been amended to allow entry of over seventeen thousand refugees annually, but reformers judged that annual total insufficient. Finally, refugee advocates wanted to curb the president's use of the parole power as a vehicle for mass admissions of tens of thousands of refugees. Eilberg and others also wanted this reform, and the promise of the end of mass paroles helped refugee advocates sell the higher annual refugee quota to those with restrictionist leanings.[7]

THE REFUGEE ACT OF 1980

Senator Kennedy introduced refugee legislation throughout the 1970s that served as the foundation for the reform efforts of 1979 and 1980. In late 1978 Kennedy's staff began working with the INS, the State, Justice, and HEW Departments, as well as with former senator Dick Clark—who now served in the Carter administration as its refugee policy coordinator—to write a draft bill. The process moved along fairly smoothly, in large part because there was much agreement among these participants.

The decision to redefine "refugee" generated remarkably little controversy, especially compared to the tortured bargaining that accompanied the discussions over the definition in the early 1950s. In the very first drafts, the legislation incorporated the definition used by the United Nations in its 1951 Refugee Convention and its 1967 Protocol Relating to the Status of Refugees, both of which identified refugees as the victims of persecution. Neither definition linked that persecution to a particular geographical region or political ideology. The United States in 1968 signed the Protocol, an empty diplomatic and public relations gambit aimed at demonstrating interest in the UN's "International Year for Human Rights." In explaining that decision, State Department officials made clear that acceding to the Protocol would not substantively alter the nation's refugee admissions or change the definition of "refugee" established in law and precedent. Thus, the decision in 1979 to define a refugee as "any person who is outside any country of his nationality . . . and who is unable or unwilling to avail himself of the protection of, that country because of persecution or a well-founded fear of persecution on account of race, religion, nationality, membership in a particular social group, or political opinion" represented an important break with the past three decades of U.S. refugee policies and laws.[8]

The draft legislation also set up a two-tiered system of refugee admissions. The first tier created a fifty thousand annual admissions quota for so-called normal flow refugees. The president and Congress could in advance of the subsequent fiscal year agree to expand that quota. The second tier provided a means to admit refugees if an unforeseen crisis emerged after the quota had been set. Later drafts, and the final legislation, clarified that the president could admit refugees via the second tier if "justified by grave humanitarian concerns or . . . the national interest." Kennedy's staff described the second tier as "essentially the parole authority codified" but on firmer legal ground. In drafting the legislation, the White House and Congress agreed on the need for a formalized consultation process to set annual admissions quotas, but little agreement existed on the shape of that interaction. The administration would not grant Congress the power to veto the annual quota, would not concede the executive branch's power to authorize emergent refugee admissions, and opposed letting Congress place numerical limits on emergency refugee admissions. The Administration acceded only to a form of consultation called "report and wait": the White House would "wait until Congress [could] respond" to its admissions plans before actually authorizing them. Questions also arose over the immigration status the government would assign to entrants under the reform legislation. This issue, of course, had developed over the previous decades as parolees were admitted with "conditional status," thus requiring Congress to pass "status adjustment" legislation in 1958 (for the Hungarians), in 1966 (for the Cubans), and in 1977 (for the Indochinese). The 1965 immigration law's refugee admissions also granted conditional status. After some discussion, the legislation reached a compromise: refugees would enter with conditional status, but each refugee—after one year in the United States—would submit to an INS examination to determine whether that refugee had earned permanent-residence status.[9]

By the spring of 1979 the reform legislation was complete and ready for consideration. It stood a good chance of passage. The ongoing Indochinese refugee crisis and the multiple parole requests of the Carter administration that seemed to come every six months left participants from all sides of refugee politics, as well as policymakers, frustrated and certain of the need for reform. Politically, the time was also ripe for a major reform effort, as the makeup of important Congressional committees and subcommittees changed. Restrictionist senator James Eastland retired from the Senate, which placed Kennedy at the head of the Judiciary Committee in 1979. In the House, Eilberg lost his re-election bid in the wake of a bribery scandal, paving the way for Holtzman's ascension to the chair of the immigration subcommittee. Finally, the Carter White House, which participated in the drafting process, supported the reform bill.[10]

Advocates of reform continued to link an expansive commitment to refugees to human rights. No one better articulated this connection than Patricia Derian, the State Department's assistant secretary of state for human rights and humanitarian affairs. Appointed as "coordinator for human rights and humanitarian affairs," Carter institutionalized the human rights portfolio—and gave it a higher profile—by promoting Derian to assistant secretary. Derian exemplified how domestic trends ultimately influenced refugee policy. She came to human rights in the same way that many American liberals had, via experience in the civil rights movement. In the 1960s, Derian, a white Mississippian, publicly criticized the white supremacist Citizens' Council; directed the Jackson, Mississippi, Head Start program; and helped form the "Loyalist Democrats of Mississippi" (a biracial organization that opposed pro-segregation Democrats). Derian believed that human rights advocacy paralleled her civil rights activism, especially because opponents of both relied on the same arguments and rationales. Short on Washington foreign policy experience, Derian assembled a State Department team that relied heavily on former Kennedy and Fraser staffers. Her tenure at the Department was rocky, however, as she battled repeatedly with Brzezinski's NSC and her State Department colleagues less interested in human rights.[11]

Derian defined refugees as persons who had been denied their human rights: "If a government is cruelly repressive, denies its citizens an opportunity to defend themselves against the life at stake, if they are tortured, discriminated against because of their race or their religion, or their political views," then these persons were refugees. When pressed whether there was a difference between "boat cases" and political prisoners from Latin America (who would qualify as refugees under the reform proposal), Derian answered, "it is a little like asking me who is hungrier, someone in the Sahara Desert, or someone in India. I think beyond a certain point of suffering, the pain is the same. And it is very hard to make a quantitative or qualitative difference in the amount of suffering." For Derian, persecution and "suffering," no matter the ideological principles expressed by the perpetrating government, created refugees.[12]

Attorney General Griffin Bell echoed Derian and drew a connection between American identity, human rights, and the admission of refugees. Bell explained the chief principles underlying the nation's refugee laws and policies: "our policy is based on humaneness, based on the historical fact that our country began as a haven." He continued, "That's why people came here. . . . they came here in the beginning seeking rights. And that's why we all believe so strongly in rights—human rights, the Bill of Rights, all rights." Thus, it was the nation's historical destiny—an expression of American-ness—to aid refugees: "As it comes to our attention that people are suffering in the sense that they are losing their rights—we are people who think of human rights—I think we ought to do our share as part of the world community to take in as many as we can of these people who are suffering." Bell's defense of a commitment to helping refugees rang not with Cold War anticommunism, but with universalist, human rights principles. Like President Carter, he believed that the protection of rights was a uniquely American virtue that could be promoted through refugee admissions.[13]

Indicative of the link between human rights and refugees, Amnesty International—the preeminent human rights organization—vigorously pushed for the new legislation. Amnesty's A. Whitney Ellsworth argued that, "The primary focus of refugee policy should be humanitarian, not political," and that AIUSA "hoped that American policy will become more consistent with the non-political, humanitarian concerns that underlie its international obligations and expressed human rights policies." Others—from religious groups like the Church World Service to refugee aid groups like the International Rescue Committee—made these arguments, but Amnesty's appearance was particularly relevant. The organization had been an increasingly powerful participant in human rights and refugee issues throughout the 1970s—especially those touching on the Indochinese, Soviets, and Chileans—and it now endorsed systemic reform of refugee policy because it embraced Amnesty's core mission.[14]

A significant rethinking of the United States' refugee laws and policies also was possible because of the remarkably light opposition to just such an effort. Congressional critics of the reform package, headed up Democrat Walter Huddleston of Kentucky in the Senate and Republican Frank Sensenbrenner in the House, argued that the United States already accepted too many immigrants (both legal and illegal), straining the country's fragile economic and social system. Huddleston's position highlighted his differences from earlier generations of restrictionists who were more ardent in their opposition to admissions and much more tied to national origins principles. The senator proclaimed the United States a country of immigrants and declared his support for American efforts to aid the Indochinese boat people. He did not, like Senator Helms, argue that refugees wrecked cultural and social unity, nor did Huddleston play overtly to racial or ethnic fears. For Huddleston, the new definition of "refugee," the lack of substantive congressional control over admissions, the fifty thousand annual visas for refugees, the poorly defined phrase "special concern" in reference to refugees to be admitted in emergent situations, and the retention of the parole statute all pointed to a flood of refugees if the reform legislation passed. Both Huddleston and Sensenbrenner, then, wanted to count any additional refugee admissions over the fifty thousand quota against the existing immigration quota and to make the president's emergency refugee admissions request subject to a veto by either the House or Senate. The reform bill's supporters accommodated a number of Huddleston's and Sensenbrenner's minor modifications, but they did not accept the meat of their demands.[15]

Such outcomes symbolized the weaknesses of the bill's opponents and the strengths of the legislation's supporters. Unlike their restrictionist predecessors, Huddleston and Sensenbrenner had few allies of consequence. Neither the American Legion nor the Daughters of the American Revolution, two stalwarts of restrictionism, protested the reforms. Even the newly created FAIR was ambivalent. On the one hand, FAIR—whose objections Huddleston noted in his attacks—worried that the bill did not go far enough in reasserting Congress's place in the policymaking process and that the vague language of "humanitarian concern" only opened the door for greater refugee admissions. On the other hand, FAIR favored passage of the bill, hoping it would curb paroles and encourage Congress to seize the immigration and refugee agenda. (FAIR's ambivalence was matched by Huddleston, who voted for the reform bill, but not by Sensenbrenner, who cast a nay vote.) FAIR's position highlighted one of the peculiarities of the debate: Critics of the parole procedure and White House predominance in refugee affairs actually shared some common ground with refugee advocates like Kennedy and Holtzman. Moreover, reform legislation—if it severely restricted the use of parole and guaranteed fifty thousand annual refugee admissions—was quite plausibly a restrictionist measure, especially compared to the post-1975 paroles. The bill's leading proponents made this point repeatedly.[16]

The paucity of opposition in Congress, the ambivalence of neo-restrictionist groups like FAIR, and the silence of traditional restrictionist voices—even with opinion polls registering public concern about the admission of newcomers—signify the low ebb of restrictionist sentiment and point to the larger and much more important conclusion. By the late 1970s a general consensus existed across the political spectrum—and across the politics of newcomers—that the United States would have, and should have, some sort of rational, formal refugee admissions. Americans came to this conclusion for a variety of reasons, and with a variety of different understandings about why this commitment was important—as the politics of refugee affairs in the 1970s demonstrated repeatedly—but consensus existed. By the late 1970s, refugee admissions were a fact of life, which was a long way from the late 1940s and early 1950s. When the Refugee Act passed both Houses in 1979—and then its reconciled version in March 1980—the votes told this story. In the Senate, the bill passed unanimously in 1979 and by voice vote in 1980. The House vote in 1979 was 328–47, with opposition scattered throughout the country. In 1980, the House passed the reconciled bill by a much smaller margin, 207–192 with 34 abstentions. But this tally was misleadingly close, reflecting concerns that the final bill granted too much control over refugee policy to the president, not disagreement with substantial annual refugee admissions or the new definition of "refugee."[17]

On March 17, 1980, President Carter signed the Refugee Act of 1980. It authorized the annual admission of fifty thousand refugees with conditional status that would, after one year and subject to INS oversight, convert to permanent resident status. Moreover, if the White House believed that the fifty thousand refugee admissions would be insufficient for the coming year, it could—after consulting with Congress—raise that limit. Finally, the law also allowed the president to admit on an emergency basis refugees of "grave humanitarian concern," again subject to congressional consultation but not approval. The Refugee Act gave the office of the U.S. coordinator for refugee affairs, an executive-branch bureaucracy recently created by Carter, new funding and authority; its head would have the rank of ambassador and would be chosen by the president and approved by the Senate. Additionally, the Refugee Act increased federal government funding for refugee resettlement.[18]

The reforms were significant on a few levels. First, the law was the culmination of congressional efforts throughout the 1970s to limit executive control of refugee affairs and admissions. While the Refugee Act's consultation procedure did not return Congress to the powerful position it had held in the 1950s under the leadership of McCarran and Walter, or give Congress a veto over White House admissions policies, it did open refugee policymaking and the setting of the annual refugee quota to congressional scrutiny. Second, the Refugee Act nearly tripled the nation's annual refugee admissions and acknowledged that in some situations the United States would likely take more. Third, the law divorced refugee affairs from immigration affairs by ending the so-called seventh preference for refugees established in the 1965 immigration amendments and by making clear that according to American law an immigrant left his or her country voluntarily, while a refugee did not. Finally, the law replaced the Cold War ideological concerns that founded the American commitment to refugees with universal, human rights–based principles. Thus the importance of the codicil that allowed the president to admit refugees of "grave humanitarian concern" and the new definition of "refugee," divorced of its Cold War political, ideological, and geographic biases. In one more nod to the new era, Congresswoman Holtzman's concerns that refugees themselves not be human rights abusers were enshrined in the new definition as well. "The term 'refugee,' " the 1980 statute read, "does not include any person who ordered, incited, assisted, or otherwise participated in the persecution of any person on account of race, religion, nationality, membership in a particular social group, or political opinion."[19]

The Refugee Act also attempted to clarify the United States' asylum policy. This reform would have important and unforeseen consequences over the coming decades. The key difference between asylum and refugee status was that foreign nationals *in* the United States claiming fear of persecution in their homelands sought asylum, while stateless foreign nationals *outside* the United States with fears of persecution sought refugee status. While the United States had been party to the United Nation's Protocol Relating to the Status of Refugees since 1968, in which signatories acknowledged a right of asylum, American law did not contain procedures by which foreign nationals might receive asylum. Instead, the Justice Department and INS handled asylum claims via rather murky administrative procedures assembled in the early 1970s. Only a few thousand foreign nationals applied for asylum annually in the United States during the 1970s, and the U.S. government more often than not rejected these claims. The Refugee Act ordered the attorney general to develop procedures by which an "alien" in the United States who met the new definition of "refugee" could apply for asylum. Moreover, the law permitted the Justice Department to reserve up to five thousand of the fifty thousand annual refugee quota for persons granted asylum, specifically so that those people could become permanent residents and, eventually, citizens.[20]

In the wake of the Refugee Act, asylum applications grew to tens of thousands per year. By 1983 the Justice Department had nearly 175,000 asylum applications on file, a tally that showed no signs of shrinking. No consensus exists on the reasons behind the surge in asylum applications, but three factors suggest themselves. First, a persecuted person faced with the choice of staying in a country and applying for refugee status or entering the United States (either legally or illegally) and applying for asylum status might choose the latter course merely because that option placed the applicant in the relative safety of the United States. Second, for those foreign nationals in the United States illegally but caught by the INS and thus subject to deportation, filing an asylum claim allowed them to stay as the government processed the claim. Third, refugee admissions were limited to the quota number, but asylum admissions technically were not. This fine, but important distinction, rested upon a reading of the Refugee Act wherein the Justice Department could only move five thousand asylum seekers toward permanent residence or citizenship per year, but could grant asylum to as many persons as it wanted. Like refugee affairs, though, the question of who deserved asylum soon became highly controversial.[21]

THE MARIEL REFUGEE CRISIS

The Refugee Act encountered its first serious test one month after Carter signed it. In late April 1980, Cubans began setting sail from the port of Mariel—just west of Havana—and arriving on Florida's shores. Over the following six months, about 130,000 Cubans arrived in the United States, initiating a new chapter in U.S.-Cuban migratory history: the Mariel Refugee Crisis. While 500,000 Cuban refugees arrived between 1959 and 1973, the influx slowed so much in the early 1970s that the United States abrogated its agreement with Cuba governing the refugee flow. Thus, during the 1970s, only 185,000 Cubans came to the United States, though they received the same welcome from American authorities as their predecessors. Mariel ended this relative quiet.

A concurrent increase in Haitians landing in Florida complicated the Mariel crisis. In fact, throughout the 1970s more Haitians than ever before came to the United States. The 1965 immigration reforms encouraged legal immigration from Haiti, so that while 35,000 Haitians came to the United States in the 1960s, more than 55,000 came in the 1970s. Moreover, between 1972 and 1980 the Haitian government—now under the control of Francois Duvalier's son, nicknamed "Baby Doc" Duvalier—adopted even more repressive tactics aimed at quashing resistance and opposition. In response, about 30,000 Haitians fled and entered the United States outside of regular immigration procedures. After landing in the United States, those Haitians tried to claim asylum. Haitians ran into a bureaucratic wall, though. The U.S. government generally did not recognize their persecution claims—they were fleeing an American ally, after all—or judged them economic migrants rather than victims of political persecution. If they did not win their asylum claim, Haitians were deported. The best estimates are that the U.S. government granted asylum status to fewer than one hundred Haitians in the 1970s, in effect reversing the informal but relatively welcoming policy of the 1960s. Critics charged both racism—the 1970s Haitian asylum claimants were black—and a double standard in asylum and refugee law that aided those fleeing the United States' Cold War opponents and shut out those escaping American allies. Just as the Mariel crisis began, Haitian landings in Florida also surged; almost twelve thousand landed in 1980 alone. The concurrent arrivals of Cubans and Haitians forced the public and policymakers to contemplate a response to two sets of persons fleeing oppressive Caribbean governments.[22]

The Cubans, though, captured the most attention. The Mariel refugee flow arose from the island's political and economic conditions and the tangled relations between the United States and Cuba. In mid-April, about ten thousand Cubans who wanted to leave the island took refuge in the Peruvian embassy, claiming that the regime endangered their lives. The international community and Cuba worked out a solution in which 3,500 of those Cubans would go to the United States directly; 3,500 others would go to eight other nations; and the rest would go to Costa Rica to await resettlement. (Costa Rica received assurances that if those Cubans were not resettled, they would be welcomed in either the United States or Peru.) The plan got under way—with numerous daily flights out of Cuba—when Castro changed the rules by declaring that all flights must go to the United States. It seems he hoped to tweak his northern neighbor. The Carter administration rejected Castro's gambit, likely because in an election year it did not want to appear at Castro's command. Castro's response echoed 1965. He encouraged all Cubans who wanted to depart to do so and he invited Cuban exiles in the United States to come and get their relatives at the port of Mariel.[23]

Between April and the end of September, about 130,000 Cubans left. The Marielitos (as they were known) differed in some important ways from Cubans who had come in the 1960s. They were disproportionately young (under the age of thirty), and 70 percent were male. They came predominantly from blue-collar, semiskilled or unskilled professions. While the majority of the Marielitos were white, as in previous Cuban refugee flows, a larger number than before—15 to 40 percent of the 1980 refugees—were black or mixed race. Most were no friends of the Cuban government, but nor were the majority long-time political opponents of Castro or in acute danger of political persecution. Rather, like the post-1965 Cuban refugees, they sought a better life in the United States. As historian Louis Perez points out, the late 1970s saw an influx of Americans and U.S. consumer goods into Cuba, which only heightened the desire among many Marielitos to head north. At the height of the crisis about thirteen thousand Cubans landed in Florida each week. Thousands of boats left southern Florida for the island during the summer of 1980, some to pick up relatives and some to grab whomever wanted to leave. A number of these crafts were not seaworthy—conditions dramatically presented to the U.S. public via now familiar images of overcrowded, rickety ships—and the U.S. Coast Guard began rescue operations in the Florida Straits.[24]

As in his 1965 announcement reopening travel between the United States and Cuba, Castro used the exodus to strengthen the Revolution and dispose of an element of popular discontent. As the Mariel crisis unfolded, it also became clear that Castro had pressed—sometimes forcibly—thousands of prisoners, drug addicts, mentally handicapped, and homosexuals to join the flow. INS studies later showed that about 24,000 of the Marielitos, roughly 19 percent, had been in jail in Cuba. Of those 24,000, about 20 percent were political prisoners and a further 70 percent were minor offenders with short sentences (for robbery or drugs, for example) or were jailed for activities that were not crimes in the United States (trying to leave Cuba, for instance.) Less than 10 percent had been convicted of serious crimes. The INS also learned that 600 Marielitos were mental patients and 1,500 were homosexual. Reading either the Cuban or American press in the summer of 1980 would have led to an opposite conclusion. The Cuban media trumpeted that the Marielitos were "scum" and social deviants that the country was happy to see depart. The American press, weirdly, mimicked its Cuban counterparts, producing story upon story that left the impression that gays, criminals, drug addicts, and mental patients were flooding Florida via the refugee flow.[25]

No matter how inaccurate those portrayals, they helped cement public discontent and antagonism toward the new arrivals. Opinion polls in May 1980 showed that 57 percent of Americans opposed the admission of Cubans, reflective of the consistent antinewcomer bias of the postwar era, the building restrictionism that would come in the 1980s, concerns about the Marielitos' pasts, and fears that the Cubans might take jobs from

Americans in a sour economy. While opposition to admission did not differ much regionally—at least in the polls—the hue and cry was loudest in Florida, the refugees' main landing destination and most likely their place of permanent resettlement. Senator Lawton Chiles of Florida reported that his mail was running 80 percent against Cuban admissions. Even the Cuban American community in Florida did not escape the controversy over the Marielitos' arrival. To be sure, many Cuban Americans welcomed the newcomers. But as more and more disparaging stories emerged about the Marielitos, Cubans who had arrived in the 1960s and 1970s expressed concern that the post-1980 migrants would wreck the flourishing Cuban American community and its hard-won reputation. All in all, this public reaction greatly complicated the Carter administration's response to the Mariel crisis, especially because it was an election year.[26]

At the same time, the Carter administration came under different criticism for its treatment of fleeing Haitians. Haitian advocates—a collection of religious groups and minority Democratic politicians, especially the Congressional Black Caucus—saw the Mariel crisis as an opportunity to point out the hypocrisy of American refugee policy. The battle to win better if not equal treatment for Haitians had begun in the years before Mariel, but by coincidence it came to a head in 1980. In 1979 the National Council of Churches won a court review of the INS's treatment of Haitian refugees, alleging that the Haitians were not granted proper procedural protections in their deportation hearings and that the government wrongly classified them as economic migrants rather than political refugees. The much anticipated decision came down in the summer of 1980, in the midst of the upsurge in Cuban *and* Haitian arrivals. In an often stinging opinion, U.S. District Court Judge James King ruled that the INS (including its highest officials) had looked only to deport the Haitians rather than considering the facts of each application, committing "a wholesale violation of due process." The judge ordered the INS to revamp the process by which it adjudicated Haitian asylum claims. King's legal bombshell validated charges long made by Haitian advocates of unfair treatment and a concerted federal government effort to deny Haitians entry into the United States and only increased pressure on the government to treat more equally Haitians and Cubans now pouring into Florida.[27]

The Carter administration's response to the Mariel crisis was like the boatlift itself: chaotic, unorganized, and haphazard. As the Mariel exodus began in late April, the INS looked to control and limit arrivals by warning and, in some cases, fining boat owners who left Florida for Mariel to pick up Cubans. Once they returned to Florida, though, the INS allowed the Cubans to disembark and claim asylum. The INS's actions angered pro-Cuban elements in the United States, leading Carter to announce that the United States would accept all Cubans who made the passage. This welcoming policy, while in line with past American efforts, did not last long in the face of increasing public concerns about the makeup of the Cuban flow and its effect on the job market. Carter, backing away from earlier statements, then took a hard line, and the INS and Customs service resumed their efforts to prevent boats from leaving Florida for Cuba, even going so far as to seize some crafts. This helped slow the exodus some in the summer of 1980. It eventually ended in late September when Castro closed Mariel to departures.[28]

The Carter administration still needed to determine which legislative mechanism would legally admit these newcomers to the United States. The one-month-old Refugee Act contained procedures by which the Justice Department could admit and confer refugee status upon an asylum claimant should he or she qualify as a refugee, but government officials quickly determined that the sheer numbers of Cubans made such administrative procedures impossible. Instead, in June 1980 Carter paroled the Cubans into the United States, and the INS assigned them a new bureaucratic category, separate from "refugee" and "asylee," called "entrants (status pending)." Carter's action provided for the Marielitos' admission and access to some basic welfare services, but left unclear their immigration status and denied them the generous resettlement funding that had aided so many previous Cubans. The "entrant" status expired after six months, and Carter left the decision of whether to extend that status in Congress's hands. Congress responded by repeatedly extending the "entrant" status and, in October 1980, providing the Marielitos with full access to government resettlement funds. In 1984 Congress finally "normalized" the Marielitos' immigration status by amending the 1966 Cuban Adjustment Act, placing them on the path to permanent residence or citizenship. Carter's and the INS's maneuvers also affected the thirty thousand Haitians who had arrived in the United States beginning in the early 1970s. Those Haitians—and eventually any Haitians who landed in the United States before June 19, 1980 (later extended to October 11 1980)— also were deemed "entrants (status pending)." Haitians entering after October were subject to the INS's revamped Haitian admission procedures. Nevertheless, for Haitians who had entered the country illegally in the 1970s, the legal limbo of "entrant" immigration status surely was an improvement over potential deportation.[29]

The Mariel refugee crisis and the concurrent changes in American policy toward Haitian refugees showed the shortcomings and successes of the 1980 Refugee Act. President Carter essentially paroled the Cubans into the United States, choosing not to utilize the legal and administrative procedures established by the 1980 law to deal precisely with this type of large-scale refugee crisis. By resorting to the parole codicil, Carter also demonstrated the limits of congressional attempts to rein in the power of

the executive branch to devise and conduct refugee policy without inter-
ference. Finally, the majority of refugees entering in 1980—the Cubans—
were admitted precisely because they fled a Cold War enemy of the United
States'. In these ways, the Mariel episode and subsequent federal government actions resembled the pre-1970s American commitment to refugees.
Yet, the events of the 1980s also showed the effectiveness of the Refugee
Act and, indeed, the sea change that had occurred in refugee affairs over
the previous decade. Most important, thirty thousand Haitians fleeing
their country's repressive, rightist, American-allied government were allowed to stay in the United States, without fear of deportation. With this
action, American admissions of refugees in fact resembled the definition
of "refugee" contained in the 1980 law. Likewise, the admission of Haitians—as victims of persecution outside of Cold War foreign policy concerns—could be counted as a triumph for the human rights ethos in American refugee policies; Haitians were exactly the types of refugees that
liberalizers like Kennedy and Holtzman believed the United States ought
to aid. Finally, the Carter administration in 1980, while retaining its prerogatives in refugee affairs, proved more willing than previous administrations to work with Congress. Cynics, of course, would note that the
Carter administration's Cuban-Haitian parole decision provided for congressional review after the "entrants" had been in the United States for
six months, making it harder for Congress to reverse the policy. It remained to be seen which of these trends revealed by the Mariel crisis
would become the norm, but such decisions would be made by President
Ronald Reagan, who took office in January 1981.[30]

President Reagan and Refugees

The Reagan Revolution that shook American politics did not have similar
seismic effects upon immigration affairs. The Reagan White House displayed an overall ambivalence on immigration issues. The Administration
was mildly liberalizer in its orientation, generally supportive of a free
flow of newcomers into the United States (which it believed would
provide businesses with cheap labor). This position resonated with the
Administration's free-market conservatism. Likewise, suspicion of government regulation and intervention in economic matters helped make
the Reagan White House very hesitant to assign government a role in
ensuring that businesses not hire illegal aliens. Just the same, the Administration did have restrictionist tendencies. Reagan and his advisers opposed extending political and social rights to those newcomers, a stance
that revealed the conservative distaste for the rights-revolution-era expansion of protections for minorities. Moreover, Reagan and his advisers

warned repeatedly that the United States faced an onslaught of immigrants, illegal aliens, and refugees. Politics surely motivated such comments—after all, cultural conservatives and Republicans in the Southwest and West were both restrictionists and Reagan voters—but the frequency and vehemence of the Administration's comments suggests more than just political expediency.[31]

Indicative of this larger straddle, Reagan only very gingerly entered the debates that produced the most important immigration legislation of the decade, the 1986 Immigration Reform and Control Act (IRCA). That law's content and passage owed much more to congressional bargaining and persistence than to the Administration's efforts. This major piece of legislation signified that the revival of immigration restrictionism in the late 1970s had blossomed by the mid-1980s into a powerful backlash against newcomers, especially in the western United States and among groups like FAIR. While the IRCA offered a general amnesty for millions of illegal aliens, it paired this reform with establishment of a mild set of sanctions on employers who hired illegals and tougher border-security measures meant to cut the flow of illegals. Restrictionists hoped that the IRCA would solve, once and for all, the illegal immigration issue, and the law clearly intended to cut the flow of newcomers, specifically illegal aliens, to the United States. The restrictionist senator Alan Simpson (R-WY), who sponsored the IRCA, exemplified the depth of restrictionist desire to radically curb immigration. Simpson originally proposed that the IRCA cap legal immigration to the United States by mandating that relatives of American citizens count against the hemispheric caps established in 1965. (This loophole had allowed immigrant admissions to supersede those caps each year.) While Simpson's gambit failed, it just as surely revealed the concerns of 1980s restrictionists.[32]

Reagan may have stayed somewhat aloof from immigration issues, but he faced an exploding global refugee population. In 1975 the United Nations High Commissioner for Refugees believed that 3 million persons were refugees. Ten years later, the number of refugees stood at 11.8 million, with 5.9 million in Asia, 3.8 million in Africa, and 1 million in Europe. While some of this growth can be attributed to the peculiarities of compiling refugee statistics, it also accurately reflects both continuing and new refugee flows. Hundred of thousands of Indochinese refugees still lived in camps in Southeast Asia, while millions of Palestinian refugees languished in the Middle East. New refugee problems also emerged in the 1980s. Political upheaval and violence produced growing refugee flows in the Horn of Africa (Ethiopia, Sudan, Somalia, Uganda, and Kenya) and in Central America (Mexico, Nicaragua, El Salvador, and Honduras). Finally, the Soviet invasion and occupation of Afghanistan in 1979 sent millions of Afghani refugees into Iran and Pakistan.[33]

The international community's response to these problems was mixed. The UNHCR spent ever larger sums to maintain camps in which refugees waited to be resettled or repatriated; its budget grew from $76 million in 1975 to $580 million in 1990. But resettlement opportunities slowed in the 1980s. In 1983 Charles Sternberg of the International Rescue Committee argued that "in more and more countries, the readiness to assist and receive refugees is diminishing. It is not just in the United States, it is a universal phenomenon." In the 1980s industrialized nations like Canada, West Germany, Great Britain, and Switzerland all toughened the criteria by which they granted asylum. Many of these same nations either reduced (Canada) or held steady (Australia) their annual refugee admission quotas. Industrialized nations, then, were happy to fund refugee camps in the nonindustrialized world, but less willing to resettle those refugees on their soil.[34]

The United States was not exempt from these trends. After 1980 the president's annual proposal for admissions under the Refugee Act became the centerpiece of refugee politics and policymaking—and thus is the ideal starting point for understanding how the Reagan administration shaped the nation's commitment to refugees. Under the Refugee Act, the president presented to Congress prior to the coming fiscal year his plan for the next twelve months of refugee admissions. The proposal identified the total number of refugee visas allotted for the upcoming year and divided that allocation among different regions. Congress offered its comments on the allocations and then the White House finalized, with some revisions, its official proposal. Reagan's annual proposals regularly surpassed the 50,000 quota and even after congressional consultation they remained well above that limit. For fiscal year 1982—the first proposal submitted by the Reagan administration—the White House set a quota of 140,000 refugees. (Their original request was 170,000.) But thereafter, the overall admissions ceiling shrank significantly. For 1983, the total was 90,000; for 1984, 72,000; and for 1986, 67,000. In Reagan's last year in office, he reversed course, requesting refugee admissions totaling 94,000. President George H. W. Bush, continued this trend, calling for the entry of 116,500 refugees in 1990.[35]

To be sure, the Reagan White House made a concerted effort to reduce refugee admissions during the 1980s. While the Reagan proposals consistently surpassed the fifty thousand limit, they did so by smaller and smaller margins as the decade wore on, even as the global refugee problem worsened. Compared to the Carter administration's paroles in the late 1970s—and Carter's one and only proposal (for FY 1981) under the Refugee Act—the Reagan administration left no doubt that it wanted smaller admissions. Such thinking flowed from domestic political factors, especially the growing restrictionist sentiment in the United States that included a significant undercurrent of opposition to refugee admissions. Indeed restrictionist politicians repeatedly linked refugee entry to the immigration problem and bashed both to build their popularity. Writing in the *New York Times*, Colorado governor and leading restrictionist Richard Lamm effectively summed up the anti-refugee position, arguing, "One refugee is a symbol; a million refugees . . . constitute a major demographic event." Lamm continued, "It's tragic that people have to live under totalitarian regimes, but we simply do not have the capacity to accept new, large infusions of refugees for resettlement on top of our regular immigrant quota." Likewise, Senator Alan Simpson, head of the Senate's Immigration Subcommittee, conceded that the United States should admit some refugees, but wanted to shrink annual admissions. In these cases, Lamm and Simpson (who, not surprisingly, also had the support of groups like FAIR) attacked generous refugee admissions as symptomatic of a larger problem: generous immigration policies and laws that allowed ever larger numbers of newcomers entry into the United States.[36]

Reagan administration officials made clear their sympathy with these critics. In explaining their planned admissions, Reagan's advisers consistently stressed that the annual quota was merely a "ceiling" that did not mean all of the visas allocated for the upcoming year would be used. Officials emphasized that refugee resettlement in the United States was the least desirable option, secondary to repatriation or resettlement in the region from which the refugees originated. Such thinking led Reagan officials, more than any of their predecessors, to highlight their work with the United Nations and other international organizations to solve the global refugee problem via mechanisms that did not involve refugees entering the United States.[37]

Even as the annual quota shrank, the Reagan administration clearly preferred to admit refugees fleeing communism and—to a lesser extent—Europeans. Indochinese refugees regularly received the highest proportion of the annual quota, followed by refugees from the Soviet Union and eastern Europe. Throughout the decade, refugees from Africa, South and Central America, and the Middle East received the smallest allocations—usually a few thousand per region annually. The Indochinese, Soviet, and eastern European allocations fluctuated, however. The Indochinese in fiscal year 1982 received 96,000 slots. By FY 1986, that ceiling had been halved (to 45,500), and it would continue to shrink, bottoming out at 38,000 in FY 1988. (It did begin to recover, to slightly over 50,000, in the late 1980s and into the early 1990s.) In the Reagan administration's FY 1982 allocation, eastern Europeans got 11,000 slots, and Soviet refugees claimed 20,000 spaces. Like the Indochinese, that allocation (the Administration combined the Soviet and eastern European quota in 1983) shrunk significantly by FY 1986, to 9,500, but rebounded strongly, so that by 1989 (the last Reagan allocation), it stood at 50,000—equal to the Indochinese quota.[38]

There were two important caveats to this "open door" for refugees from communism. First, the Reagan administration consistently reduced (and sometimes drastically) the quotas available to the Indochinese, Soviets, and eastern Europeans. Second, all Cold War refugees were not created equal in the eyes of the Reagan White House. Refugees from communism in Africa (for instance, from the conflicts in Angola and Mozambique) and in the Middle East/South Asia (for instance, Afghan refugees pouring in to Pakistan) received minuscule quotas despite their geopolitical and ideological circumstances.

The particular choices made by Reagan and his advisers as they shaped refugee policies reflected, foremost, their foreign policy aims. Reagan believed that the United States' position in relation to the Soviets had deteriorated in the 1970s, largely because of the Nixon, Ford, and Carter policies of détente. Reagan came to office determined to reverse this slide. He supported a massive military buildup to reestablish American military superiority. Reagan aggressively challenged Soviet and communist expansion in the Third World, especially in Central America. The United States under Reagan offered both rhetorical and military support to the anticommunist, American-allied governments of El Salvador (itself in the throes of a civil war) and Guatemala, as well as to the "Contras," Nicaraguan guerillas fighting against the Sandinista government closely tied to Cuba and the Soviet Union. Finally, unlike American presidents during the 1970s, the staunchly anticommunist Reagan repeatedly made clear his disdain for the Soviet political and economic system as he bitterly criticized the Kremlin. In Reagan's view, the Cold War was a contest between good and evil, a larger moral battle that framed the political, military, and economic competition.[39]

The Reagan administration's refugee policy served this last tenet of its foreign policy agenda. Reagan noted in 1982, "Nowhere in its whole sordid history have the promises of communism been redeemed. Everywhere it has exploited and aggravated temporary economic suffering to seize power and then to institutionalize economic deprivation and suppress human rights. Right now, 6 million people worldwide are refugees from Communist systems." Later that same year, Reagan declared, "one of the simple but overwhelming facts of our time is this: Of all the millions of refugees we've seen in the modern world, their flight is always away from, not toward the Communist world." (Reagan's analysis conveniently omitted the flight of ethnic Hoa from Vietnam toward communist China.) Granting large quotas to refugees from Indochina, the Soviet Union, and eastern Europe strengthened the United States' moral case in the Cold War and the battle against Soviet tyranny. For Reagan and his advisers, refugees from communism were living examples of the Soviet Union's and communism's failures. Even symbolic victories were important. Attorney General William French Smith justified the 20,000 Soviet quota requested for 1982—even though only 13,000 Soviets emigrated to the United States in 1981 and the Administration believed it highly unlikely that the 20,000 target would be filled in 1982—by asserting that the Administration wanted to "send the clearest possible signal that we do not accept restrictive Soviet emigration policies." On this score, the Reagan administration revived the efforts begun by Scoop Jackson (one of Reagan's closest, and few, Democratic allies) and the neoconservatives of the mid-1970s.[40]

Refugee policy was closely intertwined with Reagan's foreign policies toward Central America, but in a more complicated manner. The political and military upheaval and deteriorating economic conditions that wracked El Salvador, Nicaragua, and Guatemala fed a mushrooming refugee problem that topped 2 million by the end of the 1980s. At least a quarter of these refugees fled to neighboring countries, about half to Mexico. Tens of thousands of Central Americans entered the United States (some illegally) to escape the turmoil. The Administration made little effort via Refugee Act quotas to admit Central American refugees, many of whom were fleeing repression and violence in countries allied with the United States.[41] Yet Central American refugees were also tools to forward the Reagan foreign policy agenda. Reagan consistently played up fears of a Central American refugee influx into the United States as he made the case for increased American military and economic aid to the Salvadoran government and to the Contras. Reagan's argument was simple. Refugees fled communism, and if the United States failed to halt the spread of communism in Central America, then "we face a flood of refugees and a direct threat on our own southern border." At other times, Reagan warned of "feet people . . . streaming into the country, seeking a safe haven from Communist repression to our south," or "millions of refugees on our doorstep." In making these claims, Reagan effectively mixed the anticommunism of his foreign policy with the anti-newcomer sentiment of his domestic policy: the best way to stop the "flood" of newcomers was to defeat communism in Central America.[42]

Asylum cases proved increasingly numerous and just as troubling. Tens of thousands of Central Americans in the United States applied for political asylum in the 1980s, claiming that they could not return home lest they suffer persecution, and thus should be granted refugee status. A pattern quickly emerged that mirrored Reagan's refugee policies in general: the United States favored the asylum cases of Central Americans fleeing communist governments and were much more likely to deny asylum applications from those fleeing American allies. By January 1982, with

8,900 asylum applications from Salvadorans pending, 165 had been denied and 7 had won asylum. Nicaraguans fleeing the Sandinista government fared better than their Salvadoran neighbors, however. In 1984, over 8,000 applied for asylum in the United States and 1,000 won their claims. One year later, the government slowed its approvals slightly, granting asylum to 9 percent of Nicaraguan applications. (Asylum applications from eastern Europe received even better treatment. In 1985 Poles filed 1,188 asylum applications and the INS approved 451—or 38 percent.) The statistics testify not only to the anticommunist bias in asylum policies, which surely existed, but also to the general reticence to admit newcomers. The asylum admission rates of Nicaraguans (and Poles) were quite low considering the prominent place those countries earned in Reagan's foreign policy. Elliott Abrams, assistant secretary of state for human rights and humanitarian affairs defended the Administration's handling of Central American asylum cases. He asserted that the vast majority were not victims of political persecution but rather were "fleeing poverty and seeking better lives"—and thus should not win asylum and refugee status.[43]

It was as if American refugee policies—and their close sibling, asylum admissions—had returned to the early Cold War era. During the 1980s, the vast majority of refugees arrived in the United States from communist countries and the U.S. government used those admissions as weapons in their renewed offensive against the Soviet Union and communism. Reagan-era refugee admissions, then, marked a decisive and very real retreat from the human rights–influenced policies and rhetoric of late 1970s refugee affairs. Advocates of the Refugee Act designed that law specifically to give the nation's commitment to refugees a grounding in human rights rather than the Cold War, as evidenced by the law's new definition of "refugee" that lacked a reference to Cold War ideology. Yet, the Reagan administration managed to strongly reorient the nation's refugee policies and laws around Cold War principles. In part, this was the fault of the law, which left the executive branch, and specifically the White House, as the prime mover in refugee policymaking and failed to give Congress enough power to assert its prerogatives. But, just as important, the Reagan administration chose for refugee policy to reflect the White House's larger foreign policy agenda, which stressed anticommunism and turning back the Soviet threat. The Reagan White House, in other words, had no use for human rights principles as identified and defined by liberal Democrats like Kennedy and Holtzman in the previous decade.

Reagan's foreign policy agenda—and, in turn, his refugee policies—provoked great controversy and opposition among liberals and Democrats. At their bluntest, critics warned that Reagan's aggressive policies would result in nuclear war or military adventures in the Third World.

Others noted that Reagan's foreign policies allied the United States with regimes that regularly abused democratic norms and individual rights. It was a double standard, they charged, for the White House to castigate Soviet totalitarianism and human rights abuses while turning a blind eye toward America's anticommunist partners who committed similar sins. (The Administration responded that the Cold War required such alliances and that the United States' imperfect authoritarian allies could and would embrace democracy and individual rights over time, while the Soviet Union was incapable of such reforms.) Critics of Reagan's refugee policies saw similar faults. They regretted the turn away from human rights and they charged that a double standard also stood at the center of the Administration's refugee policies.

If Reagan used refugee policies to forward his foreign policy, liberals and Democrats returned the favor. They happily bashed both the Administration's refugee policies and its larger foreign policy. This symbiosis emerged most clearly in the critiques of Reagan's handling of Central America. Church groups, human rights and peace activists, and a good number of liberal Democrats like Senator Kennedy warned that Reagan's support for the Nicaraguan Contras might embroil the United States in a Vietnam-style war in Central America's jungles. These objections went hand in hand with calls for a more capacious policy toward Central American refugees and, for some, led to participation in (or, at least, support of) the "sanctuary movement," in which left-leaning religious activists sheltered Central Americans who the U.S. government wanted to deport back to their war-torn nations. This activism surely was politically astute as well. The left, liberals, and Democrats viewed Reagan's policies toward Central America and its refugees as defining issues that revealed the White House's recklessness, lack of compassion, and generally conservative nature. Few things energized Reagan's opponents and critics more than the president's handling of Central America, thus liberal Democrats had much to gain from making political noise about the fate of refugees from south of the border. Here again, domestic political and partisan considerations brought new energy to refugee politics, and vice versa.

Admissions Procedures in the 1980s

The passage of the Refugee Act did not end controversies over admissions procedures either, which came to the fore first with Indochinese admissions in the early 1980s and then with the entry of refugees from the Soviet Union and eastern Europe in the late 1980s. In both cases, the problems arose because of questions about whether applicants met the actual definition of "refugee" on the books, and whether government officials were bending the law to admit—or deny entry to—newcomers. These concerns reflected a relatively new chapter in the administration of refugee programs. In the 1950s, administrators and State and INS officials in the field focused on the security check. With the Indochinese program, the security check and the hunt for subversives had fully faded into the background, replaced by a concern with ensuring that refugees fit into a "preference" category. Now, officials at the State Department, Justice Department, and INS focused most intently on determining an applicant's eligibility under the new definition of "refugee."

In the spring of 1981, a battle erupted between the Department of State, on the one hand, and the Justice Department and the INS, on the other, over the admission of Indochinese refugees. In 1981, 317,000 Indochinese were still living in refugee camps throughout Asia. Moreover, while the arrival of boat people in the camps slowed in 1979, by early 1981 that trend had reversed as at least 10,000 newcomers arrived each month. The Carter administration reacted by pledging to admit 168,000 Indochinese in 1981 under the Refugee Act—a quota that would be largely overseen by the incoming Reagan administration. Under the entry procedures, INS officers determined whether an applicant qualified as a "refugee" and could enter the United States. In early 1981 it became clear that INS officials working in Southeast Asia had slowed the entry of the Indochinese. Interviews with the refugees had revealed that thousands of them were not victims of "political persecution," nor were they persons "of special concern" to the United States—two conditions that qualified an applicant for admission under the 1980 law. The slowdown was real. From October 1980 (the start of fiscal year 1981) through May 1981, officials deferred, or set aside, nearly 6,000 Indochinese applications. This amounted to about 8 percent of all applicants. In fact, the deferral rate after January 1981, when the Reagan administration took office, actually stood at 16 percent, showing that deferrals increased greatly in 1981.[44]

The State Department, now under the leadership of General Alexander Haig, vigorously objected to what it saw as INS and Justice Department obstructionism. American allies in the region like Thailand and Indonesia complained to the State Department that the stricter admissions policies produced ever larger camps and thus represented a retraction of the commitments that the United States made in the late 1970s to accept refugees and control the size of the camps. State Department officials were particularly exasperated because they could not understand the reasons for the stricter admissions policies. They operated under the assumption that all refugees from Indochina were "refugees" under the 1980 law—and pointed to the previous year's consultation with Congress that seemingly ratified that conclusion. Senator Edward Kennedy's public support for the State Department's position—he argued that the State Department handle admissions decisions rather than the INS because the former better understood the political conditions in a country and could thus better judge refugee status—confirmed that this was Congress's intention.[45]

The controversy ended when the Justice Department, after considerable pressure from the State Department and Haig's personal intervention, agreed that "the vast majority" of deferred applications were in fact submitted by legitimate refugees. The Department gave assurances that INS officials in Southeast Asia would not interpret the definition so stringently when it came to the Indochinese. Yet, nearly one year later, the INS established new, stricter entry requirements for Vietnamese, Cambodian, and Laotian refugees. The U.S. embassy announced that "in the future refugees will only be eligible for resettlement in the United States if they have close relatives in the United States, have worked at one time for the U.S. government or have other ties to the United States or to one of the previous noncommunist governments of Indochina and now have reason to fear persecution." An unnamed American diplomat confirmed that the change aimed to ensure that Indochinese coming to the United States were truly targets of political persecution and not just searching for better economic opportunities. Officials believed the new regulations might reduce the Indochinese applications by as much as 40 percent. The new policy, interestingly, originated in the State Department. The Thai government had earlier announced a series of measures designed to slow the refugee influx by making the Thai camps less hospitable to refugees hoping to use them as a way station to the United States. The Thais asked the United States to tighten its entry requirements as a way to further discourage refugees from setting out for the Southeast Asian camps. Once again, American foreign policy considerations and the maintenance of good relations with key allies drove admissions procedures.[46]

In 1988, questions arose about the admissions standards that governed the entry of Armenians from the Soviet Union. Under Mikhail Gorbachev, the Kremlin began easing its emigration policies, largely in the hopes of eliminating a long-standing impediment to better relations with the United States. (In fact, U.S. officials—including President Reagan—repeatedly urged Soviet leaders to permit emigrants to depart.) As a result, tens of thousands of Soviet citizens, but especially minority groups, began appearing at the U.S. embassy in Moscow to apply for visas under the Refugee Act. By late 1987 the American embassy received about 1,400 Refugee Act visa applications per month from Soviet Armenians—up from about 200 applications annually only a few years earlier. State Department officials estimated that as many as 80,000 Soviet Armenians wished to follow them. Moreover, Soviet Jews also applied for refugee visas in increasingly larger numbers in the late 1980s. In sum, these trends produced a severe crunch as the Soviet Refugee Act quota was considerably smaller. The Reagan administration eventually responded by raising the Soviet (and eastern European) refugee quota for 1989.[47]

As in the Indochinese admissions process of the early 1980s, both State Department consular officials and INS officers interviewed the applicant, but the INS determined who qualified as a refugee. Through May of 1988, the vast majority of Soviet Armenians who applied for refugee visas won them. State Department lawyers, though, believed that instead of determining whether each Armenian was truly the target of persecution, the INS granted refugee status and admission en masse. The State Department worried that such procedures evaded the intent of the Refugee Act and might produce an uncontrollable flood of refugees. INS officials who oversaw the Armenian admissions did not dispute these allegations; one asserted that Soviet Armenian admissions were "virtually automatic." One examiner apparently admitted that "in hundreds of interviews with Soviet Armenians in Rome he had not encountered a single individual claiming to have left the Soviet Union on account of persecution or fear of persecution." Liberalizers and restrictionists in Congress also attacked. The former saw the INS's relaxed admission's policies for Armenians as unfair in light of the difficulties the Indochinese faced in entering the United States. Moreover, advocates for the Indochinese saw refugee admissions as a zero-sum game: generous policies toward Soviet Armenians meant smaller quotas for the Indochinese. Restrictionist opposition arose from the belief that too many newcomers (immigrants and refugees) were arriving in the late 1980s. Senator Alan Simpson, who by the mid-1980s led the restrictionist bloc, charged, "We must distinguish between the right to leave the Soviet Union and the right to enter the United States. They are not the same."[48]

The Reagan administration muddled through this controversy before finally settling on a policy solution that while familiar to refugee affairs evaded the issue at hand. In truth, the Administration was in a tough spot. It wanted to admit refugees from communism, especially from the Soviet Union and eastern Europe, but it was not prepared for the crush of applicants, for the strictures placed on admissions by the definition of "refugee," or for a restrictionist backlash. At first the State Department announced in July 1988 that emigration of Soviet citizens to the United States via the refugee quotas would be halted until October. After October the United States began admitting Soviets as refugees, but under stricter guidelines that addressed the State Department's earlier concerns. It was not clear how many Soviets were denied refugee status in the fall of 1988. The State Department asserted only a few hundred, while resettlement organizations that assisted Soviet émigrés, especially the Hebrew Immigrant Aid Society (HIAS), claimed the denials were more numerous. With the numbers of Soviets hoping to emigrate only growing, the State Department and Justice Department finally worked out a short-term solution. The attorney general decided to parole into the United States up to 2,000 Soviets each month, while the State Department's tougher admissions standards remained in place. In essence, State, Justice, the INS, and the White House dodged the central question—whether Soviet Armenians actually qualified as refugees under the 1980 definition.[49]

While of minor order, both the Indochinese and Soviet Armenian episodes made clear several dynamics at work in the admissions process, some of which had long roots. In the 1980s, as in the previous nearly four decades of refugee admissions, INS and State Department consular officers in the field still ultimately determined who entered the United States as a refugee. And, as in the past, those officials used an interview process to ensure that applicants met specific eligibility criteria, in this case the definition of "refugee" laid out in the 1980 law. Likewise, the admissions process in the 1980s was still influenced by foreign policy considerations—especially those related to the Cold War—as well as by domestic political pressures from both restrictionists and liberalizers. Finally, refugee admissions policies engendered fierce bureaucratic battles in Washington, D.C., especially between the State Department and the INS, as policymakers looked to shape the American commitment to refugees to suit their needs.

• • •

In the late 1980s, the Cold War ended in a flurry of events: Gorbachev's embrace of political and economic reforms; arms-control agreements between the United States and the Soviet Union; the Kremlin's decision to forfeit its eastern European empire; the reunification of Germany; and the collapse of the Soviet Union. American refugee laws and policies played no role in these epochal events, yet the Cold War's end did illuminate the state of the American commitment to refugees and how far it had come since its birth in the early 1950s. Then, the Cold War—abroad and at home—was integral in shaping refugee laws, politics, and programs. But with the Cold War's conclusion, the American commitment to refugees persisted and grew, by some measures, even more capacious. The Refugee Act's annual admissions quotas grew steadily larger through the early 1990s, and over the course of the decade, the United States admitted nearly 1 million refugees, even more than in the 1980s. The American commitment to refugees had outlived the Cold War that had helped birth it, suggesting that by the 1990s that commitment was a solid and integral part of American politics, culture, and foreign affairs. At the same time, controversy remained—particularly concerning how that commitment ought to be shaped. In December 1988, the same month that Gorbachev visited President Reagan and President Elect George H.W. Bush in New York—another important summit in the Cold War's end game—the *New York Times* asked in an editorial: "Who's a Refugee?" Old questions still had relevance in a new era.[50]

The United States and Refugees
after the Cold War

REFUGEES REMAINED a fact of life in global affairs after the Cold War. The global refugee population decreased in the 1990s, and while estimates as to the size of the reduction varied by aid organizations, at least 12 million persons were refugees as the new century began. A quick review of international and regional politics confirms the changing and persistent nature of the refugee problem. With the end of the Cold War, some conflicts in Africa and Central America—which had been started, fueled, and sustained both by Soviet and American prodding and funding and (more important) by indigenous economic, political, and social motives—began to come to a close. Thus, the refugee flows that attended these conflicts also slowed. Across southern Africa, the end of violence and war in Namibia, Mozambique, and Angola permitted hundreds of thousands of refugees and displaced persons to return home. In Central America the wars of the 1970s and 1980s receded as the Cold War ended and Nicaraguans, Salvadorans, and Guatemalans (among others) also began the trek home.[1]

If good news emanated from Central America and Southern Africa, refugee crises appeared with depressing regularity during the post–Cold War 1990s. Some of these refugee problems arose precisely because the Cold War had ended. The UN estimated that with the Soviet Union's dissolution, more than 9 million former Soviet citizens moved within the fifteen new states that arose from the imperial wreckage. While some of these population flows were voluntary, many were not. A war between Armenia and Azerbaijan produced over 400,000 refugees, and civil wars and violence in the Caucusus, Tajikistan, and Chechnya destroyed the lives of hundreds of thousands. With Yugoslavia's collapse, ethnic hatreds led to genocidal wars in the Balkans and almost 1.4 million persons fled Bosnia, Croatia, and Kosovo between 1991 and 1999. In both Yugoslavia and the Soviet Union, communist governments had kept these tensions under control for decades, and the end of the Soviet and Yugoslav empires permitted them to reemerge in deadly ways. Other refugee crises in the 1990s sprung from deeply rooted political and cultural hostilities unrelated to the course of superpower relations. Rwanda erupted into awful violence in 1994 when the Hutu majority launched a genocide that killed

800,000 of the Tutsi minority in a matter of months. The successful Tutsi counterattack that halted the killings drove 300,000 Hutus into Tanzania and at least 1 million Hutus into eastern Zaire, where international aid organizations set up sprawling refugee camps.[2]

The United States' record of action in these episodes was rarely laudable, usually minimal, and sometimes morally repugnant. American diplomats helped negotiate the settlements that brought peace to southern Africa and to Central America, though the United Nations High Commissioner for Refugees led the repatriation efforts in both regions. Neither the Bush nor Clinton administrations made special efforts to resettle Central American and southern African refugees in the United States. The worst failure occurred in Rwanda. The Clinton administration refused to intervene or support international efforts that might have halted the genocide. Its efforts in the refugee crisis were paltry as well, limited to financial and material aid to international organizations that ran the refugee camps. Symbolic of the United States' engagement with the central African crisis, even those efforts went wrong; the air drops of food and supplies to the refugee camps were hastily conducted—and without warning to those below—sending Rwandan refugees and international personnel scrambling for safety from giant pallets of supplies falling from American C-130 aircraft.[3]

The United States, though, did admit over 1 million refugees between 1990 and 2000, mainly via the Refugee Act's annual quotas. Indeed, Refugee Act admissions were the main avenue by which the United States helped refugees in the former Soviet Union and Yugoslavia. Admissions peaked in the early to mid-1990s, when the Clinton administration regularly established annual quotas that exceeded 120,000. But in the second half of the decade, the annual quotas never topped 91,000 and bottomed out at 78,000 for fiscal year 1997. The United States by and large filled those quotas; annually, about 90 percent of available visas were awarded to refugees. Finally, throughout the decade, most visas went to refugees from the former Soviet Union, East Asia, and eastern Europe. Africa, South and Central America, and the Near East and South Asia received annual allocations of several thousand visas.

The Clinton administration's implementation of the Refugee Act, and its overall conduct of refugee affairs in the 1990s, then, resembled its Republican predecessors. Foremost, the annual quotas proposed by the Clinton administration shrank. Refugees from eastern Europe, the former Soviet Union, and Indochina continued in the aftermath of the superpower conflict to receive first call upon available visas. Of course, these regions suffered from significant refugee crises in the 1990s, and thus U.S. policies were understandable. But equally large and horrific refugee problems occurred in Africa during the decade, which the United States did not address via admissions. American foreign policy concerns about Europe, a continuing desire to help victims of the Cold War and the Soviet Union, and the strong lobbying of ethnic organizations—especially representing eastern Europeans or ethnic groups from the former Soviet Union—in the United States helped secure these favored admissions. American officials in the 1990s continued to stress the importance of working with organizations like the UNHCR to solve the global refugee problem. Clinton administration officials made clear that they viewed repatriation and regional resettlement of refugees as more desirable than resettlement in the United States.[4]

The Clinton administration's comments about, and its actions in, refugee affairs revealed an acute awareness of the public's concerns that the country had lost control of its borders and that too many immigrants, especially illegal immigrants, had arrived in the United States. If immigration restriction had revived in the 1980s, it peaked in the mid-1990s often on the strength of the illegal immigration question. (Even the 1990 Immigration Act, in which lawmakers increased the annual immigrant quota, was an effort not to liberalize the law, but to make it a more accurate reflection of annual admissions that had exceeded the caps established in 1965 because of loopholes.) Polling showed that between 1993 and 1995, 65 percent of Americans believed that immigration to the United States ought to be reduced. By the end of the 1990s, that percentage had fallen a little more than 20 percent, but remained historically high. Authors as diverse as Pat Buchanan and the historian Arthur Schlesinger, Jr., worried that the very cultural, political, and social bonds that united the nation were fraying under the weight of immigration (among other problems). Such sentiments played out in the political arena with real consequences. In 1992 Pat Buchanan's insurgent campaign in the Republican primary fed partly on fears of newcomers. Two years later, California voters overwhelmingly endorsed Proposition 187, which prohibited illegal immigrants from using the state's welfare services. In 1996 Congress's welfare-reform package cut legal immigrants' access to welfare programs like food stamps and Medicaid. While conservative Republicans played a key role in the 1996 legislation, pro- and anti-immigration forces remained bipartisan. Nonetheless, the right's anti-immigrant message, coupled with its growing political power, placed the Clinton administration in a very precarious position when it came to immigration and refugee issues.[5]

One Cold War refugee problem received continued attention throughout the 1990s: Cuban refugees. About 300,000 Cubans came to the United States in the two decades following the Mariel crisis, the vast majority of them receiving refugee status via an agreement between the Cuban and American governments that regulated the flow and stressed family reunification. Illegal entry into the United States did not end, but continued at rates much lower than those seen in the early 1960s and early 1980s. One upsurge occurred during the first six months of 1994 when about six thousand Cubans illegally made landfall in Florida after traversing the Florida Straits in their own crafts. This swell in illegal entries occurred because of a downturn in the island's economy. Desperate to reverse this slide, Castro threatened to encourage emigration to the United States—on the scale of 1965 or 1980—in the hopes of winning American economic concessions. The Clinton administration did not buckle to Castro's hardball, announcing that it would blockade the island if another "boatlift" began. Moreover, the Administration tried to avoid a refugee crisis by instituting what came to be known as a "wet foot, dry foot" policy. If a Cuban successfully but illegally entered the United States (that is, made it to dry land, thus the "dry foot"), he or she would be given asylum. But if the Coast Guard grabbed that refugee on the ocean ("wet foot"), then the refugee would be sent to the American military base at Guantanamo Bay, Cuba, and either returned to Cuba or allowed to leave for a third country. The decision reversed decades of policy wherein Cubans taken into U.S. custody on the ocean were paroled into the United States.[6] Important segments of the Cuban community supported the Clinton policies, and especially the Administration's decision to uphold economic sanctions and not to cave in to Castro's demands.

The Clinton administration's handling of Cuban refugee issues did not always meet the approval of the Cuban American community. A political firestorm erupted in 1999 with the spectacular controversy generated by a six-year-old Cuban boy named Elian Gonzales. He miraculously survived an ill-fated attempt to cross the Florida Straits, which took his mother's life. Gonzales stayed with his relatives in Florida while the Clinton administration decided whether to grant him (a minor) asylum or return the boy to his father, his legal guardian, who remained on the island. The Administration chose the latter course. An outraged Cuban American community—and tens of millions of other Americans—watched in horror as armed government officials under orders from Attorney General Janet Reno seized Gonzales from the home in Florida in which he was staying so that he could be returned to Cuba. The Gonzalez case and the thwarted 1994 boat lift made clear that by the 1990s the politically powerful Cuban American community centered in Florida had replaced foreign policy considerations as the key factor in the American government's Cuban refugee policy.[7]

Asylum policy in the 1990s also continued to pose challenges for the American government and court system. Asylum procedures, of course, only received a sound legal and administrative founding in the 1970s and with the 1980 Refugee Act, but they quickly became a key aspect governing the arrival of newcomers in the United States. The number of asylum applications grew markedly in the 1980s, a trend that continued in astonishing fashion in the early 1990s. From 1992 through 1996, the United States received over 100,000 asylum applications annually; in comparison, from 1980 to 1991, only once did the number of asylum applications in any one year top 75,000. As a result, a backlog of applications—sometimes numbering as high as 400,000—waited at the INS for adjudication. The upsurge in applications only fueled critics who saw asylum as a back door through which illegal immigrants tried to win legal entry into the United States by claiming refugee status. If it was a back door, it was not a large one, however. Between 1996 and 1998, the United States admitted about 10,000 asylum seekers annually. Their admission, moreover, both reflected and differed from refugee admissions in the 1990s. In 1998 more than one-third of those asylum seekers came from the former Soviet Union—replicating the bias in refugee policy—while an equally large number came from Africa, a significant departure from trends in refugee admissions.[8]

Asylum policy also emerged as the arena in which the basic principles underlying the definition of "refugee" underwent considerable reworking. Beginning in the late 1980s, a series of legal decisions promulgated by the federal courts and the separate immigration/asylum court system reinterpreted the statutory definition of "refugee" to acknowledge that gender-based persecution could be a basis for refugee status. In 1995 the INS took heed of these interpretations and issued an important administrative memo that outlined how asylum officers were to adjudicate gender-based asylum claims from women. These changes, all in all, offered a substantive change in asylum law and a broader interpretation of the definition of "refugee." The U.S. government acknowledged that gendered violence like rape (which more often is perpetrated upon women than men) and female genital mutilation were not only crimes, but might also be persecutory acts. Moreover, a woman might suffer persecution because of her membership in a social group that was either solely female and/or espoused beliefs that challenged a society's gender norms. A female asylum applicant, of course, still had to prove that the state or government did nothing to halt such persecution and that return to her homeland put her life in danger. In making this change to asylum law, the United States followed closely on the heels of Canada, which in 1993 announced that gender-based persecution could be sufficient for refugee status. A number of western-European countries quickly followed Canada's and the United States' lead.[9]

What factors led to this change? A favorable political environment emerged in the early 1990s—both in the United States and overseas—that augured well for women's-rights issues and, specifically, efforts to combat persecution of and attacks upon women. Widespread revulsion arose in North America and western Europe as the public learned that mass rapes had occurred in the Balkans and in Rwanda as parts of genocidal campaigns against persecuted populations. Relatedly, women's organizations and NGOs spoke out ever more forcefully against social practices like forced marriage and female genital mutilation in the developing world that harmed or curtailed women's rights; nowhere was concern for these issues on better display than at the United Nations' Fourth World Conference on Women in Beijing, China, in 1995. Women's rights received a greater hearing in American politics as well. Organizations like the National Organization for Women fought relentlessly for a greater government commitment to protect the rights of women, succeeding in 1994 and 1998 with the passage of major legislation aimed at curbing domestic violence against women. (It goes without saying that American antifeminists on the political right also made gains during these years, making the accomplishments of feminists all the more remarkable.) In this encouraging political environment, the Women Refugees Project—a dedicated group of American lawyers with expertise in women's-rights issues and refugee and asylum law—proposed a set of guidelines to the INS in 1994 that would integrate gender concerns into asylum claims; the guidelines became the basis of the 1995 INS memo.[10]

The changes in asylum law in the 1990s occurred because of particular events in international politics and a more favorable domestic political and cultural environment that left women's groups (and refugee advocates) more empowered to push their agenda. In a sense, these changes could only have occurred in the 1990s. The Cold War's end, and the disintegration of the Soviet empire, opened the door for 1990s conflicts that seemed to feature appalling levels of gendered violence. While gendered violence was, in fact, not new at all, the attention it received was novel. Indeed, this increase in public knowledge was possible in part because the absence of superpower conflict in international politics opened space for new issues—like the treatment of women—to achieve a better hearing. It also should be noted that human rights advocates and organizations working in the United States and internationally helped bring the new attention to women's issues. Domestically, by the 1990s, women's organizations that had formed in ferment of "second wave" feminism had achieved considerable institutional power and a degree of acceptance unknown in the 1970s, when the definition of "refugee" underwent its most significant rewriting.

At the same time, the limits of the gender revolution in asylum law were equally apparent. The changes invited a somewhat predictable backlash from restrictionist groups like FAIR who warned that an already broken asylum system would now be further overwhelmed with women from around the world pleading for asylum.[11] (No such deluge occurred.) Some advocates of women refugees claimed that the INS and courts had not gone far enough. The definition of "refugee," they believed, required an explicit reference to "gender," elevating it to equal stature with "race, religion, nationality, membership in a particular social group, or political opinion" as conditions that can lead to persecution and (ultimately) refugee status. This critique has merits and is completely understandable given the failure of asylum and refugee policy to take gender into account over the previous decades. Yet, as this book has shown, policy implementation and the administration of refugee laws and policies can bring substantive change to refugee affairs. The gender revolution in asylum law is yet another example of this phenomenon.

No events, though, have reshaped the American commitment to refugees since the end of the Cold War as greatly as the 9/11 terrorist attacks and the United States' subsequent "War on Terror." The Bush administration planned to announce its quota allocations under the Refugee Act at the end of September 2001—the first major clue as to how the new Administration might shape refugee affairs—but the attacks forced a postponement. After 9/11, the Administration ordered all refugee admissions halted immediately. In particular, the Administration closed refugee processing centers around the globe, citing concerns for the security of American personnel, and it blocked the admission of those refugees— numbering about twenty thousand—who already had been processed, won a security clearance, and given permission to travel to the United States. On this latter score, the Administration seemed to be saying that it did not trust the security checks conducted by officials in the weeks, months, and years in advance of 9/11. The Administration also began, in short order, to review and rethink all aspects of refugee admissions. A task force of Department of State and Department of Justice officials studied how to improve the safety of INS officials overseas, to toughen screening to detect security threats, and to protect against fraud and misrepresentation by refugees in the screening process. Apparently this review occurred at the highest levels of the State and Justice Departments— among officials without much experience in refugee affairs—and deliberately excluded those department officials who ran the refugee programs. Nongovernmental organizations that specialized in refugee resettlement protested that they were not consulted as well.[12]

As 2001 came to a close, the United States' refugee programs and policies were ready to resume. The Bush administration announced that it had set the refugee quota for 2002 at 70,000, the lowest quota since the mid-1980s, continuing the trend of shrinking refugee admissions begun in the mid 1990s. But the 2002 numbers did contain some surprises. The Bush administration allocated nearly one-third (22,000) of the total refugee visas to Africa; smaller but still significant numbers of visas went to the former Soviet Union (17,000) and South Asia and the Middle East

(15,000.) The Clinton administration had increased the Africa refugee quota in its last three Refugee Act proposals (from 12,000 for 1999 to almost 19,000 in 2001) and the Bush White House went even further. Refugees from three countries—Somalia, Sudan, and Liberia—received most of these visas, demonstrating a mix of American motives that echoed historically. The commitment to Somali refugees, much like the Vietnam admissions of the 1970s, flowed from the United States' disastrous efforts in that country in the early 1990s. Humanitarian needs—rather than U.S. foreign policy considerations, or a sense of responsibility generated from an abject failure in foreign policy—motivated the efforts in Liberia and Sudan. In both of those cases, but especially with Sudan, refugee advocates and nongovernmental organizations pushed for action. Among this community of pressure groups, new actors joined the long-standing Catholic, Protestant, and Jewish refugee advocates who had dominated this arena since the end of World War II. Most important, politically conservative evangelical Christians, who had in the 1980s and 1990s argued for greater admissions of co-religionists from the Soviet Union, led the call for greater action in Sudan. With the growing power of evangelical conservatives in U.S. politics generally, this group could play an important role in the future of refugee politics.[13]

It soon became clear, however, that not all was back to normal in refugee affairs. The Bush administration had fairly thoroughly reworked the admissions process, and especially the security checks and investigations into each refugee applicant, in the aftermath of 9/11. The INS and the State Department's Bureau of Population, Refugees, and Migration toughened its security checks generally. In the cases of refugee applicants of certain nationalities, the new guidelines required an FBI investigation, called a Security Advisory Opinion, of an applicant before the INS even determined if he or she even qualified as a refugee under U.S. law. Likewise, government officials more vigorously investigated the veracity of refugee applicants' claims of having family in the United States. Finally, the U.S. government ordered that all refugees be fingerprinted upon entry into the United States. The twenty thousand or so refugees who as of 9/11 had been approved for admission to the United States but had not yet entered were subject to new security checks and verification of family ties (if any) in the United States.[14]

Because of the changes in the admissions process, of the difficulty of staffing refugee processing centers around the world, and, in general, of restarting a dormant program governed by a new set of concerns and priorities, refugee admissions proceeded very slowly in 2002. By the end of the year, only 27,000 of the 70,000 slots had been used, and admissions from the Middle East moved particularly slowly. It seems likely that the shrinking admissions were part of a concerted effort to establish a much more rigorous, thorough, and ultimately time-consuming investigatory process. The annual quota was only 41 percent filled in 2003 (28,400 admissions for 70,000 spots) and 75 percent filled in 2004 and 2005. Thus the rate of admission improved, but still was significantly lower than previous admissions under the Refugee Act. Refugee advocates in the main understood the need for new procedures and a more rigorous investigatory regime, but worried that the new approach was denying and delaying entry to worthy candidates. Some also questioned whether targeting refugee admissions was the most effective way of denying terrorists entry to the United States. As Jana Mason of the U.S. Committee for Refugees noted, "You have to be a pretty dumb terrorist to decide that the way you're going to get to the U.S. is to go to Pakistan, sit in a refugee camp for six years and hope the U.S. selects you for admission." She did not need to mention that of all entrants into the United States, refugees—even before 9/11, and certainly after—faced the most arduous admissions process and security and background checks. Refugee advocates voiced these concerns in light of an equally disturbing trend: annual admissions quotas of the Bush administration's Refugee Act remained at seventy thousand from 2003 through 2006, despite protests from NGOs and members of Congress from both parties.[15]

If the Cold War was vital in birthing the American commitment to refugees, then were the 9/11 attacks a similar epochal moment? The prudent answer, of course, is that it is still too early to tell. For instance, it remains unclear whether 9/11 and the subsequent American response has reconfigured American identity to the degree that the onset of the Cold War forced Americans to redefine themselves. Yet, some preliminary observations may be made. The differences between the two eras are important and significant. First, at the Cold War's dawn, the United States had neither annual refugee admissions nor ad hoc programs. The federal government had little experience with, and few bureaucracies dedicated to, solving refugee problems. Finally, while immigration advocates surely existed in the political arena, refugee advocates were in short supply. The early twenty-first century obviously presents an entirely different set of circumstances on each of these fronts, largely because of the fifty years of American history that this book has detailed. Thus, the question is not whether to begin an American commitment to refugees, but whether—and to what degree—to maintain that commitment. Second, American foreign policy and politics in the early Cold War declared communism and the Soviet Union the chief threats to the nation's future. In the post-9/11 world, transnational terrorism has emerged as the defining threat. But as many commentators have noted, terrorism is a tactic embraced by a collection of perhaps loosely aligned nonstate actors espousing a certain brand of Islamic fundamentalism, quite different from the political and economic ideology embraced by the globe's other superpower. This distinction is important in refugee affairs because contemporary policymakers, politicians, and refugee officials working "on the ground"—in comparison to their Cold War–era predecessors—face far greater challenges in identifying the refugees they wish to help and those they wish to exclude in light of the more amorphous challenges presented by transnational terrorism.

For all of these differences, the similarities between the two eras are just as important. At the beginning of the Cold War and the "War on Terror," Americans grew more scared that subversive elements might penetrate the United States via the regular flow of newcomers. Such fears, in both cases, were central to the ways in which the nation and its leaders conceptualized a larger emerging threat to American national security that required a rethinking not only of the foundations of American foreign policy but also of important aspects of domestic politics and culture. Likewise, in both eras refugee advocates and opponents, as well as the larger immigration liberalizer and restrictionist blocs, very quickly shaped their arguments and positions to reflect this new national security paradigm; it should be noted, though, that in the post-9/11 period, opponents of newcomers, both immigrants and refugees, have more effectively accomplished this task. Just as striking, the post-9/11 era and the early Cold War years witnessed a concerted effort by government officials to use the administration of refugee laws and policies to slow the entry of newcomers. It is not hard to imagine—and, perhaps, ultimately necessary—that officials from U.S. Citizenship and Immigration Services (the successor agency to INS) and the State Department investigate the political histories and affiliations of refugees. Each of these parallels, then, points to the continuing relevance in contemporary America of some of the basic facets of Cold War refugee affairs.

But the most important continuity between the two eras is the fragility of the American commitment to refugees. Throughout the Cold War, the admission of refugees was never assured. Refugee policies, laws, and programs required constant attention, justification, and explanation, even more so because how refugee programs ran "on the ground" continually re-opened basic questions about the depth and shape of the country's commitment. This essential fragility remains today. But just as refugee admissions were worth fighting for in the Cold War, it is imperative that Americans from all walks of life—not just those with a particular interest or expertise in these issues—take up the fight anew. An "open door" for men, women, and children from around the globe who suffer from violence, persecution, and terror is an important symbol to the rest of the world, and a reminder to ourselves, of the best the United States has to offer.

Notes

ABBREVIATIONS

CSM   *Christian Science Monitor*
CR   *Congressional Record*
DDEL   Dwight D. Eisenhower Presidential Library, Abilene, Kansas
GFL   Gerald Ford Presidential Library, Ann Arbor, Michigan
HTL   Harry Truman Presidential Library, Independence, Missouri
JFKL   John F. Kennedy Presidential Library, Boston, Massachusetts
LAT   *Los Angeles Times*
LBJL   Lyndon B. Johnson Presidential Library, Austin, Texas
MH   *Miami Herald*
NYT   *New York Times*
WSJ   *Wall Street Journal*
WP   *Washington Post*

INTRODUCTION
AMERICANS AT THE GATE

1. This figure is calculated from the Department of Homeland Security, Office of Immigration Statistics, *2003 Yearbook of Immigration Statistics* (September 2004), p. 11, accessed August 24, 2007, at http://www.dhs.gov/xlibrary/assets/statistics/yearbook/2003/2003Yearbook.pdf.

2. These points build upon the thinking of Daniel Tichenor, *Dividing Lines: The Politics of Immigration Control in America* (Princeton, NJ: Princeton University Press, 2002), 176–241.

3. See, for instance, Deborah Anker and Michael Posner, "Forty-Year Crisis: A Legislative History of the Refugee Act of 1980." *San Diego Law Review* 19 (December 1981): 9–89; Norman Zucker and Naomi Zucker, *The Guarded Gate: The Reality of American Refugee Policy* (New York: Harcourt, 1987).

4. The two most important works on the history of American refugee affairs—and ones that stress the relationship between the United States' foreign policy and American refugee affairs—are Gil Loescher and John Scanlan, *Calculated Kindness: Refugees and America's Half-Open Door, 1945 to the Present* (New York: The Free Press, 1986), and Michael Gill Davis, "The Cold War, Refugees, and U.S. Immigration Policy, 1952–1965," Ph.D. Dissertation, Vanderbilt University, 1996.

5. David Wyman, *Paper Walls: America and the Refugee Crisis, 1938–1941* (Amherst: University of Massachusetts Press, 1968); Michael Marrus, *The Unwanted: European Refugees in the Twentieth Century* (New York: Oxford University Press, 1985); Leonard Dinnerstein, *America and the Survivors of the Holo-*

caust (New York: Columbia University Press, 1982); Haim Genizi, *America's Fair Share: The Admission and Resettlement of Displaced Persons, 1945–1952* (Detroit: Wayne State University Press, 1993).

6. For an example of the older scholarship that also looks at these factors, see John Higham, *Strangers in the Land: Patterns of American Nativism, 1860–1925*, (New Brunswick, NJ: Rutgers University Press, 1955). For examples of the latest scholarship, see Gary Gerstle, *American Crucible: Race and Nation in the Twentieth Century*, (Princeton, NJ: Princeton University Press, 2001); Mai Ngai, *Impossible Subjects: Illegal Aliens and the Making of Modern America* (Princeton, NJ: Princeton University Press, 2004); Tichenor, *Dividing Lines*; Aristide Zolberg, *A Nation by Design: Immigration Policy in the Fashioning of America* (Cambridge: Harvard University Press, 2006). Zolberg's comprehensive account of immigration history does not devote much attention to the historical details of refugee affairs, understandable given the breadth of his account. But he does offer very valuable and sophisticated thinking (pages 10, 18, 21)—some of which mirrors my own—explaining why the United States admitted refugees in the decades after World War II.

7. For some examples of historians who explore the intersection of the domestic and international in American history, see Kenneth Cmiel, "The Emergence of Human Rights Politics in the United States," *Journal of American History*, December 1999, 1231–50; Mary Dudziak, *Cold War Civil Rights: Race and the Image of American Democracy* (Princeton, NJ: Princeton University Press, 2000); Michael Hogan, *A Cross of Iron: Harry S. Truman and the Origins of the National Security State, 1945–1954* (Cambridge: Cambridge University Press, 1998).

8. Recent scholarship on American nationalism and national identity falls into a number of categories. The best synthetic treatment that looks at the entire twentieth century is Gerstle, *American Crucible*. Other notable synthetic works include John Bodnar, editor, *Bonds of Affection: Americans Define Their Patriotism* (Princeton, NJ: Princeton University Press, 1996); Eric Foner, *The Story of American Freedom* (New York: W.W. Norton, 1998); Michael Kammen, *Mystic Chords of Memory: The Transformation of Tradition in American Culture* (New York: Knopf, 1991). On late nineteenth-century and early twentieth century American nationalism and identity, see Matthew F. Jacobson, *Barbarian Virtues: The United States Encounters Foreign Peoples at Home and Abroad, 1876–1917* (New York: Hill and Wang, 2000); Desmond King, *Making Americans: Immigration, Race, and the Origins of Diverse Democracy* (Cambridge, MA: Harvard University Press, 2000); Cecilia O'Leary, *To Die For: The Paradox of American Patriotism* (Princeton, NJ: Princeton University Press, 1999). On post–1941 American identity and nationalism, see John Dower, *War without Mercy: Race and Power in the Pacific War* (New York: Pantheon Book, 1993); Dudziak, *Cold War Civil Rights*; Tom Engelhardt, *The End of Victory Culture: Cold War America and the Disillusioning of a Generation* (Amherst: University of Massachusetts Press, 1998); John Fousek, *To Lead the Free World: American Nationalism and the Cultural Roots of the Cold War* (Chapel Hill: University of North Carolina Press, 2000); Aaron Freidberg, "Why Didn't the United States become a Garrison State?" *International Security*, vol. 16, no. 4 (Spring 1992), 109–42; Richard

Fried, *The Russians Are Coming! The Russians Are Coming!: Pageantry and Patriotism in Cold-War America* (New York: Oxford University Press, 1998); Hogan, *A Cross of Iron*; Jane Sherron De Hart, "Containment at Home: Gender, Sexuality, and National Identity in Cold War America," in *Rethinking Cold War Culture*, Peter Kuznick and James Gilbert, eds. (Washington, DC: Smithsonian Institution Press, 2001); Michael Sherry, *In the Shadow of War: The United States since the 1930s* (New Haven: Yale University Press, 1995); Richard Slotkin, *Gunfighter Nation: The Myth of the Frontier in Twentieth-Century America* (New York: Atheneum, 1992).

9. The works listed above by Michael Hogan, Desmond King, Aaron Friedberg, and Mary Dudziak also explore how Americans actualized their conceptions of national identity.

10. Loescher's and Scanlan's *Calculated Kindness* and Davis's "The Cold War, Refugees, and U.S. Immigration Policy, 1952–1965," make this assumption. One work that takes a fleeting look at implementation—though without examining archival sources—is Anker and Posner, "Forty-Year Crisis." For an examination of the importance of the admissions process for immigrants, see Amy Fairchild, *Science at the Borders: Immigrant Medical Inspection and the Shaping of the Modern Industrial Labor Force* (Baltimore, MD: Johns Hopkins University Press, 2003).

11. This book's analysis of governance and policymaking owes much to the innovative work of historically minded political scientists like Paul Pierson and Jacob Hacker, and especially their studies of phenomena called "path dependency" and "policy feedback." As the preceding makes clear, I believe the history of refugee affairs ratifies some of the foundational conclusions of their work. But by highlighting the importance of ideology, in addition to procedures, in the development of refugee policies, this book adds to our understanding of "institutional continuity." Moreover, by stressing the importance of policy implementation, this book argues that it might be best not to overstate the continuity and stability that develops via "path dependency" and "policy feedback." For a very valuable interpretation of immigration history that applies the theories of path dependency and policy feedback, see Zolberg, *A Nation by Design*. For the political science literature on these phenomena, see Paul Pierson, "Increasing Returns, Path Dependence, and the Study of Politics," *American Political Science Review*, vol. 94, no. 2, June 2000, 251–67; Paul Pierson, "Not Just What, but *When*: Timing and Sequence in Political Processes," *Studies in American Political Development*, 14 (Spring 2000), 72–92; Suzanne Mettler, "Bringing the State Back into Civic Engagement: Policy Feedback Effects of the G.I. Bill for World War II Veterans," *American Political Science Review*, vol. 96, no. 2, June 2002, 351–65; Jacob Hacker, "Bringing the Welfare State Back In: The Promise (and Perils) of the New Social Welfare History," *Journal of Policy History*, vol. 17, no. 1, 2005, 125–54; Paul Pierson, "The Study of Policy Development," *The Journal of Policy History*, vol. 17, no. 1, 2005, 34–51; Paul Pierson, "The New Politics of the Welfare State," *World Politics*, vol. 48, no. 2, 1996, 143–79.

12. Public Law 96–212, *United States Statutes at Large, 1980*, vol. 94, pt. I (Washington, DC: U.S. Government Printing Office, 1981.)

CHAPTER 1
"THE AGE OF THE UPROOTED MAN": THE UNITED STATES AND
REFUGEES, 1900–1952

1. Eleanor Roosevelt, foreword, in Lyman White, *300,000 New Americans* (New York: Harper and Brothers, 1957), ix.

2. David Wyman, *Paper Walls: America and the Refugee Crisis, 1938–1941* (New York: Pantheon, 1985), 30–34, 43, 71; Barbara McDonald Stewart, *United States Government Policy on Refugees from Nazism* (New York: Garland Publishing, 1982), 4–7, 267–71; Michael Marrus, "Refugees, 1933–1945," in *The Encyclopedia of the Holocaust*, Israel Guttman, ed. (New York: Macmillan, 1990), 1234–36.

3. On immigration affairs in general during the first half of the twentieth century, see John Higham, *Send These to Me: Immigrants in Urban America*, 3rd ed. (Baltimore, MD: Johns Hopkins University Press, 1993); John Higham, *Strangers in the Land: Patterns of American Nativism, 1860–1925*; Roger Daniels, *Coming to America: A History of Immigration and Ethnicity in American Life*, 2nd ed. (New York: HarperPerennial, 2002); Daniel J. Tichenor, *Dividing Lines: The Politics of Immigration Control in America* (Princeton, NJ: Princeton University Press, 2002); Mai Ngai, *Impossible Subjects: Illegal Aliens and the Making of Modern America* (Princeton, NJ: Princeton University Press, 2004); Lucy Salyer, *Laws as Harsh as Tigers: Chinese Immigrants and the Shaping of Modern Immigration Law* (Chapel Hill: University of North Carolina Press, 1995); Erica Lee, *At America's Gate: Chinese Immigration in the Exclusion Era, 1882–1943* (Chapel Hill: University of North Carolina Press, 2003); Gary Gerstle, *American Crucible: Race and Nation in the Twentieth Century* (Princeton, NJ: Princeton University Press, 2001), 14–43.

4. Tichenor, *Dividing Lines*, 104, 117–21.

5. Ibid.; Higham, *Send These to Me*, 41–49; Higham, *Strangers in the Land*, 264–330; Gerstle, *American Crucible*, ch. 1.

6. Tichenor, *Dividing Lines*, 87–113; Higham, *Send These to Me*, 37–41; Daniels, *Coming to America*, 271–78; Keith Fitzgerald, *The Face of the Nation: Immigration, the State, and the National Identity* (Stanford, CA: Stanford University Press, 1996), 112–16.

7. Tichenor, *Dividing Lines*, 28–45, 65–85, 114–28; Gerstle, *American Crucible*, 103–22; Mae M. Ngai, "The Architecture of Race in American Immigration Law: A Reexamination of the Immigration Act of 1924," *Journal of American History*, vol. 86, no. 1, June 1999.

8. Desmond King, *Making Americans: Immigration, Race, and the Origins of Diverse Democracy* (Cambridge, MA: Harvard University Press, 2000), ch. 6; Gerstle, *American Crucible*, 95–122; Daniels, *Coming to America*, 283–84; Robert Divine, *American Immigration Policy, 1924–1952* (New Haven, CT: Yale University Press, 1957), 15–17.

9. David Reimers, "Refugee Policies," *Encyclopedia of American Foreign Policy*, 2nd ed., vol. 3 (New York: Charles Scribner's Sons, 2002), 357–59.

10. The League of Nations' definition (from Holborn, 680, 685) was: "Any person of Russian origin (respectively, Armenian origin, formerly a subject of the

Ottoman Empire) who does not enjoy, or who no longer enjoys, the protection of the Government of the Union of Soviet Socialist Republics (respectively, of the Government of the Turkish Republic) and who has not acquired another nationality." Louise Holborn, "The Legal Status of Political Refugees, 1920–1938," *American Journal of International Law*, vol. 32, issue 4 (October 1938), 681–86; Jon Sörenson, *The Saga of Fridjtof Nansen*, trans. J.B.C. Watkins (New York: W.W. Norton, 1932), 275–87; and generally: Claudena Skran, *Refugees in Inter-War Europe: The Emergence of a Regime* (Oxford: Clarendon Press, 1995), 109–13; Mai Ngai, *Impossible Subjects*, 9–10.

11. E. P. Hutchinson, *Legislative History of American Immigration Policy, 1798–1965* (Philadelphia: University of Pennsylvania Press, 1981), 141–42, 179, 184, 524; Reimers, "Refugee Policies," 360–61; for the 1923 definition cited in the text, see "Admission into the United States of Certain Refugees from Near Eastern Countries," Senate Report No. 1010, Sixty-Seventh Congress, Fourth Session, January 15, 1923, p. 1.

12. Wyman, *Paper Walls*, 4–5, 168–71, ch. 4, and appendix II; Bat-Ami Zucker, *In Search of Refuge: Jews and U.S. Consuls in Nazi Germany, 1933–1941* (London: Valentine-Mitchell, 2001), 40–42; Tichenor, *Dividing Lines*, 164–65.

13. Wyman, *Paper Walls*, 4–5, 168–71, ch. 4, and appendix II.

14. Ibid. ch. 4, especially 67–71, 78–79, 83–92, 116–34; Divine, *American Immigration Policy*, 101–102, and ch. 5.

15. Wyman, *Paper Walls*, 155–208 and in passim; Bat-Ami Zucker, *In Search of Refuge*, 46–61, 135–79.

16. Roger Daniels, *Guarding the Golden Door: American Immigration Policy and Immigrants Since 1882* (New York: Hill and Wang, 2004), 86–87, 91–93; Wyman, *Paper Walls*, 137–54.

17. Daniels, *Guarding the Golden Door*, 86–87, 91–93; Wyman, *Paper Walls*, 137–54.

18. "Alien Registration Act," June 28, 1940, *United States Statutes at Large,1940*, vol. 54, pt. 1, 670–76; Daniels, *Guarding the Golden Door*, 82–83; Louise London, *Whitehall and the Jews, 1933–1948: British Immigration Policy and the Holocaust* (Cambridge: Cambridge University Press, 2000.)

19. Tichenor, *Dividing Lines*, 165–67; Divine, *American Immigration Policy*, 106–107; Wyman, *Paper Walls*, 171–74, 182–97.

20. Tichenor, *Dividing Lines*, 165–67; Wyman, *Paper Walls*, 171–74, 182–97.

21. On the new conception of national security, see Michael Sherry, *In the Shadow of War: The United States since the 1930s* (New Haven: Yale University Press, 1995), 29–44.

22. Peter Novick, *The Holocaust in American Life* (New York: Houghton Miflin, 1999.)

23. Divine, *American Immigration Policy*, 110–15, Gil Loescher and John Scanlan, *Calculated Kindness: Refugees and America's Half-Open Door, 1945 to the Present* (New York: The Free Press, 1986), 2–10; Leonard Dinnerstein, *America and the Survivors of the Holocaust* (New York: Columbia University Press, 1982), 12, 77–79, 112–14; Haim Genizi, *America's Fair Share: The Admission and Resettlement of Displaced Persons, 1945–1952* (Detroit: Wayne State University Press, 1993), 67–68.

24. Genizi, *America's Fair Share*, chs. 2, 3, 5; Dinnerstein, *America and the Survivors of the Holocaust*, 101–36; Novick, *The Holocaust in American Life*, 63–103.

25. Melvyn Leffler, *A Preponderance of Power: National Security, the Truman Administration, and the Cold War* (Stanford: Stanford University Press, 1992), 1–24; Loescher and Scanlan, *Calculated Kindness*, 1–4, 15–19; Tichenor, *Dividing Lines*, 185–86.

26. Quote ("Our political institutions . . .") from John Trevor, "Coalition of American Patriotic Societies" in Dinnerstein, *America and the Survivors of the Holocaust*, 145; Revercombe quote in Dinnerstein, *America and the Survivors of the Holocaust*, 139–40; Dinnerstein, *America and the Survivors of the Holocaust*, 114–15, 137–61; Loescher and Scanlan, *Calculated Kindness*, 8–13; Genizi, *America's Fair Share*, 68–72; Michael Ybarra, *Washington Gone Crazy: Senator Pat McCarran and the Great American Communist Hunt* (Hanover, NH: Steerforth Press, 2004), 459–84.

27. Nelson Lichtenstein, *State of the Union: A Century of American Labor* (Princeton, NJ: Princeton University Press, 2002), chs. 2–4; James Patterson, *Grand Expectations: The United States, 1945–1974* (New York: Oxford University Press, 1996), 137–64; Gerstle, *American Crucible*, 139; Daniels, *Coming to America*, 305; Higham, *Send These to Me*, 198–232.

28. Genizi, *America's Fair Share*, 76; Divine, *American Immigration Policy*, 118–21, 128–29; Dinnerstein, *America and the Survivors of the Holocaust*, 174, 315–19; Loescher and Scanlan, *Calculated Kindness*, 20–21. For the law itself, see Public Law 774, *United States Statutes at Large* (Washington, DC: U.S. Government Printing Office, 1949), 1009–1014.

29. "Constitution of the International Refugee Organization," Committee Print of the Senate Committee on Foreign Relations, United States Senate, 80th Congress, 1st Session (Washington, DC: U.S. Government Printing Office, 1947), 12–13 (quotes); Public Law 774, *United States Statutes at Large* (Washington, DC: U.S. Government Printing Office, 1949), 1009.

30. Genizi, *America's Fair Share*, 82–95; Dinnerstein, *America and the Survivors of the Holocaust*, 183–216; Christopher Simpson, *Blowback: America's Recruitment of Nazis and Its Effects on the Cold War* (New York: Weidenfield and Nicolson, 1988.)

31. Dinnerstein quote, *America and the Survivors of the Holocaust*, 253; Dinnerstein, *America and the Survivors of the Holocaust*, 217–53; Divine, *American Immigration Policy*, ch. 7; Genizi, *America's Fair Share*, ch. 6.

32. Fitzgerald, *The Face of the Nation*, 199; Loescher and Scanlan, *Calculated Kindness*, 4–24.

33. "Statement by the President upon Signing the Displaced Persons Act, June 25, 1948," *Public Papers of the Presidents of the United States Harry S. Truman, 1948* (Washington: U.S. Government Printing Office, 1964), 382–85; "Special Message to the Congress on the Admission of Displaced Persons, July 7, 1947," *Public Papers of the Presidents of the United States Harry S. Truman, 1947* (Washington, DC: U.S. Government Printing Office, 1963), 327–29.

34. Tichenor, *Dividing Lines*, 176–81, 188–89; Daniels, *Guarding the Golden Door*, 112–16.

35. Gerstle, *American Crucible*, 258–59; Divine, *American Immigration Policy*, 165–85; Tichenor, *Dividing Lines*, 188–94.

36. Gerstle, *American Crucible*, 257–62, McCarran quote in Gerstle, *American Crucible*, 260; Divine, *American Immigration Policy*, 165–85; King, *Making Americans*, ch. 8, and especially 237–39.

37. Jerome Edwards, "McCarran, Patrick Anthony" in *The Harry S. Truman Encyclopedia*, Richard Kirkendall, ed. (Boston, MA: GK Hall and Co., 1989), 225–26; Dinnerstein, *America and the Survivors of the Holocaust*, 217–24; Peter Felten, "Patrick Anthony McCarran," *American National Biography*, John Garraty and Mark Carnes, eds., vol. 14 (New York: Oxford University Press, 1999), 840–42.

38. Ybarra, *Washington Gone Crazy*, 636–56, especially 639–40.

39. Hutchinson, *Legislative History of American Immigration Policy*, 297–313; Tichenor, *Dividing Lines*, 191–96.

40. Gerstle, *American Crucible*, 259; Stephen Wagner, "The Lingering Death of the National Origins Immigration System: A Political History of United States Immigration Policy, 1952–1965," Ph.D. Dissertation, Harvard University, 1986, 106–16; Harry S. Truman, "Veto to Revise the Laws Relating to Immigration, Naturalization, and Nationality, June 25, 1952," *Public Papers of the Presidents of the United States, Harry S. Truman, 1952–1953* (Washington, DC: U.S. Government Printing Office, 1966), 441–47.

41. Truman, ibid.

42. For a critique of Truman's actions during the Red Scare and McCarthyism, see Schrecker, *The Age of McCarthyism: A Brief History with Documents* (Boston: Bedford Books, 1994), 20–25. For a balanced assessment, see Donald McCoy, *The Presidency of Harry S. Truman* (Lawrence: University of Kansas Press, 1984), 83–84, 216–20, 274–76; Alonzo Hamby, *Beyond the New Deal: Harry S. Truman and American* Liberalism (New York: Columbia University Press, 1973), 468–69.

43. On the importance of anticommunism to American politics, culture, and society, see John Fousek, *To Lead the Free World: American Nationalism and the Cultural Roots of the Cold War* (Chapel Hill: University of North Carolina Press, 2000); Stephen J. Whitfield, *The Culture of the Cold War* (Baltimore, MD: Johns Hopkins University Press, 1991); Richard Fried, *The Russians Are Coming! The Russians Are Coming! Pageantry and Patriotism in Cold-War America* (New York: Oxford University Press, 1998), quote page 67; Elaine Tyler May, *Homeward Bound: American Families in the Cold War Era* (New York: Basic Books, 1988); Michael Hogan, *A Cross of Iron: Harry S. Truman and the Origins of the National Security State, 1945–1954* (Cambridge: Cambridge University Press, 1998) 419–62.

44. Jeff Broadwater, *Eisenhower and the Anti-Communist Crusade* (Chapel Hill: University of North Carolina Press, 1992), 1–25; Sean Savage, *Truman and the Democratic Party* (Lexington: University of Kentucky Press, 1997), 25–56, 97–103, 171–84.

45. Broadwater, *Eisenhower and the Anti-Communist Crusade*, 1–25; Charles Gati, *Failed Illusions: Moscow, Washington, Budapest, and the 1956 Hungarian Revolution* (Washington, DC: Woodrow Wilson Center Press, 2006), 71–72.

46. Divine, *American Immigration Policy*, 184–85; Davis, "The Cold War, Refugees, and U.S. Immigration Policy, 1952–1965," 9–15, 36, 70–78. On Italy, see "Memorandum by Commissioner Rosenfield to the Chairman of the Displaced Persons Commission, January 9, 1952," 1565–72. On Germany, see "The Director of the Bureau of German Affairs (Byroade) to the United States High Commissioner for Germany (McCloy), January 30, 1952," 1578; "The United States High Commission for Germany (McCloy) to the Director of the Bureau of German Affairs (Byroade), February 5, 1952," 1579; "Minutes of the 59th Meeting of the Policy Committee on Immigration and Naturalization, held in the Department of State . . . March 5, 1952," 1580–1586. Each of these memos can be found in *Foreign Relations of the United States, 1952–1954*, vol. I *General: Economic and Political Matters (in two parts) Part 2*, ed. William Z. Slany (Washington, DC: U.S. Government Printing Office: 1983).

47. See "Special Message to the Congress on Aid for Refugees and Displaced Persons, March 24, 1952" in *The Public Papers of the President of the United States: Harry S. Truman, 1952–53* (Washington DC: U.S. Government Printing Office, 1966), 209–15; on the relationship between the MWA and the EMP, see David D. Lloyd, "Memorandum for the President, Subject: Immigration Bills," May 3, 1952; Student Research File, Box 50 "Immigration Policy: President Truman's Veto of the McCarran-Walter Act," File 11, HTL; "Plea for DPs Faces Congress Opposition," *NYT*, March 30, 1952, Section IV, 7.

CHAPTER 2
"A MYSTIC MAZE OF ENFORCEMENT": THE REFUGEE RELIEF PROGRAM

1. "Celler Assails Refugee Relief," *NYT*, December 14, 1954, 50
2. Michael Gill Davis, "The Cold War, Refugees, and U.S. Immigration Policy, 1952–1965," Ph.D. Dissertation, Vanderbilt University, 1996, 70–78.
3. Ibid., 66, 78.
4. "Memorandum to the Secretary of State" from Dwight D. Eisenhower, March 24, 1953, Whitman File, Dulles-Herter Series, Box 1, File: "Dulles, John F., March 1953," DDEL; "Memorandum for the President," from John Foster Dulles, March 26, 1953, Whitman File, Dulles-Herter Series, Box 1, File: "Dulles, John F., March 1953," DDEL; Robert Divine, *Foreign Policy and U.S. Presidential Elections, Volume II, 1952–1960* (New York: New Viewpoints, 1974), 50–56, 81–85; Jeff Broadwater, *Eisenhower and the Anti-Communist Crusade* (Chapel Hill: University of North Carolina Press, 1992) 26–53; Charles Gati, *Failed Illusions: Moscow, Washington, Budapest, and the 1956 Hungarian Revolution* (Washington, DC: Woodrow Wilson Center Press, 2006), 71–72, 110–11.
5. The Intergovernmental Committee for European Migration, "Report of the Director on the Work of the Committee for the Year 1957," March 6, 1958, 24, 27; Howard Margolian, *The Truth about Nazi War Criminals in Canada, 1946–1956* (Toronto: University of Toronto Press, 2000), 148–86; Freda Hawkins, *Critical Years in Immigration: Canada and Australia Compared* (Kingston, Ontario: McGill-Queen's University Press, 1989), 164–65; Colin Holmes, *John Bull's*

Island: Immigration and British Society, 1871–1971 (Basingstoke: Macmillan, 1988), 211–72.

6. "Letter to the President of the Senate and to the Speaker of the House of Representatives Recommending Emergency Legislation for the Admission of Refugees," April 22, 1953. *Public Papers of the Presidents of the United States, Dwight D. Eisenhower, 1953* (Washington, DC: U.S. Government Printing Office, 1954).

7. "Memorandum by Frederick J. Mann to the Administrator of the Bureau of Security and Consular Affairs (McLeod)," *Foreign Relations of the United States, 1952–1954,* vol. I, *General: Economic and Political Matters (in two parts) Part 2,* ed. William Z. Slany (Washington, DC: U.S. Government Printing Office: 1983), 1627–29 (cited hereafter as *"FRUS, 1952–1954* vol. I").

8. "Memorandum by Frederick J. Mann to the Administrator of the Bureau of Security and Consular Affairs (McLeod)," *FRUS, 1952–1954,* vol. I, 1627–29; "Committee Print, May 15, 1953," "Emergency Immigration Program, Hearings before Subcommittee No. 1 of the Committee on the Judiciary," May 21, 22, June 8, 9, 10, and July 9, 1953, House of Representatives, 83rd Congress, First Session (Washington DC: U.S. Government Printing Office, 1953), 1–5 (cited hereafter as "House Hearings, *Emergency Immigration Program,* 1953"); "Committee Print—May 26, 1953," "Emergency Migration of Escapees, Expellees, and Refugees, Hearings before the Subcommittee of the Committee on the Judiciary," May 26, 27, 28, and July 1, 1953, United States Senate, 83rd Congress, First Session (Washington, DC: U.S. Government Printing Office: 1953), 2–6 (cited hereafter as "Senate Hearings, *Emergency Migration,* 1953"); "HR. 6481," "S. 1917," and the "Committee Bill," available in "Special Migration Act, 1953—Conference Report," *CR,* 85th Congress, First Session, page 10805.

9. See the sources cited in n. 8.

10. Ibid.; "S. 1917," May 15, 1953, Record Group 46, Records of the United States Senate, Committee on the Judiciary, 83rd Congress, First Session, Box 35, File "S. 1917," National Archives; "Confidential Committee Print NO.2 S. 1917" July 4, 1953, Record Group 46, Records of the United States Senate, Committee on the Judiciary, 83rd Congress, First Session, Box 35, File "S. 1917," National Archives; "Confidential Committee Print S. 1917," July 13, 1953, Record Group 46, Records of the United States Senate, Committee on the Judiciary, 83rd Congress, First Session, Box 35, File "S. 1917," National Archives; "Confidential Committee Print No. 3 S. 1917," July 14, 1953, Record Group 46, Records of the United States Senate, Committee on the Judiciary, 83rd Congress, First Session, Box 35, File "S. 1917," National Archives; "Committee Print S. 1917," July 20, 1953, Record Group 46, Records of the United States Senate, Committee on the Judiciary, 83rd Congress, First Session, Box 35, File "S. 1917," National Archives.

11. Maxwell Rabb, Oral History Interview, May 13, 1975, 27–28, DDEL; "Two Requests," *The Commonweal,* May 15, 1953, 138–39; "Eisenhower Refugee Measure Faces Bipartisan Changes," *WP,* 23 May 1953; David Reimers, *Still the Golden Door,* 2nd ed. (New York: Columbia University Press, 1992), 156.

12. Roger Biles, *Crusading Liberal: Paul H. Douglas of Illinois* (Dekalb: Northern Illinois University Press, 2002), 94–95; Allen Nevins, *Herbert H. Leh-*

man and His Era (New York: Charles Scribner's Sons, 1963); Steven Gillon, *Politics and Vision: The ADA and American Liberalism, 1947–1985* (New York: Oxford University Press, 1987), 57–130.

13. For the 1951 poll, see George Gallup, *The Gallup Poll, Public Opinion 1935–1971*, vol. II, 1949–58 (New York: Random House, 1972), 1029–30; for the RRA poll, see Rita Simon, *Public Opinion and the Immigrant: Print Media Coverage, 1880–1980* (Lexington, MA: Lexington Books, 1985) 36–37.

14. Rep. Robert Byrd (D-WV), *Appendix to the Congressional Record*, July 28, 1953, A4766; Secretary of Labor Martin Durkin, House Hearings, *Emergency Immigration Program*, 1953, 40–47. Representative Kenneth Keating, *CR*, July 28, 1953, 10183; Statement of the Congress of Industrial Organizations, Senate Hearings, *Emergency Migration*, 1953, 302–303; Senator Herman Welker, *CR*, July 29, 1953, 10246; Senator Olin Johnston, *CR*, July 28, 1953, 10117; "Legion for McCarran Act" *NYT*, May 1, 1953; John Cervase (Columbian Civic Club), House Hearings, *Emergency Immigration Program*, 1953, 205; Senator Herbert Lehman, *CR*, July 28, 1953, 10106.

15. Crete Anderson (American Legion), Senate Hearings, *Emergency Migration*, 1953, 124; Rep. Francis Walter, *CR*, July 28, 1953, 10154, 10171; see also, Rep. J. Frank Wilson, *CR*, July 28, 1953, 10153–10154.

16. Senator Watkins, *CR*, May 15, 1953, 4981; Rep. John Fino, *CR*, July 28, 1953, 10165; Monsignor Edward Swanstrom (NCWC), House Hearings, *Emergency Immigration Program*, 1953, 102.

17. Rep. Emanuel Celler, *CR*, July 28, 1953, 10168.

18. Judge Juvenal Marchisio, House Hearings, *Emergency Immigration Program*, 1953, 186; see also, Marchisio, Senate Hearings, *Emergency Migration*, 1953, 154–67; Peter Wagner (United Friends of Needy and Displaced People of Yugoslavia, Inc.), Senate Hearings, *Emergency Migration*, 1953, 148–49; George Washington Williams, Senate Hearings, *Emergency Migration*, 1953, 185; see also Sen. Allen Ellender, *CR*, July 28, 1953, 10121; Madeline Leetch (National Society of New England Women), Senate Hearings, *Emergency Migration*, 1953, 189.

19. Rep. Stuy Wainwright, *CR*, July 28, 1953, 10166; Rep. Emanuel Celler, *CR*, July 28, 1953, 10168.

20. Rep. Wilson, *CR*, July 28, 1953, 10153–54; Rep. Donald Matthews, *CR*, July 28, 1953, 10186–87; Crete Anderson (American Legion), Senate Hearings, *Emergency Migration*, 1953, 136.

21. Gary Reichard, *The Reaffirmation of Republicanism: Eisenhower and the Eighty-Third Congress* (Knoxville: University of Tennessee Press, 1975), 85–87; E. P. Hutchinson, *Legislative History of American Immigration Policy, 1798–1965* (Philadelphia: University of Pennsylvania Press, 1981), 317–19; Davis, "The Cold War, Refugees, and U.S. Immigration Policy, 1952–1965," 82–97.

22. The Refugee Relief Act of 1953, *United States Statutes-at-Large*, vol. 67 (1953): 401–403.

23. "Procedures Stall New Refugee Law," *NYT*, August 19, 1953, 17; "Refugee Prospect Cheers President," *NYT*, March 25, 1954, 14; John F. Dulles to Scott McLeod, September 23, 1953, *FRUS, 1952–1954*; vol. I, 1631–32; "Highlights of the Interdepartmental Meeting regarding the Refugee Relief Act," November 3, 1953, Records of the Bureau of Security and Consular Affairs, General

Records of the Department of State, Box 10, File: "Refugee Relief Program—General," National Archives II; The Refugee Relief Act of 1953, *United States Statutes-at-Large*, vol. 67 (1953): 403–406; Senator Herbert Lehman, *CR*, July 28, 1953, 10106.

24. The Refugee Relief Act of 1953, *United States Statutes-at-Large*, vol. 67 (1953): 403–406; The Immigration and Nationality Act, *United States Statutes-at-Large*, vol. 66 (1952): 184–90.

25. "Final Report of the Administrator of the Refugee Relief Act of 1953, as Amended" (Washington, DC: U.S. Government Printing Office, 1958), 30.

26. See generally, Broadwater, *Eisenhower and the Anticommunist Crusade*; David Oshinsky, *A Conspiracy So Immense: The World of Joe McCarthy* (New York: Macmillan, 1983), 262–64; Robert Griffith, *The Politics of Fear: Joseph R. McCarthy and the Senate* (Amherst: University of Massachusetts Press, 1987), 196–99; Robert N. Johnson, "The Eisenhower Personnel Security Program," *Journal of Politics*, vol. 18, November 1956, 635.

27. Eisenhower quote from Broadwater, *Eisenhower and the Anticommunist Crusade*, 64, 116, 117 (quote); McLeod quoted in "We're Cleaning Up 'The Mess' in the State Department," *U.S. News and World Report*, February 12, 1954, 62–73.

28. McCarran aide quote from Michael Ybarra, *Washington Gone Crazy: Senator Pat McCarran and the Great American Communist Hunt* (Hanover, NH: Steerforth Press, 2004) 715; quotes from Jack Minor to Scott McLeod, "Memorandum," September 22, 1953, Records of the Bureau of Security and Consular Affairs, General Records of the Department of State, Box 10, File: "Refugee Relief Program—General," National Archives II; "U.S. Opening Door to 200,000 Aliens," *NYT*, October 19, 1953, 22; "U.S. Plan to Admit Refugee Started," *NYT*, November 5, 1953, 46.

29. "Refugee Program to Be Stepped Up," *NYT*, January 30, 1954, 30; "Refugee 'Slight' Cited," *NYT*, March 26, 1954, 3; "Immigrant Program Declared in Danger," *NYT*, May 8, 1954, 35; "Third Semiannual Report of the Administrator of the Refugee Relief Act of 1953, as Amended," February 8, 1955 (Washington, DC: U.S. Government Printing Office, 1955), 11; "First Semiannual Report of the Administrator of the Refugee Relief Act of 1953," January 30, 1954 (Washington, DC: U.S. Government Printing Office, 1954), 10.

30. "Refugee Program to Be Stepped Up," *NYT*, January 30, 1954, 30; "Summary of Conference on April 5, 1954 of the Administration of the Immigration and Nationality Act and the Refugee Relief Act of 1953," April 6, 1954, RG 85, Acc # 59A 2038, File 56336/401, Box 48, National Archives II; "Nations Blamed In Refugee Snag," *NYT*, February 12, 1954, 10; "Few Refugees Benefit From Changes in Law," *NYT*, September 12, 1954, section IV, 4; "Third Semiannual Report of the Administrator of the Refugee Relief Act of 1953, as Amended," February 8, 1955, 18; "Refugee Director Backs Easing Law," *NYT*, January 14, 1955, 9.

31. "Lehman Honored for Immigrant Aid," *NYT*, February 1, 1954, 7; "Immigrant Program Declared in Danger," *NYT*, May 8, 1954, 35; "A Crack in the Door," *NYT*, July 9, 1954, 16; "These Inaccessible Shores," *Commonweal*, September 24, 1954, 598; "Refugees Are Still Blocked," *America*, January 15, 1955,

10; "Lutherans Score '53 Refugee Law," *NYT,* February 3, 1954, 26; testimony of Edward Corsi, "Investigation on Administration of Refugee Relief Act, Hearings before a Subcommittee of the Committee on the Judiciary," U.S. Senate, 84th Congress, First Session, April 14, 1955, 36–38; Stephen Wagner, "The Lingering Death of the National Origins Immigration System: A Political History of United States Immigration Policy, 1952–1965," Ph.D. Dissertation, Harvard University, 1986, 258–279; "President Offers Refugee Aid Plan and Urges Speed" (page 1) and "Text of President's Refugee Message" (page 6), *NYT,* May 28, 1955; "President Supports Refugee Act Revision," *NYT,* April 28, 1955, 1.

32. "Lehman Suggests Ouster of M'Leod," *NYT,* April 25, 1955, 15; "Lehman Bids Senate Revamp Relief Act," *NYT,* April 26, 1955, 21; for Celler's comments, see "Celler Assails Refugee Relief," *NYT,* December 14, 1954, 50; Emanuel Celler, "To Aid Refugee Entry" in "Letters to the Times," *NYT,* February 28, 1955, 18; "President Endorses Refugee Act Revision," *NYT,* April 28, 1955, 1; "Corsi Sees a Snag to Refugee Entry," *NYT,* June 2, 1955, 12.

33. "Third Semiannual Report of the Administrator of the Refugee Relief Act of 1953, as Amended," February 8, 1955, 5, 16, 18; Refugee Relief Act of 1953, *United States Statutes-at-Large,* vol. 67 (1953): 404; "Preliminary Questionnaire to Be Used in Connection with the Refugee Relief Act of 1953," U.S. House of Representatives, Committee on the Judiciary, 83rd Congress, Record Group 233, Box 1073, File: "H.R. 6481 (1 of 3 Folders)," National Archives I.

34. Anthony Micocci to Scott McLeod (and attached "Draft"), October 15, 1954, Records of the Bureau of Security and Consular Affairs, General Records of the Department of State, Box 9, File: "Implementation of the Refugee Act," National Archives II.

35. "Immigrant Case of Gottfried E. Mahlow," Box 3381, File 15 ("General File—RRA of 1953, Application of the INA"), Records of the Immigration and Naturalization Service, General Records of the Department of Justice, National Archives.

36. Ibid.

37. Ibid.

38. "Immigrant Case of Kurt Clemens Bruss" Box 3381, File 15 ("General File—RRA of 1953, Application of the INA"), Records of the Immigration and Naturalization Service, General Records of the Department of Justice, National Archives.

39. Ibid.

40. "Immigrant Case of George Faud Mantoura," Box 3381, File 56351/4.14, Records of the Immigration and Naturalization Service, General Records of the Department of Justice, National Archives.

41. Ibid.

42. The three cases discussed in the text are part of thirty refugee applications—complete with the interview transcripts—that found their way into the INS files at the National Archives.

43. Ellen Schrecker, *Many Are the Crimes: McCarthyism in America* (Princeton, NJ: Princeton University Press, 1998); David Johnson, *The Lavender Scare: The Cold War Persecution of Gays and Lesbians in the Federal Government* (Chicago: University of Chicago Press, 2004).

44. "President Offers Refugee Aid Plan and Urges Speed," *NYT*, May 28, 1955, 1; "Refugees in U.S. Far Below Goal," *NYT*, March 7, 1956, 20; "U.S. Reports Lag in Refugee Relief," *NYT*, January 4, 1957, 10; "Final Report of the Administrator of the Refugee Relief Act of 1953, as Amended" (Washington, DC: U.S. Government Printing Office, 1958), 140; on the 1954 amendment, see "Refugee Act Amendments," *The Congressional Quarterly Almanac, 1954*, vol. 10 (Washington, DC: Congressional Quarterly News Features), 283–84.

45. "Lawyer Named to Refugee Post with Orders to Speed Entry," *NYT*, June 10, 1955, 1; Gati, *Failed Illusions*, 110–11.

46. "Visa Aides Speed Refugee Plans," *NYT*, July 3, 1955, 3; "Entry of Refugees Said to Be on the Rise," *NYT*, August 30, 1955, 20; "Joint Aid Speeds Up Program," *WP*, August 5, 1955, 33; "New Speed Noted in Refugee Admissions," *WP*, August 6, 1955, 19.

47. "Final Report of the Administrator of the Refugee Relief Act of 1953, as Amended" (Washington, DC: U.S. Government Printing Office, 1958), 30–51, 139, 140; Margot Canaday, " 'Who Is a Homosexual?' The Consolidation of Sexual Identities in Mid-Twentieth Century American Immigration Law," *Law and Social Inquiry*, Spring 2003, 351–86.

48. "Man with a New Look," *NYT*, May 11, 1956, 10; "A New Expediter of the Refugee Relief Act," *New Republic*, June 20, 1955, 5; "Trouble Shooter," *U.S. News and World Report*, June 17, 1955, 16; "Pierce Gerety Sr., Ex-U.S. Aide, Dead," *NYT*, December 5, 1983, D14.

49. "Final Report of the Administrator of the Refugee Relief Act of 1953, as Amended" (Washington, DC: U.S. Government Printing Office, 1958), 51; "Eastland Fears Red Agent Influx," *NYT*, September 17, 1955, 10; "Security Screening of Refugees," Hearing before the Subcommittee to Investigate the Administration of the Internal Security Act and Other Internal Security Laws, June 9, 1955 (Washington, DC: U.S. Government Printing Office, 1955); "Celler Criticizes Stand on Refugees," *NYT*, September 20, 1955, 3.

CHAPTER 3
"FROM HUNGRY, NEW AMERICANS": THE UNITED STATES
AND HUNGARIAN REFUGEES

1. John Lewis Gaddis, *We Know Now: Rethinking Cold War History* (Oxford: Oxford University Press, 1997), 129–31, 208–209; J.A.S. Grenville, *A History of the World in the Twentieth Century*, vol. II, *Conflict and Liberation, 1945–1996* (Cambridge: Harvard University Press, 1997), 491–501, 529; Nicholas Riasanovsky, *A History of Russia*, Fourth Edition (New York: Oxford University Press, 1984), 539–43.

2. György Litván, ed. *The Hungarian Revolution of 1956: Reform, Revolt, and Repression, 1953–1963* (New York: Longman, 1996), 17–34, 52–60; Grenville, *A History of the World*, 501; Joseph Rothschild, *Return to Diversity: A Political History of East Central Europe Since World War II* (New York: Oxford University Press, 1989), 156–60; Csaba Békés, "New Findings on the 1956 Hungarian Revolution, " *Cold War International History Project Bulletin* (Issue 2), Fall 1992, 1–3.

3. Békés, "New Findings," 2 (quotes); Litván, *The Hungarian Revolution of 1956*, 64–69.

4. Rothschild, *Return to Diversity*, 159–60; Litván, *The Hungarian Revolution of 1956*, 68–73; Csaba Békés, "Working Paper #16: The 1956 Hungarian Revolution and World Politics," *The Cold War International History Project*, September, 1996, 1–43.

5. "Dead in Budapest Put at 20,000; Exile Describes Street Fighting," *NYT*, November 11, 1956, 34; for an example of a contemporary historian using the 20,000 dead figure, see Gaddis, *We Now Know*, 211. For the latest assessment of casualty figures from the Soviet intervention, see Litván, *The Hungarian Revolution of 1956*, 103.

6. While the policy of liberation was never implemented, the Eisenhower administration did support a number of covert operations designed to build and strengthen opponents of the Soviet Union and communism behind the Iron Curtain. See Stephen Ambrose, *Eisenhower: The President*, vol. II (New York: Simon and Schuster, 1984), 355. See also Békés, "The 1956 Hungarian Revolution and World Politics," 4–5; Michael Gill Davis, "The Cold War, Refugees, and U.S. Immigration Policy, 1952–1965," Ph.D. Dissertation, Vanderbilt University, 1996, 108–10. For Eisenhower quote, see "Memorandum of Discussion at the 301st Meeting of the National Security Council, October 26, 1956," *Foreign Relations of the United States, 1955–57, Eastern Europe*, vol. XXV (Washington, DC: U.S. Government Printing Office, 1990) (cited hereafter as *FRUS, 1955–1957, Eastern Europe*).

7. "Address by the Secretary of State . . ." *FRUS, 1955–57, Eastern Europe*, 318 (Dulles quote); "Ike Offers Hungary $20 Million in Food," *WP*, November 3, 1956, 1 (Eisenhower quote); "Editorial Note," *FRUS, 1955–57, Eastern Europe*, 364; Gaddis, *We Now Know*, 235; Davis, "The Cold War, Refugees, and U.S. Immigration Policy," 110–12, 118; Békés, "The 1956 Hungarian Revolution and World Politics," 27–28; Ambrose, *Eisenhower*, 355; Brian McCauley, "Hungary and Suez, 1956: The Limits of Soviet and American Power," *Journal of Contemporary History*, vol. 16, 1981 (New York: SAGE), 777–800.

8. Békés, "The 1956 Hungarian Revolution and World Politics," 27, 30–33; McCauley, "Hungary and Suez, 1956," 793; Ambrose, *Eisenhower*, 375; Gil Loescher and John Scanlan, *Calculated Kindness: Refugees and America's Half-Open Door, 1945 to the Present* (New York: The Free Press, 1986), 50–54; Davis, "The Cold War, Refugees, and U.S. Immigration Policy," 104–105, 112–22.

9. "Personal . . . From Budapest," *Saturday Evening Post*, December 15, 1956, 25; Donald Critchlow, *Phyllis Schlafly and Grassroots Conservatism: A Woman's Crusade* (Princeton, NJ: Princeton University Press, 2006), 86–88; Rick Perlstein, *Before the Storm: Barry Goldwater and the Unmaking of the American Consensus* (New York: Hill and Wang, 2001), 66–67, 105–106; Gati, *Failed Illusions*, 110–11.

10. "A Strange Communist," *NYT*, October 25, 1956, 8. For a few examples of the media's portrayal of the participants in the Hungarian revolution, see "Hungary's Agony," *New York Times Magazine*, November 11, 1956, 18–19; "A Desperate Fight For Freedom," *Life*, November 5, 1956, 37–45.

11. For estimates of the size of the refugee problem in early November, see Maxwell Rabb to Sherman Adams, November 8, 1956, Official File 154–N–2, Box 823, White House Central Files, DDEL; "Hungarians Flee Land by Thousands," *WP*, November 6, 1956, A7; "Nations Asked to Aid 15,000 Hungarians," *WP*, November 7, 1956. On Austrian concerns about the influx of Hungarian refugees, see "Memorandum for the Deputy Under Secretary of State for Political Affairs (Murphy) to the Secretary of State," *FRUS*, 1955–57, *Eastern Europe*, 326–27 (quotes.) On the interagency committee's discussions, see "Notes on the 39th Meeting of the Special Committee on Soviet and Related Problems, Washington, October 26, 1956," *FRUS*, 1955–57, *Eastern Europe*, 301; "Memorandum of a Conference with the President, White House, Washington, D.C., October 27, 1956, 11 A.M.," *FRUS*, 1955–57, *Eastern Europe*, 309–10; "Notes on the 43rd Meeting of the Special Committee on Soviet and Related Problems, Washington, November 5, 1956," *FRUS*, 1955–57, *Eastern Europe*, 395–97; "Notes on the 44th Meeting of Special Committee on Soviet and Related Problems, Washington, November 6, 1956," *FRUS*, 1955–57, *Eastern Europe*, 400–402; Gati, *Failed Illusions*, 111–12.

12. Pierce Gerety to the Acting Secretary, November 7, 1956, "Hungarian Refugee Situation," Record of the Department of State, Records of the Bureau of Security and Consular Affairs, Box 10, File "Plans and Procedures for the Settlement of Hungarian Refugees," National Archives II; Maxwell Rabb to Sherman Adams, November 8, 1956, Official File 154–N–2, Box 823, White House Central Files, DDEL; Martin Bursten, *Escape From Fear* (Syracuse, NY: Syracuse University Press, 1958), 55–56; "Man with a New Look," *NYT*, May 11, 1956, 10; "McLeod May Be Envoy to Ireland," *WP*, March 17, 1957, A7; "McLeod Job Plan Opposed," *WP*, April 3, 1957, A10; Davis, "The Cold War, Refugees, and U.S. Immigration Policy," 125.

13. On the congressional briefing, see Bursten, *Escape from Fear*, 56–57.

14. "Statement by the President concerning the Admission of Refugees from Hungary," November 8, 1956, *Public Papers of the Presidents of the United States: Dwight D. Eisenhower, 1956* (Washington, DC: U.S. Government Printing Office, 1958), 1093; "The Refugee Relief Act of 1953," *United States Statutes-at-Large*, vol. 67 (1953), 401–402 (definition of escapee).

15. "Refugees Helped to Haven in the U.S.," *NYT*, November 19, 1956, 10; "Aid Distribution in Hungary Gains," *NYT*, November 17, 1956, 9; Loescher and Scanlan, *Calculated Kindness*, 52; Freda Hawkins, *Critical Years in Immigration: Canada and Australia Compared* (Kingston, Ontario: McGill-Queen's University Press, 1989), 165; Colin Holmes, *John Bull's Island: Immigration and British Society, 1871–1971* (Basingstoke: Macmillan, 1988), 210.

16. "Department of State Memorandum of Conversation, 'Subject: Processing of Visas for Hungarian Refugees,'" Records of the Department of State, Records of the Bureau of Security and Consular Affairs, Box 10, File "Activities and Plans of Rep. Walter's Committee," National Archives II; "Flights to U.S. Being Arranged for 5,000 Hungarian Refugees," *NYT*, November 18, 1956, 30; "Inquiries Flood Refugee Office," *NYT*, November 27, 1956, 3; "60 Hungarians Welcomed at Kilmer to a New Life," *NYT*, November 22, 1956, 1; "Army at Kilmer Cuts Processing Time to 55 Minutes," *NYT*, November 30, 1956, 1.

17. Bursten, *Escape from Fear*, 58–69; "First Refugees off to U.S.; Red Tape Slashed in Vienna," *NYT*, November 20, 1956, 1; "Refugees Helped to Haven in the U.S.," *NYT*, November 19, 1956, 10; "U.S. Groups Take Aid for Hungary," *NYT*, November 18, 1956, 30; "Refugee Airlift Brings 139 More," *NYT*, December 1, 1956, 10.

18. John F. Rieger to Scott McLeod, "Screening of Hungarian Refugees in Austria," January 3, 1956, Records of the Department of State, Records of the Bureau of Security and Consular Affairs, Box 10, File "Screening Plans for Hungarian Refugees," National Archives II.

19. For Hungarian Debriefing Committee plan, see Jean J. Chenard to John F. Rieger, November 13, 1956, "Screening Plan for Hungarian Refugees in Austria," Records of the Department of State, Records of the Bureau of Security and Consular Affairs, Box 10, File "Security Screening for Hungarian Refugees," National Archives II; Pierce Gerety to Allen Dulles, November 16, 1956, Records of the Department of State, Records of the Bureau of Security and Consular Affairs, Box 10, File "Hungarian Refugees for Settlement in the U.S.," National Archives II; for Besterman comments, see "Memorandum of Conversation—Department of State, Processing of Visas for Hungarian Refugees," November 26, 1956, Records of the Department of State, Records of the Bureau of Security and Consular Affairs, Box 10, File "Activities and Plans of Rep. Walter's Committee," National Archives II.

20. Quotes from John F. Rieger to Scott McLeod, "Screening of Hungarian Refugees in Austria," January 3, 1956, Records of the Department of State, Records of the Bureau of Security and Consular Affairs, Box 10, File "Screening Plans for Hungarian Refugees," National Archives II.

21. SCA Duty Officer to Mr. Scott McLeod, November 21, 1956, Records of the Department of State, Records of the Bureau of Security and Consular Affairs, Box 10, File "Hungarian Refugees—General, 1956"; "Hungarian Move to Austria Slows," *NYT*, November 28, 1956, 1; "Aide Mêmoire from the Austrian Embassy to the United States," November 15, 1956, *FRUS*, 1955–57, vol. XXV, 457–58; "Memorandum of Conversation, Subject: Resettlement of Hungarian Refugees," November 21, 1956, Records of the Department of State, Records of the Bureau of Security and Consular Affairs, Box 10, File "Hungarian Refugees for Settlement in the United States," National Archives II; "Austria Flooded with Refugees; Pleads for Help," *NYT*, November 23, 1956, 1; "White House Weighs Increase," *NYT*, November 21, 11; "Memorandum for the Acting Secretary" from Douglas MacArthur II, November 24, 1956, Records of the Department of State, Records of the Bureau of Security and Consular Affairs, Box 10, File "Statements and Announcements by the President on Hungarian Refugees," National Archives II; "White House Statement Concerning the Admission of Additional Hungarian Refugees," December 1, 1956, *Public Papers of the Presidents of the United States: Dwight D. Eisenhower, 1956* (Washington, DC: U.S. Government Printing Office, 1958), 305–307.

22. Loescher and Scanlan, *Calculated Kindness*, 55–57; Daniel Tichenor, *Dividing Lines: The Politics of Immigration Control in America* (Princeton, NJ: Princeton University Press, 2002), 202–203; Bursten, *Escape from Fear*, 56–58. For the text of the "parole" section—Section 212(a)(d)(5)—of the Immigration

and Nationality Act, see *United States Statutes at Large*, 82nd Congress, 2nd Session, 1952, vol. 66 (Washington, DC: U.S. Government Printing Office, 1953), 188. "Memorandum for the Acting Secretary" from Douglas MacArthur II, November 24, 1956, Records of the Department of State, Records of the Bureau of Security and Consular Affairs, Box 10, File "Statements and Announcements by the President on Hungarian Refugees," National Archives II; Tyler Thompson to Douglas MacArthur II, November 26, 1956, "Possibilities for Increase in Number of Hungarian Refugees to be admitted to the United States over the Number of 5,000 as Originally Announced by the President," Records of the Department of State, Records of the Bureau of Security and Consular Affairs, Box 10, File "Statements and Announcements by the President on Hungarian Refugees," National Archives II; "Memorandum for the Secretary" by Douglas MacArthur II, November 28, 1956, Records of the Department of State, Records of the Bureau of Security and Consular Affairs, Box 10, File "Hungarian Refugees—General, 1956," National Archives II; "Memo for Sherman Adams," November 28, 1956, Records of the Department of State, Bureau of Security and Consular Affairs, Box 10, File "Statements and Announcements by the President on Hungarian Refugees," National Archives II.

23. Pierce Gerety, "Memorandum to All Members of Congress," December 11, 1956, Committee on the Judiciary, Subcommittee on Refugees and Escapees, United States Senate, 85th Congress, Box 10, File "Department of State, 1 of 2," National Archives. On Walter, see Davis, 130; "Refugees Fly In; Aid Offers Grow," *NYT*, November 25, 1956, 43; Walter to John Foster Dulles, November 27, Records of the Committee on the Judiciary, Subcommittee on Immigration and Naturalization, House of Representatives, Eighty-Fifth Congress, Box 1056, File "Hungarian Refugee Correspondence (3 of 3)," National Archives. For poll numbers, see Rita Simon, *Public Opinion and the Immigrant: Print Media Coverage, 1880–1980* (Lexington, MA: Lexington Books, 1985), 37–38.

24. "Exiles Face Delay in Screening as U.S. Officials Won't Relax Procedure," *NYT*, December 2, 1956, 36; "U.S. Expedites Program," *NYT*, December 4, 1956, 22; "1,000 Exiles a Day Due to Fly to U.S.," *NYT*, December 5, 1956, 6. Joseph Swing to Rep. Francis Walter, December 19, 1956, Committee on the Judiciary, Subcommittee on Immigration and Nationality, House of Representatives, 85th Congress, Box 1056, File "Hungarian Refugee Correspondence (3 of 3)," National Archives; John F. Rieger to Scott McLeod, "Screening of Hungarian Refugees in Austria," January 3, 1956, Records of the Department of State, Records of the Bureau of Security and Consular Affairs, Box 10, File "Screening Plans for Hungarian Refugees," National Archives II.

25. "February 19 Target Is Set for Settling 21,500 Hungarian Exiles in U.S.," *NYT*, December 23, 1956, 3.

26. "U.S. Quota Is Filled," *NYT*, December 12, 1956, 3; "Nixon Takes Off on Refugee Trip," *NYT*, December 19, 1956, 1; "Nixon in Austria Indicates a Rise in Refugee Quota," *NYT*, December 20, 1956, 1; "Eisenhower Acts to Spur the Entry of More Refugees," *NYT*, December 27, 1956, 1; "President Adds to Refugee Quota at Nixon Request," *NYT*, January 2, 1957, 1; "More Hungarians Get a Haven Here," *NYT*, January 9, 1957, 1; "Month's Goal Put at 4,000 Refugees," *NYT*, January 29, 1957, 9; "Refugees Confront U.S. with Basic Decisions," *NYT*,

February 3, 1957, 6; "Refugee Program Slowed, Not Ended, U.S. Officials Say," *NYT,* April 7, 1957, 1; "U.S. Will Admit More Refugees," *NYT,* April 14, 1957, 28; "U.S. Opens Doors for Hungarians," *NYT,* May 16, 1957, 8.

27. "U.S. Nears Ruling on Refugee Entry," *NYT,* November 29, 1956, 20 (White House quote); George Gallup, *The Gallup Poll, Public Opinion 1935–1971,* vol. II, 1949–58 (New York: Random House, 1972), 1459; "Refugees Suspected," *NYT,* December 31, 1956, 3; "Refugee Hearings Mapped by Walter," *NYT,* January 5, 1957, 3; "Walter at Kilmer to Study Refugees," *NYT,* January 10, 1957, 12; Walter's January 10 quote, "Refugee Inquiry Is Set by Walter," *NYT,* January 23, 1957, 9; "Johnston Says Reds Slip in as Refugees," *NYT,* January 16, 1957, 1. For the Lang case, see "Scope of Soviet Activity in the United States," Hearings before the Subcommittee to Investigate the Administration of the Internal Revenue Act and Other Internal Security Laws, Committee on the Judiciary, U.S. Senate, 85th Congress, First Session, Part 48, January 15, 1957 (Washington, DC: U.S. Government Printing Office, 1957), 3307–08; Arthur Markowitz, "Humanitarianism versus Restrictionism: The United States and the Hungarian Refugees," *International Migration Review,* vol. 7, issue 1, 1973, 50–52.

28. "M'Leod Defends Exile Screening," January 24, 1957, *NYT,* 5; Walter quoted in (and Swing's defense of screening) "U.S. Finds Only Three Subversives in 23,000 Hungarian Refugees," January 26, 1957, *NYT,* 3.

29. Loescher and Scanlon, *Calculated Kindness,* 58; Davis, "The Cold War, Refugees, and U.S. Immigration Policy," 133–46.

30. On the IRC, see Leo Cherne, "Thirty Days That Shook the World," *Saturday Review,* December 22, 1956, 22–23; Aaron Levenstein, *Escape to Freedom: The Story of the International Rescue Committee* (Westport, CT: Greenwood Press, 1983), 51–63. On Nixon, see "Informal Nixon Baffles Austria," *NYT,* December 21, 1956, 12; "Nixon Takes Off on Refugee Trip," *NYT,* December 19, 1956, 1; "Nixon in Austria Indicates a Rise in Refugee Quota," *NYT,* December 20, 1956, 1; "The President's News Conference of November 14, 1956," John Woolley and Gerhard Peters, *The American Presidency Project* (online). Santa Barbara, CA: University of California (hosted), Gerhard Peters (database), accessed on August 24, 2007, from the Web at http://www.presidency.ucsb.edu/ws/?pid=10702; Chester Pach and Elmo Richardson, *The Presidency of Dwight D. Eisenhower* (Lawrence: University Press of Kansas, 1991), 135–36.

31. For background on the Voorhees appointment, see Voorhees to Sherman Adams, November 8, 1956, Official File 154–N–3, Box 824, File "President's Committee for Hungarian Refugee Relief," White House Central Files, DDEL; Adams to Voorhees, November 10, 1956, Official File 154–N–3, Box 824, File "President's Committee for Hungarian Refugee Relief," White House Central Files, DDEL; Maxwell Rabb to Loy Henderson, Undersecretary of State for Administration, November 17, 1956, Official File 154–N–3, Box 824, File "President's Committee for Hungarian Refugee Relief," White House Central Files, DDEL; "President Names Aide to Expedite Refugees' Entry," *NYT,* November 30, 1956, 1; "Refugee Expediter: Tracy Stebbins Voorhees," *NYT,* November 30, 1956, 14. For CCI quote, see Murray Martin to Howard Chase, December 12, 1956, Box 11, File "Communications Counselors," Records of Presidential Committees, Commissions, and Boards, Records of the U.S. President's Committee for

Hungarian Refugee Relief, DDEL; Bursten, *Escape from Fear,* 161–69 and 193–98; Loescher and Scanlan, *Calculated Kindness,* 57–58; Markowitz, "Humanitarianism versus Restrictionism," 48–50.

32. Robert Griffith, "The Selling of America: The Advertising Council and American Politics, 1942–1960," *Business History Review,* LVII (Autumn 1993), 388–413. On the public service announcement at the end of November, see James Lambie to James C. Haggerty, November 28, 1956, Papers of James Lambie, Box 37, File "Hungarian Relief, 1957," DDEL. On the disc jockey program, see Jim Lambie to Harry Carter (with the enclosures), December 13, 1956, Papers of James Lambie, Box 37, File "Hungarian Relief, 1957," DDEL; "Disc Jockeys Aid Drive," *NYT,* December 18, 1956, 8.

33. "News of the Advertising and Marketing Business," *NYT,* January 17, 1956, 42; for Voorhees quote, see "Summary of Meeting," December 14, 1956, Box 2, File "Committee Meeting," Records of Presidential Committees, Commissions, and Boards, Records of the U.S. President's Committee for Hungarian Refugee Relief, DDEL; Murray Martin to Howard Chase, December 12, 1956, Box 11, File "Communications Counselors," Records of Presidential Committees, Commissions, and Boards, Records of the U.S. President's Committee for Hungarian Refugee Relief, DDEL. On daily activities of CCI, "CCI Progress Report to Date—Joyce Kilmer Reception Center" (undated—but obviously late 1956 because memo comments on activities planned for Christmas and New Years), Box 20, File "PIO Daily Resume of Activities," Records of Presidential Committees, Commissions, and Boards, Records of the U.S. President's Committee for Hungarian Refugee Relief, DDEL; "Status Report and Proposed Public Relations Projects—10 January 1957," Box 20, File "PIO Daily Resume of Activities," Records of Presidential Committees, Commissions, and Boards, Records of the U.S. President's Committee for Hungarian Refugee Relief, DDEL.

34. During the CCI media blitz, Foster had mixed success in getting magazines to run stories. *Reader's Digest, Sports Illustrated,* and *Vogue* published pieces that had their origins in CCI's work. *Look, Life, Time,* and the *Saturday Evening Post,* however, did not publish any more of these human-interest stories, although they did continue reporting and editorializing on Hungarian refugees and the American resettlement program. On CCI's communications with *Reader's Digest,* see A.T. Rolfe to Murray Martin, December 26, 1956, Box 43, File "Memos—Public Information Office," Records of Presidential Committees, Commissions, and Boards, Records of the U.S. President's Committee for Hungarian Refugee Relief, DDEL; Andrew Rolfe to DeWitt Wallace, January 2, 1957, Box 43, File "Memos—Public Information Office," Records of Presidential Committees, Commissions, and Boards, Records of the U.S. President's Committee for Hungarian Refugee Relief, DDEL; "CCI Public Relations Activities for the President's Committee for Hungarian Refugee Relief," Box 44, File "Radio, TV, Newspaper, etc.," Records of Presidential Committees, Commissions, and Boards, Records of the U.S. President's Committee for Hungarian Refugee Relief, DDEL. On the *Vogue* incident, see "Resume of Day's Activities," January 28, 1957, Box 20, File "PIO Resume of Daily Activities," Records of Presidential Committees, Commissions, and Boards, Records of the U.S. President's Committee for Hungarian Refugee Relief, DDEL; "Long Nights Journey into Day: Hungarians at Camp Kilmer,"

Vogue, May 1957, 159. See, also, "Hungarians in America: The Fortune of a Family," *Newsweek*, May 20, 1957, 18–43; "A Future for the Fehers," *Rotarian*, June 1957, 32–33. On the media blitz and the "to tell the story . . ." quote, see "CCI Public Relations Activities for the President's Committee for Hungarian Refugee Relief," Box 44, File "Radio, TV, Newspaper, etc.," Records of Presidential Committees, Commissions, and Boards, Records of the U.S. President's Committee for Hungarian Refugee Relief, DDEL; James Lambie to Ted Repplier (President of the Advertising Council), Box 37, File "Hungarian Relief, 1957," Records of Presidential Committees, Commissions, and Boards, Records of the U.S. President's Committee for Hungarian Refugee Relief, DDEL; Leo Beebe to Commanding General, President's Committee Staff, January 29, Box 20, File "Public Information Publicity Plans," Records of Presidential Committees, Commissions, and Boards, Records of the U.S. President's Committee for Hungarian Refugee Relief, DDEL. Foster's quote from "Report on Foster's Activities Monday, January 14th, New York City," January 15, 1957, Box 20, File "PIO Resume of Daily Activities," Records of Presidential Committees, Commissions, and Boards, Records of the U.S. President's Committee for Hungarian Refugee Relief, DDEL. On objectives for *Life* magazine quote, see B. G. to Mark Foster, "Objectives for Life Magazine Story on Hungary," January 4, 1957, Box 43, File "President's Committee," Records of Presidential Committees, Commissions, and Boards, Records of the U.S. President's Committee for Hungarian Refugee Relief, DDEL.

35. "They Pour In . . . and Family Shows Refugees Can Fit In," *Life*, January 7, 1957, 20–27. Other media outlets offered articles similar to *Life*'s "They Pour In . . ." See "Out of Hungary," *New York Times Magazine*, December 9, 1956, 12; "New Home, New Life for Three Refugees," *U.S. News and World Report*, January 4, 1957, 62–64; "From Hungary's Terror Skilled Hands for U.S.," *Business Week*, January 5, 1957, 46; "New Americans without a Hyphen," *National Council Outlook*, February, 1957, 4.

36. For the White House request concerning *Look*, see Mark Foster, "Resume of Day's Activities," January 25, 1957, Box 20, File "PIO Resume of Daily Activities," Records of Presidential Committees, Commissions, and Boards, Records of the U.S. President's Committee for Hungarian Refugee Relief, DDEL. "From Hungary—New Americans," *Look*, January 22, 1957, 49–55.

37. Gary Gerstle, *American Crucible*; Jane Sherron De Hart, "Containment at Home: Gender, Sexuality, and National Identity in Cold War America," in *Rethinking Cold War Culture*, 124–55; David Potter, *People of Plenty: Economic Abundance and the American Character* (Chicago: University of Chicago, 1954); Elaine Tyler May, *Homeward Bound: American Families in the Cold War Era* (New York: Basic Books, 1988).

38. May, *Homeward Bound*.

39. "Chairman's report to the Members of the President's Committee for Hungarian Refugee Relief," February 28, 1957, Official File 154–N–3, Box 824, File "President's Committee For Hungarian Refugee Relief," White House Central Files, DDEL. On shutting down the publicity efforts, see Harry T. Carter, "Note for File," March 25, 1957, Box 11, File "Communications Counselors," Records of Presidential Committees, Commissions, and Boards, Records of the U.S. President's Committee for Hungarian Refugee Relief, DDEL; Tracy Voorhees, "Memo-

randum for Mr. E. Frederic Morrow," April 8, 1957, Box 11, File "Communications Counselors," Records of Presidential Committees, Commissions, and Boards, Records of the U.S. President's Committee for Hungarian Refugee Relief, DDEL. For the poll, see Loescher and Scanlan, *Calculated Kindness*, 58–59.

40. Davis, "The Cold War, Refugees, and U.S. Immigration Policy," 146–58; Markowitz, "Humanitarianism versus Restrictionism," 52–56; Hutchinson, *American Immigration History*, 328–34; Loescher and Scanlan, *Calculated Kindness*, 58–60; Stephen Wagner, "The Lingering Death of the National Origins Immigration System: A Political History of United States Immigration Policy, 1952–1965," Ph.D. Dissertation, Harvard University, 1986, 331–38. For Eisenhower's 1957 State of the Union Address, see *The Public Papers of the President: Dwight D. Eisenhower, 1957*, 17–30. For Eisenhower's Special Immigration Message, see *The Public Papers of the President: Dwight D. Eisenhower, 1957*, 110–117.

41. For the "Refugee-Escapee Act," see *United States Statutes at Large, 1957*, vol. 71 (Washington, DC: U.S. Government Printing Office, 1958), 639–44. "President Notes Lag on Refugees," *NYT*, April 11, 1957, 12; "Transcript of the President's News Conference on Foreign and Domestic Matters," *NYT*, April 11, 1957, 16; "Hearings Proposed by Walter on Act," *NYT*, May 2, 1957, 3; "Ten Senators Prod Eastland for Action on Refugees' Entry," *NYT*, July 7, 1957, 1; for Eisenhower's comments, see the *Congressional Quarterly Almanac, 85th Congress, First Session . . . 1957*, vol. XIII (Washington, DC: Congressional Quarterly Inc., 1957), 670–71; "Compromise Set on Immigration," *NYT*, August 16, 1957, 3; "Congress Ready to Easy Entry for Aliens in Hardship Cases," *NYT*, August 17, 1957, 4; Davis, "The Cold War, Refugees, and U.S. Immigration Policy," 157–58; Markowitz, "Humanitarianism versus Restrictionism," 52–55; Tichenor, *Dividing Lines*, 203–207.

42. "Inquiry to Delay New Refugee Aid," *NYT*, January 19, 1957, 1. On the Gombos case, see "Hungarian Deported," *NYT*, May 30, 1957, 40. On Walter's thinking, see W. M. Besterman to Hon. Clarence Kilburn, June 19, 1957, House of Representatives, 85th Congress, Committee on the Judiciary, Subcommittee on Immigration and Naturalization, Box 1055, File "Hungarian Refugee Correspondence," National Archives.

43. Simon, *Public Opinion and the Immigrant*, 38; W. M. Besterman to Hon. Clarence Kilburn, June 19, 1957, House of Representatives, 85th Congress, Committee on the Judiciary, Subcommittee on Immigration and Naturalization, Box 1055, File "Hungarian Refugee Correspondence," National Archives.

44. The historiography on the 1958 legislation is extremely weak. Arthur Markowitz, as well as Gil Losecher and John Scanlan, curiously fail to follow the status debates beyond 1957. They conclude that because Congress rejected a status bill in 1957, Hungarian parolees were unwelcome in the United States and that the U.S. commitment to refugees was half-hearted. Of course, the story looks different a year later, after Congress passed status normalization. "Refugee Program Expiring Tuesday," *NYT*, December 29, 1957, 1; *Congressional Quarterly Almanac, 85th Congress, Second Session . . . 1958*, vol. XIV (Washington, DC: Congressional Quarterly Inc., 1958), 60, 92. "Hungarians Near Resident Status," *NYT*, February 28, 1958, 4; "Bill Opens Citizenship to Refugee Hungarians," *WP*,

February 28, 1958, A8; Michael Feighan, *CR*, 85th Congress, Second Session, February 27, 1958, 3069–70.

45. "Refugee Bill Backed," *NYT*, April 17, 1958, 8; "Hungarians Near Resident Status," *NYT*, February 28, 1958, 4; "Walter Is Critical of Hungarian Visas," *NYT*, April 9, 1958, 59; *Congressional Record—Daily Digest*, 1958, D627; Public Law 85–559, *United States Statutes at Large*, vol. 72, pt. I (Washington, DC: U.S. Government Printing Office, 1959), 419–20.

CHAPTER 4
"HALF A LOAF": THE FAILURE OF REFUGEE POLICY
AND LAW REFORM, 1957–1965

1. Meg Greenfield, "The Melting Pot of Francis E. Walter," *Reporter*, October 26, 1961, 24–28; Stephen Wagner, "The Lingering Death of the National Origins Immigration System: A Political History of United States Immigration Policy, 1952–1965," Ph.D. Dissertation, Harvard University, 1986, 323–24, and generally Chapter 5; Michael Gill Davis, "The Cold War, Refugees, and U.S. Immigration Policy, 1952–1965," Ph.D. Dissertation, Vanderbilt University, 1996, 233–34.

2. "An Obscure Congressman to Keep an Eye On," *Life*, June 4, 1965, 34; Davis, "The Cold War, Refugees, and U.S. Immigration Policy," 281–85; Wagner, "The Lingering Death of the National Origins Immigration System," 381.

3. Senator Sam Ervin, September 17, 1965, *CR*, vol. 111, pt. 18, 24231.

4. Senator Sam Ervin, "Immigration," Hearings before the Subcommittee on Immigration and Naturalization of the Committee on the Judiciary, United States Senate, 89th Congress, First Session, on S. 500, March 8, 1965 (Washington, DC: U.S. Government Printing Office, 1965), 383, 389; see also Senator Spessard Holland (D-FL), *CR*, September 22, 1965, 24776–79; Statement of Rep. O.C. Fisher (D-TX), "Immigration," Hearings before Subcommittee No. 1 of the Committee on the Judiciary, House of Representative, 88th Congress, Second Session, on H.R. 7700, Part I (Washington, DC: U.S. Government Printing Office, 1964), 281; Mrs. Cornelia Chapin and Mrs. Eleanor Gonzalez, Greenwich Women's Republican Club quoted in "Immigration," Hearings before Subcommittee No. 1 of the Committee on the Judiciary, House of Representative, 88th Congress, Second Session, on H.R. 7700, pt. III (Washington, DC: U.S. Government Printing Office, 1964), 819.

5. For the Senate vote, see *CR*, September 22, 1965, 24783; Rick Perlstein, *Before the Storm: Barry Goldwater and the Unmaking of the American Consensus* (New York: Hill and Wang, 2001); Theodore White, *The Making of the President, 1964* (New York: Athenuem Publishers, 1965), especially ch. 11; "Plank Spurring Extremists Completes Platform Draft," *NYT*, August 25, 1964, 1; "Goldwater Maps Ideological Drive," *NYT*, October 7, 1964, 27; "Goldwater Scored on Minority Attack," *NYT*, October 10, 1964, 32; "Miller Attacks Tariff Program," *NYT*, September 8, 1964, 14.

6. Ernest Van Den Haag, "More Immigration?" *National Review*, September 21, 1965, 821–22, 842; Lee Edwards, "Each Refugee, a Story," *National Review*, October 7, 1961, 229; "The Wandering of the People," *National Review*, June

19, 1962, 431; Francis Russell, "Notes on an Autumn Journey," *National Review*, December 4, 1962, 449; Politicus, "Keeping America American," *American Mercury*, July 1960, 11–20.

7. "6 Senators Offer Immigration Bill," *NYT*, July 3, 1963, 24; "4 Senators Score Immigration Law," *NYT*, January 15, 1964, 12.

8. E. P. Hutchinson, *Legislative History of American Immigration Policy, 1798–1965* (Philadelphia: University of Pennsylvania Press, 1981) 329, 353, 358, 359; "Text of President Eisenhower's Immigration Message," *NYT*, February 1, 1957, 8; "6 Senators Offer Immigration Bill," *NYT*, July 3, 1963, 24; "30 Senators Back Bill to Revise Immigration," *NYT*, February 8, 1963, 6; "President Urges Repeal of Quotas for Immigration," *NYT*, July 24, 1963, I; Davis, "The Cold War, Refugees, and U.S. Immigration Policy," 271–76; Wagner, "The Lingering Death of the National Origins Immigration System," 376–80.

9. Hutchinson, *Legislative History of American Immigration Policy*, 328–48; Wagner, "The Lingering Death of the National Origins Immigration System," 340–46, 356–58, 361–62, 376–83; Davis, "The Cold War, Refugees, and U.S. Immigration Policy," 229–31, 271–78; "Letter to the President of the Senate and to the Speaker of the House on Revision of the Immigration Laws," July 23, 1963, *Public Papers of the Presidents of the United States, John F. Kennedy, 1963* (Washington, DC: U.S. Government Printing Office, 1964), 594–97; the Administration bill as introduced by Senator Hart, July 24, 1963, *CR*, 13164–66; "President Urges Repeal of Quotas for Immigration," *NYT*, July 24, 1963, 1.

10. President Lyndon Johnson, January 8, 1964, *The Public Papers of the Presidents, Lyndon B. Johnson* (Washington, DC: U.S. Government Printing Office, 1965), 116 (quote); "President Urges a New Alien Law," *NYT*, January 14, 1964, 10; Davis, "The Cold War, Refugees, and U.S. Immigration Policy," 279–85; Wagner, "The Lingering Death of the National Origins Immigration System," 384–88; Daniel Tichenor, *Dividing Lines: The Politics of Immigration Control in America* (Princeton, NJ: Princeton University Press, 2002), 207–11; Robert Dallek, *Lone Star Rising* (Oxford: Oxford University Press, 1990), 406.

11. "Feighan Asks End to Alien Quotas Now," *Cleveland Plain Dealer*, February 5, 1965, 8; "Action at Last on Quotas," *NYT*, August 27, 1965, 28; "House Approves Bill for Immigration Reform," *NYT*, August 26, 1965, 1; "Immigration Bill Gains in the Senate," *NYT*, August 27, 1965, 9; "Senators Weigh Immigration Curb," *NYT*, August 28, 1965, 6; "Dirksen Maneuver Delays Alien Bill," *NYT*, September 1, 1965, 9; "Alien Bill Freed by Dirksen Deal," *NYT*, September 9, 1965, 1; "Immigration Bill Passes Senate with New Curbs," *NYT*, September 23, 1965, 1; Davis, "The Cold War, Refugees, and U.S. Immigration Policy," 295–300, 308–16; Wagner, "The Lingering Death of the National Origins Immigration System," 438–52; Tichenor, *Dividing Lines*, 211–15; James Patterson, *Grand Expectations: The United States, 1945–1974* (New York: Oxford University Press, 1996) 562–65.

12. "U.S. Public Is Strongly Opposed to Easing of Immigration Laws," *WP*, May 31, 1965, A2; George Gallup, *The Gallup Poll, Public Opinion 1935–1971*, vol. III (New York: Random House, 1972), 1952–53; "51 Per Cent Favor End of Change of Quota System in Immigration," *WP*, July 25, 1965, A2; Tichenor, *Dividing Lines*, 211–16.

13. President Lyndon Johnson, *The Public Papers of the Presidents, Lyndon B. Johnson*, vol. I, January 13, 1964 (Washington, DC: U.S. Government Printing Office, 1965), 124; 37; Senator Jacob Javits, *CR*, September 20, 1965, 24469 (quote); Representative Joseph Huot (D-NH), *CR*, August 25, 1965, 21787 ("millstone" quote); Representative Henry Helstoski (D-NJ), *CR*, August 25, 1965, 21786 (quote); Tichenor, *Dividing Lines*, 213, 215.

14. Representative Emanuel Celler, *CR*, August 25, 1965, 21758 (quote); Statement and Testimony of Andrew Biermiller, "Immigration," Hearings before Subcommittee No. 1 of the Committee on the Judiciary, House of Representative, 89th Congress, First Session, on H.R. 2580, May 27, 1965 (Washington, DC: U.S. Government Printing Office, 1965), 324. On the decline of anticommunism, see Donald Critchlow, *Phyllis Schlafly and Grassroots Conservatism: A Woman's Crusade* (Princeton, NJ: Princeton University Press, 2006), 89–92; Philip Jenkins, *The Cold War at Home: The Red Scare in Pennsylvania, 1945–1960* (Chapel Hill: University of North Carolina Press, 1999), 184–203.

15. Tichenor, *Dividing Lines*, 211–15; Roger Daniels, *Guarding the Golden Door: American Immigration Policy and Immigrants Since 1882* (New York: Hill and Wang, 2004), 134.

16. For general overviews of the "rights revolution" and the social and political movements of the 1960s that inform my analysis and my general conception of the 1960s, see Eric Foner, *The Story of American Freedom* (New York: W. W. Norton and Company, 1998); Charles Epp, *The Rights Revolution: Lawyers, Activists, and Supreme Courts in Comparative Perspective* (Chicago: University of Chicago Press, 1998); Patterson, *Grand Expectations*; Maurice Isserman and Michael Kazin, *America Divided: The Civil War of the 1960s* (New York: Oxford University Press, 1999); Nelson Lichtenstein, *State of the Union: A Century of American Labor* (Princeton, NJ: Princeton University Press, 2002); Reuel Edward Schiller, "Policy Ideals and Judicial Action: Expertise, Group Pluralism, and Participatory Democracy in Intellectual Thought and Legal Decision-Making, 1932–1970," Ph.D. Dissertation, University of Virginia, 1997.

17. Juvenal Marchisio, American Committee on Italian Migration, "Immigration," Hearings before Subcommittee No. 1 of the Committee on the Judiciary, House of Representative, 88th Congress, Second Session, on H.R. 7700, Part III (Washington, DC: U.S. Government Printing Office, 1964), 643 and 651; Rep. Brock Adams quoted in *CR*, August 25, 1965, 21765.

18. Senator Hiram Fong (R-HA), *CR*, September 20, 1965, 24446 (quote); Senator Ted Kennedy, *CR*, September 21, 1965, 24563 (quote); Senator Robert Kennedy, *CR*, September 22, 1965, 24777 (quote); Rep. Farbstein, *CR*, August 25, 1965, 21784 (quote). For poll numbers, see "U.S. Public Is Strongly Opposed to Easing of Immigration Laws," *WP*, May 31, 1965, A2; Gallup, *The Gallup Poll*, vol. III, 1952–53; "51 Per Cent Favor End of Change of Quota System in Immigration," *WP*, July 25, 1965, A2.

19. Public Law 89–236, "An Act to Amend the Immigration and Nationality Act, and for Other Purposes," *United States Statutes at Large, 1965* (Washington, DC: U.S. Government Printing Office, 1966).

20. Davis, "The Cold War, Refugees, and U.S. Immigration Policy," 302–305; Tichenor, *Dividing Lines*, 216; David Reimers, *Still the Golden Door*, 2nd ed. (New York: Columbia University Press, 1992), 72–73 (American Legion quote).

21. Patterson, *Grand Expectations*, 578; Rubén Rumbaut, "Passages to America," *America at Century's End*, Alan Wolfe, ed. (Berkeley: University of California Press, 1991), 208–44; Bernard Weisberger, "A Nation of Immigrants," *American Heritage*, vol. 45, February-March 1994, 75–90.

22. Public Law 89–236, "An Act to Amend the Immigration and Nationality Act, and for other purposes," *United States Statutes at Large, 1965* (Washington, DC: U.S. Government Printing Office, 1966), 913; Davis, "The Cold War, Refugees, and U.S. Immigration Policy," 307; Loescher and Scanlan, *Calculated Kindness*, 73.

23. The mandate of the U.N. High Commissioner was extremely limited. According to a memo by one of Walter's aides, the mandate covered refugees from communist dominated areas, except Chinese refugees (who largely resided in Hong Kong) and ethnic Germans expelled from eastern Europe (who were deemed under the protection of the German Federal Republic). The mandate covered Jewish refugees fleeing Egypt after the Suez crisis, but did not cover non-Jews fleeing Egypt (because they had by and large retained their nationality in other countries), nor did it cover Arab refugees from Palestine (who were under the mandate of the United Nations Relief and Works Agency). See "Who Is and Who Is Not within the Mandate of the United Nations High Commissioner for Refugees," Record Group 233, 89th Congress, Committee on the Judiciary, Subcommittee on Immigration and Naturalization, Box 329, File "Refugees—General Public Law 86–648 [1 of 2]," The National Archives; "Refugee-Escapee Act of 1957," *United States Statutes at Large, 1957*, vol. 71, 643; "Refugee and Migration Assistance Act," *United States Statutes at Large, 1962*, vol. 76 (Washington, DC: U.S. Government Printing Office, 1963), 121–24; Davis, "The Cold War, Refugees, and U.S. Immigration Policy," 183–201, 207–22, 252–63.

24. Davis, "The Cold War, Refugees, and U.S. Immigration Policy," 176–200.

25. Senator Arthur Watkins, *CR*, August 21, 1957, 15491–93 (quote); Senator Hubert Humphrey, Senator Jacob Javits, and Senator Phillip Hart, *CR*, July 1, 1960, 15390–95.

26. On the UN's 1962 report, "Report on the Eighth Session of the Executive Committee of the High Commissioner's Programme," Geneva, Switzerland, October 22–25, 1962, especially the "Statement by the High Commissioner," Annex I; see also "Refugee Problem Shifts to Africa," *NYT*, November 25, 1962, 13. On the UN's 1964 report, see "Programme of the United Nations High Commissioner for Refugees," *U.N. Monthly Chronicle*, vol. 1, no. 6 (United Nations Office of Public Information, November 1964), 50. For the 1964 quote, see "Africa Refugees Reported on Rise," *NYT*, November 23, 1964, 45. For the USCR 1965 quote, see "Refugee Problem Called Mounting," *NYT*, October 31, 1965, 35. More generally, see "Refugee Gains Seen," *NYT*, February 2, 1961, 6; "The New Age of Migrations," *NYT*, January 15, 1961, 18; Representative John Lindsay, "Still Millions of Refugees," *New York Times Magazine*, August 13, 1961, 12; "U.N. Resettled 12,155 in '61," *NYT*, May 15, 1962, 3; "The U.N. and the Refugees," *NYT*, November 18, 1962, section IV, 10; "$1.5 Million Pledged for Aid in U.N. Refu-

gee Program," *NYT*, December 1, 1963, 53; "Refugee Census Finds 7.9 Million," *NYT*, August 9, 1964, 12.

27. Edward Snyder, August 9, 1957, "To Amend the Immigration and Nationality Act," vol. 4, U.S. Senate, Committee on the Judiciary, 85th Congress, 1st Session, 163; Edward Marks, "Admission of Refugees on Parole," Hearings Before Subcommittee No. 1 of the Committee on the Judiciary, House of Representatives, 86th Congress (Washington, DC: U.S. Government Printing Office, 1960), 44; Edward Swanstrom, "Admission of Refugees on Parole," Hearings before Subcommittee No. 1 of the Committee on the Judiciary, House of Representatives, 86th Congress (Washington, DC: U.S. Government Printing Office, 1960), 57.

28. For the Kennedy administration's definition of refugee, see the Administration bill as introduced by Senator Phil Hart, *CR*, July 24, 1963, 13164–66; for another example, see Rep. John Lindsay, "Immigration," Hearings before Subcommittee No. 1 of the Committee on the Judiciary, House of Representatives, 88th Congress, Second Session, on HR 7700 and fifty-five identical bills, June 22, 1964 (Washington, DC: U.S. Government Printing Office, 1964), 121; Davis, "The Cold War, Refugees, and U.S. Immigration Policy," 276–77.

29. For Feighan's remarks, see "Admission of Refugees on Parole," Hearings before Subcommittee No. 1 of the Committee on the Judiciary, House of Representatives, 86th Congress (Washington, DC: U.S. Government Printing Office, 1960), 45; John Trevor, Jr., May 20, 1965, "Immigration" Hearings before Subcommittee No. 1 of the Committee on the Judiciary House of Representatives, 89th Congress, First Session (Washington, DC: U.S. Government Printing Office, 1965), 241; Ernest Van Den Haag, "More Immigration?" *National Review*, September 21, 1965, 821–22, 842; Lee Edwards, "Each Refugee, a Story," *National Review*, October 7, 1961, 229; "The Wandering of the People," *National Review*, June 19, 1962, 431; Francis Russell, "Notes on an Autumn Journey," *National Review*, December 4, 1962, 449.

30. Roger Jones, "Migration and Refugee Assistance," Hearing before Subcommittee No. 1 of the Committee on the Judiciary, House of Representatives, 87th Congress, First Session, on H.R. 8291, August 3, 1961 (Washington, DC: U.S. Government Printing Office, 1962), 40.

31. Trevor Philpott, "The Refugees—A World Survey," *Rotarian*, December 1960, 16–37.

32. "51 Percent Favor End of Change of Quota System in Immigration," *WP*, July 25, 1965, A2; Rita Simon, *Public Opinion and the Immigrant: Print Media Coverage, 1880–1980* (Lexington, MA: Lexington Books, 1985), 38.

CHAPTER 5
"THEY ARE PROUD PEOPLE": THE UNITED STATES
AND REFUGEES FROM CUBA, 1959–1966

1. For major interpretations of the American response to the Cuban refugee crisis, most of which stress the continuities with previous refugee programs, see Gil Loescher and John Scanlan, *Calculated Kindness: Refugees and America's Half-Open Door, 1945 to the Present* (New York: The Free Press, 1986), ch. 3;

David Reimers, *Still the Golden Door: The Third World Comes to America* (New York: Columbia University Press, 1992); Michael Gill Davis, "The Cold War, Refugees, and U.S. Immigration Policy, 1952–1965," Ph.D. Dissertation, Vanderbilt University, 1996; Félix Roberto Masud-Piloto, *With Open Arms: Cuban Migration to the United States* (New Jersey: Rowman and Littlefield, 1988.

2. The literature on the Cuban American experience in the United States focuses on the relatively seamless adjustment of Cubans to the United States, the exile community's politics, and the identity of the Cuban exile community. See Juan Clark, "The Exodus from Revolutionary Cuba: A Sociological Analysis," Ph.D. Dissertation, University of Florida, 1975; Sheila Croucher, *Imagining Miami: Ethnic Politics in a Postmodern World* (Charlottesville: University of Virginia Press, 1997), ch. 4; Maria Christina Garcia, *Havana, USA: Cuban Exiles and the Cuban Americans in South Florida, 1959–1994* (Berkeley: University of California Press, 1996); Felix Masud-Piloto, *From Welcomed Exiles to Illegal Immigrants: Cuban Migration to the U.S., 1959–1995* (Lanham, MD: Rowman and Littlefield Publishers, 1996), ch. 1; Silvia Pedraza-Bailey, "Cuba's Exiles: Portrait of a Refugee Migration," *International Migration Review*, vol. 19, issue 1, Spring 1985, 4–34; James Olson and Judith Olson, *Cuban Americans: From Trauma to Triumph* (New York: Twayne Publishers, 1995); Maria de los Angeles Torres, *In the Land of Mirrors* (Ann Arbor: University of Michigan Press, 1999), chs. 1, 3.

3. "Henchmen Pour into Florida," *MH*, January 2, 1959, 1; "U.S. Recognizes New Cuban Regime; Voices Goodwill," *NYT*, January 8, 1959, 1.

4. Loree Wilkerson, *Fidel Castro's Political Programs from Reformism to "Marxism-Leninism"* (Gainesville: University of Florida Press, 1965), 52–81; Jaime Suchlicki, *Cuba: From Columbus to Castro*, 2nd ed., rev. (Washington, DC: Pergamon-Brassey's, 1986), 155–72.

5. Richard E. Welch, *Response to Revolution: The United States and the Cuban Revolution, 1959–1961* (Chapel Hill: University of North Carolina Press, 1985); Stephen G. Rabe, *Eisenhower and Latin America: The Foreign Policy of Anticommunism* (Chapel Hill: University of North Carolina Press, 1988), chs. 7 and 9.

6. Alejandro Portes and Robert Bach, *Latin Journey: Cuban and Mexican Immigrants in the United States* (Berkeley: University of California Press, 1985), 85; Silvia Pedraza-Bailey, "Cuba's Exiles," 9–11; Loescher and Scanlan, *Calculated Kindness*, 61–62; Davis, "The Cold War, Refugees, and U.S. Immigration Policy," 235–38, 243; Wilkerson, *Fidel Castro's Political Programs*, 52–81.

7. Loescher and Scanlan, *Calculated Kindness*, 64–65; Davis, "The Cold War, Refugees, and U.S. Immigration Policy," 237; Pedraza-Bailey, "Cuba's Exiles," 11.

8. Pedraza-Bailey, "Cuba's Exiles," 13–15; Garcia, *Havana, USA*, 36; James Olson and Judith Olson, *Cuban Americans*, 59.

9. "Castro Tells Rally Cubans Are Free to Leave Country," *NYT*, September 30, 1965, 1; "Refugee Flow Continues," *NYT*, October 14, 1965, 3; "Refugees Gather in Cuban Village," *NYT*, October 14, 1965, 3; "Memorandum of Understanding," National Security Files, Country File, Latin America, Cuba, Box 30, File "Cuban Refugee Program 10/63–1/65," LBJL; "U.S. and Castro Agree to Start Refugee Airlift," *NYT*, November 7, 1965, 1; Loescher and Scanlan, *Calcu-*

lated Kindness, 74 (quote), 75; Masud-Piloto, *From Welcomed Exiles*, 58–62; Garcia, *Havana, USA*, 38; Pedraza-Bailey, "Cuba's Exiles," 15–20.

10. Public Law 85–316, *United States Statutes at Large, 1957*, vol. 71, pt. I (Washington, DC: U.S. Government Printing Office, 1958), 643.

11. Loescher and Scanlan, *Calculated Kindness*, 78–79 (quote 79).

12. Louis Perez, *Cuba and the United States: Ties of Singular Intimacy*, 2nd ed. (Athens: University of Georgia Press, 1997), 207–25.

13. Perez, *Cuba and the United States*; Masud-Piloto, *From Welcomed Exiles*, 45.

14. Fredrik Logevall, *Choosing War: The Lost Chance for Peace and the Escalation of War in Vietnam* (Berkeley: University of California Press, 1999); Rita Simon, *Public Opinion and the Immigrant: Print Media Coverage, 1880–1980* (Lexington, MA: Lexington Books, 1985), 38–39; George Gallup, *The Gallup Poll, Public Opinion 1935–1971*, vol. III (New York: Random House, 1972) 1717, 1721, 1725, 1787, 1816, 1819.

15. Pedraza-Bailey, "Cuba's Exiles," 22–24.

16. For the argument that admissions requirements for the Cuban program were lax in comparison to previous refugee programs, see Davis, "The Cold War, Refugees, and U.S. Immigration Policy," 239; Loescher and Scanlan, *Calculated Kindness*, 61–62. For the argument that Cubans faced more rigorous admissions standards than their refugee predecessors, see Felix Masud-Piloto, *From Welcomed Exiles*, 37. Senator Philip Hart, "Cuban Refugee Problem," Hearings before the Subcommittee to Investigate Problems Connected with Refugees and Escapees of the Committee on the Judiciary, United States Senate, 88th Congress, First Session, Part I, May 22, 1963 (Washington, DC: U.S. Government Printing Office, 1963), 69 (cited hereafter as "Cuban Refugee Problem, Senate Hearings, 1963").

17. James Hennessy (Executive Assistant to the Commissioner of Immigration and Naturalization), "Migration and Refugee Assistance," Hearings before Subcommittee No. 1 of the Committee on the Judiciary, House of Representatives, 87th Congress, First Session, August 3, 1961 (Washington, DC: U.S. Government Printing Office, 1961), 41–44 (cited hereafter as "Migration and Refugee Assistance" House Hearings, 1961); Mario Noto, Associate Commissioner, Immigration and Naturalization Service, July 17, 1963, "Study of Population and Immigration Problems, Inquiry into the Selection, Security Screening, Admission, Emergency Care, and Resettlement of Cuban Refugees in the United States," Committee on the Judiciary, Subcommittee No. 1, House of Representatives, Special Series No. 14 (Washington, DC: U.S. Government Printing Office, 1963), 73–74 (cited hereafter as "Study of Population and Immigration Problems—Cuban Refugees" House Hearings, 1963); Mario Noto, "Cuban Refugee Problem" Hearings, 1963, 75; see also Davis, "The Cold War, Refugees, and U.S. Immigration Policy," 243.

18. Mario Noto, "Cuban Refugee Problem," Senate Hearings, 1963, 75–76; Mario Noto, March 23, 1966, "Cuban Refugee Program," Hearings before the Subcommittee to Investigate Problems Connected with Refugees and Escapees of the Committee on the Judiciary, United States Senate, 89th Congress, Second Session (Washington, DC: U.S. Government Printing Office, 1966), 24–25 (cited

hereafter as "Cuban Refugee Program, Senate Hearings, 1966"; Raymond Farrell (Commissioner of the INS) to Senator Edward Kennedy, March 11, 1970, Records of the U.S. Senate, Committee on the Judiciary, Subcommittee on Refugees and Escapees, 1972–77, Oversight/Investigative File concerning Cuban Refugee Program, 1962–71, Box 20, File: "Cuban Refugee Program, 1970," National Archives; "Cuban Refugee Program, A Staff Report to the Subcommittee on Immigration and Nationality (Subcommittee No. 1)," 89th Congress, Second Session (Washington, DC: U.S. Government Printing Office, 1966) from Records of the U.S. Senate, Committee on the Judiciary, Subcommittee on Escapees and Refugees, 1972–77, Box 21, File: "91st Congress, Cuban Refugee Report Information," National Archives.

19. SE-180, according to Marian Smith, historian of the INS, was a regional form developed for use in the Miami INS office to deal specifically with Cuban refugees. Marian Smith to Carl Bon Tempo, January 7, 2003 (in possession of the author.) For a copy of Form SE-180, see Mario Noto, May 16, 1963, "Study of Population and Immigration Problems, Inquiry into Entries of Aliens under Administrative Discretionary (Parole) Authority of the Immigration and Nationality Act with Respect to Individual Hardship Cases, Recognized International Emergencies, and the Russian Old Believers" Committee on the Judiciary, Subcommittee No. 1, House of Representatives, Special Series No. 13, Committee Print (Washington, DC: U.S. Government Printing Office, 1964), 146. James Hennessy, "Migration and Refugee Assistance," House Hearings, 1961, 44; Mario Noto, "Study of Population and Immigration Problems—Cuban Refugees," House Hearings, 1963, 73, 89; James Hennessy, "Study of Population and Immigration Problems—Cuban Refugees" House Hearings, 1963, 68.

20. Mario Noto, "Study of Population and Immigration Problems—Cuban Refugees," House Hearings, 1963, 75 ("past activities" quote); Mario Noto, "Cuban Refugee Problem," Senate Hearings, 1963, 77, 84 ("general welfare," "internal security," "Most of the cases . . ." quotes).

21. Carlos Franqui, *Diary of the Cuban Revolution*, trans. George Felix, Elaine Kerrigan, Phyllis Freeman, Hardie St. Martin (New York: Viking Press, 1976), 163; "Ex-Batista Aide Stirs Exiles' Ire," *MH*, October 22, 1961, 12-B; "Ex-Batista Aide in U.S.," *CSM*, October 23, 1961, 5; "Mournful Mariano," *Newsweek*, November 6, 1961, 57; "Former Official of Batista Police Helps U.S. Screen Cuban Exiles," *NYT*, October 22, 1961, 1.

22. "Following Up on Colonel Faget," *CSM*, October 25, 1961, E-1; also see the sources listed in ch. 5, fn. 21.

23. "U.S. Confirms Role of Ex-Batista Man," *WP*, October 23, 1961, 17; "Former Official of Batista Police Helps U.S. Screen Cuban Exiles," *NYT*, October 22, 1961, 1; "Ex-Batista Official to Lose U.S. Post," *NYT*, October 24, 1961, 1; "U.S. Denies Firing of Cuban Red Expert," *MH*, October 25, 1961, 2A; "Case of Ex-Batista Aide in U.S. Job Is Weighed," October 25, 1961, *NYT*, 21; Hennessy quoted, "Cuban Refugee Problems" Hearings before the Subcommittee to Investigate Problems Connected with Refugees and Escapees of the Committee on the Judiciary, United States Senate, 87th Congress, First Session December 13, 1961 (Washington, DC: USGPO, 1962), 212, (cited hereafter as "Cuban Refugee Problems, Senate Hearings, 1961").

24. "Refugees Held in Opa-Locka," *MH*, November 13, 1961, 3-A; "Anti-Castro Unit to Screen Cubans," *NYT*, November 28, 1961, 22; "Anti-Fidel Leaders Help U.S. Screen Refugees," *MH*, November 28, 1961, 15-A.

25. Noto and Moore, "Study of Population and Immigration Problems—Cuban Refugees," House Hearings, 1963, 76–77; Carrera quoted in Garcia, *Havana, USA*, 18.

26. Mario Noto, "Study of Population and Immigration Problems—Cuban Refugees" House Hearings, 1963, 73, 89. For the State Department figures on nonconcurrences, see Abba Schwartz, "Study of Population and Immigration Problems—Cuban Refugees," House Hearings, 1963, 99.

27. "Memo to the President" from Frederick Dutton, January 25, 1961, White House Central Subject Files, Box 637, File "ND 19-2/CO 55," JFKL; "Text of Kennedy Plan on Cuba Refugees," *NYT*, February 4, 1961, 2; "Relegation of Authority and Assignment of Responsibility for Various Aspects of the Cuban Refugee Program," W. L. Mitchell (Commissioner of Social Security), February 20, 1961, RG 363, HEW/SRS, Cuban Refugee Program, Box 2, File "847.3 Cuban Refugee Program, February 1961," National Archives II; Ellen Winston, "Cuban Refugee Problem, Senate Hearings, 1963," 28; William Mitchell, "Migration and Refugee Assistance Act of 1961," Hearings before the Committee on Foreign Relations, United States Senate, 87th Congress, First Session, September 11, 1961 (Washington DC: U.S. Government Printing Office, 1961), 16 (cited hereafter as "Migration and Refugee Assistance Act of 1961, Senate Hearings, 1961." For 1965 figures and details on allocation of funds, see Dr. Ellen Winston, March 30, 1966, "Cuban Refugee Problem," Hearings before the Subcommittee to Investigate Problems Connected with Refugees and Escapees of the Committee on the Judiciary, United States Senate, 89th Congress, Second Session, Part I (Washington, DC: U.S. Government Printing Office, 1966), 96–97 (cited hereafter as "Cuban Refugee Problem—Part I, Senate Hearings, 1966"). For the FY 1963 budget figures, see Ellen Winston, "Cuban Refugee Problem, Senate Hearings, 1963," 36. For the total expenditures between FY 1961 and FY 1966, as well as the estimate for FY 1966, see Ellen Winston, "Adjustment of Status for Cuban Refugees," Hearings before Subcommittee No. 1 of the Committee on the Judiciary, House of Representatives, 89th Congress, Second Session, August 17, 1966 (Washington, DC: U.S. Government Printing Office, 1966), 51 (cited hereafter as "Adjustment of Status for Cuban Refugees, House Hearings, 1966").

28. On complaints from Florida politicians, see "Telephone Conversation with Senator Smathers' (Fla.) Office concerning 'Cuban Situation in Miami,' " October 6, 1960, Records of the Department of State, Bureau of Inter-American Affairs, ARA/CCA, Subject File 1960–63, Box 6, File "Exiles and Refugees, Cuba, 1960," National Archives II; Memo to the President from Frederick Dutton, January 25, 1961, White House Central Subject Files, Box 637, File "ND 19–2/CO 55," JFKL; Juanita Greene, "Cuban Refugee Problems, Senate Hearings, 1961," 72–73; "A Lesson for Refugees, Too," *MH*, November 23, 1961, 6A; "Miami Economy Strained as Cubans Hunt for Jobs," *NYT*, April 3, 1961, 1; "Miami Is Going Latin as Cubans Make Their Effect Felt in City," *NYT*, March 18, 1962, 85; "Cubans in Miami Are U.S. Concern," *NYT*, October 21, 1962, 41.

29. William Mitchell, "Migration and Refugee Assistance Act of 1961, Senate Hearings, 1961," 15–16; Abraham Ribicoff, "Migration and Refugee Assistance House Hearings, 1961," 16–17; Dr. Ellen Winston, "Cuban Refugee Problem, Senate Hearings, 1963," 23–30; Juanita Greene, "Cuban Refugee Problems, Senate Hearings, 1961," 73; Senator Phil Hart, "Cuban Refugee Problems, Senate Hearings, 1961," 112; A.A. Micocci, "Memorandum for File," March 25, 1962, "Cuban Program—Some DHEW Actions on Resettlements since November 1, 1961, to March 31, 1962," Record Group 47, Records of the Social Security Administration/Cuban Refugee Program, Box 3, File "Cuban Refugee Center, FY 1963," National Archives II; Wallace Kendall to Robert Ball, June 11, 1962, "Public Information Materials—Cuban Refugee Program," Record Group 47, Social Security Administration, Box 3, Cuban Refugee Program, File "Cuban Refugee Center, FY 1963," National Archives II; "Public Information Activities Report, Cuban Refugee Center, Miami, for Period January 1–August 20, 1962"; Philip Holman to John F. Thomas, "Report on Public information Plans for Fiscal Year 1963–1964," December 27, 1963, Record Group 363, HEW/SRS, Cuban Refugee Program, Box 3, File "040.3–040.11, 1/28/63–1964/1965," National Archives II; "Cleveland Aid to Cubans Stirs Furor," *NYT*, February 25, 1962, 38; "Cleveland Welcomes Cuban Refugees' Plane," *NYT*, February 28, 1962, 6. For secondary sources on resettlement, see Garcia, *Havana, USA*, 37, 44–45.

30. On the Advertising Council, see William Mitchell to Timothy Reardon, March 1, 1962, White House Central Files, Box 637, File "ND 19-2/CO 55," JFKL; Nell Yates (Office of Timothy J. Reardon) to William Mitchell, March 10, 1962, White House Central Files, Box 637, File "ND 19-2/CO 55," JFKL; T. J. Reardon to Theodore Repplier (Advertising Council), March 12, 1962, White House Central Files, Box 637, File "ND 19-2/CO 55," JFKL; Harold Rosenberg (Advertising Council) to Timothy J. Reardon, April 16, 1962, White House Central Files, Box 637, File "ND 19-2/CO 55," JFKL. Also useful in explaining the Ad Council's role was my correspondence (November 11, 2002, in possession of the author) with William Schriver, Graduate Assistant to the Advertising Council Archives at the University of Illinois; Frank J. Devine to Mr. Phillips, December 23, 1960, "Publicity Aspects of Refugee Relief Program in Miami," Records of the Department of State, Bureau of Inter-American Affairs, Subject Files, 1960–63, Box 5, File "Exiles and Refugees, Cuba 1960," National Archives II; J. Z. Williams to Mr. Devine, December 29, 1960, Records of the Department of State, Bureau of Inter-American Affairs, Records of the Special Assistant on Communism, Box 8, File "Cuba Refugees 1961," National Archives II. For the quotes, see Frank Devine to Mr. Ortiz, "Publicity Aspects of Refugee Relief Program in Miami," January 31, 1961, Records of the Department of State, Bureau of Inter-American Affairs, Records of the Specials Assistant on Communism, Box 8, File "Cuba Refugees 1961," National Archives II.

31. A. A. Micocci, "Memorandum for File," March 25, 1962, "Cuban Program—Some DHEW Actions on Resettlements since November 1, 1961 to March 31, 1962," Record Group 47, Records of the Social Security Administration/ Cuban Refugee Program, Box 3, File "Cuban Refugee Center, FY 1963," National Archives II ("a systematic . . ." quote); on *Reader's Digest*, see Antonio A. Micocci

to Ellen Winston, November 30, 1965, Record Group 363, HEW/SRS, Cuban Refugee Program, Box 3, File "314 Weekly 1965," National Archives II.

32. On HEW reaction to the *Parade* article, Thomas to Winston, September 1, 1964, Record Group 363, HEW/SRS, Cuban Refugee Program, Box 3, File "314 Weekly, 1/28/63–1964," National Archives II; Holman to Anderson, July 2, 1964, Record Group 363, HEW/SRS, Cuban Refugee Program, Box 3, File "041.1, 1/28/63–1964," National Archives II; Jack Anderson, "The Dramatic Story of How Heroic Men, Women, and Children Brave Terror and Torture to Escape from Red Cuba," *Parade*, August 30, 1964, 9–11.

33. "Our Refugees from Castroland," *Saturday Evening Post*, June 16, 1962, 74. On the CRP's ordering of this editorial, see "Public Information Activities Report, Cuban Refugee Center, Miami, For Period January 1–August 20, 1962" Record Group 47, Records of the Social Security Administration, Cuban Refugee Program, Box 3, File "Cuban Refugee Center, FY 1963," National Archives II. "Iowa, Si!" *Newsweek*, August 19, 1963, 75. On the desire of the CRP to use "Iowa, Si!," see John F. Thomas (Director, Cuban Refugee Program) to Mr. Osbourn Elliott (Editor, *Newsweek*) September 19, 1963, Record Group 363, HEW/SRS, Cuban Refugee Program, Box 3, File "0.43.4, A—Z, 1/28/63–1964/1965," National Archives II. Philip Holman to Ruth Lauder, July 8, 1964, Record Group 363, HEW/SRS, Cuban Refugee Program, Box 3, File "041.1 1/28/63–1964," National Archives II.

34. Juanita Greene, "The Cubans," *Miami Herald Sunday Magazine*, April 25, 1965, 4–11. For the CRP reaction, see John F. Thomas to Dr. Ellen Winston, May 4, 1965, Record Group 363, HEW/SRS, Cuban Refugee Program, Box 3, File "314 Weekly 1965," National Archives II; see also the sources listed in ch. 5, fn. 33.

35. Juanita Greene, "The Cubans," *Miami Herald Sunday Magazine*, April 25, 1965, 4–11.

36. John Thomas, "Cuban Refugee Problem, Senate Hearings, 1963," 45, 260. On concerns from Florida about the new influx of Cuban refugees see the correspondence between Florida governor Haydon Burns and President Lyndon B. Johnson, Haydon Burns to Lyndon Johnson, October 5, 1965, National Security Files, Latin America, Cuba, Box 30, File "Cuba-Refugees 10/63–1/65," LBJL; John Gardner (Secretary of HEW) to Governor Burns, October 11, 1965, National Security File, Country File, Latin America, Cuba, Box 30, File "Cuba-Refugees 10/63–1/65," LBJL; W. G. Bowdler, "Memorandum for Mr. Bundy," October 11, 1965, National Security File, Country File, Latin America, Cuba, Box 30, File "Cuba-Refugees 10/63–1/65," LBJL; W. G. Bowdler, "Memorandum for Mr. Bundy," October 14, 1965, National Security File, Country File, Latin America, Cuba, Box 30, File "Cuba-Refugees 10/63–1/65," LBJL; Ellen Winston to Secretary John Gardner (HEW), October 15, 1965, Record Group 47, SSA/CRP, Box 3, File "FY 1966 Cuban Refugee Program Resettlement General," National Archives II.

37. For the quotation, John Gardner to LBJ, "Memorandum for the President," November 4, 1965, National Security File, Country File, Latin America, Cuba, Box 30, File "Cuba-Refugees 10/63–1/65," LBJL; Donald Wheeler Jones (President, Miami Branch, NAACP) to Mayor Robert King High (Mayor, Miami),

October 13, 1965, National Security File, Country File, Latin America, Cuba, Box 30, File "Cuba—Refugees 10/63–1/65," LBJL; "New Influx of Cubans Faces Cool Reception from Many Miamians," *WSJ*, October 12, 1965, 1. On the reaction of Miamians and Floridians to the post-1965 refugees, see Garcia, *Havana, USA*, 40–42; Masud-Piloto, *From Welcomed Exiles*, 62–66.

38. Secretary Gardner Memorandum to President Johnson, June 29, 1966, Office Files of White House Aides, S. Douglas Cater, Box 95, File "Federal Task Force on Greater Miami," LBJL. On the eligibility of Cuban refugees for EOA benefits, see John Thomas to Ellen Winston, September 17, 1964, "Cuban Refugees and the Economic Opportunity Act," Record Group 363, HEW/SRS, Cuban Refugee Program, Box 3, File "051.1 1/28/63–1964," National Archives II; Thomas to Winston, October 9, 1964, Record Group 363, HEW/SRS, Cuban Refugee Program, Box 3, File "051.1 1/28/63–1964," National Archives II. On the economic opportunities for Cuban refugees, see Ellen Winston, "Cuban Refugee Problem—Part I, Senate Hearings, 1966," 99, 105–106; Wilbur J. Cohen (Undersecretary of HEW) to Rep. Manny Celler, August 10, 1966, Records of the House of Representatives, 89th Congress, 2nd Session, Committee on the Judiciary, Box 149, File "HR. 15183 [3 of 4]," National Archives.

39. Kennedy to Eastland, July 22, 1966, Records of the U.S. Senate, Committee on the Judiciary, Subcommittee on Refugees and Escapees, 1972–77, Immigration: Miscellaneous Issues, Box 130, File "Adjustment of Stats for Cuban Refugees [1of 2]," National Archives; "Dale" to "Senator," October 18, 1966, "Re: conference on Cuban bill, HR 15183—meeting at 1 pm, in Rm. S-230, Dirksen's room in Capital," Records of the U.S. Senate, Committee on the Judiciary, Subcommittee on Refugees and Escapees, 1972–77, Immigration: Miscellaneous Issues, Box 130, File "Adjustment of Status for Cuban Refugees [1of 2]," National Archives. On the persistence of anti-Castro American foreign policy, see George Ball, "Adjustment of Status for Cuban Refugees, House Hearings, 1966," 6–7; Lincoln Gordon (Assistant Secretary of State for Latin American Affairs,) August 16, 1966, "To Adjust the Immigration Status of Cuban Refugees in the United States," United States Senate, Subcommittee on Immigration and Naturalization of the Committee on the Judiciary (Washington, DC: U.S. Government Printing Office, 1966), 10–12 (cited hereafter as "To Adjust the Immigration Status of Cuban Refugees," Senate Hearings, 1966); for the Cuban Adjustment Act, see Public Law 89–732, *United States Statutes at Large, 1966*, vol. 80, pt. I (Washington, DC: U.S. Government Printing Office, 1967), 1161.

40. For "road towards citizenship" quote, see "Dale" to "Senator," October 18, 1966, "Re: conference on Cuban bill, HR 15183—meeting at 1 pm, in Rm. S-230, Dirksen's room in Capital," Records of the U.S. Senate, Committee on the Judiciary, Subcommittee on Refugees and Escapees, 1972–77, Immigration: Miscellaneous Issues, Box 130, File "Adjustment of Status for Cuban Refugees [1of 2]," National Archives; Thomas Dunn, "Cuban Refugee Problem," Part III, Hearings to Investigate Problems Connected with Refugees and Escapees of the Committee on the Judiciary, United States Senate, 89th Congress, Second Session (Washington, DC: U.S. Government Printing Office, 1966), 223. On Cuban work ethic, see John McCarthy, "Cuban Refugee Problem—Part I, Senate Hearings, 1966," 38; William vanden Heuval, "Cuban Refugee Problem—Part I, Senate

Hearings, 1966," 72; Edward Kennedy, "Cuban Refugee Problem—Part I, Senate Hearings, 1966," 115; On Cuban family values, see Philip Soskis, April 13, 1966, "Cuban Refugee Problem," Part II, Hearings before the Subcommittee to Investigate Problems Connected with Refugees and Escapees of the Committee on the Judiciary, United States Senate, 89th Congress, Second Session (Washington, DC: U.S. Government Printing Office, 1966), 195 (cited hereafter as "Cuban Refugee Problem—Part II, Senate Hearings, 1966"); James Rice, "Cuban Refugee Problem—Part I, Senate Hearings, 1966," 48. On anticommunism, see McCarthy, "To Adjust the Immigration Status of Cuban Refugees," Senate Hearings, 1966, 32–33; James Rice, "Cuban Refugee Problem—Part I, Senate Hearings, 1966," 46; CR, vol. 112, pt. 17, 89th Congress, Second Session, House of Representatives, September, 19, 1966, (Washington, DC: U.S. Government Printing Office, 1966), 22913–22; CR, vol. 112, pt. 19, 89th Congress, Second Session, Senate, October 6, 1966 (Washington, DC: U.S. Government Printing Office, 1966), 25466–68.

41. William vanden Heuvel, "Cuban Refugee Problem—Part I, Senate Hearings, 1966," 73–74; John Thomas, "Adjustment of Status for Cuban Refugees, House Hearings, 1966," 69.

42. For the Ball-Cahill confrontation, "Adjustment of Status for Cuban Refugees, House Hearings, 1966," 18; Representative Frank Chelf, "Adjustment of Status for Cuban Refugees, House Hearings, 1966," 32.

43. Peter J. Spiro, "Dual Nationality and the Meaning of Citizenship," *Emory Law Journal* vol. 46, no. 4 (Fall 1997), 1443–53; Gary Gerstle, *American Crucible: Race and Nation in the Twentieth Century*, (Princeton, NJ: Princeton University Press, 2001), 238–67.

44. On 1960s black nationalism, see Gerstle, *American Crucible*, 295–308; Eric Foner, *The Story of American Freedom* (New York City: W. W. Norton and Company, 1998) 283–84. On the *Afroyim* decision, see Spiro, "Dual Nationality," 1450–53; Russell Menyhart, "Changing Identities and Changing Law: Possibilities for a Global Legal Culture," *Indiana Journal of Global Legal Studies*, vol. 10, issue 2 (Summer 2003); Tinsley Yarbrough, *Mr. Justice Black and His Critics* (Durham, NC: Duke University Press, 1988), 42–44.

CHAPTER 6
"THE SOUL OF OUR SENSE OF NATIONHOOD": HUMAN RIGHTS
AND REFUGEES IN THE 1970s

1. Elizabeth Borgwardt, *A New Deal for the World: America's Vision for Human Rights* (Cambridge: Harvard University Press, 2005); Mary Ann Glendon, *A World Made New: Eleanor Roosevelt and the Universal Declaration of Human Rights* (New York: Random House, 2001), 193–219 and passim; Kenneth Cmiel, "The Recent History of Human Rights," *American Historical Review*, vol. 109, no. 1, February 2004, 117–35; Kirsten Sellers, *The Rise and Rise of Human Rights* (Phoenix Mill: Sutton Publishing, 2002), xiii, 38–46, 66–86; Mark Bradley, "The Ambiguities of Sovereignty: The United States and the Global Human Rights Cases of the 1940s and 1950s," paper presented at Indiana University's History of Human Rights Workshop, March 2006 (paper in possession of author). For

the UDHR, see Glendon, *A World Made New*, 310–14; for the ABA quote, see Glendon, *A World Made New*, 193.

2. Kenneth Cmiel, "The Emergence of Human Rights Politics in the United States," *Journal of American History*, December 1999, 1231–50; Gary Gerstle, *American Crucible: Race and Nation in the Twentieth Century* (Princeton, NJ: Princeton University Press, 2001) 295–308, 327–42, 349–57.

3. Robert Schulzinger, *A Time for War: The United States and Vietnam, 1941–1975* (New York: Oxford University Press, 1997), 198, 201, 246–73; James Patterson, *Restless Giant: The United States from Watergate to Bush v. Gore* (New York: Oxford University Press, 2005), 99–100.

4. Raymond Garthoff, *Détente and Confrontation: American-Soviet Relations from Nixon to Reagan* (Washington, DC: Brookings Institution, 1985).

5. For examples of Kennedy's and Fraser's leadership on human rights, see "International Protection of Human Rights," Hearings before the Subcommittee on International Organizations and Movements, Committee on Foreign Affairs, 93rd Congress, First Session (Washington, DC: U.S. Government Printing Office, 1974), 1, 219, 230; "Human Rights and the World Community: A Call for U.S. Leadership," House of Representatives, Committee on Foreign Affairs, March 27, 1974 (Washington, DC: U.S. Government Printing Office, 1974); Cmiel, "The Emergence of Human Rights Politics in the United States," 1236.

6. "Primary Defeats Portend Big Shift of House Power," *NYT*, September 14, 1972, NJ97; Sidney Milkis and Michael Nelson, *The American Presidency: Origins and Development, 1776–1990* (Washington, DC: Congressional Quarterly Press, 1990), 318–20; Patterson, *Restless Giant*, 83–87, 98; Julian Zelizer, *On Capitol Hill: The Struggle to Reform Congress and Its Consequences, 1948–2000* (New York: Cambridge University Press, 2004); Sid Milkis, "Remaking Government Institutions in the 1970s: Participatory Democracy and the Triumph of Administrative Politics," *Loss of Confidence: Politics and Policy in the 1970s*, David B. Robertson, ed. (University Park: Pennsylvania State University Press, 1998), 51–74.

7. Zelizer, *On Capitol Hill*, 156–76 ; Patterson, *Restless Giant*, 83–87; Arthur Schlesinger, *The Imperial Presidency* (Boston: Houghton Miflin, 1973).

8. John Ehrman, *The Rise of Neo-Conservatism: Intellectuals and Foreign Affairs, 1945–1994* (New Haven: Yale University Press, 1995); Mark Gerson, *The Neo-Conservative Vision: From the Cold War to the Culture Wars* (Lanham: Madison Books, 1996); James Mann, *Rise of the Vulcans: The History of Bush's War Cabinet* (New York: Penguin, 2004).

9. Cmiel, "The Emergence of Human Rights Politics in the United States," 1234–35; Sellars, *The Rise and Rise of Human Rights*, 160; Andrew Smith, *Rescuing the World: The Life and Times of Leo Cherne* (Albany: State University of New York Press, 2002), 14, 108, 110, 115–16.

10. I found no published polling data that might attest to the popularity of human rights.

11. Sidney Heitman, "Jewish, German, and Armenian Emigration from the USSR: Parallels and Differences," *Soviet Jewry in the 1980s: The Politics of Anti-Semitism and Emigration and the Dynamics of Resettlement*, Robert Freedman, ed. (Durham, NC: Duke University Press, 1989), 117; Jerome Gilison, "Soviet-

Jewish Emigration, 1971–1980: An Overview," *Soviet Jewry in the Decisive Decade, 1971–1980*, Robert Freedman, ed. (Durham, NC: Duke University Press, 1984), 3–16; Paula Stern, *Water's Edge: Domestic Politics and the Making of American Foreign Policy* (Westport, CT: Greenwood Press, 1979), 10–16; Gil Loescher and John Scanlan, *Calculated Kindness: Refugees and America's Half-Open Door, 1945 to the Present* (New York: Free Press, 1986) 89–92; Ed Koch, "Denial of Human Rights to Jews in the Soviet Union," Hearings before the Subcommittee on Europe of the Committee on Foreign Affairs, House of Representatives, 92nd Congress, First Session, May 17, 1971, 12; Peter Novick, *The Holocaust in American Life* (Boston: Houghton Miflin, 1999), 170–206.

12. Stern, *Water's Edge*, 10, 16–18, 48; Loescher and Scanlan, *Calculated Kindness*, 92–93; Garthoff, *Détente and Confrontation*, 309–10; Heitman, "Jewish, German, and Armenian Emigration from the USSR," 117; Roger Daniels, *Guarding the Golden Door: American Immigration Policy and Immigrants since 1882* (New York: Hill and Wang, 2004), 215; William Korey, "Jackson-Vanik and Soviet Jewry," *Washington Quarterly*, Winter 1984, vol. 7, no. 1, 116–28.

13. Jack Kemp, "Soviet Jewry," Hearings before the Subcommittee on Europe of the Committee on Foreign Affairs, House of Representatives, 92nd Congress, First Session, November 9 and 10, 1971 (Washington, DC: U.S. Government Printing Office, 1972), 117 (cited hereafter as "Soviet Jewry, House Hearings, 1971"); Anderson, Soviet Jewry, House Hearings, 1971, 127; Henry Jackson, *CR*, Senate, December 13, 1974, vol. 120, pt. 30, especially 39781–82; Jackson quoted in "A Risky Time for Bargaining: Interview with Senator Henry M. Jackson," *U.S. News and World Report*, June 18, 1973, 34–36; Rabbi Zev Segal, Essex County Conference on Soviet Jewry, "Soviet Jewry, House Hearings, 1971," 78.

14. Stanley Karnow, "Jackson's Bid," *New Republic*, May 25, 1974, 17–21; Meg Greenfield, "Henry vs. Henry," *Newsweek*, November 11, 1974, 46; Daniel Yergin, " 'Scoop' Jackson Goes for Broke," *Atlantic Monthly*, June 1974, 76–84; Robert Kaufman, *Henry M. Jackson: A Life in Politics* (Seattle: University of Washington Press, 2000), 266–283; "Freedom of Emigration," *Nation*, December 24, 1973, 8–9; "Soviet Exit Visas," *New Republic*, April 21, 1973, 9; "Amnesty Group in Private Soviet Talks," *NYT*, November 11, 1973, 2; "Soviet Jew Aid Lack Hit by Kennedy," *WP*, March 14, 1971, 2; "Political Prisons Hold Many Types," *NYT*, June 28, 1970, 13; "Report Criticizes Soviets on Its Political Prisoners," *NYT*, November 18, 1975, 6; Stern, *Water's Edge*, 20–21.

15. Loescher and Scanlan, *Calculated Kindness*, 95–101; William F. Sater, *Chile and the United States: Empires in Conflict* (Athens: University of Georgia Press, 1990), 159–209; Paul Sigmund, *The United States and Democracy in Chile* (Baltimore: Johns Hopkins University Press, 1993).

16. Kennedy quoted in "Refugee and Humanitarian Problems in Chile," Hearing before the Subcommittee to Investigate Problems Connected with Refugees and Escapees of the Committee on the Judiciary, United States Senate, 93rd Congress First Session, September 28, 1973 (Washington, DC:, U.S. Government Printing Office, 1973), 1–2; "Crime of Silence," *New Republic*, October 13, 1973, 14–15; "A Few in Congress Could See What the Spooks Were Doing," *NYT*, February 1, 1976, E1; George F. Will, "The Dance of Détente," *National Review*, 458; William F. Buckley, Jr., "Senator Jackson Rides Again," *National Review*,

October 27, 1972, 1200–1201; William F. Buckley, Jr., "The Chilean Refugees," *National Review*, October 26, 1973, 1198; F. Reid Buckley, "Death of a Republic: An Impression," *National Review*, August 1, 1975, 828–32; William F. Buckley, Jr., "Carpet Bombing," *National Review*, December 19, 1975, 1494–95; William F. Buckley, Jr., "Pinochet and Human Rights," *National Review*, March 18, 1977, 350–51.

17. Louis Weisner, *Victims and Survivors: Displaced Persons and Other War Victims in Vietnam, 1954–1975* (New York: Greenwood Press, 1988); Eric Chester, *Covert Networks: Progressives, the International Rescue Committee, and the CIA* (Armonk, NY: M. E. Sharpe, 1995); "Indochina: A Generation of Refugees," *Time*, May 10, 1971, 24–26; "The Refugees: Journey Without End," *Time*, June 26, 1972, 26; "Cambodia: The Uprooted," *Newsweek*, September 17, 1973, 22–23; Diane Jones, " 'Winning Hearts and Minds' in 1974: Vietnamese Refugees Return to What?" *Christian Century*, July 3, 1974, 703–704; David Kales, "The Refugees of Laos," *Nation*, January 26, 1970, 76–77; "Laos: Clearing the Plain," *Time*, February 23, 1970, 35; "Exodus on the Mekong," *Time*, May 25, 1970, 33.

18. L. F. Chapman to James O. Eastland, April 28, 1975, "Indochina Evacuation and Refugee Problems, Part IV," Staff Reports Prepared for the Use of the Subcommittee to Investigate Problems Connected with Refugees and Escapees of the Committee on the Judiciary, United States Senate, 94th Congress, First Session (Washington, DC: U.S. Government Printing Office, 1975), (cited hereafter as "Indochina Evacuation and Refugee Problems, Part IV, Senate Hearings, 1975"); Edward H. Levi to James O. Eastland, April 22, 1975, "Indochina Evacuation and Refugee Problems, Part IV, Senate Hearings, 1975," 168; L. F. Chapman to James O. Eastland, May 6, 1975, "Indochina Evacuation and Refugee Problems, Part IV, Senate Hearings, 1975," 169–70.

19. Loescher and Scanlan, *Calculated Kindness*, 102–16; Phil Habib, Assistant Secretary of State for East Asian and Pacific Affairs, April 15, 1975, "Indochina Evacuation and Refugee Problems, Part II: The Evacuation," Hearings before the Subcommittee to Investigate Problems Connected with Refugees and Escapees of the Committee on the Judiciary, United States Senate, 94th Congress, First Session (Washington, DC: U.S. Government Printing Office, 1975), 30 and passim (cited hereafter as "Indochina Evacuation and Refugee Problems, Part II, Senate Hearings, 1975"); "Congress Approves Indochinese Refugee Aid," *1975 Congressional Quarterly Almanac*, vol. XXXI (Washington, DC: Congressional Quarterly, 1976), 315–20; Public Law 94–23, *United States Statutes at Large*, 1975, vol. 89 (Washington, DC: U.S. Government Printing Office, 1977); see also the communications from L. F. Chapman to James Eastland cited in ch. 6, fn. 18.

20. "Persuading U.S. to Accept Refugees," *CSM*, May 5, 1975, 3; "On Winning Refugee-Aid Support," *CSM*, May 5, 1975, 18; Loescher and Scanlan, *Calculated Kindness*, 102, 110, 119 ; David Reimers, *Still the Golden Door*, 2nd ed. (New York: Columbia University Press, 1992), 175–76.

21. Edward Kennedy, "Indochina Evacuation and Refugee Problems, Part I: Operation Babylift and Humanitarian Needs," Hearing before the Subcommittee to Investigate Problems Connected with Refugees and Escapees of the Committee on the Judiciary, United States Senate, 94th Congress, First Session, April 8, 1975 (Washington, DC: U.S. government Printing Office, 1975), 3 (cited hereafter as

"Indochina Evacuation and Refugee Problems, Part I, Senate Hearings, 1975"); Edward Kennedy, April 15, 1975, "Indochina Evacuation and Refugee Problems, Part II, Senate Hearings, 1975," 1; "Statement on House Action Rejecting Vietnam Humanitarian Assistance and Evacuation Legislation," May 1, 1975, *Public Papers of the Presidents of the United States, Gerald R. Ford, 1975*, Book I (Washington, DC: U.S. Government Printing Office, 1977), 619; "The President's News Conference, April 3, 1975," *Public Papers of the Presidents of the United States, Gerald R. Ford, 1975*, Book I (Washington, DC: U.S. Government Printing Office, 1977), 412–13, 420–21; "Address before a Joint Session of the Congress Reporting on United States Foreign Policy," April 10, 1975, *Public Papers of the Presidents of the United States, Gerald R.. Ford, 1975*, Book I (Washington, DC: U.S. Government Printing Office, 1977), 461–63.

22. Loescher and Scanlan, *Calculated Kindness*, 119, 128–31; Barry Wain, "The Indochina Refugee Crisis," *Foreign Affairs*, Fall, 1979, 160–62, 175.

23. Loescher and Scanlan, *Calculated Kindness*, 129. George H. Gallup, *The Gallup Poll: Public Opinion, 1972–1977*, vol. II, 1976–77 (Wilmington, DE: Scholarly Resources, Inc, 1978), 1051.

24. Wain, "The Indochina Refugee Crisis," 162–69.

25. "Exodus without End," *WP*, June 24, 1979, A1; Barry Wain, *The Refused: The Agony of the Indochina Refugees* (New York: Simon and Schuster, 1981), 175; Loescher and Scanlan, *Calculated Kindness*, 138–46.

26. Wain, *The Refused*, 175; Loescher and Scanlan, *Calculated Kindness*, 138–46; Roger Daniels, *Coming to America: A History of Immigration and Ethnicity in American Life*, 2nd ed. (New York: HarperPerennial, 2002), 337; David Haines, ed., *Refugees as Immigrants: Cambodians, Laotians, and Vietnamese in America* (New Jersey: Rowman and Littlefield, 1989), 3.

27. President Jimmy Carter, Baltimore, Maryland, "Remarks and a Question-and-Answer Session at the National Convention of the Order of the Sons of Italy in America, August 7th, 1979" accessed on August 24, 2007, at John Woolley and Gerhard Peters, the American Presidency Project (online), (http://www.presidency.ucsb.edu/ws/?pid=32714); President Jimmy Carter, Bardstown, Kentucky "Remarks and a Question-and-Answer Session at a Town Meeting, July 31st, 1979" accessed on August 24, 2007, at John Woolley and Gerhard Peters, The American Presidency Project (online) (http://www.presidency.ucsb.edu/ws/?pid=32680); Cyrus Vance, "The Indochinese Refugee Problem" Hearings before the Subcommittee on Immigration, Refugees, and International Law of the Committee on the Judiciary, House of Representatives, 96th Congress, First Session, March 6, June 19 and 27, July 31, 1979 (Washington, DC: U.S. Government Printing Office, 1980), 85 (cited hereafter as "The Indochinese Refugee Problem, House Hearings, 1979"); Richard Holbrooke, "The Indochinese Refugee Problem, House Hearings, 1979," 3; "U.S. Defends Raising Refugee Admissions," *WP*, January 25, 1978, A18; "Asian Refugees' Fate Hinges on U.S.," *WP*, March 18, 1978, C27.

28. Joshua Muravchik, *The Uncertain Crusade: Jimmy Carter and the Dilemmas of Human Rights Policy* (New York: Hamilton Press, 1986); Gaddis Smith, *Morality, Reason, and Power: American Diplomacy in the Carter Years* (New York: Hill and Wang, 1986) (quote, 29); Burton I. Kaufman, *The Presidency of*

James Earl Carter, Jr. (Lawrence: University of Kansas Press, 1993), 38–42; Tony Smith, *America's Mission: The United States and the Worldwide Struggle for Democracy in the Twentieth Century* (Princeton, NJ: Princeton University Press, 1994, 239–48; David S. McLellan, *Cyrus Vance* (New Jersey: Rowman and Allenheld, 1985), 73–75; Steven Hurst, *The Carter Administration and Vietnam* (London: MacMillen, 1996), 1–17, 70–90.

29. For Carter's speech, see *Public Papers of the Presidents, Jimmy Carter, 1978* (Book II–June 30–December 31, 1978) (Washington, DC: U.S. Government Printing Office, 1979), 2161–65.

30. "Of Many Things," *America*, October 7, 1978, 1; "In Search of a Home," *America*, December 2, 1978, 401; "Bungled Benevolence in the Far East," *Christian Century*, October 5, 1977, 880–81; IRC quoted in Joyce Purnick, "Don't Let Them Drown," *New York*, July 23, 1979, 10–11; Leo Cherne, "Indochinese Refugees," Hearings before the Subcommittee on Asian and Pacific Affairs of the Committee on Foreign Affairs, House of Representatives, 96th Congress, First Session, April 5, 25, May 22, and June 13, 1979 (Washington, DC: U.S. Government Printing Office, 1979), 73 (cited hereafter as "Indochinese Refugees, House Hearings, April 5, 25, May 22, and June 13, 1979"). Bruce Grant, *The Boat People* (New York: Penguin Books, 1979), 158; Loescher and Scanlan, 130–42.

31. "... And Refugees," *WP*, June 22, 1979, A18.

32. Richard Holbrooke, "Indochinese Refugees, House Hearings, April 5, 25, May 22, and June 13, 1979," 93–95; Richard Holbrooke, "The Indochinese Refugee Problem, House Hearings, 1979," 3, 22–23; Gaddis Smith, *Morality, Reason, and Power*, 85–108; Hurst, *The Carter Administration and Vietnam*, 125–38; Christopher Brady, *United States Foreign Policy Towards Cambodia, 1977–1992* (London: Macmillan Press, 1999), 28–30.

33. "Indochinese Refugees," *New Republic*, March 25, 1978, 9–10; "Our Vietnam Duty Is Not Over," *NYT*, February 28, 1978, 32; President Jimmy Carter, Burlington, Iowa, "Remarks and a Question-and-Answer Session at a Town Meeting, August 22, 1979," accessed on August 24, 2007, at John Woolley and Gerhard Peters, the American Presidency Project (online) (http://www.presidency.ucsb.edu/ws/?pid=32783); Loescher and Scanlan, *Calculated Kindness*, 130–42.

34. "Hanoi's Shame—and Ours," *National Review*, August 3, 1979, 956–57; Patrick Buchanan, "Voyage of the 1979 Damned," *New York Daily News*, June 26, 1979, 32.

35. Edward Swanstrom quoted in Congress, House of Representatives, Committee on the Judiciary, Subcommittee No. 1, "Emergency Migration Program: Hearings before Subcommittee No. 1," 83rd Congress, 1st Session, June 8, 1953, 103; "In Search of a Home," *America*, December 2, 1978, 401.

36. Ambassador Dean Brown, "Indochina Refugees," Hearings before the Subcommittee on Immigration, Citizenship, and International Law of the Committee on the Judiciary, House of Representatives, 94th Congress, First Session, May 5 and 7, 1975 (Washington, DC: U.S. Government Printing Office, 1075), 17 (cited hereafter as "Indochina Refugees, House Hearings, May 5 and 7, 1975"); Leonard Chapman, "Indochina Evacuation and Refugee Problems, Part I, Senate Hearings, 1975," 107; Leonel Castillo, "Admission of Refugees into the United States, Part II," Hearings before the Subcommittee on Immigration, Citizenship,

and International Law of the Committee on the Judiciary, House of Representatives, 95th Congress, First and Second Sessions, August 4, 1977, January 24, March 1, April 12, 1978 (Washington, DC: U.S. Government Printing Office, 1978), 78–80, 133 (cited hereafter as "Admission of Refugees into the United States, Part II, House Hearings, 1977 and 1978"); "The Indochinese Refugee Situation August 1979," Report of a Study Mission of the U.S. House of Representatives, August 2–11, 1979 (Washington, DC: U.S. Government Printing Office, 1979), 60 ("Selection Process for Inland Camp Refugees,"); "U.S. Refugee Quota Viewed as Too Low," *NYT*, October 23, 1977, 17; James Tollefson, *Alien Winds: The Reeducation of America's Indochinese Refugees* (New York: Praeger, 1989).

37. L. F. Chapman to James O. Eastland, April 28, 1975, and Edward H. Levi to James O. Eastland, April 22, 1975, "Indochina Evacuation and Refugee Problems, Part IV," Staff Reports Prepared for the Use of the Subcommittee to Investigate Problems Connected with Refugees and Escapees of the Committee on the Judiciary, United States Senate, 94th Congress, First Session (Washington, DC: U.S. Government Printing Office, 1975), 168–70.

38. L. E. Castillo to Joshua Eilberg, September 1, 1977, "Admission of Refugees into the United States, Part II, House Hearings, 1977 and 1978," 80–81; Patricia Derian, "Admission of Refugees into the United States, Part II, House Hearings, 1977 and 1978," 128; "List of Indochinese Refugee Categories of Eligibility for Parole to the United States," "The Indochinese Refugee Situation August 1979," Report of a Study Mission of the U.S. House of Representatives, August 2–11, 1979 (Washington, DC: U.S. Government Printing Office, 1979), 61; Wain, *The Refused*, 177–81.

39. "Background Notes on the Subcommittee Staff's Findings," Records of the United States Senate, Committee on the Judiciary, Subcommittee on Refugees and Escapees, 1972–77, Box 79, File "Study Mission May 1975," National Archives I.

40. L. Dean Brown, "Refugees from Indochina," Hearings before the Subcommittee on Immigration, Citizenship, and International Law of the Committee on the Judiciary, House of Representatives, 94th Congress, First and Second Session, May 22, 1975, 190–91; Troy A. Adams to Senior Civil Coordinator, Eglin AFB Refugee Center, May 11, 1975, Record Group 220, Records of the Interagency Task Force on Indochinese Refugees, Civil Coordinators Subject File, Box 3, File "Ref-G (Registration and Screening)," National Archives II; L. F. Chapman (INS Commissioner) to Senator Daniel Inouye, May 15, 1975, Records of the U.S. Senate, Committee on the Judiciary, Subcommittee on Refugees and Escapees, 1972–77, Box 78, File: "Hearings on Evacuation and Guam S.M., May 13, 1975," National Archives I; Greene (I&NS, Washington, DC) to All I&NS Regional Offices, May 14, 1975, Record Group 220, Records of the Interagency Task Force on Indochinese Refugees, Civil Coordinators Subject File, 5/1975–9/1975, Eglin AFB, Box 3, File "Ref-G (Registration and Screening)," National Archives II; Sol Issenstein (INS, Washington, DC) to Donald M. Cameron, May 25, 1975, Record Group 220, Interagency Task Force, 1975–77, Civil Coordinators Subject File, 5/1975–9/1975, Eglin AFB, Box 3, File: "ref-G (Registration and Screening)," National Archives II; Greene to All INS Regional Offices, May 8, 1975, Record Group 220, Interagency Task Force for Indochinese Refugees,

1975–77, Civil Coordinators Subject File, Box 3, File "Ref-G (Registration and Screening)," National Archives II.

41. Civil Coordinator, Eglin AFB to Inter-Agency Task Force, Department of State WashDC, May 30, 1975, Record Group 220, Interagency Task Force, 1975–77, Civil Coordinators Subject File, 5/1975–9/1975, Eglin AFB, Box 3, File: "Ref-G (Registration and Screening)," National Archives II; "Memorandum for President's Advisory Committee on Refugees, from Ted Marrs and Roger Semerad," May 22, 1975, Record Group 220, Records of the President's Advisory Committee on Refugees, 1975–76, Subject File May 1975–January 1976, Box 4, File "Originals Memoranda," National Archives II; "Review of Vietnam Evacuation Program," Far East Branch, Honolulu, Hawaii, May 1975, Records of the U.S. Senate, Committee on the Judiciary, Subcommittee on Refugees and Escapees, 1972–77, Box 79, File "EMK Letter to Staats on Evacuation, 4/21/75," National Archives II.

42. INS head Leonel Castillo supplied these 1977 figures. See Leonel Castillo, May 25, 1977, "Indochinese Refugees—Adjustment of Status," Hearings before the Subcommittee on Immigration, Citizenship, and International Law, Committee on the Judiciary, House of Representatives, 95th Congress, First Session (Washington, DC: U.S. Government Printing Office, 1977), 41–42.

43. Testimony of James F. Greene and Sol Issenstein, December 18, 1975, "Refugees from Indochina," Hearings before the Subcommittee on Immigration, Citizenship, and International Law of the Committee on the Judiciary, House of Representatives, 94th Congress, First and Second Session, 490. For earlier testimony on this question and testimony that shows how even the INS seemed unclear about exactly how many refugees had been cleared, see the hearings above, testimony of L. Dean Brown, May 22, 1975, 190–91; testimony of L. F. Chapman, July 17, 1975, 262; testimony of L. F. Chapman, October 8, 1975, 415–16.

44. Testimony of L. Dean Brown, May 7, 1975, "The Vietnam-Cambodia Emergency, 1975, Part I—Vietnam Evacuation and Humanitarian Assistance," Hearings before the Committee on International Relations, House of Representatives, 94th Congress, First Session on HR 5960 and HR 5961 (Washington, DC: U.S. Government Printing Office, 1976), 179; see also the exchange between Rep. Long and Brown, May 8, 1975, "Special Assistance to Refugees from Cambodia and Vietnam," Hearings before a Subcommittee of the Committee on Appropriations, House of Representatives, 94th Congress, First Session (Washington, DC: U.S. Government Printing Office, 1975), 25; Eilberg, "Indochina Refugees, House Hearings, May 5 and 7, 1975," 102.

45. Michael VerMeulen, "Running with Liz," *New York*, August 4, 1980, 33–39; Elizabeth Holtzman, *Who Said It Would Be Easy? One Woman's Life In The Political Arena* (New York: Arcade Publishing, 1996), especially 68–89; John Corry, "The All-Star Race," *New York Times Magazine*, June 22, 1980, 16; "A Women Leader in Brooklyn to Challenge Celler in Primary," *NYT*, March 29, 1972, 25; "Time to Retire," *NYT*, June 15, 1972, 40; "Miss Holtzman, Vowing Reform, Prepares to Sit in Rep. Celler's Congressional Seat," *NYT*, October 2, 1972, 41.

46. Tiger cages were small bamboo cages in which South Vietnamese police and military forces held Vietcong prisoners. The existence of tiger cages—and,

more generally, horrific prisoner abuse by the South Vietnamese—came to light in 1970. Testimony of L. Dean Brown and L. F. Chapman, "Indochina Refugees, House Hearings, May 5 and 7, 1975," 28–31, 42–43, 48.

47. "Part II, Report of July 8, 1975 by Mrs. Parker," "Indochina Evacuation and Refugee Problems, Part IV," Staff Reports Prepared for the Use of the Subcommittee to Investigate Problems Connected with Refugees and Escapees of the Committee on the Judiciary, United States Senate, 94th Congress, First Session (Washington, DC: U.S. Government Printing Office, 1975), 76–77, 101–102, 67 (copy of G-646).

48. Ibid., 68 (Senate Republican quote); "A Meanness of Spirit," *WSJ*, May 8, 1980, 12; Holtzman, "Indochina Refugees, House Hearings, May 5 and 7, 1975," 48 (quote); Elizabeth Holtzman, "Letters to the Editor of the Journal," *WSJ*, May 19, 1975, 9.

49. "Survey Shows That Area Residents Favor Cut in Immigration," *WP*, August 4, 1975, A6; "Wide Hostility Found to Vietnamese Influx," *NYT*, May 2, 1975, 1; "Enmity to Refugees Puzzling," *WP*, May 3, 1975, A1; "The 'Boat People,' " George Gallup, *The Gallup Poll: Public Opinion 1979* (Wilmington, DE: Scholarly Resources Incorporated, 1980), 246–50; "Wide Hostility Found to Vietnamese Influx," *NYT*, May 2, 1975, 1; Reimers, *Still the Golden Door*, 176, 183.

50. "Agencies Run into Snags in Resettling of Refugees," *NYT*, May 8, 1975, 81; "Fund Bill Gains in House," *NYT*, May 8, 1975, 1; "Refugee Camps May Last—Eisenhower," *LAT*, May 24, 1975, 24; "30% of the 131,399 Who Fled Indochina Are Settled in U.S.," *NYT*, June 24, 1975, 4; "Resettlement Nearing End, but Not Refugee Problems," *NYT*, November 24, 1975, 73; "Wide Hostility Found to Vietnamese Influx," *NYT*, May 2, 1975, 1; "Survey Shows That Area Residents Favor Cut in Immigration," *WP*, August 4, 1975, A6; "U.S. Asked to Protect Jobs for Veterans," *LAT*, May 27, 1975, B2; "100,000th Refugee Resettled in U.S.," *LAT*, September 19, 1975, A13; "Responsibility for the Refugees," *LAT*, July 22, 1975, C6; "Refugees Caught in a New Cross Fire," *LAT*, August 11, 1975, B1; "Refugee Education: Who Pays?" *LAT*, September 12, 1975, B6; "The Melting Pot Begins to Simmer," *LAT*, January 11, 1981, OC_B1; "Wider Acts to Curb Influx of Refugees," *LAT*, June 24, 1981, OC_A1; "Welfare Dependency of Indochinese Officials Worrying California Officials," *NYT*, July 7, 1981, A10; Haines, ed., *Refugees as Immigrants*, 4.

51. "Refugee Task Force Director," *NYT*, May 24, 9; "Frequent Troubleshooter," *WP*, April 2, 1976, A14; "Ford Sets Up Unit to Aid Refugees," *NYT*, May 20, 1975, L13; Brent Scowcroft to Donald Rumsfeld, July 5, 1975, Presidential Subject File 1974–77, National Security Adviser, Box 17, File "Refugees-Indochina (2)," GFL; Eisenhower to Taft, (undated), Theodore Marrs Files, 1974–76, Box 11, File "Indochina Refugees President's Advisory Committee General (4)," GFL.

52. "Memorandum for Chairman Eisenhower, Ted Marrs, From Roger Semerad," June 17, 1975, Records of President's Advisory Committee on Refugees, Subject File 5/75–1/76, Box 4, File "Eisenhower Correspondence," National Archives II; "Memorandum for the President, through Mr. Ron Nessen, from Julia Vidalia Taft," June 9, 1975, John Marsh Files, General Subject File: Immigration, Box 19, File "Indochina Refugees—General (1) 4/75–7/75," GFL; Eisenhower to

Marrs, June 6, 1975, Theodore Marrs Files, 1974–76, Box 11, File "Indochina Refugees President Advisory Committee—General (2)," GFL; "To General Scowcroft from Jeanne Davis," June 11, 1975, National Security Adviser, Presidential Subject File, 1974–75, Box 17, File "Refugees—Indochina (2)," Ford Library; Scowcroft to Rumsfeld, July 5, 1975, National Security Adviser, Presidential Subject File, 1974–75, Box 17, File "Refugees—Indochina (2)," GFL; Lewis Shollenberger to James Delaney, June 11, 1975, White House Central Files ND 18–2/CO1, Box 65, File "ND 18–2/CO1 RF Indochina 8/8/74–6/22/75," GFL; Roger Semerad to Chairman Eisenhower, June 19, 1975, Theodore Marrs File, 1974–76, Box 11, File "Indochinese Refugees President's Advisory Committee General (3)," GFL; Semerad to Eisenhower and Marrs, June 17, 1975; Eisenhower to Taft, Undated, Theodore Marrs File, 1974–76, Box 11, File "Indochinese Refugees, President's Advisory Committee General (2)," GFL; Roger Semerad, Memorandum for the Record, July 16, 1975, Records of the President's Advisory Committee on Refugees, 1975–76, Subject File May 1975–January 1976, Box 6, File "PACR TV Spots," National Archives II; Memorandum from Paul O'Neill to Jim Connor, July 30, 1975, Records of the President's Advisory Committee on Refugees, 1975–76, Subject File May 1975–January 1976, Box 6, File "Staff Reports," National Archives II; James Delaney, Memorandum for the Record, July 31, 1975, Records of the President's Advisory Committee on Refugees, 1975–76, Subject File May 1975–January 1976, Box 6, File "Staff Reports," National Archives II.

53. Gordon King to Roger Semerad, June 18, 1975, Theodore Marrs Files, 1974–76, Box 11, File "Indochinese Refugees President's Advisory Committee General (3)," GFL; Gordon King, "A Strategy for the Integration of Indochinese Refugees into American Society," Theodore Marrs Files, 1974–76, Box 9, File "Indochina Refugees—General (1)," GFL.

54. President Jimmy Carter, August 7, 1979, Baltimore, Maryland, Remarks and a Question-and-Answer Session at the National Convention of the Order of the Sons of Italy in America, accessed on August 24, 2007 at John T. Woolley and Gerhard Peters, *The American Presidency Project* [online] (http://www.presidency.ucsb.edu/ws/?pid=32714.)

CHAPTER 7
REFORM AND RETRENCHMENT: THE REFUGEE ACT OF 1980
AND THE REAGAN ADMINISTRATION'S REFUGEE POLICIES

1. David Reimers, *Unwelcome Strangers: American Identity and the Turn against Immigration* (New York: Columbia University Press, 1998), 25–64; Daniel Tichenor, *Dividing Lines: The Politics of Immigration Control in America* (Princeton, NJ: Princeton University Press, 2002), 235–39; 276; Dr. George H. Gallup, *The Gallup Poll: Public Opinion, 1972–1977*, vol. II, 1976–1977 (Wilmington, DE: Scholarly Resources, Inc, 1978), 1051; Dr. George H. Gallup, *The Gallup Poll: Public Opinion, 1979* (Wilmington, DE: Scholarly Resources, Inc, 1980), 246–49; Dr. George H. Gallup, *The Gallup Poll: Public Opinion, 1980* (Wilmington, DE: Scholarly Resources, Inc, 1981), 122–23.

2. Tichenor, *Dividing Lines*, 224–35, 276.

3. Senator Jesse Helms, *CR*, May 6, 1975, 14852; Edward Berkowitz, *Something Happened* (New York: Columbia University Press, 2006), 169–76.

4. Rep. Frank James Sensenbrenner, December 20, 1979, *CR*, 37226; James Patterson, *Restless Giant: The United States from Watergate to Bush v. Gore* (New York: Oxford University Press, 2005), 131–45; Beth Bailey and David Farber, eds., *America in the Seventies* (Lawrence: University Press of Kansas, 2004); Edward Berkowitz, *Something Happened*; John Skrentny, *The Minority Rights Revolution* (Cambridge: Belknap Press of Harvard University Press, 2002), 337–39.

5. Rep. John Conyers, May 14, 1975, *CR*, 14348; James Patterson, *Grand Expectations: The United States, 1945–1974* (New York: Oxford University Press, 1996), 452–53, 666, 673.

6. For the confrontation between Eilberg and Bell, see "Admission of Refugees into the United States, Part II, House Hearings, 1977 and 1978," 2 (quote), and 1–31.

7. Kennedy quoted in Deborah Anker and Michael Posner, "The Forty-Year Crisis: A Legislative History of the Refugee Act of 1980," *San Diego Law Review*, December 1981, vol. 19, no. 1, 22–23.

8. Gil Loescher and John Scanlan, *Calculated Kindness: Refugees and America's Half-Open Door, 1945 to the Present* (New York: Free Press, 1986), 83–84; "Draft, 1/4/78, A Bill," Records of the U.S. Senate, Committee on the Judiciary, Subcommittee on Refugees and Escapees, 1972–77, Box 146, File "S. 643 1978–1979, Drafts," National Archives. The definition of "refugee" was the same in a Justice Department draft worked over in January 1979, and the bills S. 643 (introduced in March 1979) and HR 3610 (introduced in April 1979). For the Justice Draft, see "Memorandum, Re: Addresses, From: Doris Meissner, Deputy Associate Attorney General, January 5, 1979," Records of the United States Senate, Committee on the Judiciary, Subcommittee on Refugees and Escapees, 1972–77, Box 146, File "S. 643 1978–1979, Drafts," National Archives.

9. "Summary of the Refugee and Displaced Persons Bill Introduced by Senator Kennedy," Records of the U.S. Senate, Committee on the Judiciary, Subcommittee on Refugees and Escapees, 1972–77, Box 146, File "S. 643 1978–79, Drafts," National Archives; Attorney General Griffin Bell, "Refugee Act of 1979," Hearings before the Subcommittee on Immigration, Refugees, and International Law of the Committee on the Judiciary, House of Representatives, 96th Congress, First Session, May 3, 1979 (Washington, DC: U.S. Government Printing Office, 1979), 20–38, especially 33–34; "Memo, To: Judiciary Committee Staff, From: Jerry Tinker, June 8, 1979," Records of the U.S. Senate, Committee on the Judiciary, Subcommittee on Refugees and Escapees, 1972–77, Box 149, File "Staff Meeting on S. 643, June 15, 1979," National Archives I.

10. Memorandum "To: Senator, From: Jerry T, Re: Draft Administration Bill," December 21, 1979, Records of the U.S. Senate, Subcommittee on Refugees and Escapees, 1972–77, Bill File: Major Bill, Refugee Act of 1980, S. 643, Box 146, File "S. 643 1978–1979, Drafts," National Archives.

11. "Human Rights Spokeswoman," *NYT*, June 23, 1977, 43; Gaddis Smith, *Morality, Reason, and Power: American Diplomacy in the Carter Years* (New York: Hill and Wang, 1986), 51–52; Joshua Muravchik, *The Uncertain Crusade:*

Jimmy Carter and the Dilemmas of Human Rights Policy (New York: Hamilton Press, 1986), 9–11; John Kelly Damico, "From Civil Rights to Human Rights: The Career of Patricia M. Derian," Ph.D. Dissertation, Mississippi State University, December 1999.

12. Patricia Derian, "Admission of Refugees into the United States, Part II, House Hearings, 1977 and 1978," 269–72.

13. Attorney General Griffin Bell, "Refugee Act of 1979," Hearings before the Subcommittee on Immigration, Refugees, and International Law, Committee on the Judiciary, House of Representatives, 96th Congress, First Session, May 3, 1979, (Washington, DC: U.S. Government Printing Office, 1979), 26 (cited hereafter as "Refugee Act of 1979, House Hearings, 1979").

14. A. Whitney Ellsworth (Amnesty International, Treasurer and Former President), "Refugee Act of 1979, House Hearings, 1979," 168, 172. See also at these same hearings, Bernard Mannekin, Council of Jewish Federations, 83; Wells Klein, 248; Leo Cherne, 94, 96.

15. "Wrong Direction: Huddleston Shouldn't Like Aliens, Refugees," *Louisville Times*, April 16, 1979, A4; "Senator Walter Huddleston to Colleague," August 2, 1979, Records of the U.S. Senate, Committee on the Judiciary, Subcommittee on Refugees and Escapees, 1972–77, Box 146, File "S. 643 Amendments Huddleston," National Archives I. See also, Senator Walter Huddleston, *CR*, vol. 125, pt. 7, April 10, 1979, 7874–76; Representative James Sensenbrenner, *CR*, December 20, 1979, 37201, 37206, 37223–24; Kennedy to Huddleston, March 28, 1979, Records of the U.S. Senate, Committee on the Judiciary, Subcommittee on Refugees and Escapees, 1972–77, Box 147, File "Correspondence: Congressional," National Archives I; "S. 643: Likely Amendments and Issues to Be Raised during Floor Consideration," Records of the U.S. Senate, Committee on the Judiciary, Subcommittee on Refugees and Escapees, 1972–77, Box 146, File "S. 643 General Debate," National Archives; "Proposed Amendments," Records of the U.S. Senate, Committee on the Judiciary, Subcommittee on Refugees and Escapees, 1972–77, Box 146, File "S. 643 Briefing Book," National Archives.

16. Senator Walter Huddleston, *CR*, vol. 125, pt. 14, July 9, 1979, 17635–36; see the statement submitted for the record of Roger Conner, Executive Director of FAIR, "Refugee Act of 1979," Hearings before the Subcommittee on International Operation, Committee on Foreign Affairs, House of Representatives, September 25, 1979 (Washington, DC: U.S. Government Printing Office, 1980), 95–96; Representative Holtzman, December 13, 1979, *CR*, 35814; Representative Rodino, December 13, 1979, *CR*, 35817.

17. For a full discussion of the specifics behind passage, see Anker and Posner, "The Forty-Year Crisis," 43–64; "Senate and House Pass Refugee Entry Bills," *Congressional Quarterly Almanac*, 96th Congress, 1st Session . . . 1979, vol. XXXV(Washington, DC: Congressional Quarterly Inc., 1980), 392–395, 44–S, 198-H–199-H; "Bill Cleared to Triple Refugee Admissions," *Congressional Quarterly Almanac*, 96th Congress, 2nd Session . . . 1979, vol. XXXVI (Washington, DC: Congressional Quarterly Inc., 1981), 378–79, 30-H–31-H.

18. Public Law 96–212, "Refugee Act of 1980," *United States Statutes at Large, 1980*, vol. 94, pt. I (Washington, DC: U.S. Government Printing Office, 1981).

19. Ibid.

20. David Reimers, *Still the Golden Door*, Second Edition (New York: Columbia University Press, 1992), 196–97; Loescher and Scanlan, *Calculated Kindness*, 191–95.

21. Loescher and Scanlan, *Calculated Kindness*, 191–195; "Plan to Give More Poles Asylum Is under Study by Administration," *NYT*, March 30, 1986, 1; "Q&A on Asylum: Some of the Ins and Outs of Who Gets In," *NYT*, May 26, 1985, E5; "A Flood of Refugees from Salvador Tries to Get Legal Status," *NYT*, July 4, 1983, 1.

22. Roger Daniels, *Guarding the Golden Door: American Immigration Policy and Immigrants Since 1882* (New York: Hill and Wang, 2004), 202, 213; Reimers, *Still the Golden Door*, 186–87; Loescher and Scanlan, *Calculated Kindness*, 80–81, 188; Felix Masud-Piloto, *From Welcomed Exiles to Illegal Immigrants: Cuban Migration to the U.S., 1959–1995* (Lanham, MD: Rowman and Littlefield Publishers, 1996), 115.

23. Daniels, *Guarding the Golden Door*, 205–206.

24. Silvia Pedraza-Bailey, "Cuba's Exiles: Portrait of a Refugee Migration," *International Migration Review*, vol. 19, issue 1, Spring 1985, 22–28; Daniels, *Guarding the Golden Door*, 207; Louis Perez, *Cuba and the United States: Ties of Singular Intimacy*, Second Edition (Athens: University of Georgia Press, 1997), 256–57.

25. Pedraza-Bailey, "Cuba's Exiles," 26; Daniels, *Guarding the Golden Door*, 206; Robert Bach, "The New Cuban Immigrants: Their Background and Prospects," *Monthly Labor Review*, October 1980, 40.

26. Bach, "The New Cuban Immigrants," 39–40; Masud-Piloto, *From Welcomed Exiles to Illegal Immigrants*, 94–95; George Gallup, *The Gallup Poll: Public Opinion, 1980* (Wilmington, DE: Scholarly Resources, Inc., 1981), 120–24.

27. Reimers, *Still the Golden Door*, 189–90; "Ruling Nears in Haitians' Lawsuit Alleging U.S. Bias," *NYT*, June 12, 1980, A1.

28. Daniels, *Guarding the Golden Door*, 206.

29. "Text of State Department Statement on a Refugee Policy," *NYT*, June 21, 1980, 8; "U.S. to Let Refugees From Cuba and Haiti Remain for 6 Months," *NYT*, June 21, 1980, 1; Tichenor, *Dividing Lines*, 248; Reimers, *Still the Golden Door*, 172–73, 190, 275; Daniels, *Guarding the Golden Door*, 206–207.

30. While relatively recent history, several good overviews of refugee and immigration affairs in the 1980s exist. See Tichenor, *Dividing Lines*, and Daniels, *Guarding the Golden Door*.

31. Tichenor, *Dividing Lines*, 252–62.

32. Ibid.

33. United Nations High Commissioner for Refugees, *The State of the World's Refugees, 2000: Fifty Years of Humanitarian Action*, 105–31, 301, 310, accessed on August 24, 2007 at: http://www.unhcr.org/cgi-bin/texis/vtx/template?page=publ&src=static/sowr2000/toceng.htm); R. Bruce McColm, "The World's Unwanted," *WSJ*, September 28, 1989, A22.

34. "Committee Celebrates Fifty Years of Aiding Refugees," *NYT*, November 16, 1983, B3 (Sternberg quote); "Some Doors Are Closing," *NYT*, August 21, 1988, E3; "10 Million Refugees Crowd Camps in World's Various Trouble Zones," *LAT*, November 27, 1982, B9.

35. "U.S to Reduce Refugee Influx From Indochina," *WP*, September 23, 1981, A2; "Cut to Be Sought in Refugee Quota," *NYT*, September 23, 1981, A11. For a compendium of the Reagan figures, see U.S. Committee for Refugees, *Refugee Reports*, vol. XV, no. 12, December 31, 1994, 9.

36. Richard Lamm, "The U.S. Accepts Too Many Refugees," *NYT*, December 15, 1985, E23; Roger Conner, "Ersatz Refugees," *NYT*, July 16, 1987, A26; Walter D. Huddleston, "Refugees: We Can Only Take So Many," *WP*, October 24, 1981, A21; Alan Simpson, "The Next Step for Indochinese Refugees," *WP*, June 5, 1985, A23.

37. "Refugee Consultation," Hearing before the Subcommittee on Immigration and Refugee Policy, Committee on the Judiciary, United States Senate, 97th Congress, Second Session, September 29, 1982 (Washington, DC: U.S. Government Printing Office, 1983), 2–32; "Annual Refugee Consultation," Hearing before the Subcommittee on Immigration and Refugee Policy, Committee on the Judiciary, United States Senate, 98th Congress, First Session, September 26, 1983 (Washington, DC: U.S. Government Printing Office, 1984), 12–19.

38. "U.S. to Reduce Refugee Influx from Indochina," *WP*, September 23, 1981, A2; "Cut to Be Sought in Refugee Quota," *NYT*, September 23, 1981, A11; U.S. Committee for Refugees, *Refugee Reports*, vol. XV, no. 12, December 31, 1994, 9.

39. Raymond Garthoff, *The Great Transition: American-Soviet Relations and the End of the Cold War* (Washington, DC: The Brookings Institution, 1994); Lou Cannon, *President Reagan: The Role of a Lifetime* (New York: Public Affairs), 2000.

40. President Ronald Reagan ("sordid" quote), "Remarks on the Caribbean Basin Initiative, February 24, 1982" accessed on August 24, 2007, at John Woolley and Gerhard Peters, the American Presidency Project (online) http://www .presidency.ucsb.edu/ws/?pid=42202); President Ronald Reagan ("overwhelming facts" quote), "Address to Members of the British Parliament, June 8, 1982" accessed on August 24, 2007, at John Woolley and Gerhard Peters, the American Presidency Project (online) (http://www.presidency.ucsb.edu/ws/?pid=42614); "U.S. to Reduce Refugee Influx from Indochina," *WP*, September 23, 1981, A2 (Smith quote).

41. Daniels, *Coming to America*, 381–82; Reimers, *Still the Golden Door*, 195–97.

42. President Ronald Reagan ("flood" quote), "Remarks at a Meeting of the Council of the Americas, May 8, 1984" accessed on August 24, 2007, at John Woolley and Gerhard Peters, the American Presidency Project (online) (http:// www.presidency.ucsb.edu/ws/?pid=39887); President Ronald Reagan ("feet people" quote), "Remarks at a Mississippi Republican Party Fund-Raising Dinner in Jackson, June 20, 1983" accessed on August 24, 2007, at John Woolley and Gerhard Peters, the American Presidency Project (online) (http://www.presidency .ucsb.edu/ws/?pid=41497); President Ronald Reagan ("doorstep" quote), "Remarks at a Dinner Honoring Senator Jesse Helms, June 16, 1983," accessed on August 24, 2007, at John Woolley and Gerhard Peters, the American Presidency Project (online) (http://www.presidency.ucsb.edu/ws/?pid=41488); see also, Patrick Buchanan, "The Contras Need Our Help," *WP*, March 5, 1986, A19.

43. "Key Federal Aide Refused to Deport Any Nicaraguans," *NYT*, April 17, 1986, A1; "U.S. Officials Review Plans to Make It Easier for People Fleeing East

Bloc to gain Asylum," *CSM*, April 4, 1986, 3; Elliott Abrams, "U.S. Refugee Policy Is Nothing to Flee," *LAT*, January 17, 1985, C5; Daniels, *Coming to America*, 381–83; Reimers, *Still the Golden Door*, 195–97.

44. U.S. Committee for Refugees, "Refugee Reports" December 9, 1984, 9; "U.S. Aides Uncertainty on Rules Is Keeping Thousands in Asia Refugee Camps," *NYT*, May 17, 1981, 16; "Surge of Boat People Hits S.E. Asia," *WP*, May 19, 1981, A10.

45. "Exodus of Vietnam 'Boat People' Climbing Back to the 1979 Levels," *NYT*, June 26, 1981, A6; "Attorney General Yields on Indochinese Refugees," *WP*, May 31, 1981, A13; "U.S. Easing Curbs on Indochinese Refugee Flow," *LAT*, May 27, 1981, B14 ; "U.S. Aides Uncertainty on Rules Is Keeping Thousands in Asia Refugee Camps," *NYT*, May 17, 1981, 16.

46. "Attorney General Yields on Indochinese Refugees," *WP*, May 31, 1981, A13; "Policy That Limits Indochina Refugees Is Reversed by U.S.," *NYT*, May 31, 1981, 1; "U.S. Changes Refugee Policy to Curb Intake from Indochina," *WP*, April 28, 1982; "U.S. Tightens Entry Rules for Indochinese Refugees," *CSM*, April 26, 1982, 2; Doris Meissner, "U.S. Refugee Program," Oversight Hearings before the Subcommittee on Immigration, Refugees, and International Law of the Committee on the Judiciary, House of Representatives, 97th Congress, First Session, September 16, 1981 (Washington, DC: U.S. Government Printing Office, 1981), 8–9.

47. "U.S. Planning for Armenian Refugees," *NYT*, March 6, 1988, 3; "Soviet Armenians Let In Improperly, U.S. Officials Say," *NYT*, May 29, 1988, 1.

48. "Soviet Armenians Let In Improperly, U.S. Officials Say," *NYT*, May 29, 1988, 1 (quotes); "Tide of Emigrants from USSR Floods US," *CSM*, December 7, 1988, 7.

49. "U.S. Faces a Flood of Soviet Emigres," *NYT*, November 10, 1988, A15; "U.S. Embassy Holding Up Visas for Soviet Emigres," *NYT*, July 8, 1988, A1; "U.S. Bars Some Soviet Jews and Armenians as Refugees," *NYT*, December 3, 1988, 1; "Tide of Emigrants from USSR floods US," *CSM*, December 7, 1988, 7; "U.S. Eases Backlog in Soviet Emigration but Draws Criticism," *NYT*, December 9, 1988, A1.

50. "Who's a Refugee?" *NYT*, December 19, 1988, A16; for 1990s refugee admission statistics, see U.S. Committee for Refugees, *Refugee Reports*, December 2000, 9, accessed on August 24, 2007, at www.refugees.org/data/refugee_reports/ archives/2000/2000NovDec.pdf. Back issues of *Refugee Reports* are available at the Web site of the U.S. Committee for Refugees and Immigrants (www.refugees .org).

EPILOGUE
THE UNITED STATES AND REFUGEES AFTER THE COLD WAR

1. The UNHCR saw the refugee population shrink from 18 million to 12 million, while the U.S. Committee for Refugees placed the reduction on the order of 16 million to 14 million. "Refugees and Asylum Seekers Worldwide 1994 to 2002," U.S. Committee for Refugees, *World Refugee Survey 2003*, accessed on

August 24, 2007, at www.refugees.org/data/wrs/03/stats/SSRefugeesWorldwi-de.pdf; UNHCR, *The State of the World's Refugees 2000: Fifty Years of Humanitarian Action* (London: Oxford University Press), 133–53, accessed on August 24, 2007 at http://www.unhcr.org/cgibin/texis/vtx/template?page=publ&src=static/sowr2000/toceng.htm.

2. "What on Earth?" *WP*, May 22, 1999, A13; "9 Million Still Uprooted by Soviet Union's Demise," *WP*, April 28, 1999, A20; Gerard Prunier, *The Rwanda Crisis: History of a Genocide* (New York: Columbia University Press, 1995); L. R. Melvern, *A People Betrayed: The Role of the West in Rwanda's Genocide* (London: Zed Books, 2000); Samantha Power, *A Problem from Hell: America and the Age of Genocide* (New York: Basic Books, 2002).

3. Prunier, *The Rwanda Crisis*, 304.

4. Timothy Wirth, September 26, 2006, "Annual Refugee Consultation," Hearings before the Committee on the Judiciary, U.S. Senate (Washington, DC: U.S. Government Printing Office, 1997), 6–29; Phyllis Coven, August 1, 1995, "Annual Refugee Consultation," Hearings before the Committee on the Judiciary, Subcommittee on Immigration, U.S. Senate (Washington, DC: U.S. Government Printing Office, 1997), 1–27.

5. James Patterson, *Restless Giant: The United States from Watergate to Bush v. Gore* (New York: Oxford University Press, 2005), 297–304; Roger Daniels, *Guarding the Golden Door: American Immigration Policy and Immigrants Since 1882* (New York: Hill and Wang, 2004), 232–59; Daniel Tichenor, *Dividing Lines: The Politics of Immigration Control in America* (Princeton, NJ: Princeton University Press, 2002), 274–88.

6. Daniels, *Guarding the Golden Door*, 206–208.

7. "Resistance to the New Boatlift Surging in Florida," *WP*, August 11, 1994, A3; "Exodus Is Very Different from '80 Boatlift," *NYT*, August 24, 1994, A14; Daniels, *Guarding the Golden Door*, 208–10.

8. Roger Daniels, *Coming to America: A History of Immigration and Ethnicity in American Life*, 2nd ed. , (New York: HarperPerennial, 2002), 414, 417–18; U.S. Committee for Refugees, "Refugee Reports: 2004 Statistical Issue," vol. 25, no. 9, December 31, 2004.

9. Deborah Anker, "Women Refugees: Forgotten No Longer?" *San Diego Law Review* vol. 32 (1995), 771–817; Kristin Kandt, "United States Asylum Law: Recognizing Persecution Based on Gender Using Canada as a Comparison," *Georgetown Immigration Law Journal*, vol. 9 (1995), 137–80; Deborah Anker, "Refugee Law, Gender, and the Human Rights Paradigm," *Harvard Human Rights Journal*, vol. 15 (2002), 133–54.

10. Anker, "Women Refugees," 771–817; Anker, "Refugee Law, Gender, and the Human Rights Paradigm," 133–54.

11. "INS Expands Asylum Protection for Women," *WP*, June 3, 1995, A4.

12. U.S. Committee for Refugees, *Refugee Reports*, vol. 22, no. 9/10, September/October 2001, 1–5; "A Nation Challenged; Refugees at America's Door Find It Closed after Attacks," *NYT*, October 29, 2001, sec. A, 1; "Terrorism's Other Victims: Refugees Cleared to Join Family in U.S. Stuck in Limbo after Attacks," *WP*, December 2, 2001, C01.

13. Daniels, *Coming to America*, 417–18; "Sudan's Slow Self-Destruction," *Financial Times*, January 21, 2002, London ed., 15; "Why Sudan Has Become a Bush Priority," *CSM*, June 30, 2004, 1; "Americans Rally for Darfur," *Boston Globe*, May 1, 2006, A1; "Russian Congregation Seeks Asylum in U.S.," *Cleveland Plain Dealer*, February 13, 1999, 4F; U.S. Committee for Refugees, *Refugee Reports*, vol. 27, no. 1 (February 2006), 15.

14. "Terrorism's Other Victims: Refugees Cleared to Join Family in U.S. Stuck in Limbo after Attacks," *WP*, December 2, 2001, C01; U.S. Committee for Refugees, *Refugee Reports*, vol. 23, no. 1, January/February 2002, 1–10.

15. Mason quoted in "Terrorism's Other Victims: Refugees Cleared to Join Family in U.S. Stuck in Limbo after Attacks," *WP*, December 2, 2001, C01; "INS Pledges to Admit More Refugees," *WP*, February 13, 2002, A15; "Effects of 9/11 Reduce Flow of Refugees to U.S.," *WP*, August 21, 2002, A03; "U.S. Security Concerns Trap Thousands in Kenyan Camp," *NYT*, January 29, 2003, 3; U.S. Committee for Refugees, *Refugee Reports*, vol. 23, no. 4, May 2002, 1–6; U.S. Committee for Refugees, *Refugee Reports*, vol. 23, no. 7, September/October 2002, 1–6; U.S. Committee for Refugees, *Refugee Reports*, vol. 27, no. 1 (February 2006), 15.

Index

Abrams, Elliott, 190
Addams, Jane, 12
Advertising Council, 77–78, 81
AFL-CIO, 168, 172
Africa: refugees from, 99–100, 185, 188, 197, 204
Afroyim v. Rusk, 131–32
Agrarian Reform Act, 108
Alien Registration Act, 19
Allende, Salvador, 136
America, 152, 155
American Civil Liberties Union (ACLU), 7, 90, 168, 172
American Coalition of Patriotic Societies, 89, 91, 102
American Committee for Italian Migration, 40, 43, 95
American Federation of Labor (AFL), 13, 17, 27, 39
American Friends Service Committee, 99, 100
American identity, 5–6, 8; during the early Cold War, 26–31; before the Cold War, 11–12, 14; and Cuban refugees, 124–27, 129–32; and human rights 135, 152, 161–62; and Hungarian refugees, 61, 75, 79–81, 84; and Indochinese refugees, 164–65; after 9/11 terrorist attacks, 205–6; in the 1960s, 93–95; in the 1970s, 169–70, 175; and the Refugee Relief Program, 43
American Legion, 13, 17, 41, 89, 96, 176
American Mercury, 89
Americans for Democratic Action, 26
Amnesty International, USA (AIUSA), 139–40, 142, 143, 172, 175–76
Anderson, Jack, 124
Anderson, John, 141
anticommunism, 27–32, 55, 135, 205–6; in American identity, 5, 8; and Cuban refugees, 112, 120, 124–25; and Hungarian refugee admissions, 74–75, 80–81, 84; and immigration reform in the 1960s, 92–94; and Indochinese refugee admissions, 147, 154, 164–65; in the 1970s,

135, 138–39; in RRP administration, 46–47, 55–56; in RRP debates, 41–44
Anti-Semitism, 17–18; 23
Arab refugees, 38, 54–55
Arens, Richard, 29
Armenian refugees, 15, 193–95
Arnaz, Desi, 31, 113
Asian immigrants, 13, 27
Association of Southeast Asian Nations (ASEAN), 153–54
Asylum, 178–79, 180, 182, 189–90, 200–203
Australia, 37, 67, 150, 186
Austria, 21, 32, 65
Austro-Hungarian Empire, 15

Ball, George, 130
Ball, Lucille, 31, 113
Batista, Fulgencio, 107, 109
Bay of Pigs invasion, 109
Bell, Griffin, 171, 175
Besterman, Walter, 69–70
Black, Hugo, 131
black power, 131–32
boat people, 21, 145; American response to, 148–51; and international aid and resettlement efforts, 149–50; origins of, 148–49. *See also* Indochinese refugeesBridges, Styles, 46
Brown, L. Dean, 160
Bruss, Kurt, 52–54
Brzezinski, Zbigniew, 151
Buchanan, Patrick, 154–55, 199
Bureau of Security and Consular Affairs (BSCA): creation of, 29; and Hungarian refugee admissions, 66; and the Refugee Relief Program, 37, 45, 46, 50
Bush, George H.W., 186, 196
Bush, George W., Administration of, 203–5

Cahill, William, 130
California, 162–63, 199
Cambodia, 145, 148, 149
Canada, 19, 37, 67, 150, 186, 201
Canham, Irwin, 102–3
Carrera, Deborah, 120

Carter, Jimmy 140, 165; and human rights, 151–52
Carter Administration: and the boat people, 148–50, 154, 155; and Mariel refugees, 182–83; and the Refugee Act, 171, 174, 177, 192
Case, Clifford, 89
Case Act of 1972, 138
Casey, William, 152
Castro, Fidel, 107, 108, 109, 110, 112, 180–81, 200
Catholic Anti-Communist League, 89
Catholic Relief Services, 99, 100
Celler, Emanuel, 34, 40, 42, 43–44, 50, 87, 89, 160
Central America, 188, 189, 191, 197
Central Intelligence Agency, 143
Cherne, Leo, 75, 152
Chile, 136; refugees from, 9, 140, 142–43
Chiles, Lawton, 182
China, 18, 149
Christian Century, 152
Church World Service, 121, 172, 176
Citizens Commission on Indochinese Refugees (CCIR), 152, 172
citizenship, 129–31,Civil Rights Act of 1964, 95
civil rights movement, 5, 9, 93–96, 103, 131, 135
Clark, Joseph, 119
Clark, Richard (Dick), 173
Clinton Administration, 198–99, 199–200, 204
Cmiel, Ken, 139
Code, Dr. Augusto Fernandez, 118
Cold War consensus, 4, 104, 114, 135
Commons, John, 13
Communications Counselors, Inc., 77–81, 225n34
Congress of Industrial Organizations, 17, 26
Congress of Racial Equality, 128
Congressional Black Caucus, 182
Congressional Budget and Impoundment Act of 1974, 138
Conyers, John, 171
Corsi, Edward, 48–49, 50
Costa Rica, 180
Cruz, Ruben, 126
Cuban missile crisis, 108, 110, 116
Cuban refugee admissions, 9, 86, 147, 156; and admissions standards, 115–21; assimilation of, 126–27; and demographics of refugee flow, 107, 109–12, 114–15; 179; and the "Memorandum of Understanding", 110–12, 116, 127; in the 1990s, 199–200; opposition to, 121–23, 127–28; and public relations campaign; 121–27; and resettlement outside Florida, 122–23; and status normalization, 127–32; U.S. government response to refugee flow, 107, 109–14; and welfare, 121–22, 125–27, 128. See also Mariel refugee crisisCuban Refugee Program, 121–27, 128–30
Cuban revolution, 107–9, 112, 114–15, 181
Cuban Revolutionary Council, 119
Cuban Status Adjustment Act, 107, 128–32
Cultural pluralism, 23–24, 78, 94–95, 164–65

Daughters of the American Revolution (DAR), 13, 17, 27, 89, 176
Dean, Homer, 52, 53, 54
definition of immigrant, 1
definition of refugee, 1, 9–10; and admissions in the 1980s, 191–95; before the Cold War 15–16, 24, 26; and Cuban refugee admissions 112; and gender, 201–3; and Hungarian refugee admissions 67, 81; and immigration reform in the 1960s, 97, 100–104; in the 1970s 133, 157–58; and the Refugee Act of 1980, 172, 173, 178, 183; and the Refugee Relief Program, 39
Democratic Party: and human rights, 136–38, 140, 160; and Hungarian refugee admissions, 65; and immigration before 1952, 12, 13, 22–23, 26–27, 31–32; and immigration reform in the 1960s, 90, 91; and Indochinese refugees, 149; in the 1970s, 168–69; and Reagan's foreign policy 190–91; and the Refugee Relief Program, 40; and Soviet Jews, 142
Denver, John, 164
Department of Health, Education, and Welfare (HEW), 121, 124, 128, 173
Derian, Patricia, 174–76
détente, 136–37, 138, 140, 188
Dies, Martin, 19
Dinnerstein, Leonard, 3, 25
Displaced Person Commission, 25

displaced persons: and the Cold War, 25–26; definition of, 24; and the DP Program, 7–8, 12, 22, 24–26, 48; after World War II, 21–22
Dulles, John Foster, 35–36, 56, 63–64
Dunn, Thomas, 129
Duvalier, François, 113, 180
Duvalier, Jean-Claude "Baby Doc," 180

East Germany, 61
Eastland, James, 58–59, 88, 90, 91, 174
Economic Opportunity Act of 1964, 128
Education Systems Corporation, 164
Eglin Air Force Base, 159
Eilberg, Joshua, 148–49, 171, 172, 174
Eisenhower, Dwight D., 31, 32
Eisenhower, John D., 164
Eisenhower Administration, 8; and Cuban refugee admissions, 108–9, 112, 113, 114, 115, 121; and Hungarian refugees, 60, 63–64, 66, 70–71, 75, 82; and immigration reform in the 1950s, 89, 90, 97, 100; and the Refugee Relief Program, 35–37, 45, 47, 48, 56
Ellsworth, A. Whitney, 175–76
El Salvador, 189–90
Emergency Migration Program (EMP), 33
Equal Rights Amendment, 139
Ervin, Sam, 88, 169

Faget, Mariano, 117–19
Fair Share refugee law, 86, 98, 99, 101
Farbstein, Leonard, 95
Federation for American Immigration Reform (FAIR), 168, 169, 176–77, 187, 202
Feighan, Michael, 84, 87, 91–92, 96, 101–2
Fino, John, 42
Florida, 121–22, 127–28, 181
Fong, Hiram, 95
Ford Administration, 137, 141, 143, 145, 147, 161, 164, 171
Foster, Mark, 77–79
France, 67, 150
Fraser, Donald, 136–38, 139, 140, 142, 160
Freedom House, 139
French Revolution, 14

Gardner, John, 128
General Accounting Office, 159
General Society of the War of 1812, 43

Genizi, Haim, 3
Gerety, Pierce, 56–58, 66, 69
Germany, 15, 16, 21, 22, 32, 35, 48
Gerstle, Gary, 3, 24
Gideon v. Wainwright, 94
Goldwater, Barry, 89
Gombos, Samuel, 83
Gonzales, Elian, 200
Gorbachev, Mikhail, 193–94, 195, 196
Great Britain, 19, 37, 67, 149, 186
"Great Society," 94, 138
Great War. See World War I.Greece, 48
Greene, Juanita, 122, 123, 126, 127
Griswold v. Connecticut, 94
Gruenther, Arthur, 98
Guam, 155, 159
Guatemala, 189

Haig, Alexander, 192, 193
Haitian refugees, 113, 114, 179–80, 182, 183
Handlin, Oscar, 103
Hart, Philip, 89, 115, 123
Hebrew Immigration Aid Society, 68, 121, 172, 195
Helms, Jesse, 169
Helsinki Accords, 136, 139
Hennessy, James, 117, 118
Hernandez, Dr. Roberto, 119
Hoa, 149
Holbrooke, Richard, 151, 153–54
Holman, Philip, 124
Holocaust, 3, 21
Holtzman, Elizabeth, 160–62, 168, 171–72, 174, 177, 178, 184
House Un-American Activities Committee (HUAC), 19
Huddleston, Walter, 176–77
human rights, 9–10, 133–34; and the boat people, 151–53, 154–55, 158; and the Carter Administration, 151; and Chilean refugees, 142–43; in the 1970s, 134–40; and the Refugee Act of 1980, 174–76, 178; and Soviet Jewish refugees, 140–42, 143; and Vietnamese refugees, 147, 158, 160–62
Human Rights Watch, 139
Humphrey, Hubert, 40, 89
Hungarian refugee admissions, 8, 117, 120, 147, 156; decision to begin, 65–66; decision to continue, 73; final statistics of, 85; of other nations, 67–68; and

Hungarian refugee admissions (*cont'd*)
parole, 70–73; procedures relating to,
66–70; publicity campaign for, 75–81,
123; speed of, 68; and status normalization, 82–85, 128, 129, 131
Hungarian revolution, 61–63, 68, 73;
American response to, 63–65; casualties
during, 63

Immigration and Naturalization Service
(INS), 6, 99, 173, 178; and admissions
procedures in the 1980s, 192–95; before
the Cold War, 19–20; during the early
Cold War, 25, 29; and Cuban refugees,
116–20; and gender persecution, 201;
and Haitian refugees, 182; and Hungarian refugees, 71; and Indochinese refugees 156–57, 158–60, 161; and Mariel
refugee crisis, 181, 182–83; and refugees
after 9/11 attacks, 203–4
immigration laws, 7, 9; Act of 1917, 15,
20; Act of 1924, 13; Act of 1929, 13;
amendments of 1965, 96, 112, 127; effects of 1965 reform, 96–97; 1960s reform proposals, 90–92; and the Refugee
Act of 1980, 178; and refugee law in
1965, 97. *See also*, McCarran-Walter
Act (MWA)
immigration quotas: for immigration from
Germany, 16–17, 20; for immigration
from Great Britain, 14; for immigration
from Italy, 14; for immigration from
Russia, 14
Immigration Reform and Control Act of
1986 (IRCA), 185
immigration statistics, 1, 2, 12
Indochina Migration and Refugee Assistance Act of 1975, 146
Indochinese refugees, 133–34; and admission procedures in the 1980s, 192–93;
and admissions procedures and standards, 155–62; and admission statistics,
151; and the boat people, 148–55; and
human rights, 151–53; opposition to in
the United States, 162–65; quotas under
the Refugee Act, 187–88, 192; and the
Saigon evacuation, 145–48. *See also*
boat people
India, 102
Indonesia, 149, 155
Interagency Task Force on Refugees
(IATFR), 163–65

Intergovernmental Committee for Euro-
pean Migration (ICEM), 37, 67, 68, 99
Internal Security Act, 27–28, 42
International Rescue Committee, 68, 75,
98, 121, 130, 152, 172, 176, 186
Italy, 21, 32, 35–36, 48

Jackson, Henry, 140–42, 143, 189
Japan, 149–50
Javits, Jacob, 26, 89, 92
Johnson, Lyndon B., 91
Johnson Administration: and Cuban refu-
gees, 110–12, 113, 114, 115, 127–29;
and immigration reform, 92, 94, 104
Johnston, Olin, 73–75, 82–84
Jones, Roger, 102, 104, 110
Justice Department, 118–20, 173, 178–79,
192–93, 194–95, 203

Kádár, János, 62
Kallen, Horace, 12, 23
Keating, Kenneth, 26, 89
Kemp, Jack, 141
Kennedy, Edward (Ted): and Chilean refugees 143; and Haitian refugees, 184; and
human rights, 136–38, 139, 160; and im-
migration reform in the 1960s, 89–90;
95; and Indochinese refugees, 147; and
Reagan's refugee policies, 191, 192–93;
and the Refugee Act of 1980, 168–69,
171–72, 174, 177; and Soviet Jews, 142
Kennedy, John F., 82
Kennedy, Robert, 90, 95
Kennedy Administration, 87; and Cuban
refugees, 109–10; 112, 113, 114, 115,
118–19, 121; and immigration reform,
90–91; and refugee reform in the
1960s, 101
Khmer Rouge, 148
Khrushchev, Nikita, 61, 80
King, James, 182
Kissinger, Henry, 136, 138
Knights of Labor, 13
Koch, Ed, 140
Kossuth, Louis, 14

Lamm, Richard, 187
Lang, Gregory, 73–74
Laos, 145, 148, 149
Lawyers Committee for Human
Rights, 139

League of Nations, 15; definition of refugee, 15, 210n10
Lehman, Herbert, 40, 46, 48, 50, 90
liberalism, 40, 90, 91, 93–95, 137–38, 160, 190–91
liberalizers, 2; and the DP Program, 22; in the early twentieth century, 12–14, 16; and immigration in the 1970s and 1980s, 168–69; and the McCarran-Walter Act, 26–27; after the 9/11 attacks, 206; in the 1930s, 17; in the 1960s, 89–91, 92–93; and refugee experts, 98–100, 101–4, 171–72; and the Refugee Relief Program, 39–40, 42–43; during World War II, 21
Liberty Lobby, 89
Lodge, Henry Cabot, 13, 169
Loescher, Gil, 97, 113
Logevall, Frederik, 114
Long, Breckinridge, 20
Lourie, Donald, 46
Lutheran World Federation, 68

Mahlow, Gottfried, 51–52
Malaysia, 149, 155–56
Malcolm X, 131
Mantoura, George Fuad, 54–55
Marchisio, Juvenal, 43
Mariel refugee crisis, 179–84
Marks, Edward, 100
Marrus, Michael, 3
Marshall, George, 22
Mason, Jana, 205
May, Elaine Tyler, 80
McCarran, Patrick, 23, 25, 27–29, 38–39, 46–47, 57, 162
McCarran-Walter Act (MWA), 8, 26–32, 36, 41, 42, 51, 75, 82–83, 90–92
McCarthy, Joseph, 30, 31, 46–47
McLeod, Scott, 34, 46–47, 48, 55, 57, 66, 107, 162
Meany, George, 98, 164
"Mercy Ships" bill, 18
Mexico, 116, 189
Micocci, Anthony, 51
Miller, William, 89
Mindszenty, Josef, 62
Moore, Arch, 120
multiculturalism, 135

Nagy, Imre, 62, 65
Nansen, Fridjtof, 15

Nation, 136, 142
National Association for the Advancement of Colored People (NAACP), 128, 168, 170
National Association of Manufacturers, 168
National Catholic Welfare Conference, 42, 68, 121, 172
National Council for Individual Freedom, 89
National Council of Churches, 182
national identity. See American identity
National Organization for Women, 202
National Origins Quota Immigration System, 7, 8, 13–14, 18, 28–29, 87–88, 97
National Review, 89, 102, 143, 154
national security, 20–21
National Welfare Rights Organization, 170
Nazism 1, 7, 12, 21, 139, 161–62
neoconservatives, 138–39, 142, 143, 154–55
New Deal, 17, 26
New Republic, 58, 136, 142, 154
"New Right," 64, 89, 168
Newsweek, 125
New York Times, 154, 196
Ngai, Mai, 3
Nicaragua, 189–90, 191
9/11 terrorist attacks. See "War on Terror"-nineteenth century U.S. refugee policies, 14–15
Nixon, Richard, 31, 73, 75, 80
Nixon Administration: and Chilean refugees, 143; foreign policies of, 135, 136, 137, 138; and Soviet Jews, 140–43
Noto, Mario, 117, 120

Office of Investigations of the Refugee Relief Program (IRP), 50
Opa-Locka military base, 117, 118
Operation Phoenix, 135, 161–62
Ottoman Empire, 15

Pakistan, 102, 103
Parade, 124
parole, 70–71; of boat people, 148–49, 156–57; of Chilean refugees, 143; critiques of, 171; and Cuban refugees, 116; and Haitian refugees, 183–84; and the Hungarian refugee crisis, 70–73; and immigration reform in 1965, 97; and Mariel refugees, 183–84

Pastore, John, 89
Perez, Louis, 113, 181
Perkins, Frances, 20
Peru, 180
Philippines, 155–56, 158
Pinochet, Augusto, 136, 142–43
Platt Amendment, 114
Poland, 61, 190
President's Advisory Committee on Refugees (PACR), 163–64
President's Committee for Hungarian Refugee Relief (PCFHRR), 77
progressivism, 13
publicity campaigns, 7; for Cuban refugees, 121–27, 129; for Hungarian refugees, 75–81, 225n34; for Indochinese refugees, 164–66
public opinion, 2; and boat people, 148–49, 165; and Cuban refugee admissions, 121–23; and Hungarian refugees, 71, 74–75, 81, 83; and the Hungarian revolution, 64–65; and immigration in the 1970s and 1980s, 168, 169–70; and immigration in the 1990s, 199; on immigration reform in the 1960s, 92, 95; and Mariel refugees, 181–82; on 1960s refugee admissions, 104; and the Refugee Relief Program, 40–41; and Vietnamese refugees in 1975, 146, 162–65
Public Works and Economic Development Act of 1965, 128

Rabb, Maxwell, 38, 66, 98
Rangel, Vincent, 125, 126
Reagan, Ronald, 170
Reagan administration, 4, 10, 167; and foreign policy, 188–89; and immigration, 184–85, 189; and Indochinese refugee admissions procedures, 191–93; and the Refugee Act of 1980, 186–89, 190; and refugees from Central America, 189–90; and Soviet Armenian refugees, 193–95
Red Scare, 5
Refugee Act of 1980, 9–10, 167, 173–79, 183–84, 186–89, 191–92, 193–94, 198–99, 200–201, 203–5
Refugee-Escapee Act of 1957, 82–83, 86, 97
Refugee Relief Program (RRP), 4, 8, 97, 117, 120, 156, 162; administration of, 50–56; admissions under, 47–48, 56; "assurances" in, 45–46, 48, 57; critiques of

34; congressional debates concerning, 39–44; drafting of, 37–39; genesis of, 35–37; and Hungarian refugee admissions, 66, 68–69, 70; passage of, 45; success of, 56–59; refugees: as a global problem in the 1960s, 99–100, 185, 197–98; statistics concerning, 1, 2
Reno, Janet, 200
Republican Party 12, 31–32, 36–37, 39, 57, 64–65, 89, 168, 169–70, 199
restrictionists, 2; and Cuban refugee admissions, 121–22; and the DP Program, 23; in the early twentieth century, 12–14; and Hungarian refugee admissions, 73–75, 82–83; and Indochinese refugees, 146, 148–49, 162–65; after the 9/11 attacks, 206; in the 1930s, 17–18; in the 1960s, 87–89, 91–92, 96, 101–2; in the 1970s and 1980s, 168–71, 185, 186–87; in the 1990s, 199, 202–3; and the Refugee Act of 1980, 176–77; and the Refugee Relief Program, 41, 44, 58–59; during World War II, 21
Revercombe, William C., 23
Revolutions of 1848, 14
"Rights Revolution," 93–95, 103, 135, 168, 170–71
Rionda, Olga, 126
Rodino, Peter, 168–69
Rogers, William P., 84–85
Roosevelt, Eleanor, 11
Roosevelt, Franklin, 16, 17, 18–19, 134
Rotarian, 102
Rustin, Bayard, 152
Rwanda, 197–98, 202

Salinger, Pierre, 119
Saltonstall, Leverett, 89
sanctuary movement, 191
Saturday Evening Post, 125
Sayre, Francis, 103
Scanlan, John, 97, 113
Schlafly, Phyllis, 64
Schlesinger, Jr., Arthur, 137, 199
Schwartz, Abba, 87
security checks: and Cuban refugees, 116–20; in the Hungarian refugee admissions, 67, 68–70, 71–72, 74, 119; and Indochinese refugees, 134, 155–57, 158–60; after the 9/11 attacks, 203–5, 206; and refugees in the 1980s, 192–93; 194–95;

in the Refugee Relief Program, 48, 50–56, 57–58
segregation, 13, 27, 88
Sensenbrenner, Frank, 170, 176–77
Simpson, Alan, 185, 187, 194
Smith, William French, 189
Snyder, Edward, 100
Sons of Italy, 40
Soviet Jewish refugees, 133, 140–42
Soviet Union, 3–4, 15, 22; and Cuba, 108–9; and the Hungarian Revolution, 62–63; Jews in, 9, 133, 140; refugees from during the 1980s, 187–88, 189, 193–95; refugees from during the 1990s, 197; and the United States in the 1970s, 136–39, 140–41; and Vietnam, 154
Spain, 116
Stalin, Joseph, 61
State Department, 6, 20; and Cuban refugees, 116–17, 121, 123, 128–29; and the DP Program, 25; and human rights, 137, 151, 173; and Hungarian refugee admissions, 71–72; and immigration reform in the 1960s, 91–92; and Indochinese refugees, 145–47, 148, 153–54, 155–57, 192–93; and McCarran-Walter Act, 29; and the Refugee Act of 1980, 173–75; and refugee experts in the 1960s, 99, 102; and refugees in the 1930s, 16–18; and refugees during World War II, 18–20; and refugees after World War II, 22; and refugees in early 1950s, 32; and refugees in the 1980s, 192–95; and refugees after 9/11 attacks, 203–5; and the Refugee Relief Program, 36, 37–38
status normalization: of Cuban refugees, 107, 127–32; of Hungarian refugees, 70, 82–85, 128, 129, 131; of Indochinese refugees, 174; of Mariel refugees, 183; and the Refugee Act of 1980, 174
Sternberg, Charles, 186
subversion, fear of: in Cold War, 23, 27–28; and Cuban refugees, 117–20; in Hungarian refugee admissions, 74–75, 84–85; and immigration reform in the 1960s, 93; and Indochinese refugees, 159–60; in Refugee Relief Program, 41–42; in World War II, 19;Suez Crisis, 63
Swanstrom, Edward, 42, 100, 155
Sweden, 67
Swing, Joseph, 66, 71, 72, 74
Switzerland, 67, 116, 186

Taft, Julia V., 163–164
Thailand, 149, 155, 156, 193
Thomas, John, 130
Tichenor, Dan, 3
Trevor, Jr., John, 102
Truman, Harry, 22–23; 29–30, 32–33, 37
26th of July Movement, 107

United National Relief and Rehabilitation Agency (UNRRA), 21–22
United Nations, 67, 99, 134, 150, 202; and the 1951 Refugee Convention, 173; and the 1967 Protocol Relating to the Status of Refugees, 173, 178
United Nations High Commission for Refugees (UNHCR), 98, 99, 142, 150, 185–86, 198, 231n23
Universal Declaration of Human Rights (UDHR), 134, 136, 152
U.S. Committee for Refugees, 98, 99–100, 103, 172, 205

Vance, Cyrus, 151, 154
Van Den Haag, Ernest, 89
Vanden Heuval, William, 130
Veterans of Foreign Wars, 89
Vietnamese refugees: and admissions procedures and standards, 155–62; American government response to in 1975, 145–46; opposition to in the U.S., 162–65; Saigon evacuation, 145–48; and security check, 158–59
Vietnam War, 9, 104, 114, 135, 137, 145–46, 160–61
Voorhees, Tracy, 77, 81
Voting Rights Act of 1965, 95

Wainwright, Stuy, 43
Wall Street Journal, 161–62
Walter, Francis, 27, 57, 71, 72, 73, 82–84, 87, 90, 91, 97–98
"War on Terror," 203–6
War Powers Resolution of 1973, 138
Warren, Avra, 20
Warren, George, 103
Washington Post, 153
"Watergate Babies," 137
Watkins, Arthur, 39, 42, 98, 99
West Germany, 67, 186
Williams, George Washington, 43
Women Refugees Project, 202
women's movement, 5, 201–2

World Council of Churches, 68, 99
World Refugee Year, 97
World War I, 13
World War II, 11, 18–21
Wyman, David, 3

Yugoslavia, 197

Zelizer, Julian, 137
Zellerbach Commission, 98–99
Zolberg, Aristide, 3

POLITICS AND SOCIETY IN TWENTIETH-CENTURY AMERICA

Civil Defense Begins at Home: Militarization Meets Everyday Life in the Fifties by LAURA MCENANEY

Cold War Civil Rights: Race and the Image of American Democracy by MARY L. DUDZIAK

Divided We Stand: American Workers and the Struggle for Black Equality by BRUCE NELSON

Poverty Knowledge: Social Science, Social Policy, and the Poor in Twentieth-Century U.S. History by ALICE O'CONNOR

Suburban Warriors: The Origins of the New American Right by LISA MCGIRR

The Politics of Whiteness: Race, Workers, and Culture in the Modern South by MICHELLE BRATTAIN

State of the Union: A Century of American Labor by NELSON LICHTENSTEIN

Changing the World: American Progressives in War and Revolution by ALAN DAWLEY

Dead on Arrival: The Politics of Health Care in Twentieth-Century America by COLIN GORDON

For All These Rights: Business, Labor, and the Shaping of America's Public-Private Welfare State by JENNIFER KLEIN

The Radical Middle Class: Populist Democracy and the Question of Capitalism in Progressive Era Portland, Oregon by ROBERT D. JOHNSTON

American Babylon: Race and the Struggle for Postwar Oakland by ROBERT O. SELF

The Other Women's Movement: Workplace Justice and Social Rights in Modern America by DOROTHY SUE COBBLE

Impossible Subjects: Illegal Aliens and the Making of Modern America by MAE M. NGAI

More Equal than Others: America from Nixon to the New Century by GODFREY HODGSON

Cities of Knowledge: Cold War Science and the Search for the Next Silicon Valley by MARGARET PUGH O'MARA

Labor Rights Are Civil Rights: Mexican American Workers in Twentieth-Century America by ZARAGOSA VARGAS

Pocketbook Politics: Economic Citizenship in Twentieth-Century America by MEG JACOBS

Taken Hostage: The Iran Hostage Crisis and America's First Encounter with Radical Islam by DAVID FARBER

Morning in America: How Ronald Reagan Invented the 1980s by GIL TROY

Defending America: Military Culture and the Cold War Court-Martial by ELIZABETH LUTES HILLMAN

Phyllis Schlafly and Grassroots Conservatism: A Woman's Crusade by DONALD T. CRITCHLOW

White Flight: Atlanta and the Making of Modern Conservatism by KEVIN M. KRUSE

The Silent Majority: Suburban Politics in the Sunbelt South by MATTHEW D. LASSITER

Troubling the Waters: Black-Jewish Relations in the American Century by CHERYL LYNN GREENBERG

In Search of Another Country: Mississippi and the Conservative Counterrevolution by JOSEPH H. CRESPINO

The Shifting Grounds of Race: Black and Japanese Americans in the Making of Multiethnic Los Angeles by SCOTT KURASHIGE

School Lunch Politics: The Surprising History of America's Favorite Welfare Program by SUSAN LEVINE

Americans at the Gate: The United States and Refugees during the Cold War by CARL J. BON TEMPO